Curiosities
of the Civil War

CURIOSITIES
OF THE CIVIL WAR

Strange Stories, Infamous Characters, and Bizarre Events

WEBB GARRISON

THOMAS NELSON
Since 1798

NASHVILLE   DALLAS   MEXICO CITY   RIO DE JANEIRO

Published in Nashville, Tennessee, by Thomas Nelson. Thomas Nelson is a registered trademark of Thomas Nelson, Inc.

Thomas Nelson, Inc., titles may be purchased in bulk for educational, business, fund-raising, or sales promotional use. For information, please e-mail SpecialMarkets@ThomasNelson.com.

Library of Congress Cataloging-in-Publication Data

Garrison, Webb B.
    Curiosities of the Civil War : strange stories, infamous characters, and bizarre events / Webb Garrison.
        p. cm.
    Previously published as two separate works: Civil War curiosities in 1994, and More Civil War curiosities in 1995.
    Includes bibliographical references and index.
    ISBN 978-1-59555-359-1
    1. United States—History—Civil War, 1861–1865—Miscellanea. I. Garrison, Webb B. Civil War curiosities. II. Garrison, Webb B. More Civil War curiosities. III. Title.
E468.9.G372 2011
973.7—dc22   2010036386

Printed in the United States of America

19 LSC 11 10 9 8 7

Contents

Introduction:

EVERY ASPECT OF THE WAR PRODUCED ITS OWN CROP OF CURIOSITIES

I f the June 1865 surrender of Kirby-Smith's forces is taken as the last hurrah of the Confederacy, then the war lasted almost fifty months. It is estimated that 623,000 soldiers died during the Civil War. Fighting took place on each of the war's approximately 1,396 days from 1861 to 1865; as tabulated by Frederick H. Dyer, 10,455 military "events" took place during the war. Millions of men and thousands of encounters produced a multitude of extraordinary things.

Members of the U.S. Congress and the C.S. Congress gave frequent speeches, offered much advice, and pulled strings to get political and military favors. Editors of newspapers—from the New York *Tribune* to the Charleston *Mercury*—published thousands of editorials, and their correspondents filed reports by the tens of thousands. Men, ranging from cabinet members to buck privates in the rear ranks, wrote letters and penned diaries. Artists and photographers competed with one another to be the first to depict important events and the men who participated in them.

During the four years of frenetic activity, enough firsthand material was written and published to fill several large rooms. All major battles and many minor military events have been described in one or a score of books, and each commander who played a significant role—and many soldiers who did not—recorded their activities in detail.

Instead of offering another look at the most significant military and political events, *Curiosities of the Civil War* focuses on relatively unknown and obscure aspects of the war. Some of the subjects treated are brand new. For instance, major multi-volume works seldom include an index entry dealing with "hostages." Subjects such as "atrocities" and "appraisals by contemporaries," to say nothing of "Lincoln's appearance," are not found in standard Civil War encyclopedias and dictionaries. Even seasoned readers are likely to discover much that is new and fresh here.

Numerous chapters focus upon events or emphases that have been neglected—maybe because they're hard to locate. Except in these pages, it is all but impossible to find more than an occasional reference to banishment or deportation. If friendly fire during the Civil War has been treated earlier anywhere, I've failed to find it. Because a fellow put his life on the line when he so much as whispered about "fragging," the chapter dealing with this intramural sport of soldiers is comparatively short.

My criteria for determining what to include focused on three main points: interest, novelty, and brevity. Much of the information here is brief enough to be read aloud to a friend or family member. Inclusion of a comprehensive index allows the book to double as a special kind of reference work.

Does this collection exhaust possibilities for compilations of its sort? No. Plenty of other fast-moving, offbeat topics aren't touched here because there's a limit to the number of pages that can be used. Whether you're a lifelong addict or just beginning to get acquainted with the Civil War, you'll find a trove of conversation-starters here. I hope that as you read through *Curiosities of the Civil War*, your imagination will be challenged on every page. Certainly, the war was filled with unusual events, and I have sought to record some of the most interesting ones for your reading enjoyment. Maybe you'll want to use what few blank spots there are in this volume to add notes about other unusual aspects of the war that was launched in a fervent bid to preserve the Union.

— Webb Garrison

Part One

MEMORABLE PLAYERS IN THE NATION'S GREATEST DRAMA

One

LINCOLN AND DAVIS STARTED OUT LESS THAN ONE HUNDRED MILES APART

Abraham Lincoln liked to ask exceptionally tall men to stand with him, back to back, in order to compare measurements. He was rarely topped, because wearing a very tall silk hat, he measured almost seven feet from head to toe.

Headed for a visit with Maj. Gen. Ambrose Burnside, Lincoln stopped at Aquia Creek, Virginia, to review troops. Almost as soon as he entered the encampment, the Federal commander in chief spotted a lanky member of the Ninety-third Pennsylvania Regiment. Gesturing, the president let Mahlon Shaaber know that he wanted a word with him. "Turn around, young fellow," he is alleged to have said, "and put your back against mine while I take off my hat." As soon as their heads touched, Lincoln knew he had met a man considerably taller than he.

Carefully measured, the seventeen-year-old from Pennsylvania proved to top the six-foot, four-inch president by two and one-half inches. Together, the two men, who towered above most of those who surrounded them, gleefully measured others who considered themselves exceptionally tall. They found Brig. Robert A. Cameron to be six feet, one inch in height. To lincoln's suprise, Pennsylvania Governor Andrew G. Curtin, who was present for the review, topped Cameron by a full inch.

As a memento, Lincoln jotted down a memorandum listing the names and heights of "six-footers" on hand for the spur-of-the-moment ceremony that Shaaber never forgot.

As president of the Confederate States of America, Jefferson Davis frequently had occasion to sign orders that meant certain death for numerous soldiers. Yet intimates described the former U.S. secretary of war as being "exceptionally tender-hearted." Once when Davis was lying on a sick bed, a member of the family started reading to his son, Willie. Unable to endure the horror of the centuries-old story, Davis demanded that the reading of "Babes in the Woods" come to a halt.

Elida Rumsey, considered too old to serve as a nurse in the hospitals of Washington, became the talk of the capital because of her skill and patience in singing to the sick and wounded. When she accepted John Fowle's proposal, the upcoming wedding of a couple past the usual age of marriage was widely discussed.

Learning of the impending plans, Abraham Lincoln declared that no ordinary ceremony was good enough for Elida. Upon the initiative of the president, the wartime ceremony was held on the floor of the House of Representatives in 1863—before a joint session of Congress.

A furious fight among Democrats split the party three ways in 1860. Seasoned observers commented in advance of the Republican National Convention in Chicago that any man who won the nomination was sure to go to the White House.

Lincoln, who was not present at the convention, was the surprise victor over "Mr. Republican," William H. Seward of New York. On the heels of Lincoln's nomination, adviser's urged him to make no speeches and give no interviews. "Don't budge from Springfield," they insisted.

The President-elect followed this recommendation so faithfully that he did not meet Hannibal Hamlin until after the veteran congressional leader from Maine had been elected to serve as his vice-president.

Jefferson Davis, prominent among Democrats expected to have a chance at nomination for the presidency in 1860, had some staunch admirers in the North. One of them was Benjamin Butler of Massachusetts, destined soon to receive from Lincoln the first commission as a major general of volunteer troops entering Federal service.

Senator Davis, who placed a high value on the support of Butler, was not disappointed in him. During fifty-seven ballots, the man from Massachusetts voted in favor of pitting Davis against any presidential candidate that Republicans might choose.

Franklin D. Roosevelt is widely remembered for trying to enlarge, or "pack" the U.S. Supreme Court with justices considered likely to espouse his causes. Far less familiar to the general public is the fact that Roosevelt was not the first to attempt this strategy.

During months in which it seemed that Union military force might not be enough "to quell the rebellion," Washington was agog with talk about legal tests of matters in which Lincoln was deeply involved. Settlement of "prize cases" concerning the disposition of captured ships taken by Federal vessels was a central issue of the period.

Attorneys for owners of the ships *Amy Warwick, Brilliante, Crenshaw,* and *Hiawatha* were expected to argue that the president had pronounced a blockade without authority, because war had not been declared. Had this reasoning prevailed, the legality of the conflict itself would have been at issue.

Scheduled to be heard in March 1862, the case was deferred until Lincoln's close friend, David Davis, and two others recently named to the high court by him could take part in deliberations. Seizing an opportunity from the delay, Lincoln broke precedent by nominating and securing the confirmation of a tenth member of the judicial body.

Stephen J. Field, formerly chief justice of the California Supreme Court, had to cross the continent in order to assume his new position. He failed to reach Washington in time to participate in the debate about the prize cases, however. To the surprise of no one who remembered that four justices already on the bench had been chosen by the man from Illinois, the legality of the war he launched was confirmed by a vote of five to four. Seated after that decision was reached, Field "packed the court" as its tenth member.

On one of his numerous trips to visit military commanders and troops in the field, Lincoln told intimates that it might be expedient to go part of the way aboard the USS *Malvern*. In March 1865, it became certain that the warship would have the honor of conveying the commander in chief. Hence the chief carpenter of the vessel hastily put men to work to lengthen a bunk for the man who was more than a foot taller than most seamen of the day.

Seizure of Confederate passengers on the British mail packet *Trent* by the commander of the USS *San Jacinto* on November 8, 1861, was by far the most explosive international event of the war. England immediately announced plans to send a contingent of troops to Canada, and rumblings from the island kingdom sounded like threats of war against the United States.

During this dire emergency, Lincoln prepared his first annual message to Congress. James M. Mason and John Slidell, the Confederate commissioners to Britain who were taken from the *Trent*, were already occupying an improvised cell in Boston's Fort Warren. Dated December 3, 1861, the formal report of the president to lawmakers runs to at least seventeen printed pages in most editions of his works. Strangely, the lengthy document includes not a single word about the *Trent* affair, which was then the talk of Washington, London, and Europe.

West Point graduate Jefferson Davis, though enamored with a daughter of his commander, Col. Zachary Taylor, was not regarded as a suitable mate for Sarah. Ignoring potential consequences of the colonel's wrath, the couple eloped and Davis soon resigned his commission in order to become a Mississippi planter. To his lasting sorrow, his bride survived only three months after the wedding.

A dozen years later he met youthful Varina Howell and married her within a year. On their honeymoon, the future Confederate president took Varina for a solemn visit to Sarah's grave.

U.S. Secretary of War Jefferson Davis was open minded concerning changes in the military establishment. His decision to lengthen the term of study at West Point from four years to five years was soon canceled. Yet two of his innovations were remembered long after he left the service of the United States.

Two years after having joined the cabinet of President Franklin Pierce, he brought camels to the Southwest. Animals accustomed to desert life, he said, were likely to expand the usefulness of military units whose members were accustomed to riding horses. Shortly afterward, he introduced to the U.S. Army the newfangled rifle, which he considered superior to the time-honored musket.

Camels remained in action a few years, but were not replaced when they died. Rifles, still not in wide use at the time the Civil War broke out, eventually made muskets obsolete and contributed significantly to the defeat of Confederate forces.

The first battle of Bull Run clearly demonstrated that 75,000 ninety-day volunteers could not put down what Lincoln insisted on calling an "insurrection." Hence when Congress assembled for a special July 1861 session, the president asked Congress for 400,000 troops and $400 million.

Lawmakers enthusiastically voted to make $500 million available and James S. Gibbons published a song with a promise: "We Are Coming, Father Abraham,

Four Hundred Thousand Strong." Issued in about twenty different versions, the patriotic melody sold two million copies. Yet fewer than 100,000 men who heard its stirring words volunteered to serve in U.S. military forces. Union ranks were largely filled with men who joined up for the sake of a bounty and with substitutes whose services had been purchased by draftees.

<hr/>

Elected to the U.S. Senate in 1847, Jefferson Davis soon learned that his West Point education placed him in a minority. When he took his seat among the nation's senior lawmakers, he found that ten percent of his colleagues were graduates of a single institution: tiny Transylvania College in Lexington Kentucky.

<hr/>

Established during the Civil War as a reward for conspicuous bravery on the battlefield exhibited by noncommissioned officers and privates, the Congressional Medal of Honor soon became one of the nation's most coveted military awards. About one thousand medals were conferred during the war years, with many of them going to men who carried flags under fire or who captured Confederate flags.

Upon the death of Lincoln, War Department officials departed from tradition and awarded a few medals for service that could have been performed by civilians. These went, not to men who displayed gallantry under fire, but to first sergeants who escorted the body of the assassinated president to Springfield, Illinois.

<hr/>

Jefferson Davis never forgot that at the Democratic National Convention of 1860 at Charleston, perhaps his most devoted follower was Benjamin F. Butler. But late in 1862, the Confederate president found himself facing a dilemma. For months, Butler's name had been anathema in Richmond because of his unconventional and sometimes outrageous actions as military commander of occupied New Orleans.

Reports of financial misdeeds forced Lincoln to remove Butler from command at about the same time new stories of atrocities committed by him reached Confederates. Davis reacted by branding his one-time devotee a felon and an outlaw, not subject to the laws of civilized nations in the event of capture.

Positive proof is lacking, but many documents suggest that the strangest action taken by President Jefferson Davis came late in 1864. With the downfall of the Confederacy now seen nearly everywhere as inevitable, Davis sent Duncan Kenner to England and France on a special mission.

Much evidence indicates that Kenner was authorized to promise that slavery would be abolished in the Confederacy in exchange for diplomatic recognition by the two most powerful nations on the other side of the Atlantic Ocean. If such an overture were actually made, it came too late; Lt. Gen. Ulysses S. Grant and his men were about to crush the Army of Northern Virginia.

Within weeks of taking the oath of office as president of the United States, Lincoln received a gesture of courtesy from abroad. Having taken the helm of the world's largest and most powerful democracy, wrote Gaetano Belluri, it was only fitting that Lincoln be made an honorary citizen of San Marino, the world's smallest democracy.

Having gone aboard the tugboat *Lioness* for a short voyage of inspection in May 1862, Lincoln became the first sitting president to be exposed to enemy fire. "Having appeared out of nowhere," a party of cavalrymen in gray began firing at persons on the tugboat, in addition to members of a landing party that preceded it.

Lt. Frederick A. Rowe of the Ninety-ninth New York Regiment observed the entire incident and was surprised to see that Lincoln appeared to be unconcerned about his personal danger. Because men of Rowe's command insistently urged the president to seek a sheltered spot, he reluctantly "stepped behind the wheel-house while bullets whizzed across the deck" of the unarmed Federal vessel.

~~~

With Richmond located only about one hundred miles from Washington, presidents Lincoln and Davis spent the war years approximately as far from one another as during their earliest years in Kentucky.

Commissioned to paint an official presidential portrait, artist John Robertson made a nuisance of himself in the White House of the Confederacy. His portrait of Jefferson Davis, completed and hung in 1863 evoked a few bursts of ardent praise along with many highly critical evaluations. Most who labeled the work of art as inferior in quality did so "because it makes our President look too much like Lincoln."

~~~

Two civilians who had many other things in common shared with one another a refusal to yield to handicaps that would have put many men on the shelf.

Jefferson Davis lost the sight of one eye during the Mexican War and was subject to neuralgia so severe that during bouts of it he was all but blind. His agonizing stomach pains suggest that he had peptic ulcers. As though these handicaps were not enough, during severe attacks of head-splitting pain he sometimes was unable to use his right arm.

~~~

Some present-day medical specialists who have studied his photographs believe that Abraham Lincoln was a victim of Marfan syndrome. This hereditary condition leads to elongation of bones and abnormalities of the eyes and the cardiovascular system.

Moods brought on by Marfan syndrome would account for an otherwise puzzling incident. Departing from Springfield at age fifty-two, Lincoln told his fellow townspeople that he had grown old among them.

Everyone who knew the wartime president was aware that he was subject to severe mood swings, with periods of depression that lasted for two or three days. As if this mental-emotional handicap were not enough, as a boy he had received a kick from a mule that caused him to remain unconscious for many hours. Comments preserved by persons who observed him closely suggest that he suffered from *petit mal*, a type of epilepsy, as a result of this boyhood injury.

Two

Famous—Or Soon to Be

Kentucky-born Christopher Carson, better known as Kit, won early fame in the West. As guide to John Charles Frémont's expedition of 1842, 1843, and 1845, he made his name a household word.

Had he wanted a brigadiership, it would have almost certainly been Kit's for the asking. Instead of seeking command, at age fifty-two he became lieutenant colonel of the First New Mexico Cavalry. Carson led eight companies in the February 21, 1862, battle of Valverde, where his leadership was so significant that he reluctantly accepted a brevet, or honorary promotion, as a reward.

Frank Leslie, who was born in England in 1821, came to the United States at age twenty-seven. After working for *Gleason's Pictorial and Illustrated News*, in 1854 he launched *Frank Leslie's Ladies Gazette of Paris, London, and New York Fashions*. One year later he began putting out his own illustrated weekly newspaper, only moderately successful at first. But circulation increased dramatically when it began giving the North a battle-by-battle view of the Civil War.

Made bold by success, "the man who took the war into drawing rooms of the Union" launched numerous new publications. Soon his list included *Boys' and Girls' Weekly Sunday Magazine, Jolly Joker, Comic Almanac, Chatterbox, Ladies' Magazine,* and *Ladies' Journal.* Perhaps overextended, he was forced into bankruptcy and died as a debtor.

Today each of the more than two hundred 1861–65 issues of the illustrated newspaper is a collector's item, and since that time, *Frank Leslie's Illustrated Weekly* has been a major source of Civil War art.

⁂

Forty-two years of age at the time of Fort Sumter, Walt Whitman of New York had failed at practically everything he tried to do. He was successively an office boy, printer's devil, schoolteacher, typesetter, journalist, and editor. After publishing the book of poems *Leaves of Grass* in 1855, he cringed every time he saw a review of it.

Serving as a volunteer nurse in the hospitals of Washington, he caught an occasional glimpse of Abraham Lincoln, but spent most of his time bandaging wounds. Belated recognition of his poetic genius came first in Europe, then in the United States, after his death.

⁂

Brayton Ives signed up with the Fifth Connecticut Regiment in July 1861, later switched to the cavalry, and during four years of war rose to the rank of colonel. He fought at Deep Bottom, Five Forks, Sayler's Creek, Gaines' Mill, Bethesda Church, Cold Harbor, Opequon, and Cedar Creek. When he took off his uniform he was considered to be one of thousands of run-of-the-mill officers. Back in civilian circles, he was president of the New York Stock Exchange before winning fame in a select circle of book collectors as owner of a Gutenberg Bible.

⁂

At the outbreak of the war, ex-captain Ulysses S. Grant was a military has been who was reduced to working as a clerk in a family owned leather goods store. Nevertheless, "perennial failure Grant" became the first person since George Washington to become a lieutenant general in the U.S. Army, then spent two terms as president of the United States.

New York native Matthew B. Brady's portrait studio saw a few notables sit for the camera during the 1850s. He was all but unknown, however, outside a small circle of persons who had learned the photographic process perfected by Louis J. J. Daguerre of France.

Aware that his eyes had been damaged—perhaps by chemicals—and that he was fast losing his vision, Brady hired a group of enthusiastic younger men and sent them to war. They made thousands of photographs for which their employer took full credit. Today much material in the Brady Collection is identified by the name of the photographer who produced it. Still, no other man who envisioned capturing the war on wet plates is more closely identified with 1861–65 action that the man who personally saw very little of it.

According to the New York *Evening Post* of September 4, 1862, the Seventeenth Connecticut Regiment "left New York for the seat of war" on the previous evening. Having been organized on August 28, the unit was assigned to garrison duty until it participated in the famous "Mud March" of January 1863. (A mid-winter storm left Virginia roads in "shocking" condition.)

Among the privates who made up the regiment was inventor Elias Howe. At that time, the sewing machine he perfected was widely pirated in England and Europe, but Howe was not generally known. When his improved sewing machine won a gold medal at the Paris Exposition of 1867, the ground was laid for his later induction into the American Hall of Fame.

Bavarian emigrant Thomas Nast was just twenty-one years old at the outbreak of hostilities, but he had sketched some of Giuseppi Garibaldi's battles for *Frank Leslie's Illustrated Newspaper*. Switching to the staff of *Harper's Weekly*, the artist was on numerous battlefields and in many camps. Within a decade after the end of hostilities, he gained national fame from his attacks on the Tweed Ring in New York City. Today he is chiefly remembered for having created both the Democratic donkey and the Republican elephant.

By 1861, the name of one-time ferry boat captain Cornelius Vanderbilt was becoming familiar in U.S. shipping circles. Men who knew the business predicted that he would find a way to double the money he had made when he sold his California-to-Nicaragua shipping line.

One month after Fort Sumter, he surprised Federal authorities. In a letter to W. O. Bartlett, who was about to go to Washington, Vanderbilt authorized him to say that the steamer *Vanderbilt* would be turned over to the government on its own terms. As president of the Atlantic and Pacific Steamship Company, he offered the U.S. Navy four additional vessels. With the price of these ships to be determined by a "board of Commodores," he offered the *Ocean Queen*, *Ariel*, *Champion*, and *Daniel Webster*.

Just one year later, Vanderbilt bought a controlling interest in the New York and Harlem Railroad. From that point he had clear sailing in his quest to become one of the nation's wealthiest men.

Thomas A. Scott, superintendent of the Pittsburgh division of the Pennsylvania Railroad, took an aide with him when he went to Washington to become an assistant secretary of war. Speaking with a soft Scottish burr, his twenty-six-year-old companion quickly showed himself to be an expert in telegraphy. Soon Andrew Carnegie was put to work coordinating rail and telegraph lines of the Union.

Serving as a civilian executive in the military transportation section of the War Department, Carnegie was never forced to dodge Confederate bullets. He considered establishment of the telegraph office frequented by Lincoln to be one of his greatest contributions to the war effort.

Entering the iron and steel business in 1865, within one-quarter of a century, he had gained controlling interest in the U.S. Steel Corporation. Then the former worker for the War Department sold out and devoted the rest of his life to distributing his fortune among countless public libraries and other charitable enterprises.

Some of the Federal soldiers who were seriously wounded at Fort Donelson were taken by steamer to a St. Louis hospital. Among the civilians who visited them were sisters known only as "three maiden ladies from Philadelphia." Not until they had been doing volunteer hospital work for weeks did patients discover the trio to be numbered among the top ranks of America's bluebloods. They proved to be grandnieces of James "Commodore" Biddle, a top naval commander during the War of 1812.

Organization of the Forty-second Ohio Regiment was completed in August 1861 with the selection of its lieutenant colonel. Leading Ohio troops in numerous engagements, he won such rapid promotion that he became a major general on September 19, 1863.

Three months later, citizens of the Buckeye State elected the two-year veteran to Congress. He left Federal forces on December 5 to take the seat he had won without waging a campaign. Eighteen years later, James A. Garfield was inaugurated as our twentieth president.

John Jacob Astor Jr., grandson of the fur trader who was the first American to accumulate a great fortune, was eager to demonstrate his patriotism. He was, however, less than enthusiastic about signing up for three years of military service. Hence he negotiated a deal whereby he became a volunteer aide-de-camp to Maj. Gen, George B. McClellan.

Colonel Astor took up his duties in November 1861 and remained with the Army of the Potomac for eight months. There's no record that he ever carried a musket or was exposed to Confederate fire, but in 1865 he was awarded a brevet as brigadier general "for services rendered during the Peninsular campaign."

<hr />

Abraham Lincoln's oldest son, Robert Todd, was a student at Harvard when hostilities began. Some Illinois leaders grumbled and complained at his sheltered life, but he entered law school instead of the army after his 1864 graduation. Under tremendous public pressure, Abraham Lincoln then arranged for his oldest son to become a member of Grant's staff.

Captain Lincoln took care of visiting dignitaries, including his father, but never "saw the elephant" by engaging in combat. He was U.S. secretary of war and U.S. minister to Great Britain before heading the Pullman Car Company, then one of the nation's largest corporations.

<hr />

Missouri-born Thomas Coleman Younger was just seventeen years old in 1861. He could have entered Federal service, but he chose not to do so. Instead, the youth, whose friends called him "Cole," joined forces with guerrillas who ravaged Missouri and Kansas.

Younger gained fame as an outlaw during a dozen post-war years in which he cut a wide swath through the West. Then the Civil War veteran spent sixteen years behind bars for his part in a bank robbery at Northfield, Minnesota.

<hr />

While pastor of Plymouth Congregational Church in Brooklyn, the Rev. Dr. Henry Ward Beecher became the nation's most famous clergyman. An ardent abolitionist, he helped to create conditions that led to the widely used label "Bloody Kansas."

Hoping to cause the territory to tilt into the antislavery column when it became a state, the clergyman shipped substantial numbers of Sharps rifles to Kansas.

Some weapons seem to have gone to the West in crates that were marked "Beecher's Bibles." Hence for a time that name was applied to breech-loaders initially opposed by many Federal military leaders who believed that use of them would encourage waste of ammunition.

Confederate Brig. Gen. Ben Hardin Helm was the only Southerner whose combat death caused conspicuous mourning in Washington. Having married Mary Todd Lincoln's half-sister Emilie, he turned down his brother-in-law's offer of a commission as Union paymaster. When Helm died from wounds received at Chickamauga, the Union commander in chief and his family went into mourning.

Winslow Homer's cumulative experience of the war was derived from about eight nonconsecutive months during which he worked for *Harper's Weekly* as an artist. Though he devoted much more of his time and skill to camp life than to combat, his drawing *Sharpshooter* became one of the most famous Civil War depictions. During post-war years the man who prepared perhaps the most notable sketch of a Federal marksman turned to tranquil subjects and gained international fame as a painter of seascapes.

While serving as a nurse in a Georgetown hospital, Louisa May Alcott attracted no attention at all. She went quietly about her work, seldom talked with anyone at length, and was barely noticed by those with whom she associated. Yet letters written to her family, collected and published as *Hospital Sketches*, proved that she had more than an ordinary ability with the pen. At war's end, she gained fame with her *Little Women*, followed by *Little Men* and other novels.

Frank and Jesse James of Clay County, Missouri, signed up as members of the home guard, a pro-Confederate force under state control. Soon they found that even the lax rules of the militia were too much for them, so when Brig. Gen. Sterling Price left the state for Arkansas they become bushwhackers, or renegade raiders.

Little is known with certainty about their Civil War years, which have become embellished with legends. Many of these folk tales were spawned after the pair of cutthroats became central figures in the brief era known as the Wild West.

Edward Everett Hale, grandnephew of the Revolutionary War hero Nathan Hale, was born in 1822. A graduate of Harvard, he became a Unitarian clergyman who for six years before his death was chaplain of the U.S. Senate. He'd be largely forgotten today, however, had he not written a short story for *The Atlantic Monthly* that appeared in 1863.

Hale's fictional account of the adventures of "The Man Without a Country" was a thinly veiled report of the travails of Ohio congressmen Clement L. Vallandigham. Vocally opposed to the war, the editor-lawmaker made international news when he was banished from the United States because of his views. Today, Hale's writing is better known than is Vallandigham's name.

Frederick Douglass was born in Maryland around 1817, the mixed-blood son of a slave, Harriet Bailey, and a white father. At about age twenty he escaped from slavery and settled in Massachusetts. Having committed his life story to paper, his *Narrative of the Life of Frederick Douglass* earned him enough money to buy his freedom.

Long before Federal authorities began to look favorably on the use of black soldiers, Douglass advocated their recruitment. Nationally renowned as a champion of black Americans, he met Lincoln several times but gave only qualified support to the president's racial views.

<center>~~~~</center>

Comdr. Matthew F. Maury of the U.S. Navy was already renowned among oceanographers when he changed uniforms. Becoming a Confederate officer of the same rank, he played a key role in establishing a battery of submarines.

Today, memories of his wartime work are eclipsed by the fact the he was the first man to recognize the existence of the Gulf Stream. His pioneer work in studying the world's largest bodies of water caused the one-time Confederate commander to become known as "the Pathfinder of the Seas."

<center>~~~~</center>

Ohio-born Ambrose Bierce, a prolific writer of short stories, is today most widely remembered for his sardonic *Devil's Dictionary*. He fought throughout the war, and in its aftermath said his most vivid memory was that of Union soldiers slashed to death by Confederate bayonets at Shiloh.

<center>~~~~</center>

Throughout the nation, mid-century audiences clamored for a chance to see actor Edwin Booth. A son of famous actor Junius Booth, he performed in packed halls as Hamlet, King Lear, Brutus, Othello, Iago, and other Shakespearean figures.

Though not so well known, his brother John Wilkes Booth, also an actor, was admired and respected by critics and the public in both the North and the South. After the April 14, 1865, assassination of Lincoln, the name of Edwin's younger brother became more widely known than those of all other members of the Booth family.

At age twenty, the Harvard-educated son of one of the nation's most famous writers volunteered for military service. He survived such battles as Ball's Bluff, Antietam, and Fredericksburg, then hung out his shingle as an attorney. Appointed to the Massachusetts Supreme Court after fifteen years of practice, he was appointed to the U.S. Supreme Court in 1902. There Oliver Wendell Holmes Jr., won such renown for his minority decisions that his book about his dissenting opinions, *Collected Legal Papers*, was widely read by members of the general public as well as by attorneys.

Samuel L. Clemens had done nothing of significance by age twenty-five. As a journeyman printer and pilot of a Mississippi River steamer, he had barely managed to earn enough money for bed and board. Hence it was easy for him to turn his back on civilian life and enlist in a pro-Confederate unit that was organized in his native Missouri.

It took only a few weeks for him to decide that military life was not for him. Returning to the newspaper field as a reporter, he adopted the pseudonym Mark Twain and became the most noted American writer of the century. Despite his pro-secessionist views in early manhood, it was Twain who took a fling at publishing in order to issue successfully the autobiography of Ulysses S. Grant.

John Charles Frémont, known as "the Pathfinder," explored the West as a lieutenant in the U.S. Army Topographical Engineers Corps. By the time pioneer settlers in California elected him governor, he was already nationally famous. Republicans turned to him in 1856 and made him their first nominee for the

U.S. presidency. Small wonder, therefore, that in July 1861 Lincoln made him a major general and put him in command of the Western Department.

Frémont may have considered himself to have a wider following than the president who gained his office by support of less than 40 percent of the nation's voters. Without consulting his commander in chief, he issued an August 1861 emancipation proclamation that Lincoln forced him to rescind. Embittered at Washington and chafing at having been defeated at Wilson's Creek, the Union's most notable active general at that time resigned after just five months in uniform.

Daily prodding by New York *Tribune* headlines that demanded "ON TO RICHMOND" probably contributed to the Federal fiasco at Bull Run in July 1861. Publisher Horace Greeley heartily supported the war effort at that time, but he parted company with Lincoln over the issue of slavery.

Former warmonger Greeley, whose newspaper is widely regarded as having been the most influential in the nation, eventually headed a Northern movement whose aim was to effect a negotiated peace. After the war, he signed the bail bond of Jefferson Davis despite warnings that such a move could cut circulation of the *Tribune* in half.

Nominated for the presidency by liberal Republicans in 1872 and supported by Democrats, Greeley might have gone to the White House had his opponent been anyone other than Ulysses S. Grant.

Scores of Federal officers were awarded post-war brevets as brigadier generals. Some of the men who received this strictly honorary title had long distinguished records; others knew how to pull political strings.

Because he was not among those to whom "honorary and temporary promotions" were given, the name of Col. Eli Lilly does not appear in standard Civil War dictionaries and encyclopedias. In post-war years, however, the man who was bypassed when congressmen and senators handed out large numbers of brevets headed an Indianapolis pharmaceutical firm. Because his corporation was a pioneer in making and distributing insulin and other life-saving medications, the name of Eli Lilly is now familiar around the world.

Three

NEVER SAY DIE

Guiding his horse during the heat of battle, a line officer sometimes wished for an extra arm. That way he could use his revolver while holding his reins and waving signals to his aides.

Confederate Maj. Gen. John B. Hood tops the list of those who kept on going with inadequate body equipment. At Gettysburg, an injury to his left arm left it all but useless. Chickamauga then cost him his right leg, which was amputated very close to his trunk. Hood therefore led Confederates in the battle of Atlanta while strapped into his saddle, wearing a $5,000 French-made cork leg.

Though notoriously temperamental, drugs may have affected his judgment. Trying to cope with constant pain, he used laudanum in such quantities that some medical analysts suggest it may have produced euphoria.

Francis R. Nicholls was a Confederate double amputee who wouldn't give up. During the first battle of Winchester he lost an arm, and at Chancellorsville a Federal shell caused him to lose a foot. Assigned to post duty for a period, the brigadier became head of conscription in the Trans-Mississippi Department. Returning to Louisiana and admitting that he was "only the broken remnant of the man who marched off to fight the Yankees," he served two terms as governor before becoming head of the state supreme court.

Union Brig. Gen. Davis Tillson suffered a pre-war injury that led to amputation of a foot. Hobbling from battery to battery, he commanded artillery that defended both Cincinnati and Knoxville.

At least three well-known Confederates could sympathize with Tillson. Vice-president Alexander H. Stephens suffered all his life from a severe case of club foot. Col. Roger W. Hanson had "an especially peculiar gait" as a result of taking a bullet in his leg during a pre-war duel. Brig. Gen. Henry H. Walker lost a foot as a result of a wound at Spotsylvania.

Although many amputees and cripples gave up, others did not. Had all commanders minus the use of a leg or an arm been brought together, they'd have been numerous enough to form their own brigade.

Union Brig. Gen. Egbert B. Brown took a direct hit in the shoulder at Springfield, Missouri, in January 1863. For the duration of the war, he had only one usable arm, but he sometimes commanded cavalry forces.

An 1863 skirmish with Virginia guerrillas cost Union Brig. Gen. Martin D. Hardin his left arm. Yet he was back in the saddle in time to lead his men at Gettysburg, Falling Waters, Spotsylvania, North Anna, and Bethesda Church.

By the time he began fighting Confederates, Captain Joseph A. Haskin was accustomed to getting along without his left hand. Having lost it during the Mexican War, he continued in the army and in 1864 was made a brigadier of volunteers.

Union Brig. Gen. Thomas W. Sweeney left his right arm behind at Churubusco, Mexico, but fought at Wilson's Creek, Fort Donelson, Shiloh, Chattanooga, and Atlanta.

Union Maj. Gen. Philip Kearny had good reason to remember Mexico City, where he lost his left arm. Back in uniform at the head of a New Jersey brigade, he led with distinction at Williamsburg, Seven Pines, and Second Bull Run before being killed after having accidentally ridden into Confederate lines at Chantilly.

Union Col. Theodore Read's brevet (honorary promotion) came to him "for conspicuous gallantry before the enemy" during actions in which he took several wounds and lost his left arm. When Edward A. Wild's left arm was hit at Shiloh, he used his training as a physician to direct the amputation. As a brigadier, he later led black troops on raids and against guerrillas in North Carolina.

Severely wounded at Seven Pines, Union Brig. Gen. O. O. Howard lost his right arm but soon returned to duty with an empty sleeve. He subsequently fought at Antietam, Fredericksburg, Chancellorsville, and Gettysburg, where his leadership brought him the Thanks of Congress. When the document that conveyed one of the nation's highest honors was offered to him, he accepted it with his left hand.

Capt. James McCleary's sword arm was amputated after Shiloh, and before it fully healed, the future Union brevet brigadier was again wounded at Stones River.

One-armed fighting men were scattered throughout Confederate forces. John T. Halbert of Lincoln County, Tennessee, lost a hand at a cotton gin when he was young. So he was rejected when he offered his services to the Eighth Tennessee Regiment. Six months later, with the manpower pinch already being felt in the South, one-handed Halbert was accepted into the Forty-first Tennessee and fought with his regiment throughout the war.

Col. John Kerr of the Army of Northern Virginia lost an arm at Gettysburg but fought without it in the Wilderness, and at Spotsylvania, Cold Harbor, and Petersburg.

Seconds after he was hit at Antietam, Col. Birkett D. Fry knew his arm was shattered. Made a brigadier in 1864, he commanded two separate divisions at Cold Harbor.

Lt. Col. John C. Cheves' right arm was amputated after Gaines' Mill. Returning to duty, he was second in command of Hood's artillery at Gettysburg. He served through the Overland campaign, in the defense of Petersburg, and remained with Lee until Appomattox.

By the time he began leading troops against men in blue, Brig. Gen. William W. Loring was accustomed to using only one arm, having lost the other during the Mexican War. He fought with such distinction that Jefferson Davis made him a major general in February 1862.

Because he lost his sword arm at Churubusco, men commanded by Brig. Gen. James G. Martin called him "Old One Wing."

Swiss-born Henry Wirz enlisted in Louisiana as a private, then rose steadily in rank until his right arm was shattered at Seven Pines. After serving as commandant at Andersonville Prison, he became the only man who went to the scaffold after having been convicted of war crimes.

After Seven Pines, the right arm of Brig. Gen. James J. Pettigrew was as useless as that of Wirz. Still, he commanded a division at Gettysburg and led it in Pickett's Charge.

Minus an arm, Brig. Gen. Laurence S. Baker was in the field most of the time until 1865. After having faced Sherman and his veterans in South Carolina, he made a gallant but futile attempt to join forces with Gen. Joseph E. Johnston.

At Malvern Hill, surgeons managed to save the arm of Stephen Ramseur, but he found it to be so useless that he often said he wished they had amputated it. With his arm in a sling, he fought at Gettysburg, the Wilderness, and Spotsylvania; as a major general he led his division at Cold Harbor and in the Shenandoah Valley.

Col. Matthew C. Butler went through Antietam and Fredericksburg without injury, then saw a Federal shell take off his right foot at Brandy Station. Returning to active duty and promoted twice, he was a major general when he joined Johnston to oppose Sherman in the Carolinas.

Lt. Col. William L. Brandon left a leg behind at Malvern Hill. He later fought at Gettysburg, Chickamauga, and Knoxville before becoming a brigadier.

At Shiloh, Brig. Gen. Charles Clark was so severely injured that he never again walked without aid. Flourishing his crutches, he took off his uniform in order to become the last Confederate governor of Mississippi.

Col. Stapleton Crutchfield lost a leg on the second day at Chancellorsville, returned to active duty, and was decapitated by a Federal cannonball seventy-two hours before Appomattox.

Col. Thomas T. Eckert was leading a brigade near Atlanta when a direct hit cost him a leg. Barely having recovered, he went into Tennessee with Hood and later helped to defend Mobile.

Lt. Col. William H. Forney was crippled for life by multiple wounds to an arm and a leg at Gettysburg. While still on crutches, he was made a brigadier. His colleague, Brig. Gen. George D. Johnston, took a direct hit within hours after his promotion. Weaving clumsily on his crutches, he led a brigade into Tennessee and the Carolinas in an attempt to join forces with Johnston.

When Maj. Gen. Richard S. Ewell, who lost a leg at Groveton, returned to duty as a lieutenant general, he had to be lifted on his horse and strapped to his saddle to lead the Confederate advance into Pennsylvania. Uninjured at Gettysburg, his luck again ran out at Kelly's Ford. After another injury and a serious fall from his horse, he took charge of the defense of Richmond.

Maj. James Connor's leg was shattered by a rifle ball at Gaines' Mill. Out of action less than two months, he fought at Chancellorsville and Gettysburg before a Cedar Creek wound forced the amputation of his leg. During the final months of the war, Connor was back in the field, apparently holding a commission as major general that was never confirmed by the Confederate Congress.

Confederates weren't the only ones who lost their limbs while fighting. One-legged officers also abounded in Union forces. One of the earliest to fight after an amputation was Col. William F. Bartlett, who lost a leg at Yorktown. Twice briefly on the sidelines, in 1863 he raised a new regiment in order to join the Army of the Potomac. His leadership in the Wilderness and Cold Harbor brought him the star he was wearing at Petersburg when his cork leg was shattered by enemy fire.

Made a colonel when his leg was amputated after Gettysburg, the son of Adm. John A. Dahlgren returned to active duty on crutches. Hobbling about on a wooden leg, he led a raid against Richmond in which he was killed while carrying papers that suggested Jefferson Davis was the target of a Federal murder plot. Some Confederates were almost as interested in Ulric Dahlgren's fancy cork leg as in the incriminating documents they found on his body.

For Lt. Col. Francis M. Drake, one cost of victory at Marks' Mill was a leg. He returned to his regiment and after the war entered politics. As a result, Iowa, as well as Mississippi, had as its governor a wounded veteran who could not walk without crutches.

Col. Francis Fessenden's right leg was left behind at Monett's Bluff. Returning to duty as a brigadier, he failed to win distinction on the battlefield. Later he was one of the military judges who tried and condemned the commandant of Andersonville.

When Col. David Moore's leg was lost at Shiloh, friends urged him to retire from active service. Instead, he raised the Fifty-first Missouri Regiment and led it so successfully in Southern campaigns that it brought him a brevet brigadiership in May 1865.

Brig. Gen. Halbert E. Paine became a brevet major general after losing a leg at Port Hudson. Col. Byron R. Pierce had a leg amputated after the second day at Gettysburg, but later led his men at Bristoe and Mine Run. While engaged in the Overland campaign, he became a brigadier.

Col. A. V. Rice, also promoted after being wounded, lost his leg at Kennesaw Mountain.

Daniel E. Sickles was already a major general when he was stripped of a leg at Gettysburg, the battle he described as having "set Meade's best aides to limping."

Handicaps that did not involve amputation might not be as noticeable, but they could still be serious. Having complied with orders that required him to observe an eclipse of the sun, Union Adm. John A. Dahlgren suffered permanent eye damage. Also among Federal leaders, the secretary of the treasury, Salmon P. Chase, and Maj. Gen. Benjamin F. Butler had serious eye defects.

Confederate Brig. Gen. Felix Zollicoffer was notoriously nearsighted. When he died at Logan's Cross Roads, some of his comrades said his poor vision cost him his life, because he had approached a Federal officer he mistook for a cohort. Col. Daniel W. Adams lost his right eye at Shiloh, was rewarded with a promotion, and was among those who tried to stop Wilson's raid through Alabama and Georgia. Accidentally hit in the face by a bullet from the gun of a fellow Confederate, "Stovepipe" Johnson donned dark glasses to hide his near-blindness and continued to fight.

Some of his colleagues insisted that Confederate Maj. Gen. Theopohilus H. Holmes was stone deaf. Though the West Point classmate of Jefferson Davis indignantly denied this allegation, he admitted that he learned much more through his eyes than through his ears. That was an understatement, aides said privately. According to them, he sometimes was unable to determine whether or not a battle was in progress.

Stonewall Jackson's deafness involved only one ear, but it was serious enough to make it difficult for him to locate the origin of artillery fire.

At Allatoona, Union Brig. Gen. John M. Corse received a direct hit on the side of his face. Advised to return to civilian life, he refused and quipped, "I'm short a cheek-bone and one ear, but can still whip all hell!"

At Cedar Mountain, Union Col. Snowden Andrews was almost cut in two by a shell. When he returned to active duty ten months later, a comrade described him as "bowed crooked by that awful wound, but still able to fight like a lion."

Thomas E. Ransom became captain of the Eleventh Illinois Regiment in April 1861 and received direct hits at Charleston, Missouri, and Fort Donelson. Wounded a third time at Shiloh after having become a colonel, he almost bled to death when he refused to leave the field. Still not recovered from a fourth major wound received at Sabine Cross Roads, U.S. Brigadier General Ransom took to an ambulance in order to remain at the head of his column during the Atlanta campaign.

Even after having been made a major general, Benjamin H. Grierson suffered from what some officers in blue considered "the strangest handicap of any general officer." Having been severely injured when kicked by a horse in childhood, the man destined to gain fame as a Federal raider was afraid of horses and tried to balk when assigned to cavalry service.

During a pre-war tour of duty in Florida, William F. Smith contracted so serious a case of malaria that it seldom went into remission. Weak and depressed, he fought at Bull Run, Yorktown, Lee's Mill, Williamsburg, Fair Oaks, White Oak Swap, Savage's Station, Malvern Hill, South Mountain, Antietam, and Fredericksburg. Picked by Lincoln for advancement to the rank of major general, he failed to get Senate confirmation, probably because lawmakers knew of the seriousness of his malaria.

Brig. Gen. Alexander Schimmelfennig also had periodic bouts with malaria that put him in bed as late as the period during which he commanded Federal forces at Charleston.

Union Adm. Andrew H. Foote suffered from headaches so severe that he was sometimes out of action for two or three days.

Confederate Maj. Gen. Braxton Bragg confessed that his migraines hit him so hard that there were many days when he was unable to function. Yet there were periods in which he hardly noticed his headaches because pain from chronic boils and rheumatism blocked out consciousness of his migraine.

Edwin M. Stanton, while Union secretary of war, suffered what he described as "paroxysms of asthma." Confederate Maj. Gen. William H. T. Walker fought the same condition for most of his life. Sometimes he breathed with such difficulty that he slept in an upright position.

Compared with Union Brig. Gen. Marcellus M. Crocker, Stanton and Walker were in great health. Though he seldom missed participation in battle, Crocker probably had tuberculosis at the time of his May 1861 enlistment. He fought throughout the war, but "consumption" took him to his grave just four months after Appomattox.

Wisconsin native Rufus King, who organized and led the famous Iron Brigade, was a victim of epilepsy.

Union Brig. Gen. William H. Lawrence was not exposed to Confederate fire at Gettysburg; marching toward that destination, he suffered "a disabling case of sunstroke." Still, he took command of Columbus, Kentucky, and led the April 11, 1864, action that won the praise of Grant.

Confederate Maj. Gen. Ambrose P. Hill, far from well when the war began, remained in the field despite the fact that he was growing progressively weaker. Though frequently on sick leave, he marched with Stonewall Jackson at Chancellorsville and later led a corps at Gettysburg and through the Wilderness. Subsequently, Hill got up from his bed and fought at Petersburg with such distinction that he won universal praise. Fragmentary records have persuaded some medical specialists to conclude that he suffered from a venereal disease, contracted while a student at West Point.

West Pointer Marcellus A. Stovall, class of 1840, suffered from rheumatism so severe that he was "invalided out of the academy." When war broke out, he limped to a confederate recruitment center, became a lieutenant colonel, and fought at Waldron's Ridge and Stones River. Named a brigadier, he led his regiments at Chickamauga, Chattanooga, and Atlanta before going to Tennessee with Hood.

Confederate Maj. Gen. Richard S. Ewell may have been able to cope with the loss of a leg because he was accustomed to pain. His dyspepsia was so severe that for lengthy periods he ate nothing except cracked wheat. His fellow officer, Gen. Nathan Bedford Forrest, had recurrent bouts with boils so severe that it was sometimes all he could do to mount a horse.

One of the most unusual of severely handicapped fighting men was J. N. Ballard, a member of Mosby's Rangers. A direct hit by a Federal bullet splintered bones of one leg so badly that surgeons told him he wouldn't live without amputation.

Literally "biting the bullet" while scalpel and saw were being wielded, Ballard was considered by his comrades to be unfit for additional action. Hence they were amazed when the amputee hobbled into camp wearing the splendid cork leg found on the body of Union Col. Ulric Dahlgren when he was killed near Richmond.

Part Two

SUPPORTING MEMBERS OF THE CAST

Four

MANY WIVES DID MORE
THAN KNIT SOCKS

Mrs. Robert Anderson was aghast when she learned that her husband and his men, who had taken refuge in Fort Sumter, were likely to be starved into submission.

During the Mexican War she had come to have great confidence in Sgt. Peter Hart, who later left the U.S. Army in order to join the police force of New York City. At Mrs. Anderson's persuasion, Hart quit his job and accompanied her to Charleston. There he managed to get permission to join the civil work force inside Fort Sumter.

One of the most dramatic incidents for defenders of the fort came when a hail of Confederate hot shot set fire to wooden barracks. At the height of danger it was the sergeant-turned-policeman who took the lead in extinguishing the fire that threatened to engulf the installation.

Fanny Ricketts, wife of U.S. Army Capt. James B. Ricketts, was in or near the capital at the time of the first battle of Bull Run. When her husband didn't return with his unit, she persuaded Lt. Gen. Winfield Scott to give her a pass that permitted her to go through Union lines to the site of the conflict. However, when she reached a Confederate outpost, Scott's pass became worthless and it seemed that she would have to turn back.

Remembering her husband's friendship with J. E. B. Stuart, she managed to contact at Fairfax Court House the professional soldier now wearing the uniform of a Confederate colonel. Stuart gave her a pass that enabled her to go to the Manassas battlefield, held by victorious Confederates. Four days after the battle she found her husband in an improvised field hospital at the Lewis house, from which she accompanied him to Richmond, the Confederate capital.

These adventures would have been more than enough for many wives, but Fanny's saga was just beginning. When Federal officers were being selected as hostages for Confederates charged with piracy, Richmond's Libby Prison held an insufficient number of colonels and majors to complete the lottery. Ricketts was selected as one of the junior officers who were threatened with execution in the event that their Confederate counterparts should hang.

Fanny remained in Richmond, made friends with prison guards in order to gain visiting privileges, and was with her husband almost daily until he was exchanged for Julius A. de Lagnel in January 1862.

Largely recruited from the Irish in New York City, the Eighty-eighth New York Regiment marched off to war under the leadership of Col. Thomas F. Meagher. Because his wife had gone to great pains to secure and to present a U.S. flag to the fighting men, this unit of ninety-day volunteers was popularly known as "Mrs. Meagher's Own."

Meagher later organized and led the famous Irish Brigade. Soon a brigadier general, he served with distinction at Seven Pines, the Seven Days, Antietam, Fredericksburg, and Chancellorsville. Always fighting under his wife's flag, Meagher tried to resign when told he could not recruit new members of his command. Republican leaders refused to accept the resignation of the Democratic brigadier and kept him close to his flag until May 1865.

Mrs. John C. Breckinridge, who was at the headquarters of her husband much of the time, owned "a handsome silk dress." She vividly remembered having worn it at a state dinner in Washington when her mate was vice-president of the United States. That dress, she decided after many months at the front, would make a spectacular flag.

Formally presented to the Twentieth Tennessee Regiment, the flag of a Confederate general's wife was first exposed to gunfire at Hoover's Gap, Tennessee, in June 1863. Color bearer Ben Yeargin died that day and both Wallace Evans and Johnny Fly were wounded by gunfire directed at the emblem they carried. Three more color bearers were wounded at Chickamagua.

Finally, at Jonesboro, Georgia, every member of the color guard responsible for "the Mrs. Breckinridge flag" was killed or wounded. Wounded men not taken prisoner soon saw their general's wife headed toward them, her arms filled with lint and bandages.

Confederate Brig. Gen. Nathan Bedford Forrest was not amused when he learned the identity of a civilian taken prisoner at Holly Springs, Mississippi, in December 1862. Because Forrest was barely able to scribble a few common words, no written record of his order has survived. His oral command probably was brief and to the point: "Pass that woman through the lines, and waste no time!"

His captive, Julia Grant, is believed to have been the only wife of a Union major general to be taken prisoner by a Confederate force.

Often accompanied by their youngest son, Jesse, Mrs. Grant was with her husband in numerous camps. When Grant settled down at City Point, Virginia, for the long siege of Petersburg, it was his wife who made sure that he frequently had "good home-cooked food."

June 1862 saw Union Maj. Gen. David D. Hunter embark on a special mission. Eager to free Southern slaves, he led a force against Secessionville, South

Carolina. There he suffered so stunning a defeat that he suspended his military operations.

Upon returning to his base at Hilton Head, South Carolina, by means of a military steamer, the thwarted abolitionist received a special kind of consolation: his wife was waiting for him at the pier of the one-time Confederate stronghold.

As its name implies, the Mississippi River's Island Number Ten was downstream from nine other islands. Located close to Columbus, Kentucky, it was fortified by Confederates who planned to close the river to Federal traffic. In a dramatic ship-to-shore operation, forces under Union Maj. Gen. John Pope and Flag Off. Andrew H. Foote took over the island on April 8, 1862.

The victorious Union soldiers and sailors were dumbfounded to discover among their captives "a female invalid generally known as Harriet Redd." Questioned, she admitted to having come to the military installation to be with her Confederate husband. Refusing a pass, Harriet said she preferred to remain with him, so she joined the men in an improvised prisoner-of-war camp.

Reared near Baltimore, Hetty Cary was related to two of Virginia's "first families," the Randolphs and the Jeffersons. War forced her to choose between leaving home and facing imprisonment on suspicion of harboring Confederate sympathies, so she settled in Richmond. Soon she was a leader among those working to provide clothing, food, and other necessities for soldiers.

After nearly four years of volunteer work, her activities caught the eye of thirty-two-year-old John Pegram, who sought and won her hand. On January 19, 1865, the refugee from Maryland and the Confederate brigadier general were married. Hetty enjoyed this relationship just three weeks; on February 5, the husband she found in the course of her war work was killed in the battle of Hatcher's Run.

Russian born John B. Turchin came home one day and joyfully informed his wife that he would soon be made colonel of the Nineteenth Illinois Regiment. Eyes flashing, she instantly responded, "I'm going with you, even to battlefields."

Although at that time most of the military nurses were men, Mrs. Turchin volunteered her services and went along in an unofficial capacity. Less than a year later, now commanding a brigade, Turchin permitted his men to loot indiscriminately in Huntsville and Athens, Alabama.

Accused of having encouraged his men to plunder and rob civilians, the Federal officer went before a court-martial that recommended his dismissal from the service. Oral tradition has it that his wife promptly set out for Washington, where she managed to win an interview with Lincoln. Impressed with her account of what had taken place, the president set aside the verdict of the court-martial. Soon afterward the president submitted the name of Mrs. Turchin's husband for confirmation as a brigadier general.

Months later, during a Tennessee campaign, the Federal general, whose baptismal name was Ivan Vasilovitch Turchinoff, became so ill that he could not sit in the saddle. Veterans who served under him vowed that for a period of ten days Mrs. Turchin took command of his unit and once briefly led it in battle.

Mrs. John Charles Frémont was in Missouri with her husband when he aroused the wrath of Lincoln. On August 30, 1861, the Federal major general issued a famous "emancipation proclamation" concerning the territory over which he had military control. As soon as word about Frémont's action reached Washington, the president firmly requested that he rescind it.

Furious, Frémont's wife, the daughter of the powerful Missouri senator, Jessie Hart Benton, went to the capital to intercede. Lincoln is known to have seen Jessie Frémont on at least two occasions in early September, but he refused to modify his stand. Disappointed and angry, she returned to her husband in the war zone and remained with him until he was relieved of command in November.

August 23, 1862, found the Federal commander in chief face-to-face with the wife of an officer who had a grievance. Gabriel R. Paul, a West Point graduate and a lieutenant colonel in the U.S. Army, believed "some things in Washington were out of kilter." Over and over, he had seen men whose service had not been continuous receive promotions he felt should have gone to career officers. During the 1862 Confederate invasion of New Mexico, he commanded vital Fort Union with the temporary rank of colonel. When enlistments of his men expired, he was demoted to his former grade.

Mrs. Paul spent many nights with her husband, talking about "things wrong with the seniority system of the U.S. Army." When she felt she fully understood the situation, the wife of a man whose father and grandfather had fought with Napoleon made the long journey from New Mexico to Washington to plead with Lincoln to promote her husband over others who had not spent their careers in uniform.

After their August 23, 1862, session, the president said of Mrs. Paul, "She is a saucy woman and I am afraid she will keep tormenting till I may have to do it." On September 5, Paul's name was presented for promotion to the rank of brigadier general. Failing to get Senate confirmation, he continued to serve as lieutenant colonel until he was renominated and confirmed in April 1863.

"It took a while for her to do it," said a subordinate in the division Paul commanded, "but Mrs. Paul eventually got what she wanted for her husband."

Having been wounded at Fort Donelson, Tennessee, Lt. Col. James O. Churchill of the Eleventh Illinois Regiment found himself in a hospital bed beside that of Col. John A. Logan on the steamer *New Uncle Sam*. Soon Brig. Gen. Ulysses S. Grant's chief surgeon came aboard the headquarters steamer, examined Churchill, shook his head, and said there was nothing he could do for him.

Hours later the wounded man opened his eyes to find a woman bending over him. Having followed Federal forces as closely as the war zone permitted, Mrs. Logan had come to nurse her husband. Finding Churchill to be the more seriously injured one, she turned her attention to him. Under her constant care, Churchill recuperated so rapidly that the hospital boat *City of Memphis* took him aboard and kept him until he was able to return to his unit.

Members of the crew of the 100-ton Confederate privateer *Retribution* rejoiced on the afternoon of January 10, 1863. Having captured the coal brig *F. P. Ellicott* (or *F. P. Elliott*), they estimated how much prize money the vessel would bring when taken to port and sold.

Their elation proved to be premature. When crew members of the captured vessel were replaced by Confederates, the wife of the *Ellicott's* mate was left aboard. As soon as the *Retribution* was out of sight, she broke out a store of rum and the captors became thoroughly drunk. Then the wife (not named in official reports) put irons on Confederates and sailed the bark into St. Thomas, where she delivered it and her captives to the U.S. consul.

When attorney John S. Mosby decided to become a Confederate partisan ranger, he knew that members of irregular units were in far greater danger than conventional soldiers. Very early, Federal actions had made it clear that rangers not shot on sight would be relentlessly hunted. Undeterred by danger, Mosby's wife frequently stayed close to him even during his famous raids in the Loudoun Valley of Virginia.

Federal soldiers once broke into the house where the pair was sleeping, but found no one there but Mrs. Mosby. Warned by her to get out quickly, Mosby had climbed into a tree wearing only his underwear. He remained in his perch and kept very quiet until the Federals departed, enabling him to return to bed with his wife.

Massachusetts clergyman Stephen Barker was so stirred by Lincoln's first call for volunteers that he gave up his parish and became chaplain of the Thirteenth Massachusetts Regiment. Refusing to be left behind, his wife became a nurse. Though she had no formal training, she served in field hospitals for more than three years before becoming a superintendent for the U.S. Sanitary Commission.

Harriet W. F. Hawley, wife of a Connecticut lawyer, became a nurse when her husband donned a blue uniform, and the Hawleys managed to stay together. Harriet spent most of her days and many of her nights among the sick of the Seventh Connecticut Regiment, led by her husband.

When Hawley was sent to his native state, North Carolina, his wife found a place in the hospital at Beaufort. After following her husband to Florida and South Carolina, she went with him to Washington when his command was assigned to the Army of the James in April 1864. Soon back in North Carolina, where her husband was now in command at Wilmington, the Connecticut woman may have been the only wife of a brigadier general to spend weeks nursing former inmates of Andersonville Prison.

Union Brig. Gen. Henry W. Slocum, a Syracuse attorney who had graduated from West Point and spent four years in the artillery, headed the Twenty-seventh New York Regiment when it was raised. When his unit formed an encampment near Washington, men of the unit called the place Camp Clara, an appropriate name because Mrs. Slocum stayed with her husband much of the time—the only regimental wife to do so. Lt. Charles S. Baker graciously vacated his tent, so that Slocum and his mate could bunk together.

When Union Brig. Gen. Francis C. Barlow took a serious wound at Gettysburg, his wife moved heaven and earth in what was initially a futile attempt to go to his bedside. At that time a nurse with Union forces, in desperation she turned to Confederate Brig. Gen. John B. Gordon. Credited by Barlow with having saved Gordon's life when he lay wounded on the battlefield, the Georgia native provided Mrs. Barlow with a safe conduct that permitted her to pass through Confederate lines in order to join her husband.

Not all wives were content with occasional visits to their husbands or with work as volunteer nurses. When R. S. Brownell signed up with the First Rhode Island Volunteers, a ninety-day unit, his wife refused to be left behind. Kady accompanied her husband to Bull Run in 1861, having already won from Col. Ambrose Burnside the nickname "Child of the Regiment."

During fierce fighting near Manassas, Brownell's wife stayed on the field to attend the wounded as best she could. She was close to the standard bearer of the Sixth Regiment when he received a direct hit and dropped the flag. Seizing it, Kady was wounded while carrying it across the field. Although she relinquished the flag, the wife who went to war picked up and kept for the rest of her life a trophy that she termed "a Secessia rifle."

Agnes Elisabeth Winona Leclerq Joy, who may have been born in Canada, was in New York when the war began. She frequently visited military encampments, where she met and soon married Prussian nobleman and soldier of fortune Felix Salm-Salm.

Princess Agnes, as the colonel's wife was called, stayed with her husband throughout the conflict. She spent much of her time and energy caring for the sick and wounded, frequently ignoring regulations that forbade her presence on or near the battlefields. Having watched the Prussian's wife in action, Governor Richard Yates of Illinois was so impressed that he gave her a commission as an honorary captain.

Novelist Martha Caroline Keller, author of *Love and Rebellion*, described a pair of Confederates she believed to have been at Gettysburg. One of them, "a dreaming boy who fought with tiger fierceness," lay beside an older soldier. Instead of sleeping, "this strong, manly warrior" remained awake to "guard the resting youth."

Their comrades considered them to be father and son. Actually, Keller wrote, "This fair young soldier is the man's wife."

That account is undocumented, but similar stories are buried in records of both Confederate and Federal forces.

Some men of the Twenty-sixth North Carolina Regiment noticed that Sam and Keith Blalock seemed to have an unusually close relationship. When questioned, Keith explained that they were old friends who had grown up in the same town and were distantly related.

It was months before officers discovered that Sam's real name was Malinda. When Keith signed up to fight the Yankees, his wife put on men's attire and went with him to war.

Belle Reynolds encouraged her husband to offer his services to the Union, then insisted on going with the lieutenant when he marched off to war. Becoming a nurse with the Seventeenth Illinois Regiment, she accompanied her husband to Fort Henry, Fort Donelson, Shiloh, and Vicksburg. Belle didn't return to the land of Lincoln until Reynolds and his men were mustered out in May 1864.

Considered unfit for service—because she was female—as a nurse when she offered to go with the First Michigan Cavalry, Bridget Divers refused to take "no" for an answer. Purchasing a small supply of staple goods, she accompanied the unit as a vivandiere, somewhat like "a female sutler."

Little or nothing is known about the man she followed to war, but Bridget liked military life so well that she remained with the U.S. Army as a laundress after the end of the hostilities. Hundreds of soldiers knew Divers' wife simply as "Irish Bridget," and a smaller number persisted in calling her "Michigan Bridget."

Five

CLERGYMEN "FOUGHT LIKE HELL"

Because Federal conscription laws provided for employment of substitutes and payments of commutation fees, only about 6 percent of men drafted actually went into uniform. Also, requiring the clergy to fight remained a vexatious issue throughout the war. Governor A. G. Curtin of Pennsylvania wrestled with the issue in September 1864. About the same time, Bishop William H. De Lancey of New York asked Secretary of War William H. Stanton for a ruling. They learned that under a congressional act, "The clergy stand in the same position as members of other pursuits and professions." However, provost Marshal General James B. Fry offered to "entertain the question of detailing them for charitable and benevolent duties."

Wearers of the cloth fared differently in the Confederacy. A congressional act "to exempt certain persons from military duty" applied to "every minister of religion authorized to preach according to the rules of his sect." Some of the many other vocations to which conscription laws did not apply included: postmasters, members of state legislatures, merchant marine pilots, tanners, blacksmiths, wagon makers, millers, millwrights, and shoemakers.

In a special ruling made on November 6, 1861, Jefferson Davis said "necessities of the public defense" caused him to refuse to authorize the discharge from the army "young men who are candidates for the ministry."

Milton L. Haney was one of many Northern clergymen who went to war as a chaplain. During the July 22, 1864, battle of Atlanta, however, he relinquished his role as spiritual mentor of the Fifty-fifth Illinois Regiment. When another Federal unit withdrew from the field, leaving a gaping hole in the line, Haney took command of about fifty soldiers and stopped a potentially dangerous counterattack. Once the crisis was over, he resumed the normal duties of a chaplain and was awarded a Congressional Medal of Honor for his battlefield heroism.

Episcopal priest William N. Pendleton exchanged his robe for a gray uniform and at age fifty-one became a captain in the Rockbridge Artillery. Quickly promoted, he became chief of artillery on the staff of Confederate Gen. Joseph E. Johnston. Inordinately proud of four 6-pounder brass smoothbore cannons, he said they "spoke a powerful language." Hence he named them Matthew, Mark, Luke, and John.

On March 26, 1862, the priest-gunner became a brigadier general and was placed in charge of Robert E. Lee's artillery. Once the shooting stopped, Pendleton returned to Grace Church in Lexington, Virginia, where Robert E. Lee was briefly a member of the vestry.

Without relinquishing his title as bishop of Louisiana, Leonidas Polk became a Confederate lieutenant general. His military career, launched one grade lower, started on June 25, 1861. He fought at Columbus, Kentucky, and at Shiloh before winning a promotion just in time to be second in command to Gen. Braxton Bragg at Perryville. After having fought at Stones River and Murfreesboro, he quarreled with Bragg, who tried to send him before a court-martial.

Jefferson Davis came to the rescue of his longtime friend by assigning him to Mississippi. From that state he led his corps into Georgia in order to try to help stop Sherman's advance toward Atlanta. A Parrott gun, far more deadly than Pendleton's 6-pounders, practically took off the head of the bishop-general at Pine Mountain, Georgia, on June 14, 1864.

※

On August 25, 1862, Union Secretary of War Edwin Stanton gave a clear signal that Washington was dropping its opposition to the use of black soldiers. That day, Stanton authorized Brig. Gen. Rufus Saxton to recruit and train not more than five thousand former slaves.

In command at Beaufort, South Carolina, Saxton put Col. Thomas W. Higginson, a minister, at the head of the First South Carolina Colored Infantry. Many high-ranking officials in Washington strongly opposed to the use of black soldiers made life difficult for the colonel and his men. In spite of his fervent pleas, they were not paid for months. Following a near mutiny, the unit was disbanded.

Although Higginson failed to win distinction on battlefields, in post-war years, the clergyman who had been in uniform wrote *Army Life in a Black Regiment*, which continues to hold the interest of readers today.

※

Father Abram J. Ryan, a Catholic priest, tried to win a Confederate commission but was turned down. Undaunted, he became a freelance chaplain who wandered from one battlefield to another to administer last rites to the dying. Within a year after the war ended, he won national recognition for his poem "The Conquered Banner" and is remembered as the "poet-priest of the Lost Cause."

※

At the battle of Mine Run, chaplain Lorenzo Barber won the nickname "Fighting Parson." Members of an artillery battery were wasting ammunition by shooting over the heads of their foes. Barber took charge of a gun and with a single shot dropped a razorback hog that was rooting near the Confederate line.

Having demonstrated the proper elevation at which to fire, Barber relinquished the weapon to gunners only minutes before taking a hit from a Confederate sharpshooter.

William G. Brownlow had been a Methodist circuit rider for about ten years before becoming editor of the Knoxville *Whig*. Universally called "Parson," Brownlow was the leader of bridge-burning Unionists in East Tennessee. He never donned a uniform, but when banished to Federal territory he became sought after as an orator. As a platform speaker, his fiery messages persuaded hundreds of men to volunteer for Union service.

Perhaps the strangest facet of the extraordinary life of the parson who became a post-war governor of Tennessee and a U.S. senator was his combination of ideas. Fiercely loyal to the Union and violently opposed to secession, he minced no words in his insistence that slavery was the right and natural condition of "persons of color."

John Eaton, Jr. marched off to war as chaplain of the Twenty-seventh Ohio Regiment. Soon made a colonel and placed at the head of a regiment of black fighting men, he later became a brevet brigadier general. That honorary rank came to him as a reward for his work with runaway slaves. These fugitives had flocked to Ulysses S. Grant's army in such numbers that they seriously hampered its movements until Eaton took charge of them.

Eaton insisted that contrabands were desperately in need of both education and jobs, so he did his best to provide both. Even in the North, public opinion was only mildly favorable concerning "experiments with former slaves." This factor made it impossible for Eaton to achieve spectacular results; yet it was his work that provided the model for the Freedman's Bureau, established on March 4, 1865.

Methodist clergyman David C. Kelly was elected major when the 650 men who made up the command of Nathan B. Forrest were organized in October 1861. Early in November, Kelly's battalion left Hopkinsville, Kentucky, and soon met a Federal invasion party. Forrest achieved lasting renown as the finest cavalry leader of the war, but the only recorded victory of the Rev. Major Kelly was the seizure of a fine herd of Kentucky hogs.

The Rev. B. C. Ward, pastor of a Congregational church in Genesee, Illinois, conceived and announced a unique plan. Early in 1862, he received from the governor permission to recruit a company of infantry, all of whom were to be ordained clergymen. Ward solemnly called on "the fighting stock of the Church militant" to join him. Ministers, he urged, should "come out from behind velvet-cushioned barracks" in order to face "the hot shot of rifled artillery."

Despite wide publicity, ranks of the "clerical regiment" expanded so slowly that it was never called into service.

The Rev. Dr. Cox, a Chicago Methodist, believed his personal contribution could best be made behind battle lines. Hence he went to St. Louis and paid $37,000 for a former Presbyterian sanctuary in order to form "a purely Union church."

As announced in the St. Joseph, Missouri, *Journal*, his plans called for placing the Stars and Stripes on top of the bell tower and beginning every service by singing "Hail, Columbia!" Persons desiring to become members of his new flock would be required to say "Yes" to customary questions, in addition to the following: "Are you for the Union, and have you always been true to the flag?"

Known to his men as "the Fighting Parson," John M. Chivington was a minister who became major of the First Colorado Infantry. When the Federal unit was converted to cavalry, Chivington became its colonel. Leading his men in blue against a Cheyenne camp late in November 1864, he and his troops caught the Native Americans by surprise.

Disregarding a white flag shown by Cheyenne chieftain Black Kettle, soldiers killed right and left. In one of the least-heralded atrocities of the war, Union soldiers led by "the Fighting Parson" butchered at least 133 Native Americans.

⚬⚬⚬

Dozens of regiments first "saw the elephant," or went into battle, armed with flintlock muskets. Soon, however, a few fortunate units had weapons equipped to use percussion caps. Few who were delighted to get the more modern weapons, which were fired by means of the small metal caps, knew that they were the product of a clergyman's genius.

In 1805, the Rev. Alexander J. Forsyth of Scotland perfected this improvement in the firing system of a weapon. By 1865, nearly all fighting men on both sides were using the product of a Scottish pastor's brain.

⚬⚬⚬

Methodists, Baptists, Presbyterians, and adherents of other Protestant denominations experienced North-South divisions well before the war began. Sectional animosity among divided clergy was sometimes as fierce as that displayed in hand-to-hand combat.

According to the Mobile *Tribune*, the Rev. H. A. M. Henderson of Alabama vented his rage in an 1862 letter to the New Orleans *Christian Advocate*. Writing of a fellow Methodist named Black who was stationed in Newport, Kentucky, Henderson reported that he prayed that the Union may be preserved "even though blood may come out of the wine-presses even unto the horses' bridles."

Urging the speedy capture of Jefferson Davis and P. G. T. Beauregard, Black knew what to do with them. In an impassioned sermon he gave worshippers his formula for their treatment: "Hang them up on Mason and Dixon's Line, that traitors of both sections may be warned. Let them hang until the vultures shall eat their rotten flesh from their bones; let them hang until the crows shall build their filthy nests in their skeletons."

Henderson soon decided that actions speak louder than words. According to the Richmond *Dispatch*, by November 1861 he was busy raising a regiment. According to the newspaper published in the Confederate capital:

> He was driven from Kentucky because he would not take upon him the Lincoln yoke. It argues well for the Southern confederacy to see the clergy flying to arms.

It is stated here that one-half of the Baptist ministers of this state are in the army, so that in the convention, many vacant seats are to be found.

The Rev. William A. Pile, a Methodist minister, joined the fray as chaplain of the First Missouri Light Artillery. Just ten months later, in June 1862, he transferred to line duty as captain of the unit's Battery I. Boosted to the rank of brigadier general, the clergyman's leadership of black troops at Fort Blakely, Alabama, was so outstanding that he became a brevet major general.

Another Methodist, Granville Moody, had no interest in the chaplains' corps. When the Seventy-fourth Ohio Regiment was being formed, he was invited to become its colonel. After gaining the consent of those who made up the membership of his church, he took the post. At Stones River, his men gave him the same nickname bestowed on Lorenzo Barber and John M. Chivington: "Fighting Parson."

According to the New York *World*, the Rev. Harvey E. Chapin did much better than Moody. On October 16, 1861, he arrived at Camp Strong, leading a company of sixty-four men, most of whom were members of the congregation he left behind.

Less than a month later, editors of the Cincinnati *Gazette* described actions of the former pastor of a German Baptist church in Albany, New York. Taking leave of his flock, the Rev. A. A. Von Puttkammer "assumed command of the Havelock Flying Artillery, 160 men and six guns." Von Puttkammer, reported the Ohio newspaper, "admits none but men of Christ character into his command, and proposes to observe worship three times a day when practicable."

Pointing out that both sides customarily freed captured surgeons, Confederate lawmakers argued for similar treatment of chaplains. As a result, the adjutant general's office issued a special order on July 1, 1862: "All chaplains taken prisoners of war by the armies of the Confederate States while engaged in the discharge of their proper duties will be immediately and unconditionally released."

Pastor of a Unitarian church in Concord when the Third New Hampshire regiment was organized, the Rev. Mr. Billings donned a uniform as a chaplain. Soon he became a lieutenant colonel.

According to the New York *World*, this was the man who told residents to evacuate St. Simon's Island, Georgia. Following his orders, soldiers seized "the splendid mansion once occupied by ex-U.S. Senator and arch-rebel T. Butler King, and stripped it of everything."

A report published in the Memphis *Bulletin* said that notorious Tennessee guerrilla leader Richardson had as his chief aide the Rev. Captain Burrow, an ordained minister of the Cumberland Presbyterian Church.

Pendleton, the clergyman who became Lee's chief of artillery, seems to have first surged to prominence at Bull Run in 1861. Men who fought under his direction later swore that when a cannon was aimed to his liking he signaled for it to be fired, bowed his head, and prayed: "Lord, preserve the soul while I destroy the body."

Union Sgt. Boston Corbett survived the rigors of Andersonville Prison for five months. After recuperating, he was assigned to Company C of the Sixteenth New York Cavalry. Men from this unit formed one of the detachments sent to hunt John Wilkes Booth following Lincoln's assassination.

Corbett later testified that he found Booth in a tobacco barn and shot him against orders because he had direct instructions from the Almighty to do so. He was rewarded for his exploit, but many of his comrades—and later, analysts—said evidence showed he couldn't possibly have been Booth's killer.

In spite of questions raised by this story, the man who said he obeyed a divine order to kill claimed part of the reward offered by authorities who were seeking to capture Booth. Probably using the $1,653.85 he collected from U.S. Secretary of War Stanton, the former prisoner-sergeant travelled throughout the east before settling down in Camden, New Jersey, as pastor of the city mission.

At Hillsboro, North Carolina, Judge M. E. Manly presided over what was termed "the examination of the Rev. R. J. Graves." Having been found guilty of aiding and abetting Union forces then in control of the region, Graves was bound over to appear at court in Richmond. There he would face charges of having committed acts of treason against the Confederacy.

The Rev. Charles A. Davis fared somewhat better. Having entered Union service as a chaplain, he was expelled from the Methodist Conference of Virginia during its 1863 session at Petersburg. Though stripped of his credentials, Davis remained in uniform as spiritual counselor to his regiment.

Relatively few chaplains were killed in early action. An exception was the Rev. A. B. Fuller, chaplain of the Sixteenth Massachusetts regiment. After he was dropped by a Confederate bullet at Fredericksburg, he was given a citywide funeral in Boston.

Confederate Maj. Gen. John H. Winder, head of all Confederate prisons in 1863, issued a special order on July 4. Under its terms, two of the seventy-five Union captains then held in Libby Prison were to be selected for execution.

When prisoners assembled "in the large room on the first floor," Capt. T. N. Turner informed them of his orders and asked how they wished the choices to be made. Capt. Henry Sawyer instantly called out, "Let Chaplain Brown do the job!"

Despite an order of the previous year, the chaplain of the Fifth Maryland Regiment and two other chaplains were among those imprisoned in Richmond. As the men facing possible execution shouted their approval of Sawyer's nomination, Brown stepped forward. Described as "showing visible emotion," he reached into a box filled with slips of paper on which names had been written. Taking out a slip, the chaplain handed it to Turner without looking at it. With every man in the room frozen in attention, the Confederate commandant solemnly read: "Henry Washington Sawyer, Captain, First New Jersey Cavalry."

During a series of battles near Richmond, Captain T. L. Duke of the Nineteenth Virginia Regiment seized a musket and rushed into the fray. Soon, however, he took personal charge of a band of sharpshooters and directed their movements. In the aftermath of having proved his merit as a fighting man, Duke was made a captain of scouts and went to Mississippi with them. Post-war Confederate documents lauded him as "a double-barrel patriot."

During the final months of the struggle, numerous chaplains who never used a rifle or carried a battle flag were killed in battle or maimed for life. According to records of the Sixth Texas Cavalry, the Confederate unit lost two chaplains during a period of three years.

The Rev. Mr. Vanderhurst, "a talented young minister from Waco," was shot dead at Corinth. The Rev. Ed Hudson, who took over his duties, sustained serious wounds during the same battle. After recovering, Hudson rejoined the regiment. In an 1864 fight at Newnan, Georgia, against McCook's raiders, Hudson was hit by a shell fragment and was never again able to walk without crutches.

Six

THE ROLE OF HOSTAGES
IN THE STRUGGLE FOR SUPREMACY

Philadelphia, Dec. 13, 1861

Hon. Simon Cameron, Sec'y of War:

Days and nights of intense anxiety must prevail among all of us unhappy wives and mothers and children of those unfortunate hostages and so-called pirates. My child comes home and cries whenever he thinks of his kind and indulgent father whom he has not seen for five months.

He left home July 15 as Capt. Francis F. Keffer, Company H, First California Regiment, the late Col. E. D. Baker's brigade, and was taken prisoner at Ball's Bluff battle, October 21.

He does not complain for he knows he is not the only one who is suffering, but he wishes me to appeal to you and President Lincoln in their behalf.

Yours with respect,

Mrs. A. Keffer

P.S. Mr. Cameron, please let the President read this or have it read to him as I cannot appear in person.

By December, despairing that there would not be a quick resolution of difficulties that arose five months earlier, Mrs. Keffer dared to hope that a personal appeal would have some effect. Her plea was wasted on the chief executive who could be moved to tears at hearing that a runaway soldier was about to be executed. If Cameron ever showed the president this letter from a grieving wife and mother, he pushed it aside without responding; Keffer's name appears nowhere in Lincoln's papers.

～～

A train of events that produced Mrs. Keffer's appeal was launched on June 28, when the Confederate privateer *Jeff Davis* put to sea. Not until July 16 did the Charleston-based schooner take its first prize, the brig *Enchantress*. Put aboard the vessel as prize master, Walter W. Smith was captured—along with his crew—by the USS *Albatross* on the day after Bull Run.

Taken to Philadelphia and put on trial for piracy, there was no foot dragging like that which marked the trial of men from the first privateer to be captured, the *Savannah*. Smith's case went to court on October 22; six days later he was convicted by two judges and sentenced to death.

As soon as the man for whom the privateer was named heard about the verdict, he moved into action. At his direction, Confederate Secretary of War Judah P. Benjamin on November 9 drafted an order to Brig. Gen. John H. Winder. Under its terms, Federal officers imprisoned in Richmond were to be selected as hostages for the safety of the "pirates" held by Union authorities.

Writing a terse summary of this celebrated issue, Jefferson Davis noted that "By this course the infamous attempt made by the United States Government to inflict judicial murder was arrested."

On November 10, Winder went to Castle Thunder prison in Richmond. Federal officers being held there were assembled, and Benjamin's order of the previous day was read to them. John Whyte of the Sixty-ninth New York described events of the dramatic scene in a letter penned that evening. According to him, names of six colonels "were placed in a tin or ballot box, a cap covering it, and then well shaken."

New York congressman Alfred Ely, captured on the field after Bull Run, was chosen by Winder to conduct the lottery. At a nod, he lifted out one slip and announced, "Colonel Michael Corcoran." That made the leader of the Sixty-ninth New York hostage for the safety of Smith.

Summarizing the ceremony, Capt. Milton Cogswell listed the men who had been selected as hostages for thirteen prisoners held in New York. Five more colonels, two lieutenant colonels, and three majors were named. Because that exhausted the supply of these officers held in the Richmond prison, three captains were selected by lot in order to complete the roster of hostages.

Two of the captains chosen were found to be seriously wounded, so their names were withdrawn and a new lottery was held. As a result, John F. McQuade of the Thirty-eighth New York remained a prisoner of war and Mrs. Francis Keffer's husband took his place as "a condemned felon."

Corcoran had been captured at Bull Run, along with at least eighteen other men from his "Fighting Sixty-ninth." After a brief stay in Richmond, they were sent to Charleston's Castle Pinckney, where they were permitted to pose for a group photograph. By the time it was taken, most of the hostages were confident that some sort of trade would be arranged, in spite of the fact that "pirates" in New York had not yet gone on trial.

Because of acute embarrassment faced by Lincoln, it was one thing to reach a general understanding about "pirates" and officers held as hostages for them but quite a different matter to implement that understanding. As a result, it was not until August 1862 that Corcoran ceased to be a pawn in the North-South power struggle.

Coincidentally, a long report drafted at Martinique bore the same date as Benjamin's directive to Winder. Summarizing his experiences to date, Capt. Raphael Semmes of the Confederate raider *Sumter* detailed his capture of eighteen Yankee vessels. When he stopped at Trinidad on July 30, he wrote, he heard about the plight of Smith and the men from the *Savannah*. By the time he reached Martinique in order to land prisoners from the captured *Joseph Maxwell*, it was generally believed that no "pirate" would be executed.

Semmes recorded his delight at hearing this news at the mail station. "It has been my intention," he wrote, "had the government of the United States dared to carry out its barbarous threat of treating the prisoners of the *Savannah* as pirates, to hang members of the crew of the *Maxwell* man for man." He was glad, he said, to inform his prisoners "that this unpleasant duty had not been imposed upon me."

~~~

In the voluminous *Official Records* of the war, the term *hostage* is applied only to Federal officers who would have been killed in reprisal had Confederate "pirates" been executed. Despite the fact that the designation was so rarely employed, the conflict saw numerous instances of hostage taking. Both the North and the South seized not only men in uniform, but also men, women, and children not involved in the conflict.

Ulysses S. Grant seems to have been the first general officer to condone the practice. On August 25, 1861, he ordered Captain Chitwood to lead his men to Jefferson City, Missouri. Because that involved marching through open country believed to harbor many hostile settlers, Grant told him that "A few leading and prominent secessionists may be carried along as hostages."

~~~

November 1862 saw Confederate Brig. Gen. John H. Winder ask for the name of a suitable person to be placed in irons "as a hostage for Mr. Smith, who was connected with the burning of the *Alleghanian*." Thirty days later, twenty-six New England sea captains imprisoned at Salisbury, North Carolina, selected three from their number by lottery. Chase, Litchfield, and Kennett then became hostages for Confederates held at Alton, Illinois.

~~~

John Y. Beall fought in gray at First Bull Run, then was an acting master in the Confederate navy. He and his fourteen men were labeled pirates when captured in November 1863. Federal officers who were prisoners of war were chosen as hostages and charges of piracy were dropped; in a separate case Beall was later executed as a spy.

Civilians on both sides became deeply involved in hostage taking. James S. Wadsworth, military governor of the District of Columbia, took four Virginians as "hostages for the return of Union citizens now imprisoned in Richmond."

Confederates called Dr. William P. Rucker of Greenbriar, Virginia, "a notorious spy and bridge burner." His July 1861 arrest prompted Federals to take "three of the most respectable citizens of Greenbriar as hostages." Belligerents later reached an agreement that led to the release of both sets of prisoners.

Andrew Johnson, the leader of unionist forces in Tennessee, took over with a stern hand when he became military governor. Dealing with a hotbed of secessionist activity in May 1862, he told soldiers to hold twelve Rutherford County citizens as hostages. Jailed civilians, Johnson believed, would "secure the safety of Murfreesboro and guard against the repetition of unlawful acts."

Apparently the ploy succeeded, for a few weeks later he made a detailed report to Lincoln. Having discovered that seventy civilians from East Tennessee were imprisoned at Mobile because of unionist sentiments, he told the president that he had taken steps "to arrest 70 vile secessionists." Johnson then posed a direct question: "Does this meet with your approval?"

Keenly aware that Federal officers held as hostages would soon force him to act as though his 1861 proclamation concerning piracy had never been issued, the president sent a guarded reply to Tennessee. In it, he simply said he did not "disapprove of the proposition."

With seven Union officers being held in Richmond in August 1862, Federal judge-advocate Levi C. Turner turned to a provost marshal. Lafayette C. Baker was told to arrest fourteen citizens of Fredericksburg and "hold them in custody as hostages for the safety of the prisoners of war." Almost simultaneously, Maj. Gen. John Pope seized six citizens of the same town "as hostages for the release of Union men carried off by the rebels."

On August 27, Confederate Secretary of War George Randolph ordered the exchange of many prisoners, timed to coincide with the Federal release of seventeen hostages. Yet if civilians breathed a sigh of relief, they reacted too soon. Instead of diminishing, the hostage issue surged upward. Silas Richmond and a fellow unionist were arrested and imprisoned in Richmond. Washington responded by seizing Thomas H. Crow and William H. Carter and putting them in Fort McHenry.

Knowing many staunch secessionists to be imprisoned by the North, Richmond turned to a prison camp in North Carolina. A November 13 directive announced that "91 or 92 persons" in Salisbury were being held as "hostages for our citizens." One week later, Union Maj. Gen. T. C. Hindman reported that Maj. Gen. James G. Blunt was holding "a number of southern citizens as hostages: for Federals sick in North Carolina.

Because arrangements for the exchange of prisoners were about to be perfected, Richmond released on January 10, 1863, the names of seventy-seven men whose cases were closed. Ten more, however, were reported as being "retained as hostages for our citizens held as prisoners."

⸻

December 1863 saw black soldiers under Brig. Gen. Edward A. Wild execute Daniel Bright of the Sixty-second Georgia Infantry. Confederate Brig. Gen. George E. Pickett responded by hanging Pvt. Samuel Jones of the Fifth U.S. Colored Troops. Federal forces then made hostages of Mrs. Phoebe Munden and Mrs. Elizabeth Weeks. Enraged, Gov. Zebulon Vance of North Carolina demanded that the women be released. Union Maj. Gen. Benjamin Butler, to whom the matter was referred, graciously consented to let their husbands take their places.

⁕

Fredericksburg moved to center stage in May 1864, when sixty Federal soldiers surrendered to civilian authorities. U.S. Secretary of War Edwin M. Stanton responded by having sixty-four Virginia civilians arrested and held as hostages until his fighting men were set free.

⁕

Union Maj. Gen. Lovell H. Rousseau added a new dimension to the hostage issue during his occupation of Huntsville, Alabama. Every day, he said, "murders are committed by lawless bands who fire into railroad trains." Moving to halt this practice, on August 8, 1862, Rousseau had a dozen leading citizens placed in custody. Each morning, one of them was put on the train to discourage Confederates from shooting at it.

⁕

Richard Thomas, leader of a band of Confederate irregulars, made a name for himself by dressing as a woman and calling himself "the French Lady." When he was arrested in July 1861, Virginia authorities chose as hostages for his safety Capt. Thomas Damron; lieutenants Wilson Damron, David V. Auxier, and Isaac Goble; and privates Samuel Pack, William S. Dils, and J. W. Howe. Two years after Thomas was captured, these seven men were released in exchange for him.

⁕

When Union Capt. Emil Frey was captured at Gettysburg, he was sent to Libby Prison in Richmond. He and four comrades were chosen by lot to serve as hostages to guarantee fair treatment of imprisoned Confederates. After seventy-seven days, Washington released the men for whose safety the Federal officers were being held responsible.

Virginia Governor John Letcher read in newspapers that two of his rangers had been captured and were scheduled to be hung. Writing to Confederate Secretary of War George Randolph, he observed that "We must let Mr. Lincoln understand that for every man of this class who shall be executed we will execute in like manner one of corresponding grade selected from the prisoners in our custody."

Virginians in jeopardy held the rank of captain. Hence Letcher requested that Randolph select by lot two Federal captains "who shall be subjected to the same punishment that the Lincoln officers may visit upon Spriggs and Triplett."

Two members of the pro-Confederate Missouri State Guard had been captured and sentenced to death. An urgent plea went to Confederate Secretary of War Randolph without using the term "hostage." He simply was requested "to accomplish something for humanity by the institution of such retaliatory measures as may influence the enemy to mitigate those barbarities now so shamefully practiced, through consideration for his soldiers whom the fortunes of war have placed in our power." At Randolph's direction, Provost Marshal John Winder, who headed the Confederate prison system, saw to it that lots were cast "for two hostages of equal rank to Assistant Surgeons Foster and Vowles."

Maj. Gen. William T. Sherman devised a special role for captives. No man to treat the enemy lightly, he became furious when a buried torpedo (now known as a land mine) blew off the foot of an officer as Federal forces approached Savannah, Georgia. Sherman immediately brought bands of Confederate prisoners to the head of the column. These hostages were forced to test the ground at points where torpedoes were suspected.

During the 1864 bombardment of Charleston by Federal warships, a Confederate officer conceived a brilliant idea. Soon fifty-one Union officers who were prisoners of war were placed in range of their own artillery. One of them, Brig. Gen. Charles A. Heckman, later reported that Brig. Gen. John G. Foster put an end to that caper very quickly. Wrote Heckman: "Foster ordered down from Johnson's Island 5 Confederate generals, 15 colonels, 15 lieutenant colonels, and 15 majors" and exposed them to fire from guns of the city's defenders.

Grant had issued an order that forbade the exchange of prisoners, but in the unusual situation at Charleston, a special agreement was reached. Half a hundred officers in gray were soon exchanged for hostages in blue. Once that was done, it seemed logical to Confederates to bring more men to Charleston in order to effect another exchange.

Transportation problems prevented Confederates from implementing this scheme, but Federals at Hilton Head, South Carolina, didn't know that it had been scrapped. Consequently they brought about six hundred Confederate prisoners of war to Morris Island, near Charleston, and placed them in a stockade where they would be exposed to gunfire from Fort Sumter. After six weeks, men comprising this unique band of hostages were sent to Fort Pulaski, Georgia, and other points. In Confederate lore, they were compared with the heroes of the battle of Balaklava in the Crimean War and revered as "the Immortal Six Hundred."

When a simultaneous release was arranged during the summer of 1864, James Hamilton used his experience to offer suggestions to Edwin M. Stanton, the U.S. Secretary of War. Writing on September 2, the man who had spent thirteen months as a hostage suggested, "You might hold hostages for the negro soldiers if they refuse to exchange them." He then proposed that Virginia civilians be held hostage to procure the release of seven men still held in North Carolina.

At Fort Pillow, Tennessee, on April 12, 1864, troopers under Confederate Maj. Gen. Nathan Bedford Forrest quickly defeated its Federal defenders. Fierce fighting left 204 out of 262 black soldiers dead or so badly wounded that they were not taken prisoner. Testimony from Federal survivors strongly supported charges of a deliberate massacre.

With Washington in turmoil, Stanton endorsed a plan proposed by Secretary of State Seward. Had it been implemented, Confederate prisoners equal in number and rank to Federals who died at Pillow would have Been "set apart and held in rigorous confinement" until "perpetrators of the massacre" were identified and surrendered.

Secretary of the Treasury Chase thought this measure too mild, but Secretary of the Navy Welles opposed attempts at retaliation. Though Lincoln seems to have favored mass designation of prisoners as hostages, Stanton's idea evoked so much negative reaction that it was never implemented.

Ulysses S. Grant, probably not consulted concerning the Fort Pillow "massacre," wouldn't have hesitated to use hostages. Angry at successful raids by Confederate cavalry, Grant suggested to Maj. Gen. Phillip Sheridan a possible way to stop depredations by men under partisan commander John S. Mosby. "Seize members of their families," suggested the general in chief. "Then put them in Fort McHenry as hostages 'for good conduct' of enemy rangers."

A few prominent men triggered the most bizarre case in which prisoners of war became hostages. Confederate captains T. G. McGraw and William F. Corbin, captured in Kentucky, were executed for having persuaded Federals to desert. Richmond responded by giving the death sentence to captains W. H. Sawyer and John M. Flinn, who were then being held in Libby Prison.

When informed that these men were scheduled to die, Washington leaders rejoiced that they held two aces in the prisoner poker game.

Confederate Brig. Gen. William Henry Fitzhugh ("Rooney") Lee, a prisoner, was told that he'd hang if Sawyer should die. Simultaneously, Capt. John H. Winder was selected as hostage for Flinn.

This meant that Robert E. Lee and the son of the commandant of Richmond prisons each had a son in jeopardy. If Federals should go to the gallows in retaliation for executions in Kentucky, so would these two Confederate officers.

This delicate and complex situation was not resolved until February 1864, when both sets of hostages were freed.

Because many records were destroyed and others have not gone into print, no one knows how many hundreds of persons were held hostage during the Civil War. This much is clear, however: reported orally and in news media, each instance in which a man or woman was held as hostage—at risk of life—served to heighten sectional anger.

With the collapse of the Confederacy seen by many as imminent, Grant wrote to Lee on February 16, 1865, to protest a newspaper report stating that thirty-seven unionist civilians were being held in Richmond's Castle Thunder. Two days later, Lee responded in almost casual fashion. He said he knew nothing about the matter, but would investigate it. "If it be true that those mentioned were taken by any of our forces, I presume they are held as hostages," he concluded.

As a result of a bizarre set of coincidences, both Jefferson Davis and Abraham Lincoln were selected as potential hostages, provided they could be captured alive.

Top Union leaders—perhaps including Abraham Lincoln—seem to have approved a scheme to abduct the Confederate president. A prisoner of such importance would give the Union great leverage in demanding immediate and unconditional surrender by Confederates. So when plans were made for a

January 1864 raid upon Richmond, secret orders were given to an officer under the command of Brig. Gen. Hugh Judson ("Kill Cavalry") Kilpatrick. When felled by Confederate fire, Col. Ulrich Dahlgren was found to have on his person a set of papers that outlined a plot to kill or to kidnap Jefferson Davis.

When "the Dahlgren papers" were made public, Union officials indignantly dismissed them as forgeries. Recent investigation, has, however, turned up strong evidence in support of the charge that the incriminating documents were genuine.

Even Lee's surrender at Appomattox did not put an end to the notion of using hostages to gain concessions. John Wilkes Booth made careful plans to kidnap Lincoln and members of his cabinet in order to hold them as hostages. Only when he realized that he couldn't possibly get the president past Union lines did the famous actor turn assassin.

Well after all the shooting had stopped, the hostage concept remained alive. A band of counterfeiters made elaborate plans to steal the body of Lincoln from its Springfield, Illinois, crypt and hold it hostage for the release of their leader. However, they were thwarted because a Secret Service agent had infiltrated the band and arranged for police to be on hand when the vault was opened.

Seven

HORSES KEPT THE WAR ALIVE

U nion cavalrymen were usually provided with a government-owned horse, but an exception was found in the case of the Third Pennsylvania Cavalry, whose men rode their own steeds.

Any enlisted man who brought his own mount was entitled to fifty cents a day in extra pay. By October 1861, virtually all units were offered animals owned by the government.

One year later, the Federal government owned approximately 150,000 horses and 100,000 mules. During the first two years of fighting, Union cavalry units—which never had more than 60,000 men in the field—were supplied with about 240,000 horses. Before Lee surrendered, Federal funds had paid for an estimated 840,000 horses and at least 430,000 mules.

Confederate officers and mounted troopers were required to provide their own animals, for which they were reimbursed at the rate of forty cents per day. Its owner had to find a new one when a horse was killed, worn out, or lost; if that proved impossible, he was transferred to infantry service.

Maj. Gen. George B. McClellan transported his Union forces by water when he prepared to launch what became the Peninsular campaign. His immense flotilla carried to the field about 15,000 horses and mules along with 130,000 men. By the time Maj. Gen. William T. Sherman was ready to begin the March to the Sea, proportions had changed. He commanded only about 62,000 men, but used 28,000 horses and 32,000 mules.

At war's end, horses still represented the fastest means of transportation other than a few fine railroads. A trained cavalry mount was reported to walk at the rate of one hundred yards per minute. Trotting, an animal covered twice as much ground in the same time. When a horse was spurred to a gallop, its speed was four hundred yards per minute, equivalent to fifteen miles per hour had it been able to maintain top speed.

During the trial of Mary Surratt, accused of aiding John Wilkes Booth, many believed she was innocent even after she was convicted by a military tribunal. On the day set for her execution, Brig. Gen. Winfield S. Hancock had reason to believe that a reprieve might be issued by President Andrew Johnson. Hancock therefore established relays of horses, whose riders were to race to the grounds of the Washington Arsenal if the hanging were deferred.

Most Federal and some Confederate cavalry units rode to battle but dismounted as soon as action was expected. Because the typical horseman fought on foot, one-fourth of the manpower of most cavalry regiments was needed for the essential job of horse-holding.

When a private in an infantry unit was wounded, it was customary for an officer to dismount and provide him with a horse if he was strong enough to "retire from the field." Fighting on his own two feet instead of in the saddle proved awkward and uncomfortable—or worse—for many a colonel who accepted the unwritten code according to which "wounded men capable of survival come first."

A dead horse often formed an impromptu barricade for one or more fighting men under enemy fire. Especially when pickets were sniping at one another at short range, protection of this sort was highly prized even if the animal was "giving off odors of putrefaction."

According to Capt. Hartwell Osborn, the Federal Eleventh and Twelfth Corps traveled 994 miles by rail when sent from Washington to Bridgeport, Alabama, in 1863. With the 17,500 men went 45 guns and 717 wagons and ambulances.

Aside from horses required by officers, said Osborn, 3,402 animals were taken south to pull vehicles of the fighting units.

One of Osborn's comrades, who made the nine-day trip by rail with him, arrived at a different count. According to him:

> The Eleventh Corps had in its quartermaster's train 261 six-mule wagons, 75 two-horse ambulances, and 3 two-horse spring wagons.
>
> The Twelfth Corps carried 165 four-horse teams, 1,156 six-mule teams, and 75 two-horse ambulances.
>
> To these nearly 3,400 animals were added those of ten batteries, some 1,100 in number and the horses of the field and staff officers.

A standard U.S. Army wagon was 120 inches long (inside measurement), 43 inches wide, and 22 inches high. Such a vehicle was rated as capable of transporting a cargo of about 2,600 pounds—equivalent to 1,500 individual rations of bread, coffee, sugar, and salt.

Fully loaded, such a vehicle required a team of four horses or six mules for travel on good roads. Other loads and circumstances required more animals.

When Stonewall Jackson captured a bevy of locomotives near Harpers Ferry, he discovered that they'd have to be pulled overland to reach a Confederate railroad line. As a result, he hitched a team of forty horses to each captive locomotive for the trek to the Manassas Gap Railroad.

Veteran U.S. cavalrymen learned how to supplement information received from their scouts. "By the nervous twitching of our horses' ears," recalled a member of the expedition led into Alabama by Brig. Gen. James H. Wilson, "we learn that the enemy is near us—and soon we find him."

At the outbreak of armed conflict, the field commander of the U.S. Army was physically unable to mount a horse.

Subordinate only to the president, who was also commander in chief, at age seventy-five brevet Lt. Gen. Winfield Scott had directed the U.S. Army since 1841. Behind his back, subordinates called him "Old Fuss and Feathers." Every member of the tiny professional army knew that their leader was afflicted with gout and was too heavy to sit in a saddle.

Because no general directed his fighting men on foot, it was obvious that Scott couldn't go into combat. As much as any other factor, Scott's inability to ride contributed to George B. McClellan's October 1861 success in his campaign to supplant "Old Fuss and Feathers" as the Union's top brass.

During the Wilderness campaign, reporter Henry E. Wing of the New York *Tribune* was the only man from Union forces to reach a telegraph line with vital reports. He got there on foot, having been forced to abandon his horse when observed by Confederates. When he demanded the right to send lengthy dispatches to New York, U.S. Secretary of War Edwin M. Stanton ordered his arrest.

Abraham Lincoln countermanded Stanton's order and sent a train to bring Wing to Washington. After a dramatic 2:00 A.M. session in the White House, the president detailed for the reporter an escort of cavalry and artillery with which to return to the scene of his adventures. Wing triumphantly led them to the spot where he had hidden his horse in a thicket after he was spotted by Confederate Maj. John S. Mosby's men.

Having recovered the animal, Wing resumed the task of trying to please his publisher, Horace Greeley, and *Tribune* readers throughout the North.

According to newspaper reports from Aiken, South Carolina, the oldest surviving four-footed veteran of the war was living there in 1894. Having been sired in Sevierville, Tennessee, Old Jim took a bullet in his neck somewhere in his native state. Lieutenant McMahon later rode him to the battle of Atlanta, then to Savannah, and into South Carolina.

When the nine-hundred-pound horse became riderless in a skirmish, he wandered to the plantation of W. T. Williams. Identified long afterward by brands and saddle markings, Old Jim spent his declining years as a crowd pleaser in parades of Civil War veterans.

As a member of a wealthy New York family, Philip Kearny had nearly everything he wanted—except a military career. Forced by family pressure to become an attorney, he stuck to that vocation until his grandfather's will made him a millionaire.

As soon as he got his hands on his fortune, Kearny went to France to study at the Samur cavalry school. From that installation he went to Africa as a cavalry leader and fought with such distinction that he won the French Legion of Honor. Back in the United States, he fought in the Mexican War before returning to Europe to take part in the Crimean War.

When the Civil War erupted, Kearny's commission as a brigadier general of volunteers was backdated to May 17, 1861. Having led with distinction at Williamsburg, Seven Pines, and during the Seven Days, he was made a major general.

Few men on either side had a combat record to match that of Kearny. Still, he managed to ride into Confederate instead of Union lines at Chantilly and realized his blunder too late to spur his mount to safety. A volley from Virginians in gray brought an end to his distinguished career and his riderless horse was captured.

When Robert E. Lee learned what had taken place, he told aides that "a gesture of courtesy" was essential. When they nodded in agreement, the commander of the Army of Northern Virginia dispatched Kearny's horse and gear to the distraught widow of his opponent.

Late in the war, Egyptian dignitaries decided to send a blooded stallion to Jefferson Davis as a gift. Shipped across the Atlantic on the *Banshee*, a British-owned blockade runner, all went well until the vessel tried to slip into Wilmington, North Carolina, under the cover of darkness. When the neighing of the white Arabian horse was heard aboard a Federal blockading vessel, its crew members moved into action.

Chased into shoal water twenty miles southwest of Beaufort by the USS *Grand Gulf*, the captain of the *Banshee* chose to surrender to the men aboard the transport steamer *Fulton* rather than to the captain of the pursuing warship. As senior military officer on the vessel, Maj. James E. Bailey of the Third Rhode Island Artillery formally accepted the surrender.

Bailey's December 24, 1863, report stressed that the *Banshee* and her cargo were prizes of war belonging to the men who were on the *Fulton* at the time of her capture. However, his account of the capture failed to mention the blooded Egyptian horse bound for Richmond. As a result, official records do not indicate what became of the animal that crossed the Atlantic safely—but never bore on its back the president of the Confederacy.

Ordered to move out at night and prepare to engage the enemy on the following day, men of the Fourteenth Virginia Cavalry were ready and willing to fight. They had taken part in two dozen engagements, and were eager for more.

Col. James Cochran didn't like to disappoint his men, but he had no choice. Reluctantly, he sent a courier to headquarters to explain why orders could not be obeyed: every horse of the regiment had been turned out to graze.

At West Point, cadet Ulysses S. Grant made mediocre grades and excelled at just one skill: horsemanship. When not aboard one of his favorite mounts, he whiled away his time making sketches of horses. Though he had no training in art, Grant's work was of professional quality. He was so good that he is now listed as the only president of the United States prior to Dwight D. Eisenhower who knew how to put a horse on canvas.

Confederate Capt. S. Isadore Guillet knew that three of his brothers had been killed while riding the same horse. Desperate for a mount, he climbed aboard the animal and soon took a fatal wound. Because a horse was a valuable piece of property that any man would want to remain in his family, Guillet had willed to a nephew the horse on whose back four riders had been shot.

～～～

At Chickamauga, officers of the Ninety-eighth Ohio Regiment found themselves with a horse they labeled as "jinxed." Capt. Moses Urquhart led the unit into battle and was shot from his saddle during an early Confederate volley.

Command devolved upon Capt. Armstrong Thomas, so he mounted the same animal—only to die within minutes. Capt. John Lochry then took over, only to be killed on Urquhart's mount.

Three dead officers should have been enough, the men of the regiment later agreed. Youthful Lieutenant Milliner, the senior officer left on the field, jumped on the jinxed mount. He escaped death, but suffered all his life from an arm shattered by a Minié ball while he was in the saddle.

～～～

Military officers charged with guarding president-elect Abraham Lincoln on March 4, 1860, put their horses to special use. According to one of them, "During the march to the Capitol, by an apparently clumsy use of my spurs I managed to keep the horses uneasy. They were in such a state that it would have been difficult for even a very good rifle shot to get an aim at an inmate of the carriage between the dancing animals."

～～～

On November 23, 1863, Union Maj. Gen. George Stoneman castigated a colleague in writing. Brig. Gen. George A. Custer, he noted had a reputation for permitting men of his brigade to be "great horse-killers." Small wonder, therefore, reported Stoneman that seventeen animals "considered serviceable when they left the depot" probably were "used up as stated" in Custer's terse account of a raid.

To modern readers, such a report seems perfunctory. In 1863 it was serious, indeed. Horses were so scarce and expensive that any officer shown to have pushed them to the point of exhaustion was sure to be severely reprimanded.

Whatever the initial cost of a mount, a Confederate who took his own animal into battle faced additional expenses. According to a veteran of the gray, by 1865 it was not unusual for an officer to pay four hundred dollars in Confederate currency to have his horse curried.

Near the Chickahominy River, hungry Federal forces learned that a bridge had washed away, making it impossible to get desperately needed supplies of food to wounded men lying in a field hospital. In this emergency Brigadier General Sedgwick, affectionately known to his troops as "Uncle John," sent for Col. Daniel Hand. Long afterward, Hand himself revealed what quickly took place: "General Sedgwick gave me two cavalry horses and allowed a detail of two butcher-boys from the First Minnesota. We led the horses into a grove near the hospital, and in a very short time some beautiful beef was lying on the skins with the edges carefully turned under."

Union Brig. Gen. George W. Morgan seized strategic Cumberland Gap in June 1862. By September his men were in desperate straits; still, he reported to Maj. Gen. Horatio Wright: "Can hold Cumberland Gap 60 days by eating horses and mules."

According to some analysts, that estimate was accurate at the time it was made. Morgan, however, failed to take into account the fact that his supply of forage for the animals would be exhausted in just three days. When Union scouts reached the strategic site on June 18, they found the enemy with hungry horses had pulled out during the previous night.

When he wasn't lounging around a theater, part-time Washington resident John Wilkes Booth could often be seen going about town—riding a one-eyed horse.

Neither Confederate nor Union regulations ever stipulated that a cavalryman could doze while riding. Yet by the time the conflict was half over, leaders on both sides took it for granted that a veteran fighting man would sleep about half the time he was in the saddle.

Most officers refused to ride a white horse because it presented a tempting target for enemy sharpshooters. There were, however, conspicuous exceptions to this general practice.

At Hilton Head, South Carolina, Confederate Brig. Gen. Thomas F. Drayton's favorite mount was his white war horse. Union Brig. Gen. Joseph ("Fighting Joe") Hooker rode a huge white animal at Antietam, saying that the horse made it easy for his men to identify him.

At Fort Donelson, an aide to Union Brig. Gen. Charles F. Smith threw caution to the wind. Men on both sides shook their heads in wonder when they saw Capt. T. L. Newsham ride several times along the Union front, mounted on a noble white horse.

Many months later, Union Lt. Jim Coughlan of the Twenty-fourth Kentucky Regiment chose a white horse when he decided to lead charges at Resaca.

During the fall of 1861, Kentucky was officially—and theoretically—a neutral state. That did not prevent a woman, who some contemporaries considered greedy, from writing to Union military authorities in the state.

Her formal request for "some horses from there on the battle field" was signed, "Very Respectfully, Mrs. A. Lincoln."

After every major battle, one of the chores most dreaded by soldiers was the disposal of dead horses. Hundreds were usually found on the field, most of them having gone into the fray pulling artillery. Provided that wood and time were plentiful, crews preferred to dispose of dead animals by burning the carcasses instead of burying them.

During some of his Washington summers, Abraham Lincoln tried to get away from the heat and humidity of the city by spending his evenings at the Soldiers' Home. It was a rare evening when the chief executive consented to ride in a carriage with a military escort. Instead, he customarily mounted a horse when he was ready to leave the White House for the Civil War prototype of today's Camp David.

During bitter fighting in Mississippi in 1862, Confederate and Union commanders often found themselves in disagreement concerning procedures. By early December, however, an aide to Ulysses S. Grant was able to report to Brig. Gen. Grenville Dodge that harmony had been achieved on one issue. As a result, bulletins announced that "army surgeons who are captured have the right to retain their horses."

Memoirs and biographies cite records or claims that indicate several commanders had a number of horses shot out from under them.

At Belmont, Missouri, Union Brig. Gen. John A. McClernand was officially reported to have had three mounts shot from under him, and Col. Henry J. Hunt reported the battle loss of three mounts at Gaines' Mill, then two more at Malvern Hill.

Union Maj. Gen. Grenville Dodge ended the war with a loss of only three horses, but one of them reportedly took twenty balls before it fell. At Antietam, Union Brig. Gen. Daniel Ullman lost three mounts and sustained two wounds before being left on the field, believed to be dead.

According to some accounts of First Bull Run, Confederate Brig. Gen. P. G. T. Beauregard lost four horses during the battle. Union Brig. Gen. William T. Sherman lost a "magnificent sorrel race mare" and two other mounts on the first day at Shiloh. When a fourth was shot from under him later in the same battle, he told aides that Beauregard no longer held a record. After Shiloh, Sherman is generally believed to have lost only one more mount, for a total of five.

Topping Sherman were two Confederate brigadier generals. William B. Bate received three wounds and lost six mounts, while Alfred J. Vaughn Jr., had eight horses killed under him.

Cavalrymen who followed Confederate Maj. Gen. William W. Allen were positive that he lost ten horses. By most accounts, Union Maj. Gen. George A. Custer was wounded only once during the years in which eleven horses were shot from under him. One of his comrades in blue, Brig. Gen. Charles R. Lowell, lost an even dozen mounts. Confederate Maj. Gen. Joseph Wheeler continued to fight after having sixteen horses killed under him.

Still, the all-time record seems to have been set by Confederate Gen. Nathan Bedford Forrest. After making a meticulous study of the matter, his fellow officer, Brig. Gen. James R. Chalmers reported that Forrest was under fire more than one hundred times, during which "twenty-seven horses were shot under him." A later analysis, now widely accepted, led to the conclusion that Chalmers overlooked three dead mounts.

Without citing evidence, a writer for *Civil War* magazine said that all early estimates concerning the mortality of Forrest's steeds were too conservative. According to him, Forrest actually had thirty-nine horses killed while he was in the saddle.

Many a fighting man had one or more favorite mounts, entitled to bountiful corn and fodder, careful grooming, and a name of its own. Horses prized by some Confederates were:

Beauregard—who survived until 1883, was ridden to Appomattox by Capt. W. I. Rasin.

Fleeter—ridden by spy Belle Boyd.

Black Hawk—mounted by Maj. Gen. William B. Bate.

Dixie—battle steed killed at Perryville while being ridden by Maj. Gen. Patrick R. Cleburne.

Rifle—cherished by Lt. Gen. Richard S. Ewell.

King Philip—possibly the favorite horse of Forrest, who also owned and rode Roderick and Highlander.

Old Sorrel—formerly a Union officer's mount, was acquired by Stonewall Jackson at Harpers Ferry when she was about eleven years old. Because the mare was so small that Jackson's feet nearly dragged the ground, she was often known as Little Sorrel. Little Sorrel Lane in Somers, Connecticut, commemorates the animal Jackson was riding when he was mortally wounded.

Joe Smith—owned by Brig. Gen. Adam R. Johnson.

Fire-eater—a splendid bay Thoroughbred ridden by Gen. Albert S. Johnston when he was killed at Shiloh.

Nellie Gray—Maj. Gen. Fitzhugh Lee's mare who was numbered among the dead at Opequon.

Traveller—by all odds this best-known horse of the war was Robert E. Lee's favorite. Earlier he owned and rode Richmond, Brown-Roan, Lucy Long, and Ajax. Traveller is the purported author of a ghost-written volume that depicts the Civil War as seen through equine eyes.

Old Fox—ridden by Col. F. G. Skinner, First Virginia Infantry.

Virginia—credited with having prevented the capture of Maj. Gen.

Jeb Stuart by jumping an enormous ditch. In addition to the mare, Stuart frequently rode Highfly.

Sardanapalus—favorite mount of partisan M. Jeff Thompson of Missouri.

Union officers were as dependent on their horses as were their opponents. Had neither side been provided with mounts, the war might have fizzled out in about ninety days. Some of the animals that helped make history when carrying staunch opponents of secession were:

Old Whitey—the usual mount of "Mother" Bickerdyke, among the most famous of female nurses.

Almond Eye—ridden by Maj. Gen. Benjamin F. Butler.

Nellie—Brig. Gen. Kenner Garrard's favorite mare.

Cincinnati—presented to Lt. Gen. Ulysses S. Grant in 1864 and immediately identified as his favorite horse. When Colonel Grant rode into Springfield, Illinois, in 1861, he was astride a white horse named Methuselah. Grant first rode into battle on the back of Rondy and during the war also used Fox, Jack, Jeff Davis, and Kangaroo.

Lookout—acquired at Chattanooga and named for a battle of that campaign, stood seventeen hands high and was cherished by Maj. Gen. Joseph Hooker.

Moscow—a white horse used in battle by Maj. Gen. Philip Kearny against the advice of his colleagues may have been his favorite. Because the big horse was an inviting target, Kearny switched to a bay named Decatur and then to Bayard, whose color was light brown.

Slasher—ridden into battle by Maj. Gen. John A. Logan and depicted by an artist as dashing along a line of battle with all four feet off the ground.

Boomerang—named for his tendency to move backward, was owned
by Col. John McArthur of the Twelfth Illinois Regiment.

Kentuck—may have been the favorite mount of Maj. Gen. George
B. McClellan. There's a chance that Daniel Webster held that place
of special esteem. In addition, McClellan rode a black horse named
Burns.

Baldy—wounded at First Bull Run and at Antietam, later took Brig.
Gen. George G. Meade to Gettysburg and a promotion.
Philadelphia's Old Baldy Civil War Round Table helps to
commemorate the memory of the horse.

Aldebaron—an early mount of Col. Philip Sheridan, gave way to a
gelding named Rienzi. After taking Sheridan on his famous ride to
Winchester, the name of the animal was changed to that of the
town. Winchester (or Rienzi) was so revered that when he died, his
stuffed body was presented to the Smithsonian Institute.

Lexington—possibly the favorite of Sherman, who also rode Dolly
and Sam.

Billy—named for Sherman, was the bay war horse of Maj. Gen.
George Thomas.

⁂

One clause in the surrender terms at Appomattox in 1865 puzzled some people:
every Confederate cavalryman was entitled to take his horse home with him.
This provision, insisted on by Lee, was accepted by Grant when he was told
that once they returned to civilian life, former soldiers wouldn't be able to plant
spring crops without their war horses.

Eight

CIVIL WAR CRITTERS

Horses belonging to line officers and mules pulling wagons were by all odds the most familiar animals seen by soldiers. Not only did horses transport their masters into battle, but during lulls in fighting they also became pets of enlisted men. Next to the mule and the horse, which was in a category by itself, the most common critter seen around camp or on the march was the dog.

When the Eleventh Pennsylvania Regiment moved north to try to stem Lee's invasion of its state, the men took along their mascot. A mongrel, Sallie took to her heels during a furious Confederate cannonade at Gettysburg. She later returned to her unit and is credited with having refused to leave the dead and wounded she found on the battlefield. As a token of gratitude for her loyalty, the men she followed had Sallie's likeness placed on their regimental monument at a spot where they took a firm stand against Confederate assaults.

A mongrel was adopted as their mascot by the men of the Sixth Iowa Regiment. To make sure that the animal would win at least a footnote in accounts of their achievements, they gave it a carefully chosen name: Jeff Davis.

Records of the 102nd Pennsylvania Regiment indicate that its large black and white dog was given the commonplace name Jack. Far from ordinary in his service record, Jack went through a score of battles without injury and then took a bullet at Malvern Hill.

After his recovery from the wound, Jack and many of his two-legged comrades were captured at Salem Heights and imprisoned for six months at Richmond. During a later conflict he was again a prisoner of Confederates; this time he was freed after just six hours.

Born in Hungary, Union Brig. Gen. Alexander S. Asboth fought throughout the war without special distinction. Yet men who saw him in action at Pea Ridge, Arkansas, never forgot him. Throughout the bloody struggle, Asboth's dog York remained close to the heels of its master's horse. An artist who was impressed by the animal's fortitude carefully sketched it and its master for publication in *Leslie's Illustrated Newspaper*.

Confederates of the Fourth Louisiana Brigade picked as their mascot a black and white bird dog. Described as being of medium size, Sawbuck roamed about encampments at will. He didn't stay there, however, when bugles called for an assault on an enemy position. According to a sergeant of whom Sawbuck was especially fond, "the dog knew nearly every member of the division, and always went into battle, running up and down the lines in order to watch the fight."

A different canine spectator was present at Harris Farm in May 1864. With Confederates moving forward under terrific fire, a bulldog ran back and forth just behind the Federal line. Believed to be a pet belonging to Company D of the Fourth New York Heavy Artillery, the animal was described by a diarist as "yapping as though delighted by the show."

To the observer, who must have been endowed with a vivid imagination, it seemed that the animal "tried to jump up and snatch galls as they whizzed by him." Yet when the tail of the canine was clipped by a bullet, "he took out to the rear like a yellow streak."

During the April 1862 engagement at McDowell, Virginia, Ohio-born Capt. E. R. Monfort sadly recorded an unusual casualty. An animal described by him as "a very large Newfoundland dog" had wandered into camp and had chosen to stay with the brigade to which Monfort belonged. During the clash, he wrote, the dog "ran back and forth in front of our lines, barking and snapping at the flying missiles. Before the fight was over, he fell, pierced by a score of balls."

French-born Capt. Werner Von Bachelle, a member of an Ohio brigade, had trained his dog "to perform military salutes and many other remarkable things." Constantly at the side of its master, the pet accompanied Von Bachelle on the battlefield at Antietam. When the carnage was over, a burial crew discovered the body of the captain "abandoned by our line of men but faithfully guarded by his dog."

In at least one instance, dogs that were not a source of pleasure provided a distraction in battle. Without specifying the site of the action, Union Brig. Gen. Rufus Saxton said that bloodhounds were once set against one of his scouting parties.

"A pack of bloodhounds" belonging to a company of Rebel cavalry "attacked with great fury," said Saxton. "A well-directed volley that killed three of the hounds threw the enemy into disorder." If even one two-legged Confederate also fell during that encounter, Saxton made no mention of such a casualty.

In November 1863 men of the First South Carolina Colored Troops were forced to retreat from a site near Pocotaligo, South Carolina. Bloodhounds were brought to track them down, but the soldiers whom they chased were ready and waiting when the dogs drew near.

According to the *Rebellion Record*, the contest between men and animals was brief and bloody: "Dogs dashed into the party in advance of their comrades, the rebels. One hound was shot, and left with broken legs upon the field. Five others were impaled upon the bayonets of the Union troops, and brought as trophies into their camp."

Lt. A. O. Abbott of the First New York Dragoons was among numerous Union prisoners held at Columbia, South Carolina, during the fall of 1864. Abbott whiled away part of the time by keeping a detailed diary. According to it, an October sunrise revealed "two strangers going through the camp."

The prisoners decided that they must be killed at once, so they found an ax "and the deed was done." The bodies of the victims were shoved into an abandoned well just before guards began searching. As Abbott described the eventful morning, Confederates eventually "brought to light the missing DOGS—dead bloodhounds that were two of a pack put around camp every morning to discover if any 'Yankees' had made fresh tracks for liberty during the night."

Before donning a gray uniform, Robert E. Lee once described himself as being "very solitary." His only companions, he said in a letter to his wife, were "my dog and cats." According to the lonely cavalry officer, his dog went with him to his office every morning and lay down "from eight to four without moving."

During his U.S. Army days, Lieutenant Colonel Lee once crossed the "Narrows" between Fort Hamilton and Staten Island, New York. Halfway over the body of water, he spied a female dog with its head barely above the waves. He rescued the animal, named her Dart, and took her home with him.

One of her pups, Spec, was an alert and especially affectionate black and tan terrier who once jumped out of a high window to join the family at church. Lee was so impressed by the valor of the animal that he permitted Spec to "go into the church afterwards, whenever he wished."

Sue Chancellor, for whose family a plantation home and a major battle were named, was a girl of fourteen at the time of what some term "Lee's greatest triumph." Before she became accustomed to seeing Confederate pickets near her home, Sue later said, a large drove of sheep came running down the road one day without a shepherd.

As she recalled the incident, that to her always remained vivid, a soldier asked her if she'd like to have a pet. When she nodded, Thomas Lamar Stark of Columbia, South Carolina, picked out for her "a beautiful white lamb." Named Lamar in honor of its donor, the lamb remained with its new mistress until the Chancellor mansion was burned.

In January 1864, Lt. A. L. Cady of the Twenty-fourth New York Battery was praised in newspapers throughout the north. In Tyrrel County, North Carolina, he led a raid that resulted in the capture of five guerrillas and two Confederate officers. More important, in the opinion of the newspaper editors, "he returned to camp with one thousand sheep."

Diaries and letters reveal that men in blue as well as men in gray spent time with pets to break the monotony of camp life. Many mongrel dogs were fed scraps, and several units adopted squirrels. One of them, owned by a drummer, is said to have learned to dance to the beat of its master's instrument. Officers of a Minnesota outfit bragged to comrades that their mascot was a bear cub who "smelt powder in a dozen engagements before being sent home in good condition."

When Ohio volunteers skirmished with seven hundred secessionists at West Liberty, Kentucky, on October 23, 1861, a triumphant account published in Cincinnati reported that twenty-one enemies were killed and victors returned with an entourage.

Captured, according to the news account were "34 prisoners, 52 horses, 10 or 12 mules, two jacks—and one large bear." Like the cub kept as a mascot by another outfit, this animal was probably half tame, but was estimated to weigh about three hundred pounds.

Men of at least three Wisconsin regiments took pet badgers to war with them, and an artillery battery from the same state had a raccoon. At least one Confederate unit from Arkansas had as its mascot a wild cat, and a Louisiana regiment took a pelican to war. Members of J. E. B. Stuart's First Virginia Cavalry cautiously kept their raccoon, described as enormous, tied to a captured gun.

Confederates belonging to Company B of the Forty-third Mississippi Regiment were the envy of their comrades. From an unknown source they managed to secure a camel and used it to transport baggage of the officers' mess.

Most horses were afraid of the strange creature, so its driver was under orders to stop just outside the camp. In a forced march toward Iuka, Mississippi, just prior to the battle of Corinth, the camel blundered into the line of march and spooked horses so badly that there was a stampede in which several men were injured.

Members of Company B referred to their curious critter simply a "the camel," and apparently never conferred a name on it. To them, it seemed just as well when "the camel" was killed by a Minié ball during the siege of Vicksburg.

When there was a lull in the fighting near the Mule Shoe salient at Spotsylvania, regimental cooks butchered an ox that had wandered into Federal ranks. Because it had accompanied fighting men for several days and was regarded as a pet by the men from New York, some were so furious at the slaughter of the ox that they refused to eat its meat.

Harvard Museum in Cambridge, Massachusetts, was the recipient of an unusual gift from an unknown source. Identified as MCZ-470, a jar labeled "Richmond, Virginia, 1862" holds a lizard. How and why the creature was sent from the capital of the Confederacy to Massachusetts during heavy fighting remains a mystery.

In addition to four-legged pets, officers and men sometimes took a special fancy to feathered creatures.

Men belonging to a unit commanded by Confederate Brig. Gen. T. R. R. Cobb claimed to have taught a rooster to crow when given a signal. At Fredericksburg, reported the Savannah *Republican*, every time Federals launched an advance, the rooster responded to prompting. As a result, "Just before our sharp-shooters opened upon them, the cock's clear, shrill clarion rang out on the sulphurous air. This strange defiance, while it cheered and amused our boys, fell with a depressing effect upon the ears of the enemy."

While the Forty-second New York Regiment was encamped at Kalorama Heights, Virginia, Private Tinker captured a pigeon and made a pet of it. According to the *Rebellion Record*, the pigeon regularly followed when men of the Tammany regiment moved to another position. "Occasionally flying away at a great distance, it always returned and, when weary, would alight on some wagon of the train."

Tinker's pet reportedly went to Poolesville, Washington, Fort Monroe, and Yorktown. Staying with the regiment throughout the bloody days of the Wilderness, the pigeon is also credited with having been at Antietam and Harpers Ferry.

Some soldiers of the Army of Northern Virginia thought the most unusual animal that took part in the conflict was a barnyard hen. The fowl became so attached to Lee during his invasion of Pennsylvania that she followed him for weeks. Making her nest under his cot, she faithfully laid an egg almost every morning.

Fighting along the banks of the North Anna River in May 1864, men of Federal units were suddenly grateful, not for antics of pet animals, but for actions of farm creatures that belonged to Confederates.

A sudden rush of "frightened cattle, hogs, sheep, and turkeys" brought the running animals directly in front of Union lines. By the time soldiers recovered from astonishment as the animals charged directly over their trenches, they realized the meaning of their flight. Clearly, a massive Confederate force—of which they had no previous knowledge—was moving through the woods and driving the animals before them.

Men of the Richmond Howitzers chose as their mascot a very big crow, jet black. When their pet died, the soldiers called on their chaplain to conduct for it "a regular military funeral." Before the solemn salute was given by guns of the honor guard, the bird was eulogized in both English and Latin.

Collectively, a lamb, a bear cub, squirrels, bloodhounds, barnyard creatures in flight, and assorted small birds failed to attract attention or win renown comparable to that of a mascot cherished by the Eighth Wisconsin Regiment.

Tradition holds that during the summer months of 1860 when Democrats and Republicans were preparing for an all-out contest at the polls, Chief Sky of the Chippewa Indian tribe captured a small bald eagle. Having made a pet of it, the Native American traded it to Daniel McCann for a bushel of corn. When the eagle, known to Indians as *Me-kee-zeen-ce*, was about two months old it was sold to a farmer.

S. M. Jeffers then bought it for $2.50 and presented it to the Eau Claire Volunteers as "the Chippewa recruit." With its new owners, the eagle joined the Eighth Regiment and was consigned to the care of Pvt. James McGinnis.

Unaware that no one dared use the Republican nominee's best-known nickname within his hearing, Capt. John Perkins called the bird Old Abe. On September 13, 1861, he and his comrades and Old Abe left for St. Louis. By this time the eagle was so accustomed to living among humans that its master often turned it loose to fly above them as they drilled or marched.

By the time Company C reached Fredericksburg on October 21, Old Abe was the pride of the entire regiment. During the Unit's first clash with the enemy, Old Abe probably soared above the battle and to some Confederates became known as "that Yankee eagle."

Sometimes the big bird perched on a red, white, and blue shield fashioned for him. Often he strolled proudly about encampments, reputedly receiving a salute whenever he was encountered. When a review was held, Old Abe was likely to be found in the stand with top officers and civilian dignitaries who had come to watch.

According to regimental histories, the Eighth Wisconsin took part in the siege of New Madrid, Missouri, late in the winter of 1862. It was included in the force that besieged and captured Island Number 10 in the Mississippi River, then went to Fort Pillow. After having been briefly based at Hamburg Landing, Tennessee, the outfit took part in the siege of Corinth, Mississippi.

By this time, it was taken for granted that anytime he wished to watch the action from aloft, Old Abe would soar above the conflict just out of musket range. As described by J. O. Barrett, the bird who first "saw the elephant" (or experienced combat) weeks earlier observed his personal ritual when bullets began to fly. Wrote Barrett in 1876:

> At the sound of the regimental bugle, which he had learned to recognize, he would start suddenly, dart up his head, and then bend it gracefully, anticipating the coming shock.
>
> When conscious of its reality, he would survey the moving squadrons, and as they rushed into line his breast would tremble like the human heart.
>
> *Click* would go a thousand [musket] locks, and he would turn again, curving that majestic neck, scrutinizing the ranks, and dipping his brow forward to await the crash; and when it came, rolling fiery thunder over the plain, he would spring up and spread his opinions, uttering his startling scream, felt and gloried in by the desperate soldiers.
>
> As the smoke enveloped him, he would appear to be bewildered for a moment, but when it opened again, he would look down intently as if inquiring, "How goes the battle, boys? What of that last charge?"

Confederates who spotted the well-known bird flying overhead during the siege of Vicksburg typically cursed it as "that Yankee buzzard."

Barrett, whose biography of the eagle ran to more than one hundred printed pages, interviewed Chippewa Indians, Capt. Victor Wolfe, Lt. Burnett Demorest, and numerous men of the Eighth, in addition to McGinnis, the member of the Eighth Wisconsin Regiment who served as its keeper. Published twelve years after the end of the war, it was widely circulated in the year the United States celebrated the centennial of its birth.

According to Barrett's account, the eagle's favorite food was freshly killed rabbit. Anytime a person saw a downy white feather drop to the ground and tried to pick it up, said the Wisconsin newspaper reporter, "Abe was ready to protect his property." In such situations, "with flashing eyes and angry look," he would fly at the souvenir hunter "with perfect fury."

Old Abe observed the battle of Iuka, then returned to Corinth for another clash. Analysts who compiled the eagle's combat record concluded that he was present in at least thirty-six engagements before being presented to the governor of Wisconsin in 1864.

When the "Eagle Regiment" was mustered out at Demopolis, Alabama, on September 5, 1865, its commander soberly reported that 6 officers and 53 enlisted men died in battle and an additional 221 succumbed to disease. According to him, Old Abe weighing a little more than ten pounds, had not suffered a scratch and had not been on the sick list a single day. Yet his semicircular beak, once measuring almost three inches in length, was "somewhat reduced in size" by the time he returned to civilian life.

Back home, the now-famous war mascot was given a special perch in the capitol at Madison after having been acquired by the state of Wisconsin. A succession of ten men, most of them former infantryman, cared for the feathered veteran for nearly twenty years. They often took the celebrated bird to reunions of veterans, conventions, and expositions. He was a favorite subject of persons learning the new art of photography, and a Chicago-produced engraving of him was circulated nationally. At least two sculptors executed and mass-produced small likenesses of the Wisconsin eagle.

Artists who prepared for Union Brig. Gen. John A. Logan an enormous painting included Old Abe in it, flying over a hotly contested field. Their work of art, in which a Federal mascot is featured, now forms the centerpiece of the world-famous Atlanta Cyclorama.

Twenty years after having gone off to war with his regiment, the mascot died from smoke inhalation during a fire. A taxidermist restored the remains, which were later destroyed when the Capitol burned in 1904. Though he's long gone, countless photographs and statuettes of Old Abe still adorn museums and private collections throughout the nation whose feathered emblem is the bald eagle.

Part Three

No Two Military Events Were Identical

Nine

In the Heat of Battle

An artillery duel at long distance constituted the first battle of the war. Inside Fort Sumter, eighty-five Federals, who were aided by forty-three civilian workmen, managed to get off numerous shots at installations manned by more than 6,000 secessionists. During the thirty-eight-hour exchange of fire from sixty-nine big guns, more than 3,000 shells—some of them hot shot heated in a furnace—were fired. Not a man among defenders or attackers was killed.

Baltimore, Maryland, was the April 19, 1861, site of the first bloodshed in combat. This time, ninety-day volunteers for Federal service were pitted against civilians. Troops passing through the city on the way to Washington by train were forced to march through the streets because terminals of rail lines were not connected with one another.

Crowds of pro-secessionists blocked the path of the Massachusetts volunteers who had never been exposed to a crisis situation. Some who were present said that a melee started when bricks were thrown at soldiers; others insisted a pistol was shot by a person never identified.

Members of the militia unit headed for three months of Federal service responded by firing indiscriminately into the crowd of civilians. At least twelve civilians and four soldiers died; an accurate count of the wounded was never compiled but is believed to have exceeded a score, indicating that blood on the cobblestones of city streets marked the first site at which a significant number of casualties occurred.

～～～

Although the first battle of Bull Run has been treated in dozens of articles and books, it is the focus of an unsolved mystery. Around 2:30 P.M. on July 21, 1861, Brig. Gen. Barnard E. Bee realized that Confederate forces were gaining the upper hand. To his aides he made a remark to the effect that "Yonder stands Jackson like a stone wall; let's go to his assistance."

His hasty comment caused Brig. Gen. Thomas J. Jackson to become world famous as "Stonewall."

There is no way to determine whether he meant to compliment his colleague for resisting Federal charges or to criticize him for remaining stationary instead of moving into action. Not long after making the comment that gave Jackson his nickname, Bee received a wound from which he died a few hours later. Consequently, no one ever asked him to explain what he meant by his terse remark.

～～～

Manning F. Force, who became a brevet (honorary) major general of U.S. volunteers, started for Vicksburg from Memphis on February 22, 1863. He and the men of his Twentieth Ohio Regiment were present for the entire siege of the river city. By late June, tens of thousands of rifles and muskets were in constant use.

Force reported that during this heavy exchange of fire, "rifle balls met in the air and fell to the ground welded together." In order to silence anyone who might doubt this statement, he said that Maj. Gen. Ulysses S. Grant sent one such pair to Washington. Another, he said, was picked up by a soldier of the Seventy-eighth Ohio and presented to the Historical and Philosophical Society in Cincinnati.

Confederate Capt. Gordon McCabe of Richmond knew that anyone who heard the battle yarn about fused bullets would doubt it. Because he subscribed to the view that "seeing is believing," he photographed bullets found on the battlefield immediately after Confederates evacuated Petersburg. His souvenir, consisting of two bullets "that met in mid-air and flattened out against each other," was featured in the ten-volume *Photographic History of the Civil War* (1912).

Some accounts of meetings in combat are uncanny. A Union soldier from Iowa was amazed when he walked over part of the Allatoona Pass battlefield in October 1864. According to him: "When the battle was over one of our boys was found dead facing the enemy who had killed him. Both of them lay with their faces nearly touching, with their bayonets run through each other."

At Gettysburg, said a Confederate officer, members of the Fifth Texas Regiment were ordered to fire at will. Twin brothers belonging to Company C were standing close together. One of them took a mortal hit from a Federal marksman, so his twin caught him and "gently laid him on the ground." As the surviving member of the pair began to draw himself erect, he received a lethal ball that caused him to fall across his brother's body.

Malvern Hill, the last of the Seven Days' battles of the Peninsular campaign, was fought on July 1, 1862. Robert E. Lee had been in command of the Army of Northern Virginia exactly one month. Rifles, cartridge boxes, wagons, and other gear discarded by fleeing Federals convinced Lee that a mass attack on the hill held by the foe might break the back of the Union military effort.

He ordered his artillery forward in order to shell the hill as a prelude to an infantry charge. Gunners soon found the thickets and swamps too much for them and reported that they would be unable to follow orders. Lee promptly sent couriers to cancel plans for the advance by infantry, but some of his messages did not get through. As a result, an estimated five thousand men marched up the slope almost as orderly as though they were on review.

As they neared their objective, Federal artillery began to fire. Because they were under orders, the Confederates moved steadily forward. A few men in gray came within two hundred yards of guns that were spewing grape and canister before the assault that Lee had tried to countermand was turned back as hopeless. Their major general, Gen. Daniel H. Hill, said of the fruits of their obedience, "It was not war—it was murder."

Failure to follow orders had a fortuitous result in the November 25, 1863, battle of Missionary Ridge. Shortly after 3:00 P.M., Union Major General Grant decided to try once more to gain a few hundred yards. At a signal, men of three brigades moved forward, hoping to overwhelm the first line of their foes. Resistance proved to be less formidable than expected; the first line was soon overrun. Jubilant Federals then charged straight toward the top of the ridge held by Confederates.

Commanders of two brigades tried to stop their men. It was useless. Once launched, the charge continued for a full hour. Grant, taken by surprise, reportedly demanded of his aides, "Who ordered those men up the hill?" When he learned that they had not stopped at the point designated by him, the Federal commander muttered that "Someone will suffer for it, if it turns out badly."

His apprehension proved to be needless as the men of scattered units moved straight up the hill until they reached and secured its crest. Instead of receiving reprimands, officers and men who had acted without orders were hailed as heroes.

Lt. Stoddart Robertson of the Ninety-third New York Regiment had fought through the Wilderness, but he was not prepared for the carnage at Spotsylvania. To him the sector famous as "the Horse Shoe" was "a boiling, bubbling and hissing cauldron of death."

Musket fire was so intense, said Robertson, that undergrowth seemed to have been leveled by scythes, "and a white oak tree, twenty-two inches in diameter, was cut down wholly by bullets."

Confederate Gen. Joseph Johnston was wounded twice in late August 1862. Although he might have continued in command of the Department of the Potomac, his injuries provided Jefferson Davis with an excuse to relieve him.

It was one thing for the Confederate president to take his command from an officer with whom he had quarreled bitterly; it was another thing to choose a successor. Davis turned to the leader of the Virginia state forces and decided to replace Johnston with a comrade who had never directed a battle.

Having been put in command as a result of Johnston's wounds at Fair Oaks or Seven Pines, Robert E. Lee renamed his forces and immediately led the Army of Northern Virginia on the offensive.

A former coal dealer from Georgia who raised the Raccoon Roughs and entered Confederate service through Alabama, John B. Gordon was a colonel by the time opposing forces met at Sharpsburg, Maryland, in September 1862. Early in the action he received a minor wound when a bullet cut a hole through his cap.

Later in the day, widely called America's bloodiest, Gordon was again hit in the head. This time, he was knocked to the ground, where he bled profusely. He would have drowned in his own blood, said the future major general, had not his vital fluid drained through the hole made earlier by a Federal ball.

Men under Capt. Albert T. Torbert of the U.S. Army were strangely shielded at Gettysburg. Though many units on both sides fought so savagely that their ranks were decimated, Torbert's brigade suffered no deaths and only eleven wounded. In spite of this indication that he was little more than a spectator, Torbert was rewarded with a brevet for the battle and was made a brigadier general of U.S. Volunteers.

At Chancellorsville, Virginia, opposing forces battled during the first four days of May 1863. Brig. Gen. Joseph Hooker, commander of the Army of the Potomac, was popularly known as "Fighting Joe." With an estimated 133,000 men under his command, the Federal leader hoped to crush Lee's 60,000-man Army of Northern Virginia.

Instead of celebrating Chancellorsville as a great Union victory, Hooker withdrew north of the Rappahannock River on May 6. Men who followed him in this retreat included a force more than half the size of Lee's army that had taken no part in the fight. Far more cautious than his nickname suggests, Hooker held these men for use in an emergency and did not send them into the battle often called "Lee's masterpiece."

Hooker may have been influenced by earlier actions of Maj. Gen. George B. McClellan. At the head of a force of about 75,000 effectives, the Federal commander faced no more than 52,000 Confederates. Because McClellan held about 22,000 of his men in reserve, Antietam went into the record book as a drawn battle that logic says should have been a smashing Federal victory.

Soldiers of the Army of the Potomac's First Corps, Second Division, First Brigade, were in the thick of the action at Gettysburg. During the first day, two brigade commanders were seriously wounded, and superstitious soldiers said another officer would fall before night.

Adrian R. Root of the Ninety-fourth New York Regiment took command and became the third leader of the brigade to be taken from the field as a result of Confederate bullets fired between sunup and sundown on July 1, 1863.

At Prairie Grove, Arkansas, members of the Nineteenth Iowa regiment were in the thick of fighting on December 7, 1862. According to the Peoria, Illinois, *Transcript*, fire from Confederates forced advancing Federals to turn around and run for the protection of their battery.

After having covered about half the distance to safety, the color sergeant took a direct hit and toppled to the ground. Lt. William S. Brooks heard a foe cry, "Damn them! Take their colors!" Enraged, the man from Iowa said he shouted back and grabbed the fallen flag.

According to his account of the incident, "The cowardly rascals did not dare to close on me, but let go a volley which left nine holes in the flag and eighteen in my clothes! Four bullets passed through the cuff of my shirt-sleeve, but they could not wound the hand that held the flag."

On June 14, 1862, readers of the Boston *Transcript* pored over an account of the battle of Hanover Court House, Virginia. Part of the Peninsular campaign, the May 27 conflict at which Slash Church and Kinney's farm were landmarks, saw hundreds of men wounded. Incomplete reports don't indicate how many men were killed, but at least five hundred were dead on the field when opposing forces withdrew.

Two of the dead, according to the Boston newspaper, were sergeants. One wearing blue and the other dressed in gray, the two bodies were discovered in the woods, closely intertwined, each having his knife "buried in his opponent up to the hilt."

Numerous men who sustained serious battlefield wounds found compensation of a sort for their suffering and loss. Maj. Gen. John B. Hood, six feet, two inches tall, lost his right leg at Chickamauga. While recuperating in a Richmond hospital, his friend Jefferson Davis promoted him to the rank of lieutenant general, effective from the day he was wounded. Hood later rode into battle, strapped into his saddle, wearing a fine cork leg manufactured in France, with a spare leg carried along for emergency use.

James E. Hanger of Lexington, Virginia, was an eighteen-year-old private when he lost a leg in one of the earliest battles of the war. At Philippi, Virginia, a six-pound ball hit the ground a few feet away from him, then bounded directly toward him and mangled a leg. Left on the field when his fellow Confederates retreated, Hanger's life was saved by surgeon James D. Robison of the Sixteenth Ohio Regiment. Despite the wounded man's gray uniform, Robison took off the shattered leg just below his hip.

While recuperating, Hanger spent about ninety days with barrel staves and his pocket knife. His homemade artificial leg was so good that he began making them for others. Winning a patent, he went into business and found amputees so numerous in post-war years that at his death in 1919 the J. E. Hanger Company of Richmond had branches in four U.S. cities, as well as London and Paris.

On January 1, 1863, Confederates at Galveston realized that they had an opportunity for a coup. With the noted USS *Harriet Lane* close to land, they planned to storm the vessel and convert it to their own use.

One of the men in the boarding party, who was soon captured, told the Federals what he knew about the encounter. According to him, constant heavy fire protected attackers, who found numerous men down when they reached the deck:

Almost the first men struck down were the gallant Captain Wainwright and Lieutenant Lee, who both fought with desperation and valor.

One young son of Captain Wainwright, just ten years old, stood at the cabin door with a revolver in each hand and never ceased firing until he had expended every shot.

If that account is authentic, it may describe the actions of the youngest Civil War combatant. Despite the bravery of a ten-year-old, the ship was captured and young Wainwright became a prisoner when the Confederates captured the ship commanded by his father.

Years after the conflict came to an end, a New York reporter managed to get close enough to Sherman to ask him a quick question: "What do you regard as the bloodiest and most sanguinary battle of our Civil War?"

Without pausing in his stride, the man who conceived and executed the March to the Sea gave a one-word reply: "Shiloh!"

Officers of high rank were expected to stay behind battle lines, well out of the range of enemy fire. Some who failed to follow this pattern of action paid for their rashness with their lives.

At Antietam, however, a Confederate gun was for a time served by a high-ranking crew. Coming on a piece that had been abandoned, Gen. James Longstreet jumped from his horse and signaled for members of his staff to follow suit. For about half an hour, Longstreet aimed the gun into which his colonels had rammed charges.

Ten

BLACK SOLDIERS FELL SHORT
OF EQUALITY

B efore Abraham Lincoln took over as the nation's chief executive, it was clear that the North was badly split concerning black Americans and slavery. During his debates with Stephen A. Douglas, the man later known as "the Rail Splitter" made it clear that he did not consider blacks to be biological equals of whites. As president, he led the divided nation into war with one overpowering objective: preservation of the Union.

Ardent abolitionists never fully trusted Lincoln. In the 1860 election, more men in the North than in the South voted for his opponents. Lawmakers were also divided in their views concerning slavery, the burning issue of the day. Hence some of them were among the president's most ardent and vocal critics. Although today he is renowned through the world as "the Great Emancipator," the man who took office as president in March 1861 didn't foresee such a role for himself.

Long adamantly opposed to arming former slaves and putting them into Federal uniforms, President Lincoln was far from alone in this view. Brig. Gen. George W. Morgan (West Point, class of 1845) took off his uniform as a protest against an impending shift in national policy. Until the Emancipation Proclamation was issued and plans were made for the eventual use of black soldiers, preservation of the Union was the goal of Federal forces. By shifting to a "parallel goal" of freeing slaves, said Morgan, the administration "lost its bearings and no longer deserved to see men die for it."

Maj. Gen. John A. Logan of Illinois once threatened to lead soldiers of Midwestern birth back to their homes if blacks were permitted to fight against Confederates.

Noted as one of the best known of Lincoln's Democratic generals, Logan didn't take off his uniform when black soldiers began to become visible. Instead, he was still in action during the final campaign that ended in North Carolina. As a leader of the Grand Army of the Republic, he lived to see 100,000 black veterans became eligible for membership in the organization he headed.

From the beginning, at least one cabinet member was eager to set freed slaves against their former masters. Therefore a memorandum dispatched in the aftermath of Fort Sumter must have been signed with extreme reluctance:

WAR DEPARTMENT
Washington, April 29, 1861
Jacob Dodson (colored)
Washington City

SIR: in reply to your letter of the 23rd instant, I have to say that this Department has no intention at present to call into the service of the Government any colored soldiers.

> With respect, &c.,
> SIMON CAMERON
> Secretary of War

In October 1861, Lincoln warned against any plan that might result in "a general arming" of blacks for military service. Yet Simon Cameron laid his career on the line before the year's end. His annual report to Congress, which included a statement in favor of arming blacks, was mailed before Lincoln saw it. It was then recalled and revised at the president's direction.

A few weeks later, the secretary of war, who looked with favor on the use of black soldiers, became the first member of Lincoln's inner circle to be dismissed.

At New Orleans, during the fall of 1862, Brig. Gen. John W. Phelps conceived a plan for recruiting former slaves and free blacks to fill the rapidly dwindling ranks of Union forces. When orders arrived from Washington instructing him to put them to work instead of putting muskets in their hands, Phelps resigned.

Despite official policies, a few blacks managed to become partisans of irregular soldiers. In February 1863, Col. W. R. Penick of the Fifth Missouri Cavalry sent fifty men on a chase after guerrillas. "To test the fighting qualities of the negro," said his official report, "a contraband went with the party." Although not cited by name, that black volunteer was among the first of his race to take part in a Civil War exchange of gunfire.

According to the Leavenworth, Kansas, *Conservative*, guerrillas captured a Federal band near Shawnee Creek a month after "fighting qualities of the negro" were tested in the West. This action was newsworthy because the Confederate wagon train seized by these partisans had "an escort of thirty colored troops."

About the same time, Maj. R. G. Ward of the Second Kansas Artillery led "a party of twenty-two white men and thirty-two negro soldiers" on a foraging expedition near Sherwood, Missouri.

In both Washington and Richmond, military and political leaders were eager and willing to use all available blacks as laborers. Responding to a question about possible use of black soldiers, Union Maj. Gen. Lew Wallace gave a forthright reply.

He'd be delighted to see every Federal brigade incorporate a black regiment, said the future author of *Ben Hur*. This course of action would enable brigade officers to use black soldiers "for digging ditches and driving teams."

His expression of opinion was quite in keeping with congressional actions during the summer of 1862. In a series of qualified and ambiguous statements, lawmakers went on record as supporting the idea of making limited use of blacks. According to Congress, they could properly be employed "for labor or for military service" at the discretion of the president, who was on record as opposing the employment of blacks in the military.

Hundreds, if not thousands, of projects depended heavily on black labor. At Trent Reach on the James River, Maj. Gen. Benjamin E. Butler launched an ambitious program to build a 174-yard canal. Having coined the term "contraband of war" to label refugee slaves who gathered at Fort Monroe, he very early used contrabands for manual labor. By the time Lee surrendered, an estimated sixty thousand cubic yards of earth had been moved from the Dutch Gap Canal. Most of this work was done by blacks who could be distinguished from other members of their race only by their Federal uniforms.

In Louisiana, men of an entire black regiment were assigned to the duty of digging fortifications. Across the great river in Mississippi, black cavalrymen were told that service as cattle drovers would be their chief role in defeating Confederates.

Union Maj. Gen. Nathaniel P. Banks issued a lengthy order at New Orleans on August 21, 1863. Section V of the document stipulated that "Unemployed persons of color . . . will be arrested and employed upon the public works by the Provost-Marshal's department, without other pay than their rations and clothing."

Attitudes had not changed much by the time Sherman pushed forward to

Atlanta from Chattanooga in 1864. He resisted moves judged likely to put black soldiers into his armies, but let it be known that he was willing to employ a few hundred as laborers.

Political leaders of the self-styled nation whose soldiers fought in gray did not consider using blacks as soldiers until it was too late. They were ready and willing, however, to use their labor for defensive purposes. September 1862 saw Jefferson Davis issue a call for "a draft of 4,500 black males." He promised that they would immediately be put to work on the forts that surrounded the Confederate capital.

In July 1863, the mayor of Charleston took charge of plans to defend nearby Morris Island from Federal attack. In a special proclamation, Charles Macbeth ordered the arrest of all free blacks in the city. They were needed, he explained "to work on some unfinished defenses on Morris Island."

Confederate Brig. Gen. Hugh W. Mercer, stationed in Georgia on August 1, 1863, made it clear that owners of slaves could not withhold them from service deemed essential by military authorities. Having consulted the secretary of war, he announced his intention to "impress a number of negroes sufficient to construct such additional fortifications as are necessary for the defense of Savannah."

All slave holders of the region were ordered immediately to send to Mercer "one-fifth of their able-bodied male slaves." Transportation was to be provided, and owners would receive payment at the rate of twenty-five dollars per month for the labor of their slaves. "The Government will be responsible for the value of such negroes as may be killed by the enemy, or may in any manner fall into his hands," promised Mercer.

Not all Southerners favored the use of slaves as laborers on military fortifications. In Richmond, editors of the influential *Whig* newspaper said of them:

It has yet to appear that they can [be employed against the enemy] in any manner so effective as in raising food for our armies. Some may be occasionally used in ditching and throwing up breastworks, and it is possible a limited number might be advantageously substituted for teamsters. In the main, no doubt, the most useful function compatible with their capacities is that to which they are accustomed—food raising.

By September 1864, a few lawmakers of some Confederate states were willing to put radical views on record. According to these leaders, it was time to begin using able-bodied blacks "as pioneers, sappers, miners, cooks, nurses, and teamsters."

Unauthorized and irregular efforts aimed at the formation of black military units for Federal service began in widely separated places. As yet, there was no hint of freeing Southern-owned slaves by presidential edict.

Maj. Gen. David Hunter took command of the Department of the South on March 31, 1862. Under his leadership, Capt. James D. Fessenden of the Second U.S. Sharpshooters began recruiting former slaves. They made up the First South Carolina Volunteers, led by Col. T. W. Higginson. A second regiment was being formed when orders from Washington forced the abandonment of the effort.

Without authorization, Hunter had already issued emancipation papers to his black troops. One of them read:

HEADQUARTERS, DEPARTMENT OF THE SOUTH
Port Royal, SC, August 1, 1862
The bearer, Prince Rivers, a sergeant in First Regiment South-Carolina volunteers, lately claimed as a slave, having been employed in hostility to the United States, is hereby, agreeably to the law of the sixth of August, 1861, declared FREE FOR EVER. His wife and children are also free.

D. HUNTER
Major-General Commanding

As he had done earlier with Maj. Gen. John Charles Frémont's emancipation proclamation in Missouri, Lincoln issued a countermand.

Hunter ceased his effort to free all slaves within his department, but those who had already received "free papers" presumably kept their new status.

Without authorization, James H. Lane formed and drilled the First Kansas Colored Volunteers. Men of this regiment accompanied their white comrades on a few missions but were not accepted into Federal service until 1863.

In Louisiana, Gov. T. O. Moore enlisted at least 1,250 free blacks in the state militia. Soon after the fall of New Orleans, Union Maj. Gen. Benjamin F. Butler invited members of this "Native Guard" to join his own forces.

Brig. Gen. John W. Phelps, who had recruited many of these men, formed them into what he called the Chasseurs d'Afrique. By the time Washington got around to abolishing the units Phelps had formed, Richmond had branded him as an outlaw.

Impatient at Federal foot-dragging, Gov. John A. Andrew of Massachusetts secured permission to raise a black regiment three weeks after the Emancipation Proclamation was issued. Turning to a supporter of John Brown, Andrew persuaded wealthy George L. Stearns to take charge of the recruitment of free blacks. When the Fifty-fourth Massachusetts Colored Regiment was formed, Andrew named abolitionist Robert Gould Shaw as its colonel.

Although it was not the first black unit, the Fifty-fourth had no prototype in the North. This fact, combined with the impact of the movie *Glory*, has misled many persons to regard it as the earliest regiment composed of African Americans.

According to those who were present, no soldiers in blue fought more valiantly than did men of the Fifty-fourth Massachusetts at Battery Wagner, South Carolina (a site often erroneously labeled as a fortress).

Their series of attacks at a point less than two miles from Fort Sumter were futile. By nightfall on July 18, 1863, 40 percent of the regiment's men were casualties. At dawn, the beach was littered with the dead and dying, some of whom were described as having been "horribly mutilated" by gunfire. Describing the aftermath of the assault, a Charleston newspaper informed readers that "no battlefield anywhere has ever presented such an array of mangled bodies in a small compass."

Whether from Massachusetts or elsewhere, blacks in Federal service had to endure discrimination. All of them, including noncommissioned officers, were offered seven dollars per month in cash plus "one ration per day, of which three dollars might be paid in clothing."

William Whiting, solicitor of the War Department, studied the congressional act of July 17, 1862, and concluded that "persons of African descent" were entitled to "$10 per month and one ration daily, of which monthly pay $3 per month may be in clothing."

At that time, white volunteers received thirteen dollars in cash, free uniforms, and full rations. Incensed, men of the Fifty-fourth Massachusetts refused to accept any pay until the inequity was corrected. Even when this action was taken, "Full acceptance as equals" was usually denied to black soldiers. Letters and diaries of white soldiers are sprinkled with references to hazing and tormenting of their black comrades.

Except for Colonel Shaw and a handful of other zealots, men accepted commissions as leaders of black soldiers largely because such a role was a route to quick promotion. During the winter of 1863–64, officers of the Army of the Potomac listened to a special offer. Any man who would take a thirty-day furlough in order to receive training in Philadelphia was assured that he could learn to command "colored troops." Completion of the training course meant an automatic advancement to the rank of colonel.

Late in the war, many men switched to black units without the benefit of instruction in Philadelphia. Col. Joel A. Dewey, whose record was totally without distinction, became a brigadier as a result of leading a regiment of U.S. Colored Troops.

Capt. Charles Francis Adams, Jr., Admitted to comrades that he went to the fifth Massachusetts Cavalry (Colored) in September 1864 for the sake of advancement. Soon he became a brigadier general, but the reward was given for the part played at South Mountain and Antietam by his old outfit, the First Massachusetts Cavalry.

Capt. James S. Brisbin of the Sixth Cavalry became a colonel when he went to the Fifth U.S. Colored Cavalry in March 1864; by May 1865 he was a brigadier general. William A. Pile began his military service as chaplain of the First Missouri Light Artillery and ended it commanding a brigade of U.S. Colored Troops in the Department of the Gulf.

Charles J. Paine's first commission was as a captain of the Twenty-second Massachusetts; at war's end he was a brevet major general at the head of black troops in North Carolina. Edward A. Wild, M.D., joined the First Massachusetts on May 23, 1861, as a captain. Less than two years later, he was a brigadier general in command of the African Brigade, Department of the South.

On May 22, 1863, the U.S. War Department established a bureau for colored troops. Once a recruitment drive was launched by the new agency, numerical strength of black units rose rapidly. Brig. Gen. Lorenzo Thomas, who was heartily disliked by Secretary of War Stanton, was assigned to raise black troops in the West in March 1863. He found so many former slaves eager to fight that he organized 50 of the approximately 125 regiments made up of them.

Col. William Birney and Brig. Gen. George L. Andrews, though less spectacularly successful than Thomas, put thousands of black men into blue uniforms. In Massachusetts, once civilian abolitionist George L. Stearns had filled the ranks of the Fifty-fourth, he began recruiting for the Fifty-fifth without authorization. He then moved into Pennsylvania with his crusade, and from there he went to Tennessee, where he raised six regiments in only three months.

At war's end, with just over one million men in Federal forces, blacks made up more than 15 percent of them. One or several units of blacks fought in more than three dozen significant battles, such as Port Hudson, Olustee, Milliken's Bend, and Battery Wagner.

Because recruitment didn't begin until 1863 and many regiments were assigned to labor instead of combat, battle deaths were comparatively low. Yet the most vocal critics of emancipation by edict came to see the proclamation as an essential step toward victory over Southern forces. Coupled with Lincoln's reluctant decision to use black soldiers, the Emancipation Proclamation became the most effective single war measure adopted by the president.

Less than one hundred miles from Washington, leaders in Richmond took stern action when the Emancipation Proclamation was issued. On January 12, 1863, the Confederate Congress passed legislation designed to deal with "every white person" who as a commissioned officer commanded "negroes and mulattoes in arms against the Confederate States." Such persons, decreed lawmakers, "shall be deemed as inciting servile insurrection, and shall, if captured be put to death or otherwise punished."

Following instructions, Gen. Robert E. Lee informed Lt. Gen. Ulysses S. Grant that when "negroes belonging to citizens" were captured in uniform, they were not deemed to be subject to exchange.

Still, the "otherwise" clause in the Confederate legislation served to resolve many a dilemma faced by Jefferson Davis and his aides. There is no record that a captured Federal officer was ever executed for the "crime" of leading black soldiers into battle.

Charges of Confederate atrocities committed against black soldiers were more easily leveled than proved. Nevertheless, evidence indicates that these men in blue were subjected to special ferocity at Fort Pillow and at the Crate in Petersburg. Clearly, some were murdered rather than killed in combat. However, testimony of eyewitnesses is filled with so much confusion and contradiction that no one is likely ever to know precisely how many black soldiers were killed after combat ceased.

Like their counterparts in the Federal system, Confederate leaders used immense numbers of slaves as laborers on fortifications and other military works. Admired by its attackers as all but impregnable, the defenses of Atlanta were built from scratch by blacks who were directed by a Northern-born railroad executive. In Mississippi, Gov. John T. Pettus was authorized by the legislature to "requisition" as many as ten thousand slaves for work on the state's defenses.

Like some of their counterparts in the North, a few Southern officers made unofficial and irregular use of black soldiers. From start to finish, an estimated four hundred of them served in the Eighteenth Virginia and other units raised in the state. During the April 1862 Siege of Yorktown, Virginia, Federal attackers considered one Confederate sharpshooter especially prominent and accurate. They never learned his name, but many insisted that he was "black as soot."

Before the epochal voyage of the CSS *Shenandoah* ended, Lt. James I. Waddell added two black Americans to his crew. Partisan ranger John H. Morgan recruited a number of Mississippi blacks for his force, whose raids came to be feared throughout border states. Louisiana's Governor Moore put hundreds of free blacks into his state's militia, only to see the best of them change uniforms after the fall of New Orleans.

According to the Fort Smith, Arkansas, *Times* of September 10, 1861, some slaves willingly adopted a course of action that to Northerners seemed strange indeed: "Two companies of Southern black men have been forming in this neighborhood. They are thorough Southern men, not armed, but drilling to take the field, and say they are determined to fight for their masters and their homes."

※

After the fall of Chattanooga in November 1863, Irish-born Patrick Cleburne advocated that slaves be promised their freedom in return for military service. The Confederate major general found few supporters, in or out of uniform. One of them was Congressman Thomas J. Semmes, a cousin of the commander of the CSS *Alabama*. Another was Maj. Gen. William H. T. Walker, a Georgia native who graduated from West Point in the class of 1837.

Both Cleburne and Walker soon died in battle, and many in the South rejoiced that their radical idea had died with them.

By then, however, some staunch Confederates were admitting that their movement was doomed, so a few leaders followed the example of Lincoln.

Therefore Jefferson Davis raised the issue in November 1864. Congressman Julian Hartridge of Georgia, who served on powerful committees, was outspoken in his condemnation of the president's change of position. Congressman Henry Cousins of Mississippi, a member of the Committee on Military Affairs, vowed that he'd never permit anyone to arm a single black.

Long adamantly opposed to such an idea, many colleagues of these Confederate lawmakers seized on the use of black soldiers as a desperate last-ditch expedient. Recruitment of black soldiers was authorized by the Confederate Congress in March 1865. The bill called for putting as many as 300,000 former slaves into uniform. Nothing was said, however, about granting freedom as a reward for fighting.

Here was a classic case of "too little, too late." A few small squads of blacks drilled on the streets of Richmond and some other cities, but when Lee surrendered to Grant in April, none were ready to go into battle.

※

In both North and South, Americans fighting Americans refused for many months to endorse the concept of putting blacks into uniform. Had Confederates not been superbly led, it appears unlikely that Lincoln would have agreed to such a course of action. There is no certainty that he would have penned the Emancipation Proclamation if the end of the war had seemed to be in sight.

And the Confederates, who often were in the forefront on battlefields, lagged sorely behind with regard to the issue of black soldiers. Hence they never tapped their largest pool of unused manpower.

Eleven

SIGHTS AND SOUNDS OF COMBAT

An unidentified correspondent of the Petersburg, Virginia, *Gazette* described the Eighteenth Virginia Regiment fighting under intense fire at Bull Run in 1861:

> Men would raise their heads a few inches from the ground to peep, and would be shot in that position.
>
> The fight lasted eight hours—from nine to five. Noise and confusion of many kinds prevailed—the firing of cannon, the discharge of musketry, the whizzing of balls, the bursting of bombs, the roar of artillery, the tramp of horses, the shouts of the conquering, the groans of the dying and the shrieks of the wounded.
>
> *Our enemies are not cowards.* Many men were found with bayonets in them, some side by side, each with his bayonet in the other.

At Spotsylvania, a Federal officer found himself awed when "Added to the terrible rolls of musketry firing, and the thunder of heaven's artillery, was the deep-voiced thunder of those dogs of war, the reserve artillery. The shells shrieked and screamed over our heads, and each shell seemed to cry, 'It's you, it's you!' as it flew on its errand of death."

On November 30, 1864, infantry Capt. James A. Sexton and men of the Seventy-second Illinois Regiment dug in and waited. Entrenched near Franklin, Tennessee, Sexton described his men as "watching with anxious, nervous looks and bated breath" in a stillness that seemed oppressive.

"Look away out yonder," he wrote, "see the flashing, gleaming sunshine on polished steel in front and on the flank—it is the coming of the enemy. In close column by divisions, with flags fluttering and its army moving in echelon. See how distinct every rifle barrel, bayonet and sabre display the gleam of silver and shimmer of brass.

"We see the swinging motion, noticeable when great bodies of men move together. Thus comes this human battering ram, presenting the appearance of a huge monster closed in folds of flashing steel."

At Franklin, Tennessee, observers from a distance noticed that smoke settled on the field without drifting. Shells pouring into that pall of smoke "produced a sound rarely heard. It rose in waves above a continuous solid roar, as if the loud, grinding din of vast machinery were every few moments swelled louder and louder by traffic and prolonged explosions."

Capt. James R. Carnahan of the Eighty-sixth Indiana Regiment found Chickamauga to be unlike any battle in which he had participated before. Mingled sounds of rifles and artillery, he wrote, made him think of

> the ocean lashed to fury by the tempest, when great rolling waves come chasing one the other in their mighty rage, until they strike with a roar upon cliffs of stone, only to be broken and driven back upon other incoming waves as strong, or stronger, than they had been.
>
> So came to our ears the sound of that mighty tempest of war—volley after volley of musketry rolling in waves of dreadful sound, one upon the other, to which was added the deep sounding crash of the artillery, like

mighty thunder peals through the roar of the tempest, making the ground under your feet tremble as it came and went, each wave more terrible than the former.

⸙

In the Wilderness, wrote a participant, the battle raged fiercely over a small space for the entire forenoon. "Musketry fire was so hot and fierce that the ground was bared of bushes, as with a scythe.

"The ground drank its full of blood and grew slippery to the foot. Heaps of dead, pools of blood, and terrific volleys of musketry were too much for man's endurance. To advance was impossible; to hold our position was *grand*."

⸙

Maj. Gen. James H. Wilson led his raiders through much of Alabama and Georgia in the spring of 1865. At one point, they made direct contact with the most feared of enemy cavalry commanders. Confederates nearby when the opposing forces met said they saw "General Forrest surrounded by six Federals at one time, and they were all slashing at him with their sabres.

"One of them struck one of his pistols and knocked it from his hand. Private Dodd was fortunately near and shot the Federal soldier who was so close upon him, thus enabling General Forrest to draw his other pistol, with which he killed one after another of his attackers."

⸙

Following the May 1862 battle of Williamsburg, Felix A. Brannigan of the Seventy-sixth New York wrote home: "We were so close to the rebels that some of our wounded had their faces scorched with the firing. Fierce, short, and decisive was the struggle. As we rush on with the tide of battle, every sense of fear is swallowed up in the wild joy we feel thrilling through every fibre of our system.

During Brig. Gen. John H. Morgan's raid into Ohio, most of the forces trying to stop him were untested members of state militia. Near Marrowbone, these men turned and tried to escape. According to a participant, "For eight miles there was a desperate running fight, until men in retreat rallied around Colonel Jacob. At once there began desperate hand to hand combat between the opposing forces, with the clubbed gun and pistol."

Capt. Henry M. Neil of the Eleventh Ohio Battery guided his guns close to Confederates at Iuka, Mississippi, before being caught by surprise. "Instantly an entire rebel division concentrated its fire upon the battery with the intention of annihilating it before it could unlimber. As we emerged from the cut this sudden concentration of rifle fire gave me the impression of being in a violent hail storm."

Lt. Leander Stilwell of the Sixty-first Illinois Regiment doubted that any participant could accurately describe the sounds of battle. So many other things demanded attention that no one had time to stand still and listen. He wrote:

> The handling, tearing, and charging of his cartridge, ramming it home, the capping of his gun, the aiming and firing, with furious haste and desperate energy—for every shot may be his last—these things require the soldier's close personal attention and make him oblivious to matters transpiring beyond his immediate neighborhood.
>
> Moreover, his sense of hearing is well-nigh overcome by the deafening roar going on around him. The incessant and terrible crash of musketry, the roar of cannon, the continual zip, zip of the bullets as they hiss by him,

intermingled with the agonizing screams of the wounded, or the death-shrieks of comrades falling in dying convulsions—these things are not conducive to serene and judicial equipoise.

〰〰

A second lieutenant in the First U.S. Colored Cavalry received his baptism of fire at Jones Ford on the Chickahominy River:

> On a ridge our people planted a couple of 20 pounder Parrott guns and opened with them on the enemy. This fire the enemy's artillery quickly returned, and I was sitting on my horse lazily watching our men work the pieces and the constantly recurring puffs of white smoke as the Confederate shells burst over their heads.
>
> Suddenly I noticed a commotion among the gunners, who came running back down the pike with their rammers and swabs in their hands. Then the teams with the caissons and limbers came back on the run and immediately the Confederate infantry swarmed over the guns.
>
> It looked as if the cavalry was going to have a chance to win more glory, but our infantry was too quick, and with a counter charge they at once retook the guns. The gunners and the teams ran back, and immediately the guns were again jumping like mad creatures under the recoil of their discharge.

〰〰

Rufus R. Dawes, later a brevet brigadier, was in the army led by Maj. Gen. Joseph Hooker in September 1862. They crossed Antietam Creek shortly after daybreak on the 17th, and were warned that they were in open range of Confederate batteries.

Hurriedly they began to change directions, said Dawes, "When whiz-z-z! bang! Burst a shell over our heads; then another; then a percussion shell struck and exploded in the very center of the moving mass of men. It killed two men and wounded eleven. It tore off Captain David K. Noyes's foot and cut off both arms of a man in his company."

Describing the beginning of the battle of Antietam, he said, "Men and officers of New York and Wisconsin are fused into a common mass, in the frantic struggle to shoot fast. Everybody tears cartridges, loads, passes guns, or shoots. Men are falling in their places or running back into the corn.

"Men are loading and firing with demoniacal fury and shouting and laughing hysterically. A long, steady line of gray comes sweeping down through the woods. They fire. It is like a scythe running through our line. It is a race for life that each man runs for the cornfield."

William P. Hogarty entered the conflict as a lieutenant in Company D of the Twenty-third New York Volunteers and later transferred to an artillery unit. His most vivid experience came at Antietam Creek on September 17, 1862—a day that began with "an eerie silence." Wrote Hogarty:

Not a bugle-note stirred the quiet air with its mellow tones. Not a drum rattled its staccato taps of ever-unwelcome "First Call." No revile filled the air with untimely rollicking tunes of frolicsome joys.

Suddenly, from out the stillness came the short sharp, warning crack! crack! crack! of the watchful picket-line, that never sleeping guardian of the army. Then followed a rattle of musketry.

Then followed the command of our officers: "By piece from left into column, march! trot! gallop!! To the limit of speed, run!!"

Then six guns, each drawn by six spirited horses in fine fettle, their drivers mercilessly plying whip and spur, flew through the air. Fire streamed from their steel-tired wheels as they hit a macadamized road.

No chariot ever raced for gain or glory, no fire patrol ever rushed through fire and smoke to the rescue of life or the protection of property, more gallantly than did Battery B to save the right of the Army of the Potomac at Antietam!

Chaplain Frederic Denison of the First Rhode Island Cavalry moved forward with the riders at the battle of Groveton on August 28, 1862. They found their sabers useless, so they waited, helpless, for Confederate gunners to find their mark.

> "The affair seems like a mixture of earthquake, volcano, thunder storm and cyclone," wrote Denison. "Music that was made came from mingled howls, growls, moans, groans, screeches, screams, and explosions. With six or eight shells in the air at a time, above and around us, it was impossible to catch the key-note of the harmony. It might have been a tune for demons to dance to.
>
> "Lieutenant Lorenzo D. Gove of Troop K had his horse killed under him. He calmly unbuckled the saddle, took it on his shoulder and found his place with his troop, waiting to find a spare horse. Corporal Thomas Linerhan of Troop A had the cantle of his saddle cut off by a ricocheting shot that passed over his horse. He saw the missile as it approached him and sprang forward to escape it.
>
> "William Keating of Troop A had an exceedingly nervous horse that reared and pitched at the music of the shells and turned his head from the front, so that his rider was unable to turn him again into position. A cool comrade said: 'Let him be; turn around yourself in your saddle and face his tail, and be ready for action.'"

Glorieta, New Mexico, was in 1862 the site of small-scale battle later described as being "fully as furious as Gettysburg." According to a survivor, "Before the issue was settled, men on both sides fought with knives, bare hands, rocks, and teeth."

After the battle of Malvern Hill, a Georgia private wrote to a relative: "I never heard such a noise in all my life. It sounded like a large cane brake on fire and a thunder storm with repeated loud thunder claps, one clap following another."

In the battle of the Crater at Petersburg, the Federal mine exploded before dawn on July 30, 1864. Col. Charles G. Bartlett, commanding the 199th U.S. Colored Troops, recorded in his diary his recollection of the action:

> Got into the crater. Took the first and second lines of the enemy. Held them till after one, when we were driven back by repeated charges.
>
> I fought them for an hour after they held the whole line, excepting the crater where we were, their flag within seven feet of ours across the works. They threw bayonets and bottles on us, and we returned, for we got out of ammunition. A shell knocked down a boulder of clay onto my wooden leg and crushed it to pieces, killing the man next me.

No newspaper correspondent ever gave readers an authentic firsthand description of the explosion of the Petersburg mine. But an Illinois private who was near the spot later universally known as the Crater gave an eyewitness account. When thousands of pounds of gunpowder were ignited at the end of a long tunnel directed toward Confederate fortifications, he recalled:

> A shock like that of an earthquake was felt along the lines. The whole side of the earth seemed to be in the air. Guns, caissons, men, and heaps of earth were thrown an incredible distance into the air, and the whole descended with a sullen thud, burying beneath, in a mass of ruins, all that had been before a confident stronghold.
>
> When the smoke cleared away a chasm thirty feet deep by one hundred feet in length, with some mutilated men and fragments of woodwork and camp equipage, was all that stood in place of the fort.

Capt. George Clark of the Eleventh Alabama Regiment signaled for his men to move at top speed toward the Crater at Petersburg. Remembering that day, Clark wrote, "Our men poured over into the crater and the ring of steel and bayonet in hand-to-hand fighting began. Men were brained by butts of guns, and run through by bayonets."

Giving formal testimony concerning Gettysburg, Pvt. James Wilson remembered, "Every man picked out his man. That lasted a short time, then what was left of them fell back. . . . I saw an officer cut off the head of a Confederate color-bearer and take his banner."

Writing from the Army of the Potomac, a soldier whose notes are preserved in the *Rebellion Record* tried to describe what seemed to him to be peculiar music made by bullets:

> I caught the pitch of a large-sized Minnie yesterday—It was a swell from E flat to F, and as it passed into the distance and lost its velocity, receded to D—a very pretty change.
>
> One of the most startling sounds is that produced by the Hotchkiss shell. It comes like the shriek of a demon. It is no more destructive than some other missiles, but there is a great deal in mere sound to work upon men's fears.

Federal Maj. Gen. Lewis Wallace did not find the sounds made by field artillery especially interesting. But he confessed to intimates that to him, sounds of naval gunfire were "a source of positive pleasure."

Lt. Robert S. Robertson of the Ninety-third New York Regiment went through the Wilderness without injury, then found himself trapped at Spotsylvania. Describing his position as he "lay hugging the slope of the earth-work," he said that "to advance was impossible, to retreat was death, for in the great struggle that raged there, there were few merely wounded. . . . The bullets sang like swarming bees, and their sting was death."

At Nashville, Tennessee, in December 1864, Col. John H. Stibbs was in command of the Twelfth Iowa Regiment. While members of a battery were trying to get the range, a caisson in front of the unit exploded.

> "We saw the explosion and the cloud of smoke," wrote Stibbs, "and before the sound of the explosion reached us, we saw a man thrown into the air fully twenty feet high, and with arms and legs extended he was spinning around after the fashion of a school boy doing the wagon wheel act."

At Gettysburg's Wheat Field, a member of the 148th Pennsylvania had one especially vivid memory. "I was struck," he said, "by the way ears of wheat flew in the air all over the field as they were cut off by the enemy's bullets."

Capt. Frank Holsinger of the Nineteenth U.S. Colored Volunteers noted that nerves became unstrung as men waited in silent tension for the beginning of a battle. "Breathing a silent prayer, our hearts having ceased to pulsate," he wrote, "someone makes an idiotic remark. There is a laugh, it is infectious, and we are once more called back to life."

According to Holsinger, a quite different mood affected large groups of men when victory had been achieved or was believed to be near. Describing himself and his comrades at such a moment, he said: "The battle when it goes your way is a different proposition. We rush forward. We cheer. We are in ecstasy. While shells and canister are still resonant and while miniés are sizzling spitefully, this is one of the supreme moments of existence."

Lt. William A. Morgan of the Twenty-third Kentucky Regiment was among a group of men exposed to a cannonade from an estimated fifty Confederate guns. "The bursting projectiles seem to compress the air," he wrote, "and one's head feels as if bound with iron bands."

In fiction, the war's most famous sound was the "Rebel Yell." Brig. Gen. Ben McCulloch insisted that it was first heard during an early engagement at Springfield, Missouri: "The incessant roll of musketry was deafening, and the balls fell thick as hail stones; still our men pushed onward and with one wild yell, broke upon the enemy, pushing them back and strewing the ground with their dead."

Confederate Col. Keller Anderson, a member of Kentucky's famous Orphan Brigade, described the yell as he heard it at Chickamauga: "Then arose that do-or-die expression, that maniacal maelstrom of sound; that penetrating, rasping, shrieking, blood-curling noise that could be heard for miles and whose volume reached the heavens—such an expression as never yet came from the throats of sane men, but from men whom the seething blast of an imaginary hell would not check while the sound lasted."

At a Florida convention of the United Daughters of the Confederacy just before the end of the nineteenth century, it was decided "to have the Rebel Yell preserved for posterity by means of a victrola record."

A reporter for the New Orleans *Times Picayune* wrote of the yell: "It paragons description, that yell! How it starts deep and ends high, how it rises into three increasing crescendos and breaks with a command of battle."

Col. J. Harvey Dew of the Ninth Virginia Cavalry heard the Rebel Yell so many times that he tried to analyze it. According to him, it "was nothing more nor less than the well-known fox-hunter's yell, prolonged on the high note and more continuously repeated."

Dew was careful also to note what many observers did not.

"There was also a Federal or Yankee Yell," he said, "but it lacked vigor, vocal breadth, pitch, and resonance."

Pvt. W. W. Gish of the Twenty-sixth Ohio Regiment did not agree with that verdict. "There was a Yankee Yell as well as a Rebel Yell," he wrote, "and we always thought we put more volume into our yell than did our opponents across the works. To me their voices seemed pitched on a higher key than ours."

Near Macon, Georgia, men under Maj. Gen. George Stoneman "dashed down upon the enemy's flank with a yell and with sabres flashing." Capt. William L. Curry of the First Ohio Cavalry said that at Farmington, Tennessee, men "dismounted, raised the Yankee Yell and charged."

Lt. Alfred Pirtle of the Tenth Ohio Regiment wrote that when fighting men became sure that a Federal victory was imminent at Missionary Ridge, a spontaneous yell arose. Joyful at believing a defeat to have been avenged, "such cheering as was never before heard pealed from thousands of throats, and 'Chickamauga! Chickamauga!' followed in thunder tones the flying foe."

Perhaps the strangest of battlefield sounds made by fighting men was neither the Rebel Yell nor the Yankee Yell.

Rather, it came from throats of men in northern Zouave regiments, who, when charging enemy lines liked to shout with all their might: "Zou! Zou! Zou!"

Twelve

"THE WAR IS TO BE ILLUMINATED BY BURNING CITIES AND VILLAGES"

L t. Roger Jones of the U.S. Army's Mounted Rifles realized by April 1861 that he faced difficult choices.

His tiny band of soldiers at the Harpers Ferry armory could try to fend off an anticipated attack by secessionists, or he could make plans to abandon the place, knowing that his defensive measures would be hopelessly inadequate.

Writing to the assistant adjutant general in Washington, he put his decision on record. He had taken measures designed to apprise him of any impending advance on the Federal installation, he said. Once he received such news, he planned to destroy whatever he could not defend and to lead his men into Pennsylvania. "Steps I have taken to destroy the arsenal and 15,000 stand of arms," he reported, "are so complete that I can conceive of nothing that will prevent their entire destruction."

Buildings crammed with machines, tools, muskets, parts of weapons, and raw materials dominated the Virginia village of Harpers Ferry. In the entire United States, only the armory at Springfield, Massachusetts, was of comparable size and importance. Come what may, Jones decided, the contents of the arsenal must not fall into hands of secessionists.

A terse report went to Lt. Gen. Winfield Scott from Chambersburg, Pennsylvania on April 19. According to that report, at 10:00 P.M. on the previous day Jones destroyed the arsenal and its contents before withdrawing before an estimated 2,500 Virginia troops. Conservative estimates placed the value of buildings and their contents at more than $2 million in a period when the pay of a private in Jones's command was $13 per month.

~~~~~

Wholesale destruction of enemy facilities was a familiar keynote of the following fourteen hundred or so days of the Civil War. Targets were cities, towns, bridges, railroads, horses, cattle, baled cotton, even crops in the field—anything potentially useful to the other side.

Maj. Gen. Benjamin Butler's warning came early: "The war is to be illuminated by burning cities and villages." His terse intimation of wholesale destruction proved to be accurate. Union forces deliberately stripped the Shenandoah Valley of everything that could be used or eaten, and Sherman's March to the Sea left a sixty-mile path of devastation. Both of these actions were directed against civilians considered to be hostile.

Less familiar than the fulfillment of Butler's prediction is the fact that incredible havoc resulted from the principle put into practice at Harpers Ferry: If there is even a remote chance that the enemy can make use of something, try to destroy it before it can be captured.

Lieutenant Jones's plans to destroy the armory at Harpers Ferry were not so well developed as he had hoped; much of the sprawling Federal installation remained when the fires he had set were extinguished. Yet Jefferson Davis soon mounted a formal protest. According to him, Union soldiers had destroyed public buildings that belonged not to the nation, but to each state equally with the others.

U.S. Secretary of War Simon Cameron saw actions taken at the Virginia armory in a different light. Writing to Jones in the name of Abraham Lincoln, on April 22 he commended him and members of his command for their "judicious conduct."

That should have ended the Harpers Ferry affair, but it did not.

~~~~~

When Confederate forces evacuated the place more than a year later, they burned the armory for the second time.

~~~

Gosport Navy Yard in Virginia, along with its contents, was worth at least $400 million in today's dollars. Still, Federal defenders decided that it was better to destroy everything than let it fall into the hands of secessionists. So they did their best to render the facility and its warships useless when they left hurriedly on April 20, 1861. Among the vessels that burned to the water line that night was the mighty USS *Merrimack*.

Secessionists seized what was left of the navy yard, then raised and rebuilt the warship as an ironclad called the CSS *Virginia*. Military reverses soon led the new occupants again to burn the biggest facility of its sort in North America. That left the *Virginia* without a home, so a principal in the most famous naval duel of the war was torched for the second time in May 1862.

~~~

Maj. Robert Anderson seems to have been the first Civil War officer who tried to destroy military equipment to keep it from falling into enemy hands. Before leaving Fort Moultrie for Fort Sumter on December 26, 1860, he had every gun in the place spiked; then he destroyed the gun carriages.

~~~

Many Federal ships and much matériel were destroyed rather than have them captured by the enemy. On November 25, 1862, when it appeared that Confederates would capture the sidewheel steamer USS *Ellis*, it was destroyed in North Carolina's New River.

Worth $9,000,000 by today's calculations, the 822-ton *Westfield* was purchased from Cornelius Vanderbilt by Federal agents. Converted for battle use, it cost the equivalent of an additional $2.7 million to fit her out for naval service.

Yet when Confederates seemed likely to capture her at Galveston, the *Westfield* was destroyed by her crew. During the same engagement, Commander W. B. Renshaw succeeded in blowing up his vessel—and was killed in the explosion.

April 1864 saw the USS *Eastport* damaged by a Confederate torpedo. Unwilling to leave the hulk to be salvaged by Confederates, Adm. David Dixon Porter blew up the seven-hundred-ton warship.

At the Federal supply base of Johnsonville, Tennessee, Confederate Gen. Nathan B. Forrest shelled gunboats, barges, transports, and warehouses on November 4, 1864. His gunners missed their targets much more often than they hit them. Yet Union officers put the torch to everything they feared might fall into the hands of Forrest and his men. Destruction of their own ships and supplies cost Federals at least $6.5 million—equivalent to their president's salary for 260 years.

Maj. Gen. George B. McClellan hastily changed his base from White House to Gaines' Mill, Virginia, after having accumulated huge quantities of supplies. Unable to move equipment and supplies at the pace of his army, the Federal commander ran railroad trains loaded with food and ammunition off an embankment into the Pamunkey River.

Confederates were even more zealous than Federals in trying to destroy whatever might be useful to the enemy. Said the Charleston, South Carolina, *Courier* of December 28, 1862: "The lighthouse, situated on Morris' Island and which for many years has guided the mariner to the harbor, was blown up tonight by order of the military authorities." With Federal warships converging on the city, Confederates didn't dare risk letting it stand as a possible guide to naval gunners.

In January 1862, Confederates in Kentucky established a "scorched earth" policy. Aimed at unionists, it made victims of persons favoring neutrality. To prevent anything of potential use from falling into enemy hands, self-styled Southern patriots burned the depot, blacksmith shop, and general store at Horse Cave. Moving on to Cave City, they torched the depot, hotel, and stables.

Frightened civilians in the area fled to Munfordville. They had been told that soldiers under Colonel Hammond would return in a day or so and "burn every house that could be used by the Union army in its advance as a hospital or quarters." Secessionists kept their promise, but they didn't stop with homes and stores. A contemporary account declares, "They also burned up all the hay, oats, and fodder stacks along the road, and drove off or killed all the cattle, horses, and mules to be found."

Confederates established a policy of burning all cotton likely to be captured, and they soon surpassed Federals in sinking their own ships. In addition to the *Merrimac/Virginia*, more than a dozen went to the bottom on orders of their commanders: The CSS *Arkansas, Charleston, Chicora, Fredericksburg, Louisiana, Milledgeville, Mississippi, Neuse, Palmetto State, Pee Dee, Richmond, Virginia II,* and *Wilmington.* Much of the money used to build some of these warships had been raised by Confederate women who held "gunboat fairs" throughout the South.

Early in 1862, the Charleston *Mercury* issued a special broadside, requesting that it be reprinted in newspapers throughout the South. Addressed simply to "Cotton Planters," it made the following urgent appeal:

> It becomes now the duty of all planters to display more than ever their patriotism and devotion to their country. They have sealed that devotion upon the battle-field. Now let us fight our enemies as well, by burning and destroying every bale of cotton upon the river or rivers liable to capture.

William W. Adams of Kentucky was active in the unsuccessful effort to bring his state officially into the Confederacy.

He served in semi-independent reconnaissance duty in Mississippi and Tennessee before becoming chief of artillery for Brig. Gen. Earl Van Dorn.

Elevated to the rank of brigadier as a reward for his service in the siege of Vicksburg, Adams led his brigade into Alabama late in 1864. He was in command at Montgomery when it became clear that Federal raiders were likely to take the city. In this emergency, Adams ordered the burning of the city's stored cotton. Sherman had considered the seizure of 25,000 bales in Savannah sufficiently important to warrant a telegram to Abraham Lincoln. When New Orleans fell, warehouses in the South's largest city held about 15,000 bales. Learning that Montgomery held an estimated 90,000 bales of the South's most precious product, Adams ordered that warehouses be set afire. In post-war days, the man notorious for "having made half of Alabama stink" was shot and killed on the streets of Jackson, Mississippi, by a newspaper editor with whom he had quarreled.

<hr />

Commercial vessels and blockade runners using Southern ports fared even worse than warships. No one knows how many were burned or blown up by their own crews, or what they were worth. A handful were salvaged, but dozens went to the bottom, often with their holds crammed full of weapons and valuables.

On May 1, 1863, the schooner *Sarah* tried to run the blockade at remote Bull's Bay, South Carolina. Spotted by a lookout aboard the USS *Onward*, members of her crew ran the *Sarah* aground.

Before boats from the *Onward* could reach their objective, the Confederate vessel was blazing. Members of its crew escaped while the ship was burning to the water line.

A few weeks later, the Union gunboat *Currituck* and the transport steamer *Seth Low* made a run up Virginia's Pamunkey River. Intelligence reports had indicated that two Confederate steamers, plus a number of smaller vessels, were anchored at or near Casey's Point, approximately ten miles below Newcastle.

Apparently having been alerted, the enemy vessels were moving as rapidly as possible toward Newcastle when they were spotted within a mile of that point. Confederate crews, having seen that their enemies were rapidly gaining on them, set all vessels on fire to prevent their capture.

Famous for having tried to re-supply Fort Sumter in January 1861, the sidewheel steamer *Star of the West* soon fell into Confederate hands. Months later, members of the vessel's new crew took her into Mississippi's Tallahatchie River. They did so in full knowledge that Union warships were likely to appear at any moment. Hence advance preparations were made for destruction of the famous vessel. More than two hundred holes were drilled into oak timbers that formed the side of the steamer. Then a plug was carefully inserted into each hole to keep out the water.

When fear of impending approach of Federal vessels turned into reality, Lt. Azro Stoddard signaled for a special crew to move into action. Its members quickly jerked out the plugs, one by one, so that water would pour into the *Star of the West* at a rate slow enough to permit the crew to escape before she went to the bottom of the river.

⁓

No one has compiled a list of bridges that were burned or blown up in an effort to slow the advance of enemy forces. Among the hundreds that suffered that fate, two situated in Nashville, Tennessee, were typical.

Confederate loss of Forts Henry and Donelson caused civilians in the Tennessee capital to fear that Brig. Gen. John B. Floyd would order the destruction of "our city's vital life lines." Hence a delegation of prominent citizens went to the Confederate leader to beg that he spare the railroad and suspension bridges that crossed the Cumberland River.

Floyd reluctantly agreed to let the structures stand for a few hours, for military purposes. When "a large number of cattle and some troops had been brought from the north side of the river," Floyd ordered that the bridges be demolished on the night of February 19, 1862.

Soon after dark the wooden floor of the suspension bridge was set on fire.

Just to make sure that it couldn't be used by advancing Federals, cables were then cut in such a fashion as to plunge the entire structure into the river below. By 3:00 A.M. on the following day, Floyd recorded triumphantly in his journal that the railroad bridge vital to operation of two lines—the Louisville & Nashville and the Edgefield & Kentucky—was totally destroyed.

During a period of less than one month, men under Stonewall Jackson destroyed at least seventeen bridges. One of them, situated at Jackson's Harpers Ferry base, measured 837 feet in length. Another, the only crossing of the Opequon River for miles, triggered a fresh idea in Jackson's mind when it went up in flames. He was holding a vast number of railroad cars, many of them fully loaded, that he couldn't get to a Confederate line. If abandoned, they would surely fall into the hands of Federal forces who would make good use of them.

Because coal was vital to the war effort—most notably for its use in locomotives and in steamships—the Confederate leader ordered his men to run fifty loaded coal cars into the gap created by the destruction of a Potomac River bridge. He then had the wrecked cars and their loads of coal torched. A correspondent for the *National Intelligencer* came on the scene while the region was still covered with smoke and wrote that Confederates had:

> . . . kindled huge fires around the cars, burning all the woodwork and a great deal of the iron. They were all fine coal carriers, holding twenty tons each. Here and there the road led above them, and, looking down we could see the inside—a mass of red hot coals.
>
> We counted the line of locomotives, red and blistered with the heat, and found 41 or 42. The destruction is fearful to contemplate.

Countless civilian facilities were destroyed by Confederates in order to prevent them from falling into Federal hands. An account in the *National Intelligencer* of December 24, 1860, is typical. According to the newspaper, published in Washington:

> A party of rebels from Gen. [Sterling] Price's army destroyed about one hundred miles of the Missouri railroad. Commencing eight miles south of Hudson, and continuing to Warrenton, they burned the bridge, wood-piles, water-tanks, ties, tore up the rails for miles, bent them, and destroyed the telegraph line.

If the New York *Times* is to be believed, Confederates burned Hampton, Virginia, "rather than have it fall into the hands of the enemy." A region nine miles between Newport News and Watts Creek constituted "the garden spot of Virginia" before the outbreak of hostilities. A report in the New York *Commercial* said that "National troops" who pursued Confederates through this area were astonished. They found it "now perfectly devastated, and but one house left standing. The houses, fences and trees had been burned by the retreating rebels."

When confederates were forced to evacuate Pensacola, Florida, they tried to emulate the Federal action at Harpers Ferry by setting fire to the fort, navy yard, barracks, and marine hospital.

At nearby Fort Pickens, Union forces launched a bombardment that eventually halted the destruction. Fort McRae, the hospital, and navy yard were reduced to rubble, and the steamers *Bradford* and *Neaffle* were burned at the dock. Big guns fired from Fort Pickens saved only the barracks, a blacksmith shop, and a small foundry.

Very early, self-destruction became a guiding principle for treatment of Confederate towns and cities in danger of seizure. Maj. Gen. Leonidas Polk burned Columbus, Kentucky, when he evacuated in February 1862. Barely one month later, the railway station in Jacksonville, Florida, went up in flames—along with the business district, warehouses, machine shops, hotels, and foundries.

Still, the apex of destruction aimed at preventing enemy use was not reached until late in the war when major cities were about to be captured. Departing Confederates put the torch to their capital during the night of April 1, 1865. When Federal forces occupied Richmond on the following day, they found smoldering ruins where one thousand buildings had once stood.

Precisely what took place earlier in Columbia, South Carolina, no one knows. Debate still rages over the degree to which Maj. Gen. William T. Sherman's men were responsible for the 1865 fires that leveled much of the city. Many authorities argue that most of the damage was caused by Confederates who put huge stocks of cotton to the torch in order to prevent its capture.

Atlanta was the site of the devastating fire in 1864 depicted in *Gone With the Wind*. Abandoning Atlanta to her civilian defenders, ten weeks earlier, Confederate Maj. Gen. John B. Hood felt that he didn't dare let a railroad train fall into Federal hands. When he ordered his men to put the torch to it, eighty-one cars were burned, at least twenty-eight of them crammed with ammunition.

This destruction to prevent capture of the train was the work of the man charged with the defense of Atlanta. Pulling out of the city hastily, Hood couldn't take his train with him—so he put it to the torch.

Thirteen

Outmoded Weapons Made "Sitting Ducks" of Many Users

An unidentified political leader in Pennsylvania had what seemed to him to be a great idea. Because men were volunteering so rapidly that there were not enough muskets to go around, why not supply some of them with lances like those used by knights errant of old?

Prodded by Governor Andrew G. Curtin, the U.S. War Department let a contract for a manufacturer to turn out one thousand lances adapted from an old Austrian pattern. A nine-foot staff of Norway fir, tipped with a three-edged blade nearly a foot long, seemed formidable indeed. Citizens of Philadelphia were so delighted with the weapon calculated to put a quick end to the war that they contributed bright red swallow-tailed pennons to embellish each lance.

Organization of a new unit of fighting men was completed in October 1861. Those splendid lances were given to members of the Sixth Cavalry Regiment, led by English-born Col. Richard H. Rush. On May 25, 1862, the men of Company C charged a Confederate picket line, lances at the ready, and pretended they didn't notice that men in gray doubled up with laughter when they saw them coming.

Men of Rush's lancers later took their cumbersome weapons to Gaines' Mill, Savage's Station, White Oak Swamp, Malvern Hill, Harrison's Landing, Antietam, Fredericksburg, Chancellorsville, Brandy Station, and numerous other battlefields. A remnant of the regiment, then armed with rifles, was present at Appomattox.

Heavy and awkward lances, not known to have accounted for a single Confederate death, were discarded in May 1863 as "unfit for the wooded country of Virginia." When these weapons were abandoned, lancers strapped on sabers to replace them.

Col. Arthur Rankin, a Canadian abolitionist eager to fight for the Union, secured permission to raise a large regiment. From the beginning, Rankin made it clear that he expected his men to fight with lances.

Newspaper editors in Toronto soon accused him of deliberately setting out to violate the Neutrality Act. Authorities refused his request for a leave of absence as commander of the Ninth Military District, Canada West. Because of these rebuffs, the sixteen hundred Canadian lancers expected by Washington to help put a quick end to the fray never entered it.

In the Roman Empire, the pike became the standard weapon of infantrymen. Only about six feet long, it could be thrown, jabbed, or used defensively. Long obsolete among European armies, this was one of the weapons with which John Brown hoped to establish his new American Nation.

Brown's liking for the pike would seem to have been enough to turn all Southerners away from it, but it was not. In the weapons-short Confederacy, manufacture of pikes was in full swing within a year after Fort Sumter. An act of the Confederate Congress, never implemented, provided that each regiment should include two companies armed with pikes.

Although they didn't turn the tide in a single battle, pikes continued to be regarded as fearful. When Federal forces captured Knoxville, they found a stockpile of about one thousand of these weapons carefully stored for future use.

Governor Joseph E. Brown of Georgia had so many pikes made for the use of state-controlled troops that the weapons took his name. Two pieces of timber banded together with iron and tipped with a spring-activated blade fifteen inches long constituted the "Joe Brown pike." Described as being "ready for use in the event the state should be invaded by men in blue," the Georgia-produced weapon was not employed against General Sherman's army.

⁕

Describing the death of Richard Dale in the Wilderness, one of his comrades said that the Federal lieutenant colonel "was last seen at the head of his regiment, sword in hand, leading his men across the Rebel earthworks."

While at Fort Henry, Tennessee, Brig. Gen. Ulysses S. Grant was presented with a sword. Purchased by officers of his command, the weapon was described as being "of the most exquisite workmanship, manufactured at great expense." Men of the Twenty-fifth Massachusetts paid $1,000 for a less ornate sword they gave their colonel when he left the regiment in October 1862.

Despite its ornamental and symbolic roles, the sword was little more than an object an officer could wave when he urged his troops forward. Stonewall Jackson so seldom drew his blade from its scabbard that it reputedly rusted there. Robert L. Dabney, briefly a member of Jackson's staff, was contemptuous of the weapon made famous by Romans. So instead of strapping a sword to his side, Dabney carried an umbrella. Maxcy Gregg had no more use for the sword than did Dabney, so the brigadier from South Carolina went into battle wearing a scimitar.

Regardless of what it cost and how it was decorated, an officer's sword was all but useless against muskets and rifles. Even the special short sword issued to gunners seldom drew blood; it was designed for use in disemboweling horses that overran a position, but it was rarely flourished.

⁕

A Confederate veteran disputed claims that no Federal officer was killed by a Confederate swordsman. According to N. B. Hogan, the obsolete weapon played a dramatic role in the battle of Frayser's Farm. He reported, "Lieutenant Mickey of the Eleventh Alabama Infantry became engaged in a hand-to-hand fight with a Union captain who used both sword and pistol."

Hogan, who said he watched the entire affair, was positive that Mickey had no weapon except a sword. When the two men confronted one another, fast and furious action erupted:

> After receiving a ball from the captain's pistol in the right arm, a sword thrust in the cheek, and a cut which laid bare the skull bone on the crown of his head, Lieut. Mickey made a desperate thrust with his bright and flashing sword. It penetrated the body of the gallant captain, who staggered back and in a moment fell a lifeless corpse among the hundreds of slain.

By all odds the most frequent function of the sword was to serve as a symbol in surrender ceremonies, yet it played no part in one of the most solemn. Robert E. Lee had at his side a sword described as "very handsome" when he went to Appomattox. Grant appeared without the symbolic weapon and is said to have explained to Lee that he had left it in a wagon several miles to the rear.

Many times, war correspondents and combatants wrote in almost poetic fashion about "the thunder of many hoofs striking the ground in unison and the squealing of leather as riders leaned forward, their sabers lifted in order to split the skulls of their enemies."

Although the tips of many dress swords were slightly curved, these blades lacked the elegance of the traditional weapon of cavalrymen. Sabers varied widely in weight, length, and curvature but were alike in one respect. Few of them inflicted wounds upon foes, despite vivid and glowing accounts of their use in diaries, letters, and official reports.

Capt. George N. Bliss of the First Rhode Island Cavalry is the only authority for an account according to which an American-born officer made good use of his saber. Near Waynesboro, Virginia, he dashed directly into a group of Confederates. "As I rode," he said later, "I kept my saber swinging, striking six blows, right and left. Two of the enemy escaped by quickly dodging their heads, but I succeeded in wounding Captain William Moss and three others."

Robert H. G. Minty, an Irish-born soldier of fortune who was colonel of the Fourth Michigan Cavalry, was one of a kind, having learned to use the saber when fighting for the queen in Africa. At a Georgia spot identified only in legend—perhaps Calf Killer River or Pea Vine Bridge—he led one of the war's few successful saber charges. Despite the fact that it was a feature of an all but forgotten 1863 engagement, it gave his outfit a lasting nickname: "the Saber Brigade."

By 1863, Federal Brig. Gen. Benjamin H. Grierson's cavalry brigade included three regiments. Collectively, men of these units carried seventeen hundred sabers. By this time, however, the fabled charge of mounted men waving sabers was a thing of the past. Grierson's cavalrymen typically dismounted in order to fight, and ignored their sabers in favor of revolvers and carbines.

⁂

Claims that they made good use of their bayonets were registered by thousands of soldiers. One of the most vivid occurred at the famous battle of the Crater at Petersburg. Confederate Brig. Gen. William Mahone reported that he sent his men into the fray as soon as their bayonets were attached. They used them so effectively, he said, that a bloody hand-to-hand struggle caused Federal forces to retreat hastily or to surrender.

At Gettysburg, Union Col. Joshua L. Chamberlain's regiment had managed to repel six separate charges. To his consternation, he then saw men in gray preparing to make another assault. Realizing that he had no other alternative, Chamberlain ordered a bayonet charge.

He later said that voicing the name of the weapon electrified his men: "Bayonet' ran like fire along the line, from man to man, and rose into a shout, with which they sprang forward upon the enemy, now not 30 yards away, with fixed bayonets."

Regulations called for every musket or rifle to be equipped with either a socket or a saber bayonet. These weapons differed in shape and strength, but they were regarded as equally deadly. Actually, enemy fire was likely to halt a bayonet-wielding soldier before he could get close enough to his foes to use it.

Describing the weapon that earlier was decisive in many a major battle, Capt. S. P. Snider of the Thirteenth U.S. Colored Infantry used realistic rather than romanticized language:

> The bayonet was a piece of glistening steel attached to the musket, upon which the volunteer was to impale his enemy. The bayonet is under some circumstances uncomfortable to look upon, but many of its bloodstains were received in fierce charges on the long-nosed, fleet-footed Southern hog, while its other utilitarian qualities as a candle-stick or a coffee-mill were not to be despised.

In spite of numerous personal accounts of bayonet charges made by men in both blue and in gray, the weapon played an insignificant role. Edged weapons—lances, pikes, swords, sabers, and bayonets—are believed to have accounted at most for one wound out of twenty inflicted. Some experts calculate that bayonets were responsible for only about .5 percent of battlefield wounds.

Knives were not issued as weapons by contending governments, but hundreds of thousands of them went into battle as personal property. Factory-made blades predominated among Northern forces, but vast numbers of Southern fighting men fashioned their own from saws and other pieces of sheet steel.

Just as officers were frequent recipients of presentation swords, so enlisted men often received knives as gifts from fellow townsfolk. Each resident of

Ashby, Massachusetts (and many other communities), was solemnly presented with a Bowie knife at the time of his enlistment.

Officers and members of cavalry units frequently preferred knives equipped with "stone hooks," which enabled them to remove pebbles from the hooves of horses.

Predating today's Swiss Army Knife, many a Civil War blade folded into a bone-covered compartment that also held a fork and spoon.

According to accounts penned by Federal participants, "wagon loads of great ugly-looking knives were picked up on the battle-field of Shiloh where they had been thrown away." Similar reports from the August 1864 encounter at Athens, Tennessee, indicate that many troops discarded their knives when they went into battle.

Regardless of their size or shape, many large blades were called "Bowie knives." Men from Mississippi who fought in Missouri may have been the only combatants who took into battle big, clumsy "cane knives," which they had used during time of peace to cut stalks of sugar cane. Useless as these and Bowie knives were in battle, some of them came to be prized when their owners needed to cut up beef or pork.

Members of artillery batteries, North and South, found the common hand-spike indispensable. A long wooden post, it was used as a lever to maneuver a gun around by its tail.

At least twice, the handspike became an offensive weapon. Lt. James Campbell of the Charleston Brigade is credited with having seized one at Secessionville, using it to drop at least two Union soldiers who were charging his position.

Men under Union Col. J. B. Rogers were incensed to learn that guerrilla chieftain John F. Bolin had used handspikes in a fierce fight at Round Pond,

Missouri. After John Bolin and Nathan Wright killed three men with these bizarre weapons, pro-Federal forces hunted down Bolin's guerrillas.

They killed seven men, captured John Bolin, and watched with approval as a lynch mob strung up the handspike-wielding guerrilla.

During the early months of combat, many a Confederate soldier went into combat carrying no forearm except his own shotgun. Governor Isham Harris of Tennessee in November 1861 called on citizens to surrender "every double-barrel shot-gun to arm the troops now offering themselves for service."

Maj. Gen. Sterling Price of the Missouri State Guard repeatedly complained that of his 7,000 to 8,000 men, "Several thousand had no arms of any kind; the rest were for the most part armed with the shot-guns they had brought from their homes." As late as December 1862, Confederate Maj. Gen. John B. Magruder voiced the same charge concerning weapons provided for members of his cavalry units.

Col. Allen C. Redwood of the Fifty-fifth Virginia Regiment considered the civilian-designed shotgun better than nothing. When his company was called into camp, no man had any other firearm. Because they were brought by their owners or requisitioned from the community, these weapons were literally a hodgepodge of fire. According to Redwood, they ranged "all the way from a piece of ordnance quite six feet long and which chambered four buckshot, through various gages of double-barrels, down to a small single-barrel squirrel gun."

Factory-made ammunition was not available for squirrel rifles or shotguns. Redwood and his comrades eventually received powder, balls, and buckshot in bulk. Then, said the Virginian, "each man made cartridges to fit the arm he bore, using a stick whittled to its caliber as a 'former.'"

Union Brig. Gen. James A. Garfield seized a Confederate encampment in 1863. Describing what he found at the hastily evacuated Cumberland Mountain site, the future president listed as his most significant capture "subsistence stores together with some three hundred squirrel rifles."

At least once, at Sinking Creek Valley in Virginia, a victorious Federal unit found on abandoned ground "a very fine double barreled London twist shotgun containing 18 large buckshot in each barrel, intended for some Yankee."

Yet even expensive imported guns such as this were not powerful enough to be effective in battle. Against an enemy force, a shotgun of any kind was barely one grade ahead of a pea-shooter.

With a Federal fleet approaching during the winter of 1863, Confederate Gen. P. T. G. Beauregard called for citizen volunteers to protect Charleston and Savannah. In a February 18 proclamation he urged: "Let all able-bodied men from the sea-board to the mountains rush to arms. Be not too exacting in the choice of weapons. Pikes and scythes will do for exterminating your enemies."

There is no record that Confederates ever went into battle armed with scythes, but at Ringgold Gap, Georgia, Christopher Cleburne and other men in gray tried to stop attackers by throwing stones at them. At Franklin, Tennessee, Pvt. W. P. Peacock was seen by comrades to lose his musket. Peacock then seized an axe, rushed toward Federal Lines, and was never found.

At Gettysburg, men of Federal batteries fought attackers hand-to-hand with spikes, ax handles, and rammer staffs. In other engagements, men on both sides resorted to use of heavy old pistols that required ramrods in order to be loaded.

In a minor battle at Ream's Station, Confederate Capt. Shade Wooten of the Twenty-seventh North Carolina Regiment resorted to perhaps the most primitive of all weapons employed during the war.

"Three times," reported a fellow officer, "he found an enemy poling his gun up to shoot him. Wooten then grabbed a handful of dirt from the embankment, dashed it into the eyes of his opponent, and saved his life."

Newspaper notices hint that obsolete and outmoded weapons, combined, didn't approach the number of smoothbore muskets carried into battle. Col. George Clark and 950 men of the Eleventh Massachusetts Regiment, said the New York *News* of June 30, 1861, "are all armed with new smooth-bore muskets. In point of equipage, no regiment has exceeded the Eleventh."

When the Twentieth and Twenty-first Indiana Regiments left Indianapolis late the following month, the Louisville *Journal* said that, except for men of two companies, these volunteers were "armed with smooth-bore muskets, which will be exchanged for rifled guns as soon as the Government can obtain them."

In the New York *World* of August 9, men of the Fourteenth Massachusetts Regiment were described as "armed with the Springfield musket of the pattern of 1842." Less than one week later the New York *Herald* reported that 1,046 men of the Fifteenth Massachusetts marched from Camp Scott with the same weapon.

An August issue of the New York *Tribune*, reported that the First Long Island Regiment was "armed with the common smooth-bore musket."

More than five years prior to August 1861, the tiny U.S. Army equipped its men with muzzle-loading Springfield rifles. When Abraham Lincoln called for 75,000 volunteers to augment the 16,000-man U.S. Army, there simply were not enough rifles of any kind to go around.

Muskets of the "Brown Bess" variety, made at Springfield or Harpers Ferry, had an effective range of about two hundred yards. Confederates lucky enough to have Enfield rifles imported from England could hit their targets at one thousand yards.

At the outbreak of the war, Confederates held an estimated 22,000 rifles and about 250,000 smooth-bore muskets. Federal forces had fewer than 30,000 rifles and at least 300,000 muskets. Smoothbores were of two main varieties, an 1822 flintlock and an 1842 percussion model. Some weapons issued to men in gray were even older. Brig. Gen. Lloyd Tilgham managed to recruit about four thousand men for the defense of Fort Henry, but he ruefully reported that most of them carried shotguns and hunting rifles. His best-equipped unit, he said, had flintlock muskets of the "Tower" variety that had seen service in the War of 1812.

Desperate for weapons from any source, Confederates sent purchasing agents to England and Europe, where they secured large quantities of Enfields and other rifles.

Union Brig. Gen. James W. Ripley had used smoothbores in the War of 1812 and regarded them as adequate. Echoing views of many of his contemporaries, he reluctantly turned to the use of rifles, but resisted breechloading weapons. Use of them, said Ripley and other veteran officers, would encourage fighting men to waste ammunition. After fourteen months as head of the U.S. Ordnance Department, Ripley reported having purchased more than 700,000 rifles. He failed to say that of these, less than 10,000 were breechloading models.

Upon becoming field general in chief of U.S. forces in March 1864, Ulysses S. Grant protested bitterly about the weapons with which his men were forced to fight. Confederates had the finest imported breech loading rifles, he alleged, while many a man in blue was still carrying a muzzleloading musket whose barrel had been rifle bored.

Grant's verdict was based on less than objective observations. Yet many analysts later concluded that had U.S. authorities purchased all available foreign-made rifles at the outbreak of hostilities, the Civil War would have been shortened by two or perhaps even three years. Forced to fight with far less than the best, tens of thousands of men on both sides marched into battle knowing that to enemies with superior weapons they would be "sitting ducks."

Fourteen

STRANGE NEW WEAPONS

Federal purchasing agents were gleeful when they managed to buy a shipment of big Belgian muskets. Issued without being tested, the pieces that weighed half again as much as the U.S. model of 1842 proved to have a powerful "kick." When these clumsy pieces were fired, the weapons knocked so many men down that they soon went into storage.

Builders of the USS *Monitor* equipped the first Federal ironclad with a battery of hoses. They were linked to boilers of the warship, and when a valve was turned, scalding water was spouted. Members of the crew planned to use their hoses to repel Confederate boarders, but they soon found that such an attempt would never be made.

In Louisiana, imaginative artisans tried to tie together a locomotive and an air-powered cannon. Steam from the engine was expected to be used in lieu of powder, already scarce in 1862. Before preliminary plans were on the drawing board, promoters promised that Henry Cowling's invention would bring a quick end to the conflict.

"In the open field," they said of the contrivance, "it may well be called a flying artillery. It can run through any ranks, either of infantry or cavalry, and open a lane fourteen feet wide."

Cowling's immense weapon never went into production, but in Maryland wealthy secessionist Ross Winans had a prototype steam gun built. Winans took over the invention of Charles S. Dickinson and confidently expected to mass-produce guns capable of using steam to "throw two hundred balls a minute a distance of two miles." Shielded by a protective cone of iron, the "Winans steam-gun" was designed to run on ordinary railroad tracks.

Before a field test showed that it didn't work, it aroused immense interest. Soon, however, Winans was jailed in Fort Monroe as a political prisoner. Lincoln then is said to have offered him his freedom in exchange for the steam gun being built in iron works operated by the pro-Southern industrialist.

⚬⚬⚬

Confederates of the Tenth Arkansas Regiment marched off to war wearing immense "saber pistols." From beneath the barrel of a heavy one-shot weapon, a short saber could be moved into position "in order quickly to finish off any Yankee who survived the bullet." After being used in battle, most or all of these pistols were thrown away.

⚬⚬⚬

No attempt was ever made to implement some of the most imaginative war-born ideas about weapons. Near Jeffries' Creek, South Carolina, a would-be inventor devised a plan for breaking the Federal blockade. As published in the Charleston *Mercury*, his concept may have been the earliest American proposal for aerial bombardment of enemy positions:

> Prepare a number of large iron shells, loaded with one hundred pounds of powder. Let the shells be heavier on one side, and let this side be fitted with nipples for percussion caps.
>
> Take these shells up in balloons, and when at a convenient altitude above

the blockading squadron, allow them to descend upon the enemy's decks.

Even if this plan were impracticable upon the seas, it might serve to clear our harbors, such as Tybee and Port Royal.

A related and equally radical proposal, also never implemented, went to Confederate Secretary of War L. P Walker. On June 4, 1861, Pvt. Isham Walker of the Ninth Mississippi Regiment proposed sending a balloon over Federal-held Fort Pickens, Florida.

It should be firmly anchored at an altitude of two miles, suggested the soldier in the ranks of "the Jeff Davis Rifles." From that position, it would be feasible to drop "Poisonous Bombs into the fortress and the [Federal] fleet."

Both the secretary of war and the chief executive for whom Walker's unit was named seem to have received detailed proposals. Even had they been interested, the Confederacy lacked the technological and industrial capacity to become the world's first nation to engage in aerial bombardment.

James Woodruff, a carriage maker and manufacturer of knapsacks, was troubled when he learned that men of Federal units were often forced to drag field artillery into position when horses were shot. Before the conflict was a year old, Woodruff succeeded in producing a piece that he said soldiers could easily pull. Weighing only 256 pounds, the smoothbore was designed to throw a two-pound missile.

Lincoln saw demonstrations of the Woodruff gun and indicated interest in it, but he never demanded that it be put into use. Still, Woodruff sold thirty of his featherweight weapons for use by the Sixth Illinois Cavalry. A few of these easily moved pieces went with men under Brig. Gen. Benjamin H. Grierson when they raided Mississippi in 1863.

Had it gone into mass production and general use, the Woodruff gun would have proved invaluable in densely wooded areas and on steep terrain. For the most part, commanders refused even to consider using so light a gun; hence it was never subjected to meaningful tests.

Viewed from some perspectives, the most bizarre weapons employed with regularity were first found by Federals at Centreville, Virginia, in June 1861. When Brig. Gen. Irvin McDowell's forces occupied the village that had been a Confederate center, they discovered the cannon they had seen at a distance to be "Quaker guns." These consisted of big logs, painted black and mounted at angles, used to imitate Parrotts and other heavy weapons.

Quaker guns played significant but indecisive roles in numerous engagements. They were especially prominent at Munson's Hill and on the Potomac River at Shipping Point. At the latter site, Confederates mounted sixteen fake weapons. Three of them, carefully fashioned from white oak, were believed to have been made to deceive observers who scanned the place from Federal balloons.

During the siege of Vicksburg, General Grant found himself woefully short of heavy weapons. Adapting the concept of the Quaker gun, he had artisans bore holes in big logs. Banded with iron to form improvised Coehorn mortars, some of these pieces were fired numerous times before they burst.

Two kinds of hand grenades were made, but they saw little use in combat. One of them, patented in August 1861, carried a percussion cap and an activating "plunger" that was not inserted until it was about to be thrown. Rated as effective at a distance of about twenty-six yards, this explosive piece was known by the name of its inventor, Ketchum.

A more sophisticated grenade, "the Excelsior," was developed in 1862 by W. W. Hanes. Its cast-iron shell held fourteen nipples, to each of which a percussion cap was attached before it was thrown. Hanes insisted, correctly, that at least one cap was sure to trigger an explosion. In practice, men trying to use his device often hit a cap accidentally and had a hand or arm blown off. As a result, it seems never to have been used in battle.

Soldiers who may or may not have heard of the Ketchum grenade or the

Excelsior sometimes improvised similar weapons. At Vicksburg, Confederates in Louisiana units stuck short, lighted fuses into 6- and 12-pounder shells, then rolled them into ranks of Union sappers.

One demonstration of this weapon was enough to make believers of opponents. Confederate Capt. John M. Hickey said that when one of the city's forts was stormed, "the air was made black with hand grenades which were thrown at us by every Federal soldier who got inside the works." Similar explosive devices were made on the spot by Federals at Knoxville.

Unionists from Texas didn't fare well when they tried to use explosive shells without guns, or "tubes," with which to launch them. Confederates, who had invaded New Mexico in 1861, were viewed as threatening the entire territory. At Valverde on February 21, 1862, they were met by a motley bunch of opponents who called themselves Graydon's Independent Spy Company.

Their captain was James ("Paddy") Graydon, a former saloon operator at Fort Buchanan. Col. Edward R. Canby, head of the Department of New Mexico, listened intently as Graydon suggested a novel way "to mow down boys in gray like ripe wheat." When his commander approved Garydon's scheme, he moved into action.

A number of 24-pounder howitzer shells were packed into wooden boxes, then lashed to the back of a pair of army mules.

Under cover of darkness, a squad of Graydon's men moved across a river with the heavily laden animals. Soon they were within an estimated 150 yards of unsuspecting Confederates. Jerking the mules to a halt, Federal partisans lighted fuses, gave each animal two or three hard smacks, and ran for their own lives. To their consternation, the mules moved quickly into action—following their drivers instead of going forward.

An unidentified participant in one of the war's most unusual attempts at a cannonade summed up the affair wryly.

"Every one of them shells exploded on time, but there were only two casualties—the mules."

Describing some of the action near Chattanooga, Union Col. P. C. Hayes said an assault by troops under Confederate Lt. Gen. James Longstreet reached a deep ditch dug by Federals. Confederates, he said, jumped into the ditch in order to raise scaling ladders. According to him, "This action was fatal to them. Our men, being unable to reach them with their heavy guns, lit the fuse of the shells, which they threw by hand into the ditch, where they exploded, slaughtering the helpless occupants by the wholesale."

Records do not indicate the number of engagements in which improvised explosives were rolled or thrown against foes. Nevertheless, they were employed frequently enough to show that although technology to produce suitable hand grenades did not exist, the concept behind those weapons was fully developed by men in both gray and blue.

Before the outbreak of hostilities, English inventor William Hale perfected a self-propelled missile that he called a rocket. His radical new weapon was used by the British during the Crimean War. Once full-scale war erupted in North America, he offered to come to Washington to supervise manufacture of his device. His offer was turned down, but Federals produced enough 6-pound rockets similar to Hale's to put them into limited combat use.

Confederates also manufactured a few rockets, but on both sides leaders branded them as "puny, by comparison with conventional guns."

Lincoln, who frequently prodded his commanders to try innovations, was intrigued by incendiary chemical called "Greek Fire." He put his life at risk by watching two 13-inch shells that were charged with it spew fire over a circular area about fifty feet in diameter. At his insistence, a few of these shells were used experimentally by Federal forces.

Confederates denounced this early form of chemical warfare as "inhuman." Yet when they sent teams of arsonists into New York City in a plot to burn its major buildings, Greek Fire was used to start the blazes. The expedition ended in failure because the chemical didn't ignite properly.

———

Working with both small arms and big guns, men in blue and men in gray tried to get their hands on rapid-fire weapons. One of them, the English-made .44 Kerr revolver, could be fired five times in rapid succession. A handful of these, used by Confederate officers, functioned but were not abundant enough to have significant impact.

Far more available and successful, the Northern-made Spencer rifle carried seven cartridges. Awed Confederates exposed to its fire described it as capable of being "loaded on Sunday and fired all week." Top ordnance officials in Washington were less than enthusiastic, however. A soldier armed with a Spencer had to take along one hundred cartridges instead of forty, so Washington never ordered the weapon in quantity. Men of several regiments bought it as personal expenditures of about $50 per man. When it was used, it often proved to be a decisive factor.

———

Both the 16-shot Henry rifle and the 5- or 6-chamber Colt revolving rifle cost at least eight times as much as imported muskets. Though both rapid-fire weapons saw limited use late in the conflict, neither played a decisive role in a major battle.

———

Muskets, rather than rifles, were still dominant when opposing forces met at Gettysburg. These clumsy weapons had many drawbacks, and many of the men who wielded them had received little training.

When the carnage was over, squads of Federal soldiers went over the battle-field to recover abandoned weapons. Maj. T. S. Laidley of the U.S. Army Ordnance Department later reported that more than 27,000 muskets were found on the field.

Of these, he said that an estimated 24,000 were still loaded—not always with a single charge. According to Laidley, about 12,000 of the Gettysburg muskets that were recovered had two charges in their barrels. Another 5,000 or more carried three to six charges, and one musket left behind by a soldier was jammed with more than twenty loads.

The barrel of another abandoned musket was found to hold twenty-two balls, sixty-two buckshot, and "God only knows how many cartridges." Weighting evidence from the battle that proved to be the most decisive of the war, Laidley concluded that a military unit is only as good as its weapons—and not nearly that good unless men know how to use them.

Experimenting with ways to increase the power of large guns, Pvt. John Gilleland of Georgia's Mitchell Thunderbolts developed a double-barreled cannon. Balls linked by a chain were designed to "mow down Yankees as a scythe cuts rye." When put to use, however, it was found that precise coordination of firing was impossible. In a few test rounds, linked cannon balls "whizzed around in erratic fashion" and killed two or three Thunderbolts.

This experimental weapon is commemorated by a historical marker on the campus of the University of Georgia at Athens.

In a bid for greater mobility, Union metal workers fabricated special sheet-iron cars big enough to hold cannon. Several of these "railroad batteries" were put into service, but it was found that big guns confined to rails were seldom able to train their fire on the enemy.

At Rochester, New York, the Billinghurst Company produced a gun with its barrels mounted side by side on a metal platform. The Requia—called a battery because it employed twenty-five individual tubes—required a crew of three. Operated by experienced men, the contrivance could get off 175 shots per minute. Because there was no cover for the powder train, dampness rendered it inoperative in combat. Hence this early rapid-fire gun was employed effectively only at Chicamauga.

Lincoln investigated the single-barrel .58 Ager gun, popularly known as "the coffee-mill" because it was fed from a hand-turned hopper. Seeing firsthand that it could deliver at least one hundred bullets per minute, with an effective range of about one thousand yards, the president was so impressed that he ordered a few. There is no record that the Ager gun played a significant role in a major engagement.

Numerous generals who had little or no military training or experience viewed war from the perspective of business, and they reasoned that it was well for their men to expend as little ammunition as possible. In this respect, they concurred with James Ripley, Union chief of ordnance, who considered breechloading rifles wasteful of ammunition. In many instances, a man going to battle was permitted to take only forty rounds with him. What's more, he might be given an oral commendation if he came out of the fight with his cartridge box half full.

North Carolina physician Richard J. Gatling, who said he was motivated by humanitarian purposes, gave his name to a rapid-fire weapon that blended some of the best features of several earlier ones. When he demonstrated it at

Indianapolis in 1862, Governor Oliver P. Morton urged War Department officials to adopt it at once. Institutional inertia, combined with prejudice against a Southern-born inventor, prevailed in high circles.

Among high-ranking officers, only Maj. Gen. Benjamin F. Butler was enthusiastic about giving the Gatling gun a chance to prove itself. He paid $1,000 each for a dozen of the rapid-fire weapons, but War Department approval did not come until more than a year after the end of hostilities.

During the war the Gatling had no genuine field test except at Petersburg. Too late for use by Federal forces, it was found to be so effective that the physician who invented it is generally known as "the father of the machine gun."

Several attempts were made to use large amounts of powder in order to blow holes in enemy fortifications or positions.

By all odds the most spectacular of these experiments with "ammunition that carried no ball or shell" took place at Petersburg, Virginia.

Under the prodding of experienced coal miners, Federal leaders gave the go-ahead to dig a vast tunnel that was expected to reach beneath Confederate lines. When the tunnel was finished, "the gun was loaded" with 320 kegs, each of which held twenty-five pounds of powder

At 3:30 A.M. on July 30, 1864, the fuse was lighted by Lt. Col. Henry Pleasants of the Forty-eighth Pennsylvania. To observers, it seemed that it took an eternity (several minutes in reality) for fire to run through the fuses. Though 278 Confederates died in the blast, "the Petersburg mine" was one of the worst fiascos of the war. Men who rushed into the hole created by the explosion fought hand-to-hand for hours; some were gunned down from its edges. Confederate casualties are believed to have exceeded fifteen hundred—but more than twice as many Union Soldiers died or were wounded in the aftermath of the war's biggest explosion.

At Mobile Bay in August 1864, Union Rear Adm. David G. Glasgow Farragut gained a special kind of immortality. Knowing his ship could have a hole blown in it any second, he reputedly cried to his subordinates: "Damn the torpedoes! Full speed ahead!"

Explosive devices to which Farragut referred weren't remotely like present-day self-propelled explosive tubes. Rather, they were powder-filled stationary devices designed to detonate on contact.

Confederate Gen. Gabriel J. Rains, who began experimenting with explosives soon after his 1827 graduation from West Point, was largely responsible for their use by the Confederacy during the Civil War. Some of his early "sub terra torpedoes," which would today be called land mines, accounted for a number of Federal casualties at Yorktown, Virginia. Early "submarine mortar shells" tested by Rains were precisely what the name implies: ordinary mortar shells made waterproof and rigged to explode under the surface.

Political and military leaders on both sides of the conflict denounced the use of the "fiendish" devices fashioned by Rains. Still, he put underwater varieties to use in the James River not long after Yorktown. Soon a great hue and cry was raised in both the North and the South about employment of "diabolical" hidden explosives.

Disgruntled at official reaction to his torpedoes, Rains was for a time assigned to duty as chief of Richmond's Bureau of Conscription. After May 1863, however, he resumed work on his explosive devices and developed types that held three hundred pounds of powder and were detonated when an electrical switch was moved. Before the conflict ended, expert workmen on both sides were manufacturing "horological torpedoes" equipped with timing devices so they could be set to go off at a desired moment.

Federals who at first castigated the use of torpedoes quickly went to work devising varieties of their own for use on land and in the water.

No other radical innovation challenged the torpedo for first place as an ultramodern tool of battle. Again and again it was found to be effective against infantry, cavalry, and naval vessels.

In Georgia's Ogeechee River, the USS *Montauk* was headed downstream at moderate speed on the morning of February 28, 1863. A report made by her second assistant engineer detailed what happened at 9:35:

> A violent, sudden, and seemingly double explosion took place. Water gained rapidly on the steam pumps; in a short time it was from 5 to 6 inches deep on the engine room floor. Assistant Engineers R. Potts, McCartney, and Greene came from their stations in turret, reporting that it was a torpedo that had exploded under the vessel.
>
> The gunboats *Seneca*, *Dawn*, and *Wissahickon* sent men to assist. When floor plates at the side of the boiler were removed, I found the center of effect from the torpedo's explosion to be directly in a vertical line. Force had driven the rib of the vessel up about 6 inches. The plate-iron shell or bottom of the vessel had fractured along a line of rivets from about 2 feet to port side of center and then again diagonally, starboard and aft.

By 6:00 P.M., "the amount of leak was reduced so much that one steam pump kept the bilge clear of water."

Numerous other ironclads were much less fortunate than the *Montauk*. At Mobile Bay, a single torpedo sent the *Osage* to the bottom. Two or more exploded almost simultaneously to destroy the USS *Tecumseh* early in the same battle.

During the long siege of Charleston, perhaps the most spectacular Confederate success stemmed from having sunk a mighty battleship with a single torpedo. This explosive is believed to have been of an unusual "barrel" shape perfected late in the conflict.

Only a fraction of the torpedoes put into service found their prey, however. At Charleston, defenders of the port city shouted with joy when they saw Adm. Samuel F. DuPont's flagship, the USS *New Ironsides*, cast anchor directly over a torpedo that held two thousand pounds of powder. Their elation was premature; before the device could be detonated, a wagon ran over a wire. Once the wire was broken, the torpedo was impotent.

Today the torpedo is associated exclusively with naval warfare. During the Civil War it was the only new weapon to be almost universally used on land and in water late in the conflict. The long-range impact of a Confederate general's device almost equals that of making wooden warships obsolete by shielding them with coats of iron.

Fifteen

OFFICERS WERE OF MANY VARIETIES, BUT ONLY ONE COLOR

By September 1862, a serious crisis had developed among Federal officers. Governors of states had failed to appoint replacements for many who had fallen in battle. Maj. Gen. Henry W. Halleck therefore issued a circular to these executives, urging them to forget about political favors and act quickly to name deserving noncommissioned officers and privates to vacant spots.

Comparatively few governors responded quickly and positively; most preferred to select field officers likely to give them political support in the future.

In October 1862, a bill was introduced into the Confederate Congress, which failed to pass, directing Confederate soldiers never to take a Federal officer alive after the Emancipation Proclamation took effect on January 1, 1863. Lincoln had announced in September that if the rebelling states had not returned to the Union by that date, their slaves would be freed.

Nearly all states that provided soldiers who fought in blue jealously guarded their privilege of permitting the men to elect their officers below the rank of colonel. Most colonels were appointed by governors, but states had no control over officers of higher rank. General officers were selected in Washington or on the field of battle, with congressional confirmation required before the rank became permanent.

Of the nearly eleven hundred officers of the U.S. Army on duty at the time South Carolina seceded, more than three hundred resigned to enter Confederate service. Of the remainder, only one in twenty achieved the rank of general. Most of the army officers were graduates of West Point who were "frozen" in their units as a result of policies adopted in Washington.

Approximately one hundred graduates of West Point, no longer in the army, joined units of state volunteers upon the outbreak of hostilities. Because these men were not affected by policies that applied to U.S. Army officers, fully half of them became generals.

If a Union officer aspired to high rank, the best way to get it was to be at Fort Sumter during April 1861. Ten officers were on hand when the Confederate bombardment began. All of them survived the fierce assault, and six of them became major generals.

Confederate Lt. Col. Richard L. T. Beale of the Ninth Virginia Cavalry didn't like the multitude of rules and restrictions under which he fought. Therefore he submitted his resignation twice, without effect. When he wrote his third letter of resignation in 1862, he said he'd very much like to re-enlist in a company of independent rangers as a private.

Instead of granting his request, Richmond ordered him to stay with the men he already led. Two years later the would-be private became a brigadier general.

When Abraham Lincoln reluctantly agreed to permit blacks to enter Federal fighting forces, many of his generals shared his doubts that they would make good soldiers. As a result, nearly 180,000 black soldiers fought under white officers. About sixty black men are believed to have become noncommissioned officers.

Describing the organization of the Twelfth Regiment, U.S. Colored Troops, Henry V. Freeman casually interpolated, "The officers of the regiment were all white men, of course."

When the state of Ohio raised a unit known as the Fifth United States Colored Troops, Milton M. Holland eagerly enlisted. Fighting under Maj. Gen. Benjamin F. Butler, he was promoted to the rank of regimental sergeant major.

At the battle of New Market on September 19, 1864, all of the officers of his former company—white, of course—were killed or seriously wounded. Without authorization, Holland assumed battlefield command of Company C, then led his comrades with conspicuous bravery. As a result he became one of only twenty-one blacks to win the Congressional Medal of Honor for Civil War gallantry—but he did not receive a commission.

Maj. W. H. Chamberlain of the Eighty-first Ohio Regiment was puzzled at the inability of one of his men to make up his mind. According to Chamberlain, during the battle of Jonesboro, Georgia, J. C. Michie wore the chevrons of a sergeant. In his pocket, however, he carried three commissions, giving him the option of becoming a major of colored troops, a captain of volunteers, or first lieutenant of the Fifty-second Ohio Regiment.

Veteran political leader Abraham Lincoln won less than 40 percent of the popular vote in the election of 1860. Long before he faced re-election, he realized he needed the support of every special interest group he could muster. This influenced him to select brigadier generals from various ethnic groups in the Union.

Germans were the most numerous newcomers, so three of them became major generals: Carl Schurz, Julius H. Stahel, and Franz Sigel. Irish voters were pleased to see Michael Corcoran and Thomas Meagher become brigadier generals. Because their number was smaller, French citizens were represented by only one conspicuous appointment, Brig. Gen. Philip Regis de Trobriand.

Roger A. Pryor, sometimes cited as the person who fired the first shot at Fort Sumter, denied that he had done so. Without military training or experience, he became a brigadier and fought with distinction at Williamsburg, Seven Pines, and Antietam.

His brigade having been virtually wiped out, Pryor resigned his commission and enlisted as a private in the Virginia cavalry.

Official Records indicates that the Second Massachusetts Regiment suffered an extremely high rate of casualties among its officers. Of the sixteen known to have been killed or to have died of wounds or disease, thirteen were graduates of a single college—Harvard.

John H. Martindale became a brigadier general of volunteers in August 1861, fighting with distinction on the Peninsula and at Yorktown. At Malvern Hill, however, he was charged with favoring surrender rather than retreat. An angry Maj. Gen. Fitz-John Porter relieved him of command and sent him before a court of inquiry. Cleared by the court, Martindale was brevetted a major general.

Porter, on the other hand, underwent court-martial when charged with "disobedience, disloyalty, and misconduct in the face of the enemy." Maj. Gen. John Pope saw to it that he was dismissed from military service. Porter fought the dismissal for twenty-five years, and in 1886 was reappointed—as an infantry colonel, retired.

Desperately seeking officers to command his hastily assembled fighting forces, President Jefferson Davis made Albert S. Johnston a full general. That action on August 30, 1861, was taken with full knowledge that General Johnston had never commanded troops in battle.

Born in New York, mapmaker Jedediah Hotchkiss was regarded by Stonewall Jackson as exceptionally capable, so he was given a commission as captain. By the time Robert E. Lee surrendered at Appomattox, the Northerner without military experience had been promoted.

Prior to the surrender, Hotchkiss was arrested by Federal soldiers who forwarded to Ulysses S. Grant some of the maps made by Hotchkiss. Grant immediately released him and later paid him for the privilege of copying some of his maps. This made Major Hotchkiss the only Confederate officer ever to receive royalties from a Federal lieutenant general.

Texas-born Ben McCulloch fought for Texas independence and in the Mexican War. When his state seceded, he became a colonel of state troops that were later transferred to the Confederacy. Soon McCulloch became a brigadier general and was sent to Pea Ridge, Arkansas. There the Confederate officer died from the bullet of a sharpshooter and went to his grave without ever having worn a uniform.

A single Ohio household, that of a former U.S. secretary of the interior, produced four Union generals. Hugh B. Ewing, born in 1826, was the youngest of the quartet and became a brigadier late in 1862. Thomas Ewing Jr., three years older, won his command early in 1863. Charles Ewing, born in 1835, waited for his promotion to the rank of brigadier until March 1865.

Their foster brother, informally adopted by their father at an early age, topped all of them in rank. Reared by John Ewing as a son, William Tecumseh Sherman married his foster sister, Ellen Ewing. He became a major general in 1862 and barely four years after the end of hostilities was a full general.

Col. James H. Carleton led his men on a march from California to Mesillo, on the Rio Grande River. For that exploit he was made a brigadier general of volunteers on April 28, 1862. He remained in uniform throughout the war—but never met a Confederate unit in battle.

Prussian-born Alexander Schimmelfennig enlisted with the Seventy-fourth Pennsylvania Regiment as a colonel and became a brigadier general in November 1862. His most widely publicized exploit consisted of hiding for more than two days during the battle of Gettysburg. Some accounts say he took refuge in a stable, but others insist that he hid in a pig pen.

Attorney Alfred H. Howe enlisted as colonel of the Second Connecticut Regiment. He was in so many engagements and held so many posts that a page of fine print is required to list them. In mid-January 1865 he received one of the most extraordinary promotions of the war. Never having served a day in the U.S. Army, he was made a brigadier general of regulars.

Spanish-born Edward Ferrero loved dancing so passionately that he became a professional dance instructor. That may be why the U.S. Senate refused to confirm his appointment as brigadier general despite his achievements at Antietam and Fredericksburg.

His temporary promotion of September 1862 having expired the following March, he was reappointed in May. This time, the new rank was confirmed, thus enabling the former dance instructor to play a central role in the Federal fiasco of the Petersburg mine explosion.

Benjamin H. Grierson, once a music teacher, was decidedly uneasy around horses. That didn't prevent the governor of Illinois from making Grierson a major in a cavalry unit. With no military training, he became perhaps the most successful of all Federal officers who led his men on horseback raids.

During one of them, he and his men made an eight-hundred-mile foray that stretched from La Grange, Tennessee, to Baton Rouge, Louisiana. As a reward for his 1864 exploits that did much to break the back of the Confederacy, the former music teacher was made a major general in the U.S. Army.

Many a Confederate general officer died in battle after a few weeks or months. Their ranks became so thin that no appropriate commander was available for a division at Bentonville, North Carolina, in March 1865. As a result, Col. John G. Coltart was hastily placed at the head of the division—two command levels above his rank.

A battlefield emergency led to Coltart's informal promotion. In several instances, however, Confederate officers decided questions by holding an impromptu lottery. If two men were given the same commission on the same

day and neither was a veteran of earlier military expeditions, they threw dice or
drew straws to determine who would have seniority.

Field officers of infantry units, both North and South, customarily rode
horses. What's more, many of them stayed behind battle lines where they were
out of the range of enemy fire. There were many exceptions to this cautious
behavior, otherwise there would not have been so many casualties among
their ranks.

Maj. Gen. Philip Sheridan ignored established traditions at Cedar Creek,
Virginia, in 1864. According to Maj. Gen. Wesley Merritt, Sheridan "took his
colors in his hand, and where the fire was hottest led the men on, his horse
plunging wildly under him."

In both Federal and Confederate forces, field officers were carefully set apart
from the men they led. Many an officer had a private wall tent furnished with
carpets and mirrors, while private soldiers and noncommissioned officers were
herded into small tents with no comforts. Officers had the best food available
and could drink alcohol even when it was forbidden to their men.

Yet the most bizarre of distinctions had nothing to do with shelter and
food. Many an officer in Northern forces, as well as his Southern counterparts, went off to battle accompanied by a personal servant, usually, but not
always black.

Nowhere in the 1,087-page index to volumes of the *Official Records* of the two
armies does the term *bodyguard* appear. Yet numerous high-ranking officers had
bodyguards who functioned much as do members of the U.S. Secret Service
who are assigned to presidential duty. Possibly the largest of all bodyguards was

the three-hundred-man unit whose chief duty was the protection of Federal Maj. Gen. John Charles Frémont.

The ranks of some Confederate units were so decimated that an officer of high rank might be limited to an escort of a single comrade.

⁂

When Robert E. Lee decided to take the war far into enemy territory, fifty-one other generals accompanied him across the Pennsylvania state line. Returning to a relatively safe position in Virginia after Gettysburg, the commander of the Army of Northern Virginia had only thirty-four generals with him.

In the decisive Pennsylvania battle, seventeen Confederate generals died.

⁂

Most authorities say that more than one thousand men became general officers of opposing forces. A majority of them posed for a photographer at least once, and a huge collection of portraits is held by the U.S. Military History Institute at Carlisle Barracks, Pennsylvania.

A survey of these generals whose images were caught by the camera reveals that only about half a dozen sat for the photographer while wearing spectacles.

⁂

Long before the conflict was over, fighting men realized that there was a significant distinction between men who commanded on land and those who commanded on water.

It was taken for granted that the general who directed movement of an army would remain in a relatively safe place where he could observe the action from a distance. At sea, a commander of a fleet of warships, on the contrary, was expected to face precisely the same danger as did his sailors.

⁂

Because dress of officers varied so widely, the Confederate adjutant general, Samuel Cooper, issued a special bulletin on June 8, 1862:

> Officers of the field are permitted to wear a fatigue dress, consisting of the regulation frock-coat, without embroidery on the collar, or a gray jacket, with the designation of rank upon the collar. Only caps such as are worn by the privates of their respective commands may be worn by officers of the line.
>
> Officers of all grades are reminded that unnecessary exposure in time of battle, on the part of commissioned officers, is not only unsoldierlike, but productive of great injury to the army and infinite peril to the country.

At Fredericksburg, Union Maj. Gen. Winfield Scott Hancock noted with alarm that his officers were being killed on an almost hourly basis. As a result, he issued a special bulletin.

In it, he noted that rifle fire from Confederates had become so intense that "scarcely a pigeon" could live through it. He therefore urged all mounted officers to leave their horses behind when they went into action. A man on foot presented a less visible and tempting target than did a man astride a horse, he pointed out.

Confederate Col. Eppa Hunter found himself physically unable to stay on a horse after having undergone surgery. As a result, in the battle of Ball's Bluff, Virginia, he was the only officer positively known to have directed his regiment while lying in the bed of a wagon.

Union Col. Frederic Utassy is believed to have been the only regimental commander who frequently issued orders in seven languages. Fifteen European countries were listed as the place of birth of men in Utassy's Thirty-ninth New York Regiment.

In the early months of the war, Federal leaders wouldn't accept a man for military service unless he had a working knowledge of the English language. However, as the manpower pool shrank and as more and more recent European emigrants accepted bounties in order to become soldiers, this requirement was dropped.

Therefore, numerous line officers couldn't have handled their men had they not sometimes used a language other than English. Utassy was, however, the only colonel known to have been fluent in more than half a dozen languages.

On January 12, 1863, Jefferson Davis issued a public announcement that included his assessment of the Emancipation Proclamation. Calling it "the most execrable measure recorded in the history of guilty man," Davis realized that it would inevitably lead to the use of black soldiers by Federals.

Anticipating this result, the Confederate president tried to make a clear distinction between Union enlisted men and their officers. Enlisted men, he said, should be treated "as unwilling instruments in the commission of crimes." Hence, after being captured, they should be subject to discharge and returned to their homes on parole.

Federal officers, said the same document, deserved special treatment. Because they could be found at the head of black troops some day, a captured commissioned officer should be "dealt with in accordance with laws providing for the punishment of criminals engaged in exciting servile insurrection."

Col. Thomas Wentworth Higginson was one of the few Union officers who gave up command of an elite regiment of white troops in order to take over a black unit without a promotion in rank.

An ordained clergyman, Higginson went into the war as an ardent abolitionist who was willing to risk his life in order to help do away with slavery. To his regret, he soon found that relatively few of his comrades in arms shared his goal. Many officers were fighting to preserve the Union; others were in uniform because they saw the war as a good way to get ahead financially.

***

Federal generals who were in field command theoretically had power to promote or to demote their subordinates. In practice, their actions were subject to approval or rejection by Lincoln.

Early in 1863, Maj. Gen. Ambrose Burnside decided at one fell swoop to rid himself of nine men whom he considered incompetent or insubordinate. He dismissed from military service Gen. Joseph Hooker and removed from command Generals W. T. H. Brooks, John Newton, and John Cochrane. Simultaneously, Burnside ordered that Generals W. B. Franklin, W. F. Smith, S. D. Sturgis, and Edward Ferrero be relieved of their duties, along with Col. J. H. Taylor.

Hastily going to Washington from Fredericksburg, Burnside managed to see the president but was given no answer when he requested a final verdict. Lincoln refused to make a hasty decision, asked his commander to return the next day, and promptly shelved papers calling for the officers to be dismissed or relieved.

***

In prison, officers and enlisted men usually received different treatment. Especially in the North, enlisted men went to designated camps, while officers were sent to prisons set aside for them.

Numerous accounts by captured Union officers report that when a newly captured man arrived, the inmates who had been there for weeks or months gave him a standard greeting. "Fresh fish! Fresh fish!" they shouted in chorus.

***

In the western theater, Union Maj. Gen. W. B. Franklin and Confederate Gen. Richard Taylor reached an informal agreement.

Ignoring directives from Richmond, they agreed to exchange captured officers who had led black as well as white units.

This arrangement worked briefly as a result of a special bulletin issued by Taylor. In it, he notified Franklin—aware that the Union commander knew it to be untrue—that he had on hand "no prisoner who is an officer of a negro regiment."

⁓⁓⁓

Ardent abolitionist Edward A. Wild, M.D., donned a uniform on May 23, 1861. Initially captain of Company A of the Massachusetts Militia, he had become a brigadier general in less than two years, responsible for recruitment of black soldiers in North Carolina.

Wild might have been promoted much faster, had he not frequently created turmoil by his racial views. Harsh treatment of Confederates brought him a transfer to the Norfolk area, where he was arrested on June 19, 1864. Brig. Gen. Edward W. Hinks charged him with having used excessive force in dealing with citizens who sympathized with the insurrection.

A court-martial was hastily convened and he was quickly convicted of insubordination. Wild would have been stripped of his stars and faced other penalties had it not been for Maj. Gen. Benjamin F. Butler of his home state. Butler threw out the brigadier's conviction, correctly pointing out that a special panel was required to hear evidence against an officer who led black troops. Prejudice against such men was so great that they were not to be judged except by other officers who commanded blacks.

Sixteen

SHIPS, SEAS, AND RIVERS

Knowing that the Confederacy would soon complete construction of an ironclad vessel, Federal naval authorities accelerated their schedule for building the USS *Monitor*. Thus it was en route to Norfolk when the CSS *Virginia* (formerly the USS *Merrimack* and then the *Merrimac*) went into action against wooden warships.

Its builders weren't completely confident about the ability of the *Monitor* to make its way through heavy seas. Therefore the Federal vessel destined to take part in the first battle between ironclads didn't go to the fight under its own steam. Instead, it was towed the entire distance from New York City to Hampton Roads, Virginia, by the tug *Seth Low*.

At the outbreak of hostilities, only England and France had navies more modern and more powerful than that of the United States. During less than a decade, Washington built and commissioned more steamers than any other nation.

These included the sloops of war *Brooklyn, Dacotah, Hartford, Iroquois, Lancaster, Pawnee, Pensacola, Michigan, Narragansat, Richmond, Seminole,* and *Wyoming*. As though to prove to the world that sailing vessels were rapidly becoming obsolete, during the same period the U.S. Navy acquired six great steam-powered frigates: the *Colorado, Merrimac, Minnesota, Niagara, Roanoke,* and *Wabash*.

To the surprise of the nautical world, Abraham Lincoln announced in mid-April 1861 that ships of the U.S. Navy would blockade the coastlines of seceded states. Experts in Europe, as well as commanders of U.S. vessels, were astonished. Most vessels not in dry dock under repair were in faraway waters, leaving only two ships on hand to blockade the coasts of South Carolina, Georgia, Florida, Alabama, and Louisiana.

Chosen by Jefferson Davis to become the first Confederate secretary of the navy, Stephen R. Mallory of Florida made a lasting reputation as an innovator. He pioneered in the construction of ironclad warships and encouraged many other novel steps. On his first day in office, Mallory realized that if he hoped to give the U.S. Navy trouble, he'd have to take new and daring steps, because the "navy" of which he took charge didn't then include a single gunboat.

Recognizing the urgency of assembling a flotilla of armed river boats, Federal authorities entered into a contract with St. Louis builder James B. Eads. He agreed to construct seven ironclads of special design, name each for a river city or town, and have them ready for use in just one hundred days.

To the surprise of nearly all concerned, Eads met the schedule. But by the time the first of his vessels was about to be launched, an unexpected problem arose. New ships, widely known as "Eads rams," would be under the control of the U.S. Navy and commanded by its officers. However, due to the perpetual shortage of seamen, the Navy didn't have enough men to provide crews.

Most personnel put aboard Eads-built river boats were members of the U.S. Army or of volunteer forces sent by Union states. Naval vessels were frequently attached to armies, whose commanding generals had overall authority.

Bickering between naval and military officers was constant and sometimes reached the point of furious quarrels over who would give orders to whom.

⁓⁓⁓

After serving fifteen years in the U.S. Navy, Lt. James Bulloch left in 1854 to work as a civilian. When war broke out, he was commanding the mail steamer *Bienville*. Almost immediately he informed his subordinates that loyalty to the state of Georgia required him to give up his job and offer his services to the Confederacy. He did just that as soon as he completed a chore he felt honorbound to perform—delivering the mail steamer to New York before turning his back on it.

⁓⁓⁓

Seventeen members of Ohio's McCook family fought for the Union. Only one of them, Roderick, served on water. Yet he had the honor of becoming prize master of the *Savannah*, the first Confederate privateer to be captured.

McCook's prize figured largely in the North/South quarrel over whether or not men aboard a privateer were pirates for whom a hangman's noose was waiting. This issue triggered the first, but far from the last, instance in which hostages were used in a bid to win concessions from foes.

⁓⁓⁓

Known to friends and foes alike as "Dirty Bill," Como. William Dixon Porter of the U.S. Navy was less than happy at being assigned to command river boats. He wanted action that he believed would be found only on such vessels as the USS *St. Mary's*, on which he once served in the Pacific Ocean.

Itching to fight, he challenged a trio of Confederate gunboats near Columbus, Kentucky, on January 11, 1862. When his foes withdrew, Porter devised a ritual unlike any observed on other fighting vessels. Each day, he hoisted an insulting taunt or a cartoon on a special mast with the hope that he would provoke Confederates into an all-out fight.

Without a doubt, the strangest craft seen on the Mississippi River was launched by Union Rear Adm. David Dixon Porter. Working from his rough drawing, during a twelve-hour period in February 1863 workmen completed a mock ram that resembled the USS *Lafayette*. Inside each of its smokestacks the Federal vessel—if it could be called that—had a big iron pot filled with oakum and tar. When it was set adrift near Vicksburg, smoke was belching from the craft.

Confederate sentinels who spotted it after dusk confessed astonishment that no gun was ever fired from the ship they'd never seen before. Porter later laughed that had they taken a good look, they would have discovered that his shell of a gunboat was unarmed. Questioned, he admitted that it served no purpose except possibly "to distract the enemy for a few hours" before floating on down the river. Comparing it to the fake guns fashioned from logs, many authorities refer to Porter's craft as "the Quaker gunboat."

According to the New York *Tribune*, one of the strangest vessels that went to war was commanded by Greytown Hollins. Called "the Hollins turtle" because it somewhat resembled the shape of the familiar water creature, it was built to destroy the USS *Brooklyn*.

Because the big Federal vessel was not an ironclad, Hollins equipped his turtle with "a steam borer or auger, about the size of a man's arm above the elbow, intended to make a hole in the side of its target." To prevent crew members of its opposing warship from firing on its tiny attacker, the turtle carried twenty-five sets of hose designed "to throw boiling water over the *Brooklyn*."

One of the most colorful of Federal vessels was the *Star of the West*. President Franklin Buchanan's attempt to resupply Fort Sumter early in 1861 revolved around the speed and maneuverability of this ship. Having sailed under sealed orders, it reached Charleston harbor before dawn on January 9. As day broke, cadets of the city's Citadel Military Institute spotted the ship and opened fire, preventing her from performing her mission.

After later successful voyages, the *Star of the West* ran aground on a sandbar close to the shore of Texas. There, to the mortification of her commander, the Federal vessel was boarded and captured by Confederate Col. Earl Van Dorn and two companions, all three of whom were cavalry officers who had never spent a day at sea.

Subsequent to its entry into Confederate service, the *Star of the West* was scuttled by her own crew in an effort to prevent recapture by Union forces.

Capt. John Worden told friends that he was honored to assume command of the first U.S. ironclad vessel on January 15, 1862. Soon he received his initial set of orders from Secretary of the Navy Gideon Welles: "Proceed with the U.S. steamer *Monitor* to Hampton Road, Virginia. . . ."

He would gladly have obeyed instructions, Worden later confessed ruefully, except for circumstances that prevailed when the Welles telegram arrived. At that time the *Monitor* had no provisions on board, no crew, and no ammunition. Though provided with a small battery of guns, its weapons had not undergone routine testing when it was ordered to meet the CSS *Virginia*.

During the second year of conflict, Charleston shipbuilder Theodore Stoney designed a craft unlike any ever seen on an ocean or river. Armed with a spar torpedo, his little boat rode very low in the water in order to avoid big guns of the vessels comprising the Federal blockading squadron.

From the beginning of the attack vessel's career, Confederates hoped to use it to send huge warships to the bottom. Casting about for a suitable name, someone remembered the biblical conflict between David and Goliath. Because

Stoney's vaunted experimental vessel was tiny, all similar torpedo boats sent against Federal giants took the name "David."

Rear Adm. John A. Dahlgren took the little vessels seriously, as each could put approximately one hundred pounds of explosives against the side of a warship. Early in 1864 Dahlgren proposed that the Federal government offer a reward of $30,000 to any person who captured or destroyed a David.

Naval engineer John Ericsson, who entered into a contract to build for the U.S. Navy its first ironclad vessel, agreed to have it ready for action in one hundred working days. He was barely one day late in making delivery of the finished warship. When the *Monitor* moved into New York's East River on January 30, 1862, with the Stars and Stripes flying from both its flagstaff and turret, one long clause of the contract had not been fulfilled. Though she was steam-powered, naval leaders had insisted that the vessel built to withstand the CSS *Virginia* must be equipped with masts and sails. Ericsson balked, violated his contract, and never provided the stipulated gear for this novel warship.

No all-out battle between armored warships led to more than a fraction of the casualties from the explosion of a river boat. At least sixteen hundred men— perhaps more—died when the boilers of the *Sultana* exploded late in April 1865. She left Camp Fish, near Vicksburg, with an estimated 1,866 soldiers aboard; many of them had been prisoners of war.

Because no rolls were kept, there is no official record concerning the number of casualties. But one of the passengers, Capt. A. C. Brown of the Second Ohio Regiment, may have had an accurate count. According to him, the ship's clerk said that the vessel headed for Cairo, Illinois, with 2,580 men aboard.

Regardless of her passenger load, in addition to men in uniform, the *Sultana* carried a crew of eighty-five and about seventy-five civilians. Her hold included a cargo of at least one hundred hogs and fifty or so horses and mules.

Explosions came shortly before 3:00 A.M., when the vessel was some ninety miles from Memphis. A lengthy inquiry led to the conclusion that overloading led to the tragedy.

Officials responsible for overseeing the transportation of soldiers admitted, under questioning, that the total load of the *Sultana* was too great for her boilers. They carefully avoided introducing into evidence details of the reason for the vessel's late arrival at Camp Fish. Fresh from St. Louis, she was delayed en route by boiler trouble.

March 9, 1862, brought the clash between ironclads that experts say changed the history of naval warfare by making wooden vessels obsolete. During four hours of fighting, each of the experimental vessels used all of her firepower against her opponent.

So many direct hits were scored that when approaching darkness caused the duel to end for the day, commanders of both vessels suffered under the same error. Capt. Franklin Buchanan was convinced that his *Virginia* had inflicted mortal damage on the *Monitor*, and Capt. John Worden was positive that his *Monitor* had put the *Virginia* out of commission.

Post-battle inspections showed that neither of the vessels was gravely damaged.

The America's Cup, perhaps the most famous world yachting championship, is named for the *America*, which gained fame in 1851 by taking the "Queen's Cup." A decade after her victory that stunned the nautical sporting world, the *America* was still very much in service. This time, however, instead of racing against Europe's best, the vessel was a blockade runner scurrying back and forth between Confederate and foreign ports with cargoes of weapons, ammunition, clothing, and food.

Mighty as she was, the CSS *Virginia* was afloat for only two months before Confederates sank the vessel to avoid capture. During most of this period she was in dock or was laid up for repairs. As a result, and due to injuries suffered in battle, the Confederate vessel that fought in the first duel of ironclads had three commanders during her short life. Her first, former Union naval officer Franklin Buchanan, lasted just three days.

Union naval officer Louis M. Goldsborough began his career as a midshipman in 1817 at age eleven. His father, who was chief clerk of the Navy Department in Washington, was keenly aware that promotions and pensions were often tied to length of service. So the elder Goldsborough pulled some strings and secured for Louis a warrant that was predated to 1812. Had it been taken literally, that document would have attested that Goldsborough became a naval officer when he was just six years old.

At first, Federal authorities relied on ninety-day volunteers to fill military ranks. This process, soon shown to be ineffective, eventually made conscription the law of the land. Among many unusual aspects of Congressional acts governing conscription, until 1864 there was no provision to credit enlisted seamen to states against their quotas.

Because any man who entered the army was counted as having helped to fill the quota of his state, hundreds or thousands of veteran seaman were forced to fight on land. Naval volunteers became so scarce that all-out efforts at recruitment were made; in a few instances, a man who had never spent a day on the water received a bounty of $1,000 when he agreed to join the crew of a warship.

Struck in 1864 by a sudden and devastating illness that was never diagnosed, Como. William D. Porter took to his bed in New York City. After being photographed three times by the famous Matthew Brady, the Union naval officer didn't have money enough to buy the portraits.

Consequently he sent word that he wanted members of three gunboats he had commanded (the *Choctaw*, *Essex*, and *Lafayette*) to pass the hat. If men of each vessel would deliver $30 to him, he said, he'd be able to take possession of the Brady photos and die happy.

Late in February 1861, the officers and men of the Union revenue cutter *Henry Dodge* let it be known that they were ready and willing to abandon the service of the nation and to put themselves at the disposal of the state of Texas.

Texas leaders, not yet ready to take drastic action on secession or other issues, stalled. Eventually they said they'd take the Federal crew into state service—provided crew members would wait until March 1 to enter it, meanwhile collecting pay in the amount of $900 from the U.S. government.

Ever wonder why so many U.S. warships of the Civil War era bore American Indian names? Builder Alban C. Stimers is largely responsible. When he agreed to supervise the construction of twenty ironclads, he let contracts in which special clauses stipulated that each vessel should be given an Indian name.

As an acting rear admiral, David Dixon Porter of the U.S. Navy for a time used the USS *Blackhawk* as his flagship. Aboard the warship, in addition to members of the crew and customary supplies, he carried his hunting dogs, a team of horses, a buggy, and a cow.

~~~

Confederate inventors and builders managed to put together more than one early submarine. But even the famous CSS *Hunley* was less than a howling success, because it took its crew to the bottom with it when it went down.

Efforts of Federal naval leaders were even less fruitful. One prototype that was initially regarded as offering a potential breakthrough had no engine and was designed to be propelled by eight oars on each side.

~~~

Many of the most famous vessels in the Confederate Navy were built in English ports, while a few were built or purchased in other overseas cities. Some of these ships, renowned for successful cruises of thousands of miles, never entered a Confederate port.

~~~

One of the most successful and noted of Confederate raiders was the CSS *Alabama*, which wreaked havoc among U.S. mercantile ships. Normally a vessel captured by the *Alabama* was sold as a prize or burned, but October 1862 saw her commander depart from usual practices.

Having captured the *Tonawanda*, bound for Liverpool from Philadelphia, Capt. Raphael Semmes found it crowded with women and children. He pondered his alternatives and decided that he had no way to care for these passengers, so he reluctantly sent the Philadelphia-based vessel on its way to Liverpool.

~~~

Newspapers from England carried unusual stories in May 1863. According to their reports, considerable excitement prevailed in seacoast cities and villages because three British-owned vessels had been destroyed by a Confederate raider. Striking in South American waters, the vessel that was responsible for the damage was the *Alabama*—built in England and sold to the Confederacy.

Mention of ship-to-shore engagements typically evoke memories of such struggles as the siege of Charleston by Federal warships. Some land-and-water events were far less spectacular. During the early months of 1863, Arkansas guerrillas, led by James McGhee, turned their attention to the water. By boarding from flatboats or attacking at landings, these land-based irregular troops managed to seize at least six Federal steamers that operated on the Mississippi River. After plundering the captured vessels, guerrillas burned them.

December 1863 brought publication of a list of all Mississippi River steamers destroyed since the beginning of the conflict. In many newspapers it occupied three columns of type, for the list ran to nearly two hundred vessels that had burned or sunk during a period of thirty months.

One of the northernmost captures by a Confederate vessel operating off the North American coast took place in July 1861. Guided by Capt. Louis M. Coxetter, the privateer *Jefferson Davis* captured the schooner *S. F. Waring* at a spot about 150 miles east of the entrance to New York Harbor.

Because he was born in Campbell's Station, Tennessee, David G. Farragut was viewed with suspicion by Federal naval authorities. His Southern background, many of them agreed, made him unfit for service in the U.S. Navy during the era when its ships were sure to fight those of the Confederacy.

Farragut had another problem. Residing in Norfolk, Virginia, when the war began, his neighbors told him that his Union sympathies made him unwelcome.

U.S. Secretary of the Navy Gideon Welles pondered Farragut's case and decided that despite his Southern background he was loyal to the Union. As a result, the man who was initially viewed with suspicion on both sides of the Mason-Dixon Line had a Civil War career without parallel.

It was the Tennessee native who captured New Orleans barely more than a year after Fort Sumter fell. That victory made him a rear admiral and brought him the formal Thanks of Congress.

In 1864, Farragut took his ships into Mobile Bay, well aware that its waters were filled with torpedoes, or mines. After the USS *Tecumseh* was sent to the bottom by a Confederate explosive, Farragut took unprecedented action. He had himself lashed to the rigging of the USS *Hartford* and ordered the vessel to move forward, despite the danger.

More than any other single event, his capture of Mobile caused the man whose loyalty to the Union was once questioned to become the nation's first full admiral.

Seventeen

"RALLY ROUND THE FLAG, BOYS!"

Flags dominate much battlefield art. A typical piece showing the clash of forces, whether produced on the field or sketched in a studio, will include five or more flags. They are featured more often than batteries of artillery, bayonet charges, or generals on horseback.

Flags do not dominate sketches and drawings as a result of an artistic convention. Instead, they appear prominently because they played special and vital roles in the conflict. In today's political and social climate, when desecration of the flag has been ruled to constitute an exercise of the right of free speech, it is all but impossible to view flags from the perspective of fighting men during 1861–65.

Even then, there were two quite different views of Old Glory. All but worshiped in the North, it was hated in the South. Today, the Confederate battle flag occupies somewhat the same position. Many white Southerners who would be indignant at being called racists revere this flag; great numbers of other citizens abhor it and continue to try to get it removed from sight.

George F. Roote was sure he had a winner when he wrote "The Battle Cry of Freedom," made up of only two stanzas and a brief chorus that began with a buoyant promise: "Yes, we'll rally round the flag, boys, we'll rally once again, shouting the battle cry of freedom."

Partly because Old Glory was universally revered in Union territory and among Union fighting men, Roote's song is regarded as having been one of the top three favorites among Federal troops.

In 1988, Oxford University Press published James M. McPherson's one-volume history of the Civil War. Destined for universal praise and a Pulitzer Prize, the book borrowed from Roote and was published as *The Battle Cry of Freedom*.

At Gettysburg, Maj. Edward Pye of the Sixth Wisconsin Regiment gave the order: "Charge!" Describing the dramatic moment, one of his officers wrote: "Any correct picture of this charge would represent a V-shaped crowd of men with the colors at the advance point, moving firmly and hurriedly forward. The only commands I gave, as we advanced, were, 'Align on the colors! Close up on that color! Close up on that color!'"

"A stand of colors," or a flag complete with staff and ornaments, was considered the most valuable possession of a regiment. When it was placed within enemy lines, or "planted," it became a symbol of victory. Lowered or cut down by a shot, absence of the flag from view was taken to signal defeat.

Because it was likely to mark the spot at which enemy fire was most concentrated, the flag frequently spelled death to its bearer, who typically went into battle unarmed. Confederate Lt. P. E. Drew of a Louisiana battery was described by comrades as "rushing into the jaws of death at Franklin."

Four color bearers having previously been shot down, a fifth took a direct hit. Drew "instantly dropped his gun, caught the colors from the ground and rushed forward with them. He was pierced through the heart just as he reached the second line of works."

Kady Brownell, the wife of a member of the First Rhode Island Regiment, was among the handful of women who succeeded in going to war without assuming a male disguise. When the regiment was encamped, Kady cooked, washed clothes, and performed other routine chores.

Her comrades swore that at First Bull Run she exchanged her washboard for a rifle and rushed into the fray. Tradition asserts that during one period of furious fighting, it was Kady who functioned as color bearer for the regiment.

Without using field glasses, an experienced observer could tell from a distance whether or not an attacking unit was moving rapidly. When its flag bobbed up and down jerkily, that was a signal that the color bearer was "on the double-quick."

At Antietam, a Federal unit found itself facing a furious charge launched by men of the Sixth Georgia Regiment. Union color bearer George Horton had been shot through the arm two days earlier at South Mountain. Suddenly a Minié ball crashed into his ankle, giving him reason enough to abandon the fight.

Because his role gave him unique responsibility, he shook his head at offers of assistance. As an officer described the vivid moment:

> Horton had gone down, his foot shot off.
> The colors he had firmly planted in the ground.
> Several of us begged him to give us the colors, that we might save them.
> "Stay and defend them," was his answer.
> The enemy rushed on the colors. Horton with pistol held the flag upright, defended. It was a grand fight. A member of the Sixth Georgia, when not over a rod from the colors, fired, and Horton fell dead.

On the first day at Gettysburg, nine color bearers died carrying the regimental flag of the Twenty-fourth Michigan Regiment. During the same period, men of the Twenty-sixth North Carolina Regiment saw one comrade after another assume the crucial role; when darkness fell, their tally showed that fourteen color bearers had been shot.

At Gaines' Mill, Virginia, for a brief time the action was almost as spirited as at Getttysburg. Here, however, the men of the regiment led by Col. A. M. Smith were not content simply to count the number of men who carried the blue flag of South Carolina. Carefully listed in sequence and given capsule descriptions, these color bearers were:

James Taylor, a boy hero who had his breast fatally pierced by a bullet after being twice wounded.

Daring Young Shubrick Hayne, who took the flag from Taylor's dying grasp and briefly caused it to float on high.

Fearless young Alfred Pinckney, from whose nerveless grasp the flag dropped when he fell mortally wounded.

Gadsden Holmes, who sprang forward to rescue the precious emblem and was pierced by seven balls before he reached it.

Lion –hearted Dominick Spellman, who seized the fallen standard and bore the Palmetto through the remainder of the fight.

Because the color bearer usually had all he could do to manage the flag without using a weapon, he was protected by a color guard. Usually made up of a sergeant and five to eight corporals, this body functioned just as its name implies. Men of the color guard went into action at "shoulder arms," but lowered them as soon as resistance was met. In some Confederate units whose ranks had been thinned in battle, the color guard was reduced to two men.

Whether wearing blue or gray, members of this elite body went into action knowing that their chance of survival was only a trifle greater than that of the color bearer.

During the Mexican War, in many regiments young lieutenants vied for the honor of serving as color bearer. At Chapultepec the U.S. flag was carried into a defensive moat by Lt. James Longstreet. When knocked from his feet by a bullet, he handed the emblem to Lt. George E. Pickett.

Neither officer then could foresee that Gettysburg would once more see them fighting side by side—this time as generals in gray.

During the Civil War, numerous officers on both sides seized regimental colors in order to lead charges. Confederate Capt. John C. Carter, later a brigadier, followed this course of action at Shiloh. At Five Forks, it was a major general who did the same thing. One of his men described the action in which George A. Custer was a central figure:

> When the line was steadied and moving forward to the attack, he took his colors in his hand and where the fire was hottest led the men on, his horse plunging wildly under him, mad with excitement of the warring musketry, the hissing of the leaden shower, and the crashing of the troops through the woods.

A flag led to the first widely publicized Union fatality of the war. Col. Elmer Ellsworth of the Eleventh New York Regiment ("Fire Zouaves") led his men into Alexandria, Virginia, on May 24, 1861. During this first Federal invasion of Southern soil, Ellsworth spotted a Confederate flag on the roof of the

Marshall House tavern. He dashed to the roof, removed the offending symbol, and on his way back down the stairs was shot and killed by tavern proprietor James T. Jackson.

National forces occupied the largest city of the Confederacy in April 1862. Soon after Maj. Gen. Benjamin F. Butler took command of New Orleans, he announced that no activity or gesture in support of secession would be tolerated.

Professional gambler William B. Mumford decided to take a chance by violating the edict. At the U.S. Mint, he chopped a staff in two in order to get the hated flag out of his sight. True to his warning, Butler promptly dragged Mumford before a military tribunal, whose members found him guilty of treason. Hanged at the site of his "heinous crime," Mumford is often listed as the only man to be tried, convicted, and executed for treason in the United States since 1812. Persons who challenge that special niche for the flag-hater often forget that John Brown of Harpers Ferry was convicted of treason—not against the United States, but against the state of Virginia.

At least one Confederate flag flew over a combat unit for more than six months after Appomattox. James I. Waddell, commander of the CSS *Shenandoah*, literally burned his way around the world destroying Northern-owned commercial vessels. From a British captain he learned on August 2, 1865, that Lee had surrendered. Waddell took his craft to Liverpool, and before turning it over to authorities on November 6, he reluctantly ordered his flag to be lowered.

According to the New York *Tribune* of June 26, 1861, an especially dramatic ceremony took place at Hagerstown, Maryland, on June 23. Col. John C.

Starkweather had his ninety-day volunteers pass in review, then challenged them to follow him to the death.

Soldiers of the First Wisconsin Regiment responded by shouting their willingness to die, if necessary. Starkweather then signaled for the regimental colors to be brought beside the flag. When the officer knelt at the foot of the flag to offer a prayer, one by one his men spontaneously followed his example in symbolic renewal of their pledge to defend the flag with their lives.

When Federal forces occupied Milledgeville, Georgia, their first act was to burn the capitol and its records. Most able-bodied men were away at war, but a knot of women gathered to watch flames consume the building in which state government had been centered. A member of the arson squad, accustomed to keeping a detailed diary, observed that "The ladies were quite numerous but they were very rebellious. One of them covered her face as the stars and stripes were carried by."

Oral tradition in Akron, Ohio, preserves a capsule account of unexpected action in the city. During a Sunday school class, members were told by their teacher to stand and recite their favorite Bible verses. According to folk history, a boy of eleven darted up when his turn came and promptly recited: "If any one attempts to haul down the American flag, shoot him on the spot!"

Sgt. Gilbert Bates of the Wisconsin Heavy Artillery shook his head in disagreement when a comrade in arms insisted late in 1867 that the South hated the Union flag. In order to prove himself correct, early in January the thirty-year-old combat veteran went to Vicksburg, Mississippi, by train. There he unfurled an American flag, placed its staff over his shoulder, and set out to walk with it to the nation's capital.

In Montgomery, Alabama, citizens of the city that was briefly the capital of the Confederacy turned out en masse to cheer the flag bearer. His journey through South Carolina took him along part of the path of Sherman's march, but nowhere was he threatened or subjected to verbal abuse. At the border between South and North Carolina, he was met by an "honor guard" made up of twenty-five Confederate veterans.

After having walked for three months and worn out several pairs of shoes, Bates reached Washington on April 14, the anniversary of the day secessionists fired on Fort Sumter. Although his daring odyssey was undertaken far too early to have any effect on the course of Reconstruction, throughout the North it was hailed as a demonstration that sectional hatred was in the process of dying.

On the day before the first shot was fired at Fort Sumter, crowds gathered in the streets of Philadelphia. Civilians listened to Mayor Henry promise, "By the grace of Almighty God, treason shall never rear its head or have a boot hold here." Once the oratory was concluded a mob marched to the post office and angrily reprimanded the postmaster, who that morning had forgotten to run up the U.S. flag.

At Ford's Theater in Washington, decorative flags were installed at the beginning of the war. Their positions were sometimes changed, but for the duration of the conflict they were draped on walls and ledges.

After he shot Abraham Lincoln, John Wilkes Booth leaped from the presidential box in a bold bid to make a quick escape. He might have succeeded, had not one of his spurs caught in folds of a flag. Thrown off balance, he landed on the stage so awkwardly that he broke a bone in his leg and had to hobble toward his horse. Some of the Federal soldiers who captured and killed the man believed to have been Booth credited their exploit to the torn flag that radically altered his plan of escape.

The death in Alexandria of Col. Elmer Ellsworth threw the White House into mourning almost as great as that triggered by the later death of the Lincolns' twelve-year-old son. Members of the Federal force that captured the nearby town in Virginia escorted Ellsworth's body to the Executive Mansion.

While there, someone tried to offer Mary Todd Lincoln the bloodstained Confederate flag that had cost her husband's young protégé his life. Observers said the First Lady took a fleeting glance at the souvenir, shook her head vigorously, and then closed her eyes, refusing to look at it.

According to her own account of exploits "in camp and prison," Confederate spy Belle Boyd shot and killed a Union soldier over a Confederate flag. Prominently displayed outside her Martinsburg, Virginia, home it was the target of a July 4, 1861, raid by a squad of Federals said to have stayed too long at the tavern. A blast from Belle's hunting rifle leveled the leader of the group, at which the rest turned tail and ran—leaving the offending emblem waving in the breeze.

More than a year later, at about age nineteen, the spy in skirts was sent to Baltimore by train. During the entire journey, she waved a small Confederate flag from her window.

New Orleans, site of the only known legally sanctioned execution brought about by "disrespect to the Stars and Stripes," harbored thousands of ardent secessionists. One of them fashioned for herself a dress from the Confederate flag then pranced along the street in defiance of the military commander, General Butler. When the Federal officer learned what she had done, he sent a squad to seize her, then sentenced her to deportation on Ship Island for two years.

Defeat or surrender was symbolized by the disappearance of a flag, whether it was deliberately hauled down or was shot away. So long as an emblem continued to fly from its staff, it signaled "No surrender!" That's why Lieutenant Morris of the USS *Cumberland* proudly said of his ship, riddled by fire from the CSS *Virginia*, "We sank with the American flag flying at her peak!"

The symbolic impact of the Confederate flag was as potent as that of the Stars and Stripes. Henry G. Benson of North Carolina found that time in a Northern prison passed faster when his mind was occupied, so he laboriously wrote, rewrote, and edited a tribute to the battle flag of the Confederate States of America:

> The colors drop, are seized again—again drop and are again lifted, no man in reach daring to pass them by on the ground—colors, not bright and whole and clean as when they came first from the white embroidering fingers, but as clutched in the storm of battle with grimy, bloody hands, and torn into shreds by shot and shell.
>
> Oh hot it thrilled the heart of a soldier to catch sight of his red battle-flag, upheld on its white staff of pine, its tatters snapping in the wind!—that red rag, crossed with blue, with white stars sprinkling the cross within, tied to a slim, barked pine sapling with leather thongs cut from a soldier's shoe!

It's doubtful that most who carried the Confederate battle flag or saw it in later years realized the full meaning of its stars. Though only eleven states seceded from the Union, the flag bears thirteen stars—one for each seceded state and one each for divided Kentucky and Missouri.

Union Maj. Gen. George B. McClellan, informed that the Seventy-ninth New York Regiment had engaged in mutiny at Bull Run, inflicted a special punishment on the unit. He took away its flag, then authorized newspaper reporters to tell the North about the regiment's shame. His decision of August 17, 1861, was reversed on September 14, when he restored their regimental flag to chastened volunteers.

Prior to his promotion that made him field commander of Federal forces, McClellan and his men trounced secessionists in the mountainous regions of what is now West Virginia. In the exhilaration of triumph, the then brigadier dispatched to his wife a treasured souvenir that consisted of "scraps of a dirty rebel flag captured at Rich Mountain."

Dorothea Dix worked hard to persuade Union officials to permit her to serve as a volunteer nurse at a time when most military nurses were men. She eventually overcame prejudice sufficiently to be named superintendent of the nursing corps. When she felt that her work was finished, she returned to civilian life and as her only reward accepted a U.S. flag from Maj. Gen. William T. Sherman.

Starved out rather than subdued by artillery of secessionists, Union Maj. Robert Anderson reluctantly agreed to yield Fort Sumter. Under the terms of surrender, he requested and got permission to fire a salute of one hundred guns before lowering the U.S. flag.

In the Sunday ceremonies, all went well until the tribute to the flag reached its halfway point. Sparks then ignited so much gunpowder that the "national salute" was halted and never resumed. A member of the garrison became the first man to die in the Civil War—a casualty of a salute to the flag.

Confederate Maj. Gen. "Stonewall" Jackson, mortally wounded at Chancellorsville, was universally recognized as being irreplaceable. Speaking of his death, General Robert E. Lee said, "I have lost my right arm."

Admirers of the battlefield hero arranged for formal funeral services to be held in the Presbyterian Church of Lexington, Virginia. Casting about for a suitable tribute, it was decided to drape his coffin with a Confederate flag believed to be the first one ever made.

Richmond's Libby Prison, reserved when possible for captured Federal officers, was the site of a secret ceremony held in 1863. Col. G. W. Shurtleff, who had been there for some time, was deeply impressed when he learned that a new inmate had succeeded in smuggling into the prison a tiny U.S. flag.

"We hid it," he later reported, "and made daily pilgrimages to it and secretly feasted our eyes and comforted our hearts by looking on its stars and stripes undiminished and untarnished."

Many months earlier, Confederate Spy Rose Greenhow wrapped her body with a Confederate flag when she was ushered into Old Capitol Prison in Washington. She reputedly waved that flag from her window almost every day, and again wrapped it around her torso when she went from the capital to Fort Monroe as a political prisoner.

When Reconstruction had run its course, a new and divisive issue surfaced. Initially one by one and later in groups or "camps," Confederate veterans began to press for the return of flags captured by Federal troops during the war.

Congress several times turned down measures stipulating that some or all of these flags be restored to the states from which they came. President William

McKinley, a Civil War veteran, took the lead in urging that "decency and honor required this gesture of courtesy." By 1910, most flags held by Federal agencies and institutions had been returned, but some states refused to give up those held within their borders.

Eighteen

ANALYSIS, PREDICTION,
AND WISHFUL THINKING

January 27, 1843: "Resolved: That the compact which exists between the North and the South is a covenant with death and an agreement with hell, involving both parties in atrocious criminality, and should be immediately annulled."

William Lloyd Garrison, at the
Massachusetts Anti-Slavery Society

March 1858: "Sir, you dare not make war on cotton. No power on earth dares make war upon it. Cotton is king."

J. H. Hammond, speech in U.S. Senate

December 24, 1860: "I can but believe that there is still enough patriotism in the land, North as well as South, to save the present Union under the existing Constitution. All that is wanting is a little time and patriotic forbearance."

Letter of Alexander H. Stephens,
destined to become vice-president of the
Confederate States of America

February 15, 1861: "Notwithstanding the troubles across the river, there is really no crisis, springing from anything in the government itself. In plain words, there is really no crisis except an *artificial one!*"

> *President-elect Abraham Lincoln,*
> *speaking at Pittsburgh on his way to*
> *Washington from Springfield*

March 4, 1861: "No State, upon its own mere motion can lawfully get out of the Union. Resolves and ordinances to that effect are legally nothing. I therefore consider that the Union is unbroken. There needs to be no bloodshed or violence; and there shall be none, unless forced upon the national authority."

> *President Abraham Lincoln, after*
> *taking the oath of office*

April 1861: In a series of editorials, the New York *Times* assured readers that the "local commotion" in the South could be put to rest "effectually in thirty days."

May 2, 1861: "When our services were rendered [to the Federal government for ninety days], all were of the opinion that no more men were needed and that those already accepted by the State of New York could alone put down the Rebellion."

> *G. H. Seymour*

May 1861: Reacting to the president's call for 75,000 men who would augment the U.S. Army for ninety days, editors of the Chicago *Tribune* repeatedly asserted that in sixty to ninety days, the West alone could put an end to the sectional disturbance.

June 19, 1861: "The probabilities are, that the next few days will witness the most momentous developments in the history of the continent. Of one result we feel assured, and that is, of the final success of our great and glorious cause, and of the eventual defeat and humiliation of our vaunting enemies."

> *Cherokee chieftain John Ross, in a*
> *proclamation announcing the formation*
> *of an alliance with the Confederate*
> *States of America*

June and July 1861: Day after day, headlines in the New York *Tribune* prodded political and military leaders by demanding "On to Richmond!"

June 18, 1861: "Invasion of Virginia [by Federal troops] and our inability to repel them, have been the result of the strange notion that we are engaged in a five years' war."

> *Charleston Courier*

June 29, 1861: "When [printers of the Wisconsin Regiment] finish up the war on hand, these American soldiers will return to the desk and the case. The next number will be issued 'The day after the editors get to Richmond!'"

The Camp Record, published at
Hagerstown, Maryland

June 30, 1861: "When we have fairly fought out our independence, of course all foreign nations will acknowledge us."

New Orleans Picayune

Late June 1861: In Washington, U.S. Secretary of War Simon Cameron refused to accept into Federal service numerous companies of militia. They were offered from states whose quotas in Lincoln's call for 75,000 volunteers had already been filled.

July 1, 1861: "We went into the war on principle. Let us come out on principle, but not until we have left a mark upon our enemies that will secure for us for all time to come the respect of the world."

Charleston Courier

July 5, 1861: A clerk read to a special joint session of Congress a lengthy message from Lincoln. It drew brisk applause only once, when lawmakers heard the chief executive's promise that the conflict would be short and decisive.

July 27, 1861: "If slavery is as disagreeable to Negroes as we think it is, why
don't they all march over the border, where they would be received with open
arms? It all amazes me. I am always studying these creatures. They are to me
inscrutable in their way and past finding out.

Diary of Mary Boykin Chestnut

July 30, 1861: "Thanksgiving Day was celebrated in the Confederate States
for the success of our arms and the deliverance of our homes from the menacing hordes that have hung upon our borders like wolves upon the outskirts of
the forest."

Memphis Appeal

August 6, 1861: A giant rally having been held in New Orleans, the gist of
the principal speaker's remarks were passed along to readers of the New York
Times. Persons attending the rally were told that the present struggle would
not lead to protracted war because "such a war would bankrupt any nation in
one year."

August 9, 1861: "The well-considered judgments of military men of the highest rank and repute warrant a confident expectation that the war, prosecuted
with energy, courage, and skill, may be brought to a termination before the
close of next spring."

U.S. Secretary of the Treasury Salmon
P. Chase, in an appeal for the purchase
of treasury notes

August 21, 1861: "Northern abolitionists will have to be scourged into good behavior. The sooner this shall be done the better. All the mighty energies and resources of the South should be put forth to crush out the Northern conspiracy against her. The bombardment of a few Northern cities will bring our enemies to their senses."

Memphis Avalanche

September 10, 1861: "Soldiers: We have had our last retreat. We have seen our last defeat. You stand by me, and I will stand by you, and henceforth victory will crown our efforts."

Maj. Gen. George B. McClellan,
addressing Pennsylvania regiments
before a review.

September 16, 1861: "Our troops will not be withdrawn from Kentucky."

Gen. Albert S. Johnston, writing to
Jefferson Davis concerning the
Kentucky governor's demand that
Confederate forces leave the state

October 26, 1861: "Ranks of the Northern army have been broken forever; no trumpet will call them to battle again. However new forces may be mustered and new generals commissioned, the decree of Manassas cannot be reversed; Southern independence is assured."

Charleston Mercury

November 1, 1861: "I trust and feel that the day is not far distant when I shall return to the place dearest of all others to me, there to spend the balance of my life. The war cannot last long."

> Gen. George B. McClellan, speaking in
> Washington to a delegation from
> Philadelphia

November 11, 1861: "Chances are a hundred to one that [Confederate commissioners Mason and Slidell] will reach their destination in safety. The malice of our Yankee enemies will thus be foiled, and the attempt to capture them fail of success."

> Richmond Examiner, whose editors
> were not yet aware that the British
> mail steamer Trent had been stopped
> by the San Jacinto three days earlier

November 30, 1861: "The campaign of 1861 may be considered as over. In a fortnight the enemy can do no more."

> Richmond Examiner

March 10, 1862: "I heard a man belonging to the cavalry say yesterday, that he believed by the first of July, two thirds of the Southern people would be back in the Union, and peace would be made."

> Letter written at Camp Lee, North
> Carolina, and left behind when
> Newbern was abandoned

April 4, 1862: "The Federal army is rapidly becoming demoralized on account of the constant killing of their pickets, and the approach of summer. This is reliable."

Knoxville, Tennessee, Register

April 11, 1862: "I have seen enough of war. God grant that it may be speedily terminated."

Diary of Confederate soldier
W. S. Hillyer

May 10, 1862: A document found at Yorktown, Virginia, after it was evacuated by Confederates was addressed "To the Future Yankee Occupants of this Place" and challenged them:

"When you arise as high in the scale of created beings as a Brazilian monkey, we will allow you sometimes to associate with our negroes; but until then Southern soil will be too hot for the sons of the Pilgrims.

"The only dealings we will have with you is, henceforth, war to the knife."

Missouri Democrat

May 24, 1862: "Comrades: Our campaign opens auspiciously. The enemy is in full retreat, with consternation and demoralization devastating his ranks.

"Tennesseans! Your State and capital are almost restored without firing a gun. You return conquerors."

Confederate Gen. Braxton Bragg at
Sparta, Tennessee

June 2, 1862: "Five million white men fighting to be relieved from oppression will never be conquered by twenty million actuated by malice and pecuniary gain, mark that."

Lt. F. Scott of the South Carolina
Infantry, writing at Fort Pillow,
Tennessee

June 8, 1862: Perusing a lengthy editorial, readers of the Paris, France, *Constitutionnel* were assured that it was impossible for the South ever to be conquered. "Meditation alone will succeed in putting an end to a war disastrous to the interest of humanity," the editors said.

June 10, 1862: "By means of iron-clad boats [Federal forces] will succeed, occasionally, in effecting landings upon the Mississippi river. This will give each man, of whatever age, calling, or occupation, an opportunity to become at once an efficient soldier.

"He can take his gun, ascertain the places most likely to be frequented by the Yankee thieves, conceal himself in ravine, thicket, or undergrowth, and pick them off by the wholesale. This will be fine sport—better, indeed than hunting wild game."

Jackson Mississippian

June 23, 1862: "Whatever may be the result of the civil war in America, it is plain that it has reached a point where it is a scandal to humanity. Utter destruction may be possible or even imminent, but submission is as far off as ever."

London Times

August 7, 1862: At Blackburn, England, a rally was held "for the purpose of considering the advantages of recognizing the Southern States of America, with a view to bringing about an early termination of hostilities."

One of the principal speakers, R. R. Jackson, told his audience, "It is impossible for the North to vanquish the South."

A few days later, the House of Commons debated a bill offered by the Honorable Member Lindsay, urging formal British offers to mediate the American struggle. Lindsay told fellow lawmakers, "It is clear that the South cannot be conquered, and it is still more clear that it can never be brought back into the Union."

September 17, 1862: An analysis of the invasion of Pennsylvania by Lee's Army of Northern Virginia was made public on this day:

"By advancing into Pennsylvania with rapidity, our army can easily get possession of the Pennsylvania Central Railroad, and break it down so thoroughly that it cannot be repaired in six months.

"Let retaliation be complete, that the Yankees can learn that two can play at the game they themselves have commenced."

Richmond Dispatch

December 4, 1863: As reported in the *Rebellion Record*: "Separation is final; North Carolina will never consent to reunion at any time or upon any terms."

Resolution adopted by the North
Carolina House of Commons

July 24, 1864: "There seems to be now a great rage for investing in Confederate bonds. In Lincolndom everybody is avoiding government paper."

Savannah News

April 7, 1864: In Raleigh, North Carolina, Jefferson Davis issued "An address to the people of the confederacy." In it, he implored everyone to stand by him during a time of reverses and not become disheartened. He would steer them through, promised Davis.

November 7, 1864: Speaking to members of the Confederate Congress on the first day of its new session, an orator was in an upbeat mood. Ignoring the fact that Sherman was on the way to Savannah, he told the lawmakers:

> . . . if we had been compelled to evacuate Richmond as well as Atlanta, the Confederacy would have remained as erect and defiant as ever. Nothing could have been changed in the purpose of its government, in the indomitable valor of its troops, or in the unquenchable spirit of its people.
>
> There are no vital points in which the continued existence of the Confederacy depends. There is no military success of the enemy which can affect its destruction.
>
> Not the fall of Richmond, nor Wilmington, nor Charleston, nor Savannah, nor Mobile, nor of all combined, can save the enemy from the constant and exhaustive drain of blood and treasure which must continue until he shall discover that no peace is attainable unless based on the recognition of our indefensible rights.
>
> *Jefferson Davis*

Nineteen

PROVIDENCE, FATE, OR CHANCE?

B orn and reared in Pennsylvania, Wesley Culp later moved to Virginia. There he enlisted in the state's defensive forces, later incorporated into the Army of Northern Virginia.

When Robert E. Lee invaded his native state, Culp went along as an aggressor. Everything went well until the third day at Gettysburg; then, Culp fell during an assault in which his regiment charged the enemy and in the process crossed his father's farm.

Stephen A. Douglas gave up his Congressional seat from Kentucky in 1844, at which time the state legislature chose William A. Richardson to finish the unexpired term. Still in the House of Representatives in 1863, Richardson resigned on January 29. He did so in order to step into the U.S. Senate seat made vacant by the death of Douglas.

Joseph Howard Jr. moved to the city desk of the Brooklyn *Eagle* after having gained experience as a reporter for the New York *Times*. Working with journalist Francis A. Mallison, Howard drafted a bogus presidential proclamation and reproduced it on counterfeit Associated Press Letterheads.

As prepared by Howard, the Lincoln proclamation called for a national day of fasting and prayer as a prelude to a call for an additional 400,000 troops. Numerous editors were wary of the fake document, but in New York both the *Journal of Commerce* and the *World* published it on May 18, 1864.

As a result, the price of gold jumped 10 percent in a matter of hours; having bought the precious metal in quantity, Howard picked up what for the period was a small fortune. Two days later, he and Mallison were arrested and imprisoned in Fort Lafayette.

Influential friends gained their release after ninety days. Only then did Washington insiders confess to intimates that on the day the bogus proclamation was published, Lincoln had on his desk a paper that called for immediate conscription of 300,000 more men.

At Honey Springs (or Elk Creek) in the Indian Territory, Union and Confederate forces clashed on July 17, 1863. Forces led by Union Gen. James G. Blunt attacked units commanded by Confederate Brig. Gen. Douglas H. Cooper. Before the melee came to a close, officers on both sides realized that the largest engagement in the territory had pitted Native Americans wearing blue against other Native Americans in gray uniforms.

According to the *Rebellion Record* (Vol. 6), the president of the Confederacy was born out of wedlock. An account reprinted from the Nashville *Union* has it that "Old Davis [father of Jefferson] was a man of bad character, a horse-trader, a swindler, and of very low habits." Said the newspaper: "Jeff Davis is his illegitimate son, born some miles distant from his father's house, and taken home by him when several years of age."

A Democratic publication of 1863, issued in preparation for the election of 1864, solemnly informed readers that Abraham Lincoln was the son of a man named Inlow rather than the son of Thomas Lincoln. According to Lincoln's longtime law partner, William Herndon, the president went to his grave believing himself to be illegitimate.

*

In July 1861, farmer Wilmer McLean heard what he believed to be the sounds of musket shots, so he rode out to investigate. Soon he found himself and his land caught up in the battle of Bull Run. Tradition has it that at least one cannon ball crashed through his home, although it was some distance from the fiercest fighting. Known by his neighbors to be a man of peace, McLean was distressed at having been caught up in a conflict in which he wanted no part. Hence he put his farm on the market and set out to locate a spot so remote from the struggle that "the sound of battle would never again reach him and his family."

Almost four years later, a man in uniform approached McLean at his new residence and demanded that he vacate it immediately. When the civilian complied, his Appomattox Court House residence was used for surrender ceremonies. This time, he didn't escape with damage from a cannonball. Union officers stripped his parlor bare of furniture, each piece of which became a prized souvenir of Lee's capitulation to Grant.

*

Lord Cornwallis and his redcoats once patrolled the roads leading into Yorktown, Virginia. When the village was captured by the despised Yankees in 1781, it became a major center of Colonial forces.

Less than a century later, Yorktown was again under attack by Yankees—this time wearing blue uniforms of the Union Army. One of the campgrounds occupied by men of the Army of the Potomac in 1863 was the site at which British notables had camped in 1781.

*

During more than one thousand days of fighting, Union forces saw only one commander of an army fall during battle. Maj. Gen. James B. McPherson, head of the Army of Tennessee, was killed during the July 22, 1864, battle of Atlanta.

Only one commander of an army whose men fought in gray was killed in battle. Hit in the leg at Shiloh, Gen. Albert Sidney Johnston, who headed the entire western theater, bled to death before he could be examined by a surgeon.

Union Brig. Gen. Edward H. Hobson considered his greatest feat to be the 1863 capture of Confederate Brig. Gen. John Hunt Morgan. Taken near New Lisbon, Ohio, on July 26, 1863, the Confederate leader was hustled to the Ohio State Prison, but his stay was brief. He escaped on November 26.

Eleven months after being taken prisoner, Morgan and his men captured a body of Federal troops at Cynthiana, Kentucky. Their commander was Edward H. Hobson.

Every available Confederate vessel was ordered into service when it became clear that Union gunboats under David G. Farragut would attempt to open the lower Mississippi River.

Aboard a lightly armed steam barkentine known as the *McRae*, Confederate Comdr. Thomas B. Huger was killed by a shot from the Mighty USS *Iroquois*. A few months prior to Huger's death, he was serving as first lieutenant of the warship whose big gun fired the shell that took his life.

"Soldier Life and Secret Service" are described in Volume 8 of the famous *Photographic History of the Civil War*. According to Fenwick Y. Hedley, once adjutant of the Thirty-second Illinois Regiment, a citizen of his state was a central figure in a drama that took place more than thirty years after the war:

An Illinoisan went into the heart of Arkansas to bury a favorite sister. After the funeral service, Northerner and Southerner discovered that, in one of the fiercest battles of the first war year, their respective regiments had fought each other all day long; that they were similarly engaged in the severest battle of the Atlanta campaign, and finally in the last battle in North Carolina, in 1865; also that, in the first of these, as determined by landmarks recognized by each, the two men had probably been firing directly at each other.

Alban C. Stimers, chief engineer aboard the USS *Roanoke*, was ordered into detached service on November 5, 1861. As an assistant to Swedish-born engineer John Ericsson, he helped to complete the USS *Monitor* in time for it to meet the CSS *Virginia* on March 9, 1862. Earlier, Stimers had served aboard the Confederate vessel, which was then the USS *Merrimack*, which was partly burned at Norfolk, then reconstructed and plated with iron.

Felled by a bullet from a derringer, unconscious Abraham Lincoln was carried across the street to the home of Washington tailor William A. Petersen. A room rented by Pvt. William T. Clark of the Thirteenth Massachusetts Regiment was vacated for the wounded president.

Lincoln died on a hastily commandeered bed once occupied by John Wilkes Booth when a friend of his was renting from Petersen.

Union Brig. Gen. Henry H. Sibley spent the war years in the Indian Territory, and as a result never saw men in Confederate uniforms unless they were prisoners of war.

Confederate Brig. Gen. Henry H. Sibley also served largely in the West, where his subordinates sometimes made fun of him by showing him pictures of his namesake in blue.

⁓

When Abraham Lincoln went to Washington from his Illinois home to become chief executive of the nation, he was accompanied by a number of persons. Among them was Maj. David Hunter of the Union Army.

Four years and two months later, the body of the assassinated president was sent to Illinois by train. One of those who accompanied the slain chief executive was Maj. Gen. David Hunter.

⁓

During the American Revolution, Richard Anderson led the defense of Fort Moultrie when the Charleston installation was attacked by the British. In April 1861, his son, also named Richard Anderson, was the commander of Fort Moultrie who withdrew to Fort Sumter because of impending attack by Confederates.

⁓

Robert E. Lee's famous lost order (Special Order # 191, September 9, 1862) was found lying on the ground. Detailed information concerning Lee's plans was included in the document, which was in a small parcel wrapped with paper that also included three cigars.

In February 1864, Union Col. Ulric Dahlgren was killed while attempting to penetrate Richmond. Papers found on his body, and much later pronounced authentic, contained details of a plot to destroy part of the Confederate capital and to kill or kidnap Jefferson Davis. Now famous as "the Dahlgren Papers," they were discovered in a cigar case.

⁓

Confederate Gen. Joseph E. Johnston died of pneumonia after attending a lengthy funeral service. He was there to mourn the passing of Union Maj. Gen. William T. Sherman, to whom he surrendered his army in 1865.

When the Black Hawk War erupted in 1832, Abraham Lincoln enlisted in an Illinois unit and served for several weeks without experiencing combat. When the uprising of Native Americans was quelled, Jefferson Davis led the detachment of soldiers who escorted Chief Black Hawk to prison at Jefferson Barracks, Missouri.

Union Major Garesche, heavily involved in the siege of Vicksburg, wrote frequent letters home. In them his chief source of unhappiness was the fact that he was separated from his brother, a lieutenant colonel, by almost one thousand miles.

December 29, 1862, saw Major Garesche killed close to the Mississippi River; two days later Lieutenant Colonel Garesche fell in Tennessee.

Abraham Lincoln and Jefferson Davis were born in Kentucky within one hundred miles and one year of each other. On February 11, 1861, Lincoln left his Springfield, Illinois, home on a train bound for Washington and his inauguration as president of the United States. While he was en route to the capital, he learned that at Montgomery, Alabama, Jefferson Davis had been inaugurated as president of the Confederate States of America.

Davis left his Brierfield plantation in Mississippi for the temporary Confederate capital on February 11.

Twenty

TIME DOESN'T ALWAYS FLY

Born in St. Bernard Parish, Louisiana, P. G. T. Beauregard made his state proud when he became superintendent of the U.S. Military Academy at West Point, New York, on January 13, 1861. During his fourth day on the job, he was removed from office because of his outspoken sympathy for seceded states.

Well before the first battle of Bull Run, Federal forces had expected to put an end to the conflict somewhere in the neighborhood of Manassas, Virginia.

Nearly all the troops led by Brig. Gen. Irvin McDowell were ninety-day volunteers who had responded to Abraham Lincoln's call in April.

Members of the Fourth Pennsylvania Infantry Regiment had been mustered into service late in April. As a result, on the eve of the July 21 battle, McDowell reported to Washington that he was "embarrassed"—or handicapped—by the expiration of the term of service of many units.

"The Fourth Pennsylvania goes out today and others succeed rapidly," he wrote. Although required to relinquish weapons provided by Federals, sturdy Pennsylvania fighting men who had put in their ninety days turned their backs on the enemy and returned home without smelling gunpowder.

Col. John F. Hartranft remained on the field when men of his Fourth Pennsylvania Regiment marched to the rear on the eve of Bull Run. Because the gallant officer stayed to fight, he was rewarded with a Congressional Medal of Honor—bestowed twenty-five years later.

~~~

Brig. Gen. Joseph Hooker of the U.S. Army quarreled with Maj. Gen. Henry W. Halleck over the use of ten thousand men stationed at Harpers Ferry, then resigned hastily on June 28, 1863. George G. Meade, head of the army's Center Grand Division, was chosen to succeed him as commander of the Army of the Potomac. Three days later, far from the site of conflict, Meade learned that his forces were facing the Army of Northern Virginia at Gettysburg.

~~~

Brig. Gen. Fitz-John Porter of New Hampshire was relieved of command and arrested for having failed to obey an order to attack Stonewall Jackson's men at Second Bull Run. Put on trial, he was found guilty on January 10, 1863, and as a result received a dishonorable discharge. It took him twenty-four years to clear his name and win reinstatement as an infantry colonel without back pay.

~~~

When Gen. Joseph E. Johnston was wounded on June 1, 1862, his command devolved on Gen. Robert E. Lee. During thirty-two months, Lee frustrated his Federal opponents and twice invaded the North. He was finally made commander in chief of Confederate forces on January 28, 1865. He held that post less than three months before surrendering at Appomattox Court House.

~~~

Taken prisoner by Federal troops on May 10, 1865, Jefferson Davis was imprisoned at Fort Monroe, Virginia. Accused of having participated in the assassination of Abraham Lincoln, he never got a chance to defend himself. Instead of going on trial, he was released on bail after having spent more than seven hundred days behind bars.

⁓

Pickett's Charge at Gettysburg saw Confederates "mowed down like ripe grain." Yet Maj. Gen. Martin T. McMahon considered a Federal assault at Cold Harbor, Virginia, to be the most terrible moment of the war. According to him, during a period "not over eight minutes in length," at least seven thousand men were killed or wounded.

⁓

After just fifteen months of war, Jefferson Davis lost the third man to serve him as secretary of war.

As successor to George W. Randolph, the Confederate president picked a Kentucky-born graduate of West Point. Gustavus W. Smith accepted the high post, then submitted his resignation four days later.

⁓

Leading his brigade at Pea Ridge, Arkansas, Confederate Brig. Gen. Ben McCulloch of Texas was dropped by a Federal sharpshooter. Brig. Gen. James McIntosh succeeded him in command and was killed fifteen minutes later.

⁓

After the Confederate States of America was defeated, Jefferson Davis was stripped of his citizenship. He considered it futile to petition for clemency, so he died as a man without a country. His citizenship was restored by Congress during the administration of a post-war president—Jimmy Carter.

On June 13, 1865, Robert E. Lee addressed a letter to "His Excellency Andrew Johnson" and a similar one to Lt. Gen. Ulysses S. Grant. In both he pointed out that he was excluded from provisions of a federal proclamation of amnesty and pardon. As a result, he asked to be given the same treatment accorded to other ex-Confederates.

Grant replied on June 20, 1865, saying that in his opinion the terms of surrender to which the two commanders had agreed protected Lee from trial on charges of treason. He was simultaneously requesting, said the Union commander, that all indictments against paroled prisoners of war be quashed.

Almost as a footnote, Grant pointed out that Lee's oath of allegiance was not being forwarded because "the order requiring it had not reached Richmond" when he wrote his lengthy letter.

Subsequent efforts to have Lee's citizenship restored failed because that all-important piece of paper could not be found.

At the Library of Congress, Elmer O. Parker discovered Lee's oath that had "for a century remained buried in the nation's archives."

Dated October 2, 1865, and duly notarized, it constituted the former Confederate's solemn vow to protect and defend the Constitution and the Union of the States.

He simultaneously promised to "abide by and faithfully support all laws and proclamations with reference to the emancipation of slaves."

When that vital written vow was presented to lawmakers, Congress took another vote. When the tally was made, it showed that Lee's citizenship was formally restored—105 years after he took the oath of allegiance.

Adm. Franklin Buchanan of the Confederate Navy commanded the ironclad *Merrimac* (or *Virginia*) in its battle of March 8, 1862, and fought Farragut at Mobile Bay. Because he was wounded in both actions, he was engaged in combat during only two days of the war.

U.S. War Department policy barred acceptance into Federal service of an officer above the rank of colonel. Lee's invasion of Pennsylvania, however, led to the hasty agreement to use three regiments of the state's national guard and their commander. Brig. Gen. John Ewen and his men were mustered in on June 18, 1863—and were discharged on July 20 without having been in combat.

Confederate Brig. Gen. Richard Taylor became violently ill on June 26, 1862. With the battle of Gaines' Mill (also known as Chickahominy and Cold Harbor) pending, Col. Isaac G. Seymour took command.

For the former mayor of Macon, Georgia, this meant the fulfillment of a dream. His elation lasted only a few hours, however; during his first day at the head of a brigade he was shot and killed.

Maj. Gen. Julius Stahel entered Federal service on November 12, 1861. After having been at First Bull Run as an officer of the New York militia, he fought Stonewall Jackson in the Shenandoah Valley. Other engagements in which he took part included Cross Keys and Second Bull Run.

At Piedmont, Virginia on June 5, 1864, he was wounded during action in which his cavalry drove Confederate skirmishers seven miles to Port Republic. For that action a grateful nation bestowed upon him the Congressional Medal of Honor—twenty-nine years later.

Col. George C. Burling of the Sixth New Jersey Infantry was in temporary command of a brigade at Gettysburg. Decidedly unhappy at not winning a promotion, he resigned on March 4, 1864. More than a year later, civilian Burling was named a brevet brigadier general as a reward for his role in the defense of Sickles' salient at Gettysburg.

Richard H. Anderson entered Confederate service as a brigadier and during four years of nearly continuous fighting advanced to the rank of lieutenant general. He missed one day of action in Virginia; his command having been wiped out at Saylor's Creek, Lee sent him home twenty-four hours before Appomattox.

Col. Joshua B. Howell of New Jersey fought at Yorktown, Williamsburg, Seven Pines, the Seven Days, Fort Wagner, and the Bermuda Hundred without receiving a major wound or a promotion. His horse fell on September 12, 1864, and injured him so seriously that he lived only two more days. His longed-for promotion to brigadier general came through six months later.

When Confederate Maj. Gen. Jubal Early started toward Washington on June 27, 1864, he knew that the clock was ticking. Every minute counted, for it meant that Union forces had an additional sixty seconds in which to rush defending forces to the capital.

Reaching Frederick, Maryland, Early offered to spare the town from burning if residents would pay him $200,000. He got the money, after having waited twenty-four hours for it. That delay was just long enough to permit an additional 8,000 men in blue to face the Confederates at Monocacy. Often credited with having saved Washington, the battle of Monocacy wouldn't have been fought had Early not dawdled in Frederick while town fathers collected the ransom he demanded.

U.S. Secretary of War Stanton became angry when he realized that two corps of the Army of the Potomac were idle. They were desperately needed for what he was sure would be a major battle in the West.

It took much persuasion of Abraham Lincoln and Stanton's fellow cabinet members for him to get permission to make an unprecedented shipment by rail. Stanton was given permission to act, however, and he wasted no time.

Using seven railroads, he sent about twenty thousand men, three thousand horses, and ten artillery batteries to Chattanooga. They reached the "western" city after just eleven days of travel—an unprecedented movement of Civil War troops.

During the first hour of the July 1864 battle of Peachtree Creek, both sides lost a top commander.

James B. McPherson, commander of the Army of the Tennessee, ran into a band of Confederates by mistake. When they shouted for him to surrender, he spurred his horse into action—and was almost instantly shot.

Confederate Brig. Gen. William H. T. Walker had been praised by Joseph E. Johnston as "the only officer in the West who is competent to command a brigade." After a brief lull in fighting, he led his men toward Federal lines—and died within an hour of McPherson.

No one is sure of the exact number of brevet promotions made by Congress in the aftermath of the Civil War. In some respects, the most unusual of hundreds was that of Col. William M. Graham.

He got that brevet on March 13, 1865, as a reward for valiant service in leading a regiment of infantry at Molino del Rey, Mexico, on September 8, 1847.

During the 1864 battle of Resaca, Georgia, one Confederate officer paused long enough to count Federal shells that were raining down on his unit. Lt. William McMurray of the Twentieth Tennessee Regiment ascertained that "intervals between shells from Union batteries ranged from three to six seconds, only."

Having fought the CSS *Virginia* to a draw in the world's first clash between ironclad warships, the USS *Monitor* saw only limited action after March 6, 1862. While on the high seas headed toward a new assignment, the mighty vessel went down off Cape Hatteras, North Carolina, on December 31, 1862. Its rusting shell lay on the bottom of the Atlantic Ocean for ninety-one years before the U.S. Navy officially listed it as "out of commission" in September 1951. Then in 1974, scientists from Duke University located its rusting remains lying 220 feet underwater, fifteen miles off Cape Hatteras. While it is not feasible to try to raise it, experienced skindivers are allowed to view it.

Twenty-one

OF LIFE AND DEATH

Born in Tennessee and educated in Texas, attorney John A. Wharton enlisted in May 1861 as a captain of the Eighth Texas Cavalry. He fought at Shiloh, Perryville, Murfreesboro, Chickamauga, and in the Red River campaign without receiving a serious injury.

On April 6, 1865, George W. Baylor, his former subordinate, shot and killed him during a quarrel.

~~~

War correspondent Albert Deane of the New York *Tribune* was captured at Vicksburg and sent to the Salisbury, North Carolina, prison. After remaining there for eighteen months, he managed to escape and walked four hundred miles through hostile territory to a Federal outpost in Tennessee.

Although emaciated when he returned to New York, Deane was pronounced to be in good health. He became enamored of a woman recently divorced, and received a fatal wound from a pistol in the hand of his lover's former husband. On his deathbed, the survivor of a Confederate prison camp went through a wedding ceremony performed by noted clergyman Henry Ward Beecher.

~~~

One-time harness maker Amos Humiston of New York survived Chancellorsville but died on the first day at Gettysburg. Retreating through streets of the town with other members of his brigade, he took a bullet from an unidentified source. Not until he had lain on cobblestones for several days did a burial detail find the dead sergeant, clutching a photograph of two small boys and a small girl.

Authorities seeking to locate Humiston's family circulated the photograph through the North. His widow and children were eventually found and notified of his death. By that time, hundreds of copies of the photo found in the dead man's hand were treasured as souvenirs of the war. So much interest was generated by eight-year-old Franklin, his small sister Alice, and brother Frederick that a movement was launched to establish a home for the orphans of Federal soldiers. When it was established at Gettysburg in 1866, Mrs. Amos Humiston was the first matron.

Born in Cuba, Julius P. Garesche won an appointment to West Point, where one of his close friends was William S. Rosecrans. After Garesche's graduation in 1841, he served in the artillery of the U.S. Army for a decade, then was called into the office of the Adjutant general.

When Rosecrans became commander of the Army of the Cumberland, he persuaded Garesche to become his chief of staff. At Murfreesboro, Tennessee, the twenty-one-year veteran of the U.S. Army took a direct hit from a Confederate cannonball and died before the end of his first battle.

Union Brig. Gen. Nathaniel Lyon was killed during the August 1861 battle of Wilson's creek. In the confusion of their retreat, Federal forces eager to get wounded men to field hospitals took the body of their commander from a wagon and left it behind on the field.

Confederates who found and recognized the body sent it to their foes in

Springfield under an armed escort. Soon Federals based in the town beat a hasty retreat to Rolla, again leaving behind the body of the dead general. It was stored in an icehouse belonging to Congressman John Phelps when secessionists for the second time found and returned the remains of the man most of them put at the top of their "most hated" list.

Barrel-chested William McKinley of Niles, Ohio, entered the conflict as a private in the Twenty-third Ohio Regiment. During four years of constant action, he became a brevet major.

McKinley fought at Antietam, Cedar Creek, and numerous other battles, yet considered his greatest danger to have come when he carried orders to the front under fire at Winchester, Virginia. Back in Ohio and queried about his experiences, he usually smiled and said he spent four years in uniform without a day in a hospital bed from illness or a wound.

Years later, while a resident of the White House, he went to Buffalo, New York to speak at the Pan American Exposition. While in a receiving line in the Temple of Music he was approached by unemployed mill worker Leon F. Czolgosz. Two bullets fired by the twenty-eight-year-old civilian from a .32 revolver ended the life of the veteran president who went through the Civil War without a scratch.

Everyone knows that Abraham Lincoln's life was at risk day after day during an era when there was little concern about security of the president. Not so familiar is the fact that his oldest son, later president of the Pullman Company, barely escaped accidental death during the war years.

Shielded from battle because he was the son of the president, college student Robert Todd Lincoln was at a New Jersey railroad station waiting to board a train. Forced by the mass of other passengers to lean from the platform against the side of the train, he suddenly felt it begin to move.

The motion of the train spun young Lincoln off his feet and caused him to slide downward into the open space between the car and the platform. Suspended helplessly, he suddenly felt a hand grab his coat and lift him to safety.

Turning around to thank the bystander who had rescued him, he recognized the famous actor Edwin Booth—brother of the man who a few months later took the life of his father.

～～～

Henry A. Barnum (no relation to the famous showman) enlisted in the Twelfth New York Regiment as a private. Before the end of his first day, May 13, 1861, he was elected captain of his company. He led his men at Blackburn's Ford, Bull Run, and Malvern Hill before being seriously wounded.

Captured and imprisoned in Richmond, his name was soon recorded on the death list. Burial services were held and when word reached relatives they arranged for a funeral oration in his honor. Soon afterward they learned with astonishment that he had been made colonel of the 149th New York Regiment. Having buried another man in his name, authorities in charge of the Confederate prison released Barnum in June 1863.

～～～

Before the end of 1865, efforts were made to locate graves of men who had died during the conflict. An early tabulation showed that more than 9,000 Confederate prisoners of war were buried in Northern cemeteries. Most of these graves were marked. Yet "from some unknown cause" a relatively small graveyard near the Alton, Illinois, prison was reported by Lt. Asa B. Isham of the Seventh Michigan Cavalry to hold an astonishing 662 unidentified bodies of men who fought in gray.

～～～

Every state involved in the Civil War has at least one national cemetery. A painstaking tabulation issued in 1908 indicates that, collectively, they hold the bodies of 315,830 Federal soldiers. Of these graves, 148,833 were labeled "unknown" when *A Compendium of the War of the Rebellion* was issued.

≈≈≈

Former U.S. naval officer Catesby R. Jones supervised placement of the armament protecting the CSS *Virginia*, converted from the partly burned USS *Merrimac*. He remained on active duty without serious illness or injury until 1864, when he resigned.

Soon after the conflict ended he settled in Selma, Alabama. There his children reputedly quarreled with those of a neighbor and business partner. Angry at the neighborhood disturbance, J. S. Harral used just one bullet to kill the veteran whose twenty-eight years of naval service under two flags were spent without a serious injury.

≈≈≈

When the dust settled after the famous Baltimore Riot of April 1861, numerous participants had been wounded and four members of the Sixth Massachusetts Regiment lay dead in the streets. Responding to an urgent telegram from Governor John A. Andrew of Massachusetts, the mayor of Baltimore had the bodies of slain volunteers packed in ice for shipment to the Bay State.

≈≈≈

During three days of fighting at Gettysburg, opposing forces suffered an estimated 51,000 casualties. By Sunday, July 5, 1863, the abandoned battlefield was dotted with souvenir hunters. Among them were two small boys whose attention was attracted by an abandoned rifle that seemed to be in perfect condition. Looking it over, the older of the pair accidentally pulled the trigger. That shot made three-year-old Edward Woods the youngest person to die as a result of the mammoth conflict.

At Andersonville Prison the death rate exceeded that of many skirmishes and engagements. Malnutrition and disease claimed many prisoners, while dozens of others are believed to have been shot by guards when they crossed a clearly marked deadline. During a period of two months, an average of 127 persons died each day, meaning that bodies were pitched into trenches and graves at the rate of one every eleven minutes.

Union Col. Ulric Dahlgren, son of a rear admiral who commanded the South Atlantic Blockading Squadron in 1863, was shot during an attempted raid on Richmond. Before Confederates buried him in an unmarked grave, they stripped the body of its blue uniform and replaced it with a gray shirt and trousers.

Confederate Maj. Gen. Earl Van Dorn fought near Manassas, at Pea Ridge, Corinth, Vicksburg, and Holly Springs. Sitting tall in the saddle after nearly two years of continuous fighting, he led his men into middle Tennessee. There he became the only general officer on either side to be killed by a jealous civilian. Apparently Dr. George B. Peters didn't like attentions paid by Van Dorn to Mrs. Peters at Spring Hill.

In life, Abraham Lincoln spent a great deal of his time on legal circuits that centered around Springfield, Illinois. After his assassination, an elaborate funeral trail followed a circuitous route back to the city where he had practiced law.

His body was placed in a Springfield crypt, but it remained there only briefly. Counterfeiters headed by Jim Kenealy made plans to seize the body and use it as a hostage to secure release of gang members. Their elaborate plans might have succeeded had not a member of the U.S. Secret Service infiltrated their ranks.

Partly for security reasons, and partly because of changes and renovations in the Springfield cemetery, Lincoln scored a record after his death. Before his body was permanently laid to rest it was moved seventeen times during the thirty-six years that followed his assassination.

⁓

The contemporary term that describes the killing of an officer by one of his own men, "fragging," was not in the Civil War vocabulary. That didn't prevent an occasional disgruntled fighting man from turning his weapon on his own leader.

Confederate guerrilla leader Hanse McNeill survived many an encounter with Union forces. When he attacked men guarding a bridge near Mount Jackson, Virginia, he expected an easy victory. McNeill didn't live to see the outcome of the struggle, however. One of his own men dropped him with a bullet in the back of the head.

⁓

Most generals who died in combat were caught up in action so furious that names of their killers were never known. Among the exceptions to this general rule were a commander in gray and another in blue.

Ben McCulloch of Tennessee lived much of his pre-war adult life in Texas. Made a brigadier general on May 11, 1861, he fought at Wilson's Creek and then at Pea Ridge. During the latter engagement, he died soon after taking a direct hit from a musket or rifle. Long attributed to some unknown sharp-shooter, recently discovered documents say that his death came from Pvt. Peter Pelican of the Thirty-sixth Illinois Regiment.

Connecticut native John Sedgwick became a professional soldier and served in the Seminole and Mexican wars before becoming an Indian fighter. Made a brigadier general on August 31, 1861, he survived the bloody Peninsular campaign. Later he fought at Fair Oaks, Savage's Station, and Antietam before being promoted.

Major General Sedgwick, although wounded several times, lived through the action at Chancellorsville and Gettysburg. At Spotsylvania, the veteran of many battles paused to direct the placement of artillery and was spotted by Confederates. There a single shot from a member of the Fourth Georgia Regiment, fired by a man identified only as "Sergeant Grace," killed Sedgwick on the spot.

Part Four

EYE OF THE BEHOLDER

Twenty-two

NO ONE CALLED LINCOLN HANDSOME

No other key figure in the Civil War was so frequently described as the self-taught Illinois attorney who became commander in chief of the U.S. armed forces.

Photographs of President Abraham Lincoln are universally familiar. Before 1860 he was sometimes photographed, but the face that appears in these images is not widely known. Cartoonists of every variety depicted him; best of all, word portraits were drawn by persons ranging from schoolmates to Union soldiers.

Katie Robie, who knew Lincoln well during his late adolescence, was awed by his huge hands and feet and his extremely long arms and legs. Describing him at this time of his life, she said:

His skin was shriveled and yellow. His shoes, when he had any, were low. He wore buckskin breeches, a linsey-woolsey shirt and a cap made from the skin of a squirrel or coon.

His breeches were baggy, and lacked by several inches meeting the tops of his shoes, thereby exposing his shinbone, sharp, blue and narrow.

A few years later, while working in a general store, Lincoln's trousers were usually about five inches too short. Though a vest or coat was customary, he wore none—and frequently had only one suspender. "He wore a calico shirt, tan brogans, blue yard socks and straw hat—old style, without a band."

———

D. H. Wilder of Hiawatha, Kansas, didn't meet the future president until he was a well-known attorney. Wilder was far from impressed with Lincoln, about whom he wrote: "He had legs you could fold up; the knees stood out like that high hind joint of the Kansas grasshopper; the buttons were off his shirt."

———

Stephen Trigg, Lincoln's second law partner who was stingy with words, said only that "He was very tall, gawky, and rough looking; his pantaloons didn't meet his shoes by six inches."

———

Emilie Todd, a younger half-sister of Mrs. Lincoln, was flabbergasted when she first caught sight of her brother-in-law as he entered a room carrying his small son in his arms. Putting the child on the floor, as he arose:

> I remember thinking of "Jack and the Bean Stalk," and feared he might be the hungry giant of the story—he was so tall and looked so big with a long, full black cloak over his shoulders, and he wore a fur cap with ear straps which allowed but little of his face to be seen.
>
> Expecting to hear "Fe, fi, fo, fum," I shrunk closer to my mother and tried to hide behind her skirts.

———

As a rising politician, Lincoln managed to stage a series of debates with the great Stephen A. Douglas. One citizen who saw and heard them found the clothing and voice of the Springfield attorney intriguing:

> His clothes were black and ill-fitting, badly wrinkled—as if they had been jammed carelessly into a small trunk.
>
> His bushy head, with the stiff black hair thrown back, was balanced on a long and lead head-stalk, and when he raised his hands in an opening gesture I noticed that they were very large.
>
> He began in a low tone of voice as if he was afraid of speaking too loud. He said "Mr. Cheerman," instead of "Mr. Chairman," and employed many other words with an old-fashioned pronunciation.

A correspondent for the New York *Evening Post* covered some of the now-famous debates. From him, readers of the newspapers received a terse description of the man they didn't dream would soon become the nation's chief executive: "Built on the Kentucky type, he is very tall, slender, and angular, awkward even, in gait and attitude. His face is sharp, large-featured and unprepossessing. His eyes are deep set, under heavy brows; his forehead is high and retreating, and his hair is dark and heavy."

William H. Herndon, Lincoln's law partner, offered a detailed word picture that was anything but flattering. According to him, the fifty-one-year-old man then living in Springfield "had no gray hairs, or but few, on his head." Said the attorney of his partner:

> He was thin, wiry, sinewy, raw, and big heavy-boned, thin through the breast to the back and narrow across the shoulders. Standing, he leaned forward, was what may be called stoop-shouldered.

His body was well shrunk, cadaverous and shriveled, having very dark skin, dry and tough, wrinkled and lying somewhat in flabby folds; dark hair, the man looking woe-struck.

He had no spring to his walk; he walked undulatory, up and down in motion. The very first opinion that a stranger would form of Lincoln's walk and motion was that he was a tricky man, a man of cunning, a dangerous shrewd man, one to watch closely and not to be trusted.

His arms and hands, feet and legs, seemed in undue proportion to the balance of his body. It was only when Lincoln rose on his feet that he loomed up above the mass of men. He looked the giant then.

✼

Charles Francis Adams first saw president-elect Lincoln on February 14, 1861. Son of John Quincy Adams and grandson of John Adams, the man who soon would become U.S. ambassador to England was horrified. He said to his family: "A door opened, and a tall, large-featured shabbily-dressed man, of uncouth appearance slouched into the room. His much-kneed, ill-fitting trousers, coarse stockings, and worn slippers at once caught the eye."

✼

Walt Whitman paid little or no attention to the clothing of the man destined to become the mysterious central figure of the Civil War. Concentrating on Lincoln's face, Whitman said that it was "seam'd and wrinkled yet canny-looking." To the poet, "his dark-brown complexion" and "his black, bushy head of hair and disproportionately long neck" made a fascinating combination.

✼

After the inauguration of 1860, British journalist William H. Russell found the attire of Lincoln somewhat eye-catching. His verbal portrait of the president depicted for readers in England an American chief executive who was "dressed

in an ill-fitting wrinkled suit of black, which put one in mind of an under-
taker's uniform at a funeral; round his neck a rope of black silks was knotted in
a large bulb, with flying ends projecting beyond the collar of his coat."

One of Russell's London colleagues went into much greater detail in telling British readers about the nearly unknown man chosen to head the United
States in a time of great crisis. He wrote:

> To say that he is ugly is nothing; to add that his figure is grotesque is to con-
> vey no adequate impression.
>
> Fancy a man about six feet high, and thin in proportion, with long bony
> arms and legs, which somehow seem always to be in the way; with great rug-
> ged furrowed hands, which grasp you like a vice when shaking yours; with a
> long scraggy neck and a chest too narrow for the great arms at his side.
>
> Add to this figure a head, coconut shaped and somewhat too small for
> such a stature, covered with rough, uncombed hair, that stands out in every
> direction at once; a face furrowed, wrinkled, and indented as though it has
> been scarred by vitriol; a high narrow forehead, sunk beneath bushy eye-
> brows, too bright, somewhat dreamy eyes that seem to gaze at you without
> looking at you; a few irregular blotches of black bristly hair, in the place where
> beard and whiskers ought to grow; a close-set thin-lipped, stern mouth, with
> two rows of large white teeth, and a nose and ears which have been taken by
> mistake from a head twice the size.
>
> Clothe this figure then in a long, tight, badly-fitting suit of black, creased,
> soiled, and puckered at every salient point, put on large ill-fitting boots,
> gloves too long for the long bony fingers, and a hat covered to the top with
> dusty puffy crepe, and then add to all this an air of strength, physical as well
> as moral, and a strange look of dignity coupled with grotesqueness, and you
> will have the impression left upon me by Abraham Lincoln.

Journalist Noah Brooks, who had known the president before he entered the
White House, saw him in Washington and wrote, "His hair is grizzled, his gait

more stooping, his countenance sallow, and there is a sunken, deathly look about the large, cavernous eyes."

Frank M. Vancil of Montana was so surprised by the appearance of the president of the United States that he penned a vivid account of what he saw:

He was six feet and four inches in height, the length of his legs being out of all proportion to his body. When he sat on a chair he seemed no taller than the average man but his knees were high in front.

He weighed about 180 pounds, but was thin through the breast and had the general appearance of a consumptive. Standing, he stooped slightly forward; sitting, he usually crossed his long legs or threw them over the arms of the chair.

His head was long and tall from the base of the brain and the eyebrow; his forehead high and narrow, inclining backward as it rose. His ears were very large and stood out; eyebrows heavy, jutting forward over small, sunken, blue eyes; nose large, long, slightly Roman and blunt; chin projecting far and sharp, curving upward to meet a thick lower lip which hung downward; cheeks flabby and sunken, the loose skin falling in folds, a mole on one cheek, and an uncommonly large Adam's apple in his throat.

His hair was dark brown, stiff and unkempt; complexion dark, skin yellow, shriveled and leathery.

William H. Herndon, Lincoln's longtime law partner, insisted that he wore a size 7 1/8 hat, "his head being six and one-half inches from ear to ear." Almost invariably black and tall, the hat accentuated his height. "Little grey eyes in the right place" surmounted a mole just above the right corner of his mouth. Other facial features that intrigued the Illinois attorney were:

. . . high, sharp and prominent cheekbones; heavy and prominent eyebrows; long, upcurved and massive jaws; a large, long, and blunt nose a little awry toward the right eye; eyebrows cropped out like a huge jutting rock from the brow of a hill; a long, narrow, sallow, and cadaverous face whose flesh was shrunken, shriveled, wrinkled, and dry; a lower lip that was thick and very red—the red being a good sign of a tendency to consumption.

In August 1862, editors of the London *Times* received and studied a collection of photographs from the Brady Studio in New York. To readers they reported:

Turning to the volume of portraits, the eye is first arrested by Mr. Lincoln, sitting in company with an ink-bottle at a table, which does not conceal that foot which he is so often said by the papers "to put down" on various questions. . . . an odd, quaint face, sagacious not with-standing the receding brow, and kindly despite the coarse, heavy-lipped mouth, but with such capillary arrangements that, in combinations with the long-limbed, narrow body and great extremities, there is a gorilla expression produced by the *ensemble.*

Brig. Gen. Carl Schurz, who took time to jot down his impressions of the man whose views and decisions determined the course of the war, was strongly impressed by "that swarthy face with its strong features, its deep furrows, and its benignant, melancholy eyes."

On Lincoln's head, wrote Schurz, "he wore a battered 'stove-pipe' hat. His neck emerged, long and sinewy, from a white collar turned down over a thin black necktie." His large feet and extremely long arms, concluded the German-born Federal leader, went well with his "lank, ungainly body."

Reviewing troops at Harrison's Landing, Virginia, in April 1865, Lincoln made a vivid impression on an officer who kept a detailed diary. He confessed himself to be greatly impressed by the six-foot, four-inch commander in chief who "walked with a shambling western slouch" and wore an unusually tall hat that seemed designed to magnify his height.

As described only weeks before his assassination, Lincoln's eyes were set so deeply that their sockets seemed to be bruised.

An overwhelming impression was triggered by a close look at the face that sat above a "wry neck." That day at Harrison's Landing, he seemed to have "a clown face—a sad face."

Firsthand descriptions of a few of Lincoln's generals were penned by colleagues and subordinates. Surviving impressions made by Confederate leaders are scarce. In no instance did the wartime appearance of a general officer lead to more than two or three verbal portraits. In this respect as in many others, Abraham Lincoln stands alone among Civil War figures.

Having soaked up the descriptions offered here and having distilled their essence, poet Carl Sandburg offered what may be the best summary. Immense armies were directed by a frontiersman whom Sandburg said seemed "like an original plan for an extra-long horse or a lean and tawny buffalo."

Lincoln's seemingly total unconcern about his clothing may have stemmed from his early life. On the western frontier where he grew up, it didn't matter a hill of beans how a boy or girl, man or woman dressed.

Descriptions of his grotesque body strongly suggest that he suffered from Marfan syndrome. Efforts to make DNA tests in order to determine whether or not he actually inherited this rather rare malady have so far been thwarted.

If the genetic disorder was responsible for the physique of the man who put everything he had into preservation of the Union, it also offers a tentative explanation of some of his behavior.

All accounts indicate that he ignored repeated attempts to provide for his personal security. His "premonitions" of his own early demise could have been triggered by bodily signals. Cardiac disorders, associated with Marfan syndrome, often lead to sudden and early death. This suggests that had John Wilkes Booth not resorted to a derringer, the ill-dressed and awkward looking man who ran the Civil War might not have lived to complete his hard-won second term in the White House.

In death as in life, visual impressions of the Great Emancipator varied greatly. J. C. Buttre issued for sale a print that depicts Lincoln standing beside a bust of Washington. As shown in it, however, the Civil War president's head rests on the body of Andrew Jackson.

James Bodtker, one of Buttre's competitors, went a step beyond the Jackson/Lincoln composite. His print entitled "The Father, and the Saviour of Our Country" shows the first and the sixteenth presidents standing side by side. Yet the Lincoln who is featured here is not the man from Springfield; rather, the body of states' rights advocate John C. Calhoun of South Carolina is surmounted by the head of Lincoln.

Noted portrait painter Joseph A. Ames wanted to depict the Great Emancipator, but had nothing with which to work except a photograph of his head and shoulders. Undaunted, Ames employed a lanky model, dressed him in a frock coat, and proceeded with his Lincoln painting.

One of the most unusual paintings of Lincoln is held by the Museum of the Grand Army of the Republic in Philadelphia. It depicts the wartime commander in chief leaning on a table, and is termed "strange" by some puzzled visitors.

If it actually is strange, that's because the painter who was eager to capitalize on the market created by martyrdom hastily put Lincoln's head on the body of John C. Frémont. Reproduced, this was sold as a "remembrance portrait" of the slain president.

Even in Washington's world-famous Lincoln Memorial, awed visitors never fully glimpse the real man who welded a strong central government from a conglomeration of semi-independent states.

Daniel Chester French created the immense statue of the seated commander in chief. Much evidence indicates that the sculptor was familiar with a bronze cast of Lincoln's right arm and hand that was made on the Sunday after his nomination for the presidency. As the gigantic statue neared completion, French seems to have found himself unwilling to depict Lincoln's long and bony fingers.

As a result, visitors from around the world who pause at the Lincoln Memorial do not see the long and bony fingers of the hand, swollen from much shaking, that signed the Emancipation Proclamation. Instead, the most awesome of memorials in Washington exhibits the right hand of sculptor French.

Twenty-three

FROM THE SUBLIME
TO THE RIDICULOUS

Several Confederate line officers seem to have vied with one another for the honor of "best dressed." Brig. Gen. Jeb Stuart liked to appear in a scarlet-lined cape that he fastened with a yellow sash. His plumed hat, jack boots, and gauntlets might have been worn by a European commander of the Napoleonic era.

Brig. Gen. Thomas C. Hindman, whose height topped five feet by only one inch, leaned toward clothing such as that worn by affluent civilians. He sported ruffled shirts under a tight-fitting coat and didn't like to be seen unless he was also wearing patent-leather boots.

Despite his Texas background, Confederate Brig. Gen. Ben McCulloch fancied patent-leather, too—but insisted on wearing high-top instead of regular length boots. He rolled his long stockings over the tops of his boots, and demanded that his tailor use black velvet in making his suits. Because this outfit was topped by a white felt hat, a few of his men compared him with "a very big and very bald eagle."

Confederate Brig. Gen. Turner Ashby was fond of glittering accessories. His battle outfit typically was not considered complete until he donned gauntlets, then hung a brass spyglass on one side of his saddle and a fox-hunting horn on the other.

〰️

Gen. Robert E. Lee somehow managed to keep an elegant dress uniform clean during months in which he took it along on campaigns. As though he had watched over it for use on a very special occasion, he donned it in order to meet Grant at Appomattox.

〰️

Capt. George Armstrong Custer of the U.S. Army wore a regulation outfit. Made a brigadier of volunteers in June 1863, he promptly hunted up the best tailor he could find.

Custer's new uniform of blue velvet, heavily trimmed in gold, may have been the most resplendent of any general officer on either side.

〰️

Having fought in Algeria, where he was made a member of France's Legion of Honor, Union Brig. Gen. Philip Kearny never tired of telling about his experiences overseas. A millionaire by inheritance, he took to war a wardrobe of twenty custom-tailored uniforms. Wearing one of them and topped by a gold-braided kepi of French style, when Kearney rode into battle he looked more like a European nobleman than a member of New York City's upper crust.

〰️

At both Chancellorsville and Gettysburg, Union Col. Augusto Fogliardi took to the field wearing bright blue trousers ornamented with broad stripes of red.

The collar of his dark green coat, as well as its cuffs, were trimmed with red. To top this spectacular outfit he wore a kepi. Far from ordinary, Fogliardi's dark green headpiece was decorated with three bold stripes of gold.

—⁓—

Perhaps the most ridiculous dress donned in preparation for meeting the enemy in battle was worn by officers of numerous Zouave units that were raised in the North. When Col. John L. Riker led his men from Camp Astor to a Washington-bound train, he was a sight to see. His light blue trousers, extremely baggy, were topped by a loose jacket of darker blue. Wearing a crimson shirt, the Zouave officer displayed on his head a red fez whose long blue tassel was decorated with gold.

Ohio-born Union Maj. Gen. William S. Rosecrans scoffed at the "ostentatious display" of Zouave leaders. He usually selected black breeches and a blue coat, but underneath the coat liked to display a snow-white vest.

—⁓—

Col. Michael Corcoran of the Sixty-ninth New York Regiment wanted no one to forget that he and most of his men were Irish. Unlike officers of the Seventy-ninth Highland Regiment, Corcoran rarely wore kilts. His coat was, however, conspicuously decorated with crimson and green; and he rode proudly in the shadow of a green flag displaying an embroidered harp of Erin.

—⁓—

A "uniform" used by Sen. James Lane of Kansas was the antithesis of the dress worn by men willing to kill to quell secession. As commander of the Frontier Guards, he was briefly responsible for the security of the president and his family.

With his men quartered in the White House, Lane swaggered about in denim overalls and a leather vest. Regardless of the season, when he went outside the house he pulled on a bearskin overcoat.

A contender for "worst dressed officer" might have been Confederate Brig. Gen. William E. Jones. Having outfitted his cavalrymen of the Washington Mounted Rifles in plain homespun uniforms, Jones donned blue jeans, a hickory shirt, and a homespun coat.

At Wilson's creek, Missouri, Maj. Gen. Sterling Price of the Missouri Home Guards had no uniform. When he met Federal forces, he wore a suit of rough linen, a black plug hat, and a pair of "citizen's breeches" held up by suspenders.

Ulysses S. Grant would have been the easy winner in a quest for the title of "least soldierly looking commander." Sometimes he wore part of a uniform, but frequently he did not.

Looking much like a farmer or cattleman who had just been captured by men in blue, the Union leader was likely to be seen in "a simple blouse without any symbol to indicate his rank." Had Confederate officers not known him by sight, he might have found it difficult to participate in the surrender ceremonies at Appomattox.

Union Maj. Gen. Winfield Scott Hancock had strong ideas about shirts. Usually wearing garments of regulation issue, aides said he took a dozen with him wherever he went.

If a shirt became soiled with gunpowder or blood during a battle, he went to his tent and changed into a clean one as soon as possible, even if the guns were still roaring.

Many general officers who fought for the Confederacy didn't care if their shirts were fresh from the laundry. Some of them, though, were downright ornery about displaying what they considered to be the right color or pattern.

After the first few months of conflict, Sterling Price acquired a varicolored plaid hunting shirt. Because he didn't like to go into battle without it, aides called it his "war coat."

When in camp, Confederate Maj. Gen. Ambrose P. Hill was often wearing a fatigue jacket of gray flannel. When he prepared to meet the enemy, however, the red-bearded commander put it aside and insisted on wearing a shirt that came close to matching the color of his facial hair.

Confederate Maj. Gen. John B. Gordon was reluctant to go into battle unless he was wearing a battered shirt of checkered pattern, and Gen. Braxton Bragg didn't care what hue his rough hunting shirt was, so long as it was gray.

"Bloody Bill" Anderson and many other western guerrilla leaders affected a shirt made to special order. Such a garment usually had an open front, was likely to have been embroidered by female admirers, and was equipped with four big pockets. Each pocket was just the right size to contain revolver cylinders, loaded and ready to be slipped into guns.

Compared with hats, shirts worn by officers were relatively unimportant in variety. Grant seldom donned any head covering other than the regulation U.S. Army, or "slouch," hat. Kearny's kepi though distinctive, was an integral part of gear that caused him to look like a French commander ready to take on Austrians or Prussians.

Union Brig. Irvin McDowell tried to take good care of a headpiece made especially for him from bamboo and canvas. He needed it to shield his head from heat, he explained to anyone who inquired about it.

Cavalryman Alfred Pleasonton used straw for the same purpose, but this Union major general's narrow-brimmed hat was described as "imparting to him a most jaunty air."

Pro-Union Kansas Charles R. Jennison, leader of a band of Jayhawkers, was a tiny fellow. When riding at the head of a column, he typically wore an enormous fur cap that made him appear tall.

Confederate officers affected hats at least as varied as those of Federals. Gen. P. G. T. Beauregard didn't like to be seen unless shaded by a kepi. Maj. Gen. John C. Breckinridge could be identified at a great distance by means of his broad-brimmed felt hat. Col. John R. Mosby also preferred felt, but he fastened a long ostrich plume to his hat. Maj. Gen. Jubal Early's felt displayed a plume, but it was black and of unknown origin. Gen. Joseph E. Johnston wore more than one kind of hat, never appearing at the dinner table without one; he didn't like for observers to see that he was going bald.

Whatever a man's taste in dress might be, his individuality was often most prominent during early weeks or months of fighting. Grant reported for duty wearing a uniform made for him by his wife, Julia, when he became recruitment chairman in Galena, Illinois.

Wearing Mexican War uniforms, officers of the Eighth New York Regiment proudly marched off to lick the secessionists.

Joseph Hooker witnessed the Federal disaster at First Bull Run as a civilian. Given a commission as brigadier, he added to his outfit a brilliant red sash and shoulder straps of gold embroidery. Soon he replaced his lavish shoulder straps with metal substitutes, then ruefully confessed that sun and rain had caused his sash to turn purple.

Confederate Brig. Gen. Albert Pike was sworn in while wearing wide and flowing trousers and a hat that to observers seemed to have come from days of the American Revolution.

When he first appeared on the battlefield, Stonewall Jackson was wearing the dingy uniform of a professor at the Virginia Military Institute.

Jeb Stuart was dressed in his U.S. Army uniform when he accepted a Confederate commission. He was still wearing it when opposing forces clashed at Falling Waters, Virginia, in July 1861.

Some of the miscellaneous gear worn by officers seems to have been dangerous because it attracted enemy bullets; other pieces were simply ludicrous. Confederate Brig. Gen. Felix Zollicoffer's white raincoat made him an easy target for enemy marksmen. When he fell at Mill Springs with his precious raincoat riddled, he became the first general officer to die on Kentucky soil.

Confederate Capt. Jennings Wise affected a cape lined in brilliant scarlet, which may have caught the eyes of Federal marksmen who killed him at Roanoke Island, North Carolina.

Despite his conspicuous yellow gloves, Union Maj. Gen. Nathaniel P. Banks fought throughout the war without receiving a major injury. His carping critics said he made that record by carefully staying well behind lines of fire.

At Blackburn's Ford, Virginia, Congressman John A. Logan of Illinois—not yet a brigadier—used his musket freely, while wearing a frock coat and a plug hat. By the time he became the central figure in the painting originally called "Logan's Great Battle," he was wearing a regulation uniform. That is how he appears in Atlanta's world-famous Cyclorama, which depicts the battle that led to the Confederate loss of the city.

Though he never fired a gun against Confederates, U.S. Secretary of the Navy Gideon Welles may have displayed the most distinctive of all Federal apparel. His expensive wig grew too large with wear and frequently slipped to one side during heated discussions among members of Lincoln's cabinet.

Early in the war, many entire units were admiringly hailed as being "sights for sore eyes." Members of the Charleston Zouave Cadets, among the most colorful of Confederate outfits, had bold red stripes on their uniforms. They also wore red caps and immense cross-belts of white.

Led by Col. Philip Regis de Trobriand, men of the Fifty-fifth New York Regiment displayed uniforms as eye-catching as their commander's name. Because red was used generously on trousers of their French garments, comrades called this outfit "the red legged Fifty-fifth."

Many soldiers of the famous Philadelphia Brigade initially wore gray. Soon, however, the drab outfits were exchanged for bright blue cut-away jackets that surmounted blue pantaloons with red stripes. To complete the visual effect, they wore brilliant scarlet shirts and white leggings.

Kilts were preferred by men of the Seventy-ninth New York, while the Garibaldi Guards, who snickered at them, marched stiffly under rounded headgear decorated with green cock feathers.

Berdan's Sharpshooters were not acquainted with the term *camouflage*, but they set out to make themselves "blend with woods and fields." Hence their special green coats, caps, and trousers caused them to look like American versions of Robin Hood.

Blue uniforms of a unit of New Jersey cavalry were so ornately decorated in yellow that its members were derided as "butterflies."

Still, the most eye-catching of Federal forces may have been the 155th Pennsylvania. As described by artist Frederick Ray after he sketched them, the trousers of the fighting men were "shaped not unlike the bloomer costume worn by some women." Each pair, said Ray, required at least enough fabric to make two pairs of "ordinary pantaloons."

Dark blue jackets of men who comprised this unit were heavily trimmed with gold: down the fronts, around the wrists, and at the collar. Their yellow-trimmed red sash had no precise counterpart among fighting forces; approximately ten inches wide and ten feet long, it was designed to be wound about the waist.

Despite jacket and sash, the artist regarded their turban as "the greatest and most impressive part of the uniform." A foot-wide piece of white flannel fully ten feet long was wound in such a way that it perched on a red fez from which a blue tassel dangled.

Typical Confederate units were likely to be at the other end of the dress spectrum. Men of the Eleventh Alabama were among the most distinctive, because manufacturers of their uniforms dyed them "the color of coppras." As a result, they were known to comrades as "Yellow Dogs."

At Wilson's creek, opposing forces clashed before most units had an opportunity to adopt uniforms of any kind. Some members of the Missouri state militia wore blue, while others were in gray. Federals of the First Iowa took to the field in gray, while Confederates of the Third Louisiana wore blue.

A secessionist who took part in the August 1861 battle carefully described his apparel:

A hat made of brown jeans, quilted, and which when soaked took in half a gallon of water; a check cotton shirt that did not meet about my neck and had no button on the collar; a jacket with ventilator in its back; trousers, fringed with scorched strings from knee to ankle; socks with no feet; shoes, in which sole and upper were held together by strings.

As some Federals had done earlier at Big Bethel, Virginia, numerous Confederates at Wilson's Creek tied strips of white cloth around their left arms as means of identification.

Many a Federal unit could be distinguished at a glance because of its distinctive headgear. Instead of the regulation "Hardee hat" of felt carrying a feather, members of the highland Brigade wore Scots caps. Men of the Sixth and Eighth Massachusetts marched under enormous shakos—but so did volunteers who made up the Confederacy's Fourth Georgia.

At least one Iowa regiment was equipped with regulation black felts that were modified by attaching to each "a tin bull's eye, the size of a sauce plate, which displays the red, white, and blue."

Because veteran woodsmen largely made up the Fourth Michigan, it was natural for them to go to war displaying knitted caps with tassels. Each man of another unit from a nearby state carefully sewed a tuft of deer hair on his hat, causing the outfit to become universally known as the Pennsylvania Bucktails.

Confusion over colors prevailed at First Bull Run (Manassas) as well as at Wilson's Creek. In the Virginia struggle, a Federal battery of artillery was captured because uniforms of attackers looked almost identical to those of defenders. Some units fought in broadcloth frock coats, and both blue and gray were found on each side. In a few regiments of Federal volunteers, each company had its distinctive garments; men of one company might fight in blue, while those of other companies dotted the battlefield in uniforms of gray, white, and even red.

Two years later, when uniforms of both forces were generally standardized, color came to play a special role.

Uniforms trimmed with red indicated that their wearers were members of the artillery. A uniform trimmed with blue gave the automatic message: "This man belongs to the infantry." Yellow trimmings labeled the soldier who bore them as a member of the cavalry.

In one of the few cases where officials in Federal and Confederate forces saw eye-to-eye, both adopted the same pattern of color codes.

Twenty-four

WAR MAKERS AS APPRAISED
BY THEIR CONTEMPORARIES

Lt. Hugh J. Kilpatrick of the Union Army thought he would rise in rank faster as a leader of volunteers. Keeping his commission but switching to the Fifth New York Regiment, of which he was made captain, he became the first officer from the regular army to be wounded in action.

Again transferring he was made lieutenant colonel of the Second New York Cavalry. As a leader of mounted men he soon became widely known as "Kill Cavalry" because he pushed his men to the limit of their endurance.

In early 1864, now a brigadier, he was sent to the western theater at the request of Maj. Gen. William T. Sherman. In assessing the move, Sherman said, "I know Kilpatrick is a hell of a dammed fool, but I want just that sort of man to command my cavalry."

In the aftermath of Fort Sumter, the New York *World* offered readers a capsule appraisal of P. T. G. Beauregard, whose guns brought surrender of the Federal installation:

> One result of the Charleston fight will be to restore Beauregard to favor of the southern people. Truly he is boastful, egotistical, untruthful, and wanting in tact, but he is certainly the most marvelous engineer of modern times.

By his genius and professional skill, he has erected batteries in Charleston harbor that would sink all the wooden fleets of the world did they come under fire.

⁂

Sent to the West by Lincoln, who failed to consult generals already on the field, the arrival of Brig. Gen. John McClernand was not welcomed by Grant. Of the political appointee, the future general in chief said, "He's entirely unfit for the position of corps commander, both on the march and on the battlefield.

⁂

One after another Federal commander was whittled down to size by a contemporary. Assessing the veteran military leader whom Lincoln chose as his chief of staff, Secretary of the Navy Gideon Welles said of Henry W. Halleck, "He originates nothing, takes no responsibility, plans nothing, suggests nothing; in short, he is good for nothing."

At least once, Halleck originated something. With troops preparing to assault Corinth, Mississippi, he insisted that many of them devote their energy to digging trenches. Once the town fell, Brig. Gen. John A. Logan of Illinois solemnly swore that "My men'll never dig another ditch for Halleck except to bury him."

No man to bite his tongue, Henry Halleck, the leader whom Welles accused of doing nothing, appraised Brig. Gen. Franz Sigel after Confederates defeated his forces at New Market, Virginia. Said Halleck: "Sigel will do nothing but run. He never did anything else."

⁂

Abraham Lincoln, who as commander in chief chafed at inaction, was both cryptic and caustic when he berated Maj. Gen. George B. McClellan. Said the president who gained posthumous fame as a humorist: "McClellan has the slows."

Many months and scores of military events later, Lincoln framed a terse appraisal of Ulysses S. Grant: "This man fights."

U.S. Secretary of War Edwin M. Stanton, who despised McClellan even more than Lincoln did, drew up a list of reasons why he believed the commander of the Army of the Potomac should be relieved. When he showed his analysis to Welles, the secretary of the navy responded, "McClellan ought to be shot!"

McClellan, wrote Maj. Gen. John Pope to Halleck, was largely responsible for the chaos in Federal forces. "He is the greatest criminal," he charged. Anticipating that a victory by Pope might lead to his elevation in command, McClellan wrote to his wife, "I don't see how I can remain in the service if placed under Pope; it would be too great a disgrace."

U.S. Secretary of the Navy Gideon Welles was not happy at the prospect that after having become a major general, Pope could be placed at the head of the Army of Virginia. "He sits and smokes and swears and scratches his arms," the secretary of the navy wrote of Pope.

Brig. Gen. Samuel D. Sturgis was even more emphatic in expressing his opinion of Pope. During the disastrous Federal campaign that ended with the second battle of Bull Run, Sturgis volunteered that "I don't care for John Pope one pinch of own dung."

Lincoln, who was responsible for Pope's elevation to a major command, soon showed less tolerance for him than he had displayed toward McClellan. Referring to the fact that his new top commander was seldom seen except on horseback, the president remarked that "Pope has his headquarters where his hindquarters ought to be."

Defending his sudden decision to place Maj. Gen. George G. Meade in command of forces charged with repelling Lee's invasion of Pennsylvania, the president commented, "Meade will fight well on his own dunghill."

~~~

Maj. Gen. "Fighting Joe" Hooker endeared himself to Lincoln by showing his willingness to do something, even if it was wrong. Others saw his frenzied activity in a different light. Brig. Gen. Fitz-John Porter charged that "Hooker is looking for promotion to be General-in-chief, and will turn a somersault to get it." U.S. Ambassador to England Charles Francis Adams Jr., wrote that the commander with a reputation for willingness to fight was "little better than a drunken West Point military adventurer."

~~~

Maj. Gen. William S. Rosecrans of Ohio was the target of frequent jibes. Brig. Gen. George Cadwalader termed him "a military demagogue of the most pronounced type." McClellan dismissed his colleague as "a silly goose." Charles A. Dana refused to be so brief in his critique of Rosecrans. "His mind scatters," charged the assistant secretary of war; "there is no system in his use of his busy days and restless nights. There is no courage against individuals in his composition."

~~~

Refusing to single out one or two Federal generals whom he thought remiss in their leadership, Attorney General Edward Bates lumped all of them together. "The thing I complain of is a criminal tardiness, a fatuous apathy, a captious bickering rivalry among our commanders," he wrote. According to Bates, these leaders who were collectively eager for honors and promotions "overlook the lives of their people and the necessities of their country."

Gilbert S. Lawrence heartily agreed with that verdict, especially as it applied to two men he watched closely. Consequently he went on record as saying that

"I have no confidence in General Hooker. Burnside was stuck in the mud, and he will be stuck worse." Published in the New York *Tribune*, these quotes caused the once-praised general to be relieved of command.

Maj. Gen. Benjamin F. Butler created such an uproar as military governor of New Orleans that throughout the South he came to be known simply as "Beast." Union Brig. Gen. Rutherford B. Hayes was equally scathing but more loquacious. Referring to the post-war political defeat of his comrade-in-arms, Hayes said, "The crushing defeat of Butler was one of the best events that has happened since the war. Unscrupulous, able, rich, untiring, he was the most dangerous and wicked demagogue we have ever had."

Years earlier, Brig. Gen. William F. Smith registered a formal complaint when Grant decided to put Butler in command of forces operating between Richmond and Petersburg. "I want simply to ask you," Smith wrote to Grant, "how you can place a man in command of two army corps who is as helpless as a child on the field of battle and as visionary as an opium-eater in council."

Grant himself, though made the first full lieutenant general since George Washington, was not always seen as a great leader. When Massachusetts-born Pvt. Warren H. Freeman caught his first glimpse of Grant, he described his commander to his father: "He is rather an ordinary looking man, I should sooner take him for a chaplain than a great general."

Because he cared little about his appearance, the man who looked like a chaplain was severely rebuked by Congressman Elihu Washburn. Writing to Lincoln, the lawmaker said,

> I am afraid Grant will have to be reproved for want of style. On this whole march for five days he has had neither a horse, nor an orderly, nor servant, a

blanket, or overcoat, or clean shirt, or even a sword; that being carried by his boy 13 years old. His entire baggage consists of a toothbrush.

Sherman who couldn't have cared less how Grant looked, waited until the war was over to speak his mind to Maj. Gen. James H. Wilson. He had known the Federal commanding general for many years, Sherman pointed out, before arriving at a verdict about him:

I am a damn sight smarter man than Grant.

I know a great deal more about war, military history, strategy, and grand tactics than he does. I know more about organization, supply, administration, and about everything else than he does.

I'll tell you, though, where he beats me and where he beats the world. He don't care a damn for what the enemy does out of his sight, but it scares me like hell!

Mary Todd Lincoln, who agonized over the slaughter of her Southern relatives and the rising death rate among men in blue, blamed Grant for much of the carnage. "He is a butcher," she told the president. "He manages to claim victory, but if he remains in power, he will depopulate the North."

Confederate officers of high rank may have considered it ungentlemanly to speak bluntly about their colleagues, and much of what they said or wrote was not preserved. Whatever the reason for their apparent silence, comparatively few biting appraisals have been preserved.

A native of Mississippi, who shielded himself from identification, was downcast when transferred into the force led by Gen. Nathan B. Forrest. Said his new subordinate:

The dog's dead. I must express my distaste at being commanded by a man having no pretension at gentility—a negro trader, gambler—an ambition man, careless of the lives of his men. He may be the best cavalry officer in the West, but I object to a tyrannical, hot-headed vulgarian's commanding me.

~~~

Of Maj. Gen. Braxton Bragg, Maj. Gen. Jones M. Withers said, "He is a good officer, a man of fair capacity," before characterizing him as "utterly self-willed, arrogant and dictatorial."

~~~

Jefferson Davis, who had been a close friend of Albert S. Johnston since their West Point days, made him a full general and never expressed regret. Johnston, said the Confederate president, "is the greatest soldier, the ablest living man, civil or military, Confederate or Federal."

~~~

Mary Boykin Chestnut, diarist and wife of a top civilian aide to Davis, confessed that she never ceased to be awed when she was in the presence of Gen. Robert E. Lee. "He looks so cold and quiet and grand," she wrote of him.

After Gettysburg, Maj. Gen. George E. Pickett saw his commander as somewhat less than quiet and grand. Asked what he thought of Lee, Pickett summed up his verdict in seven words: "that old man had my division massacred."

~~~

Civilian leaders were not universally admired, even when in positions of great power. Of Ohio Senator Benjamin F. Wade, head of the powerful Joint Congressional Committee on the Conduct of the War, the Chicago *Times* wrote:

"His assurance is boundless. There is no place in the government that he would not undertake to fill. And there is none he is fit to fill."

~~~

Chief Justice Roger B. Taney of the U.S. Supreme Court ignored criticism in Washington newspapers for having issued the 1857 Dred Scott decision. Seven years later, editors had the final word when they announced, "The Hon. old Roger B. Taney has earned the gratitude of the country by dying at last."

~~~

Benjamin F. Butler of Massachusetts, famous as the first Democrat to be made a general by Lincoln, failed to impress some of his officers. One cavalry leader looked him over carefully and then wrote: "He is by all odds the most shockingly disreputable general I have ever clapped my eyes upon. He wears his hat perched sideways on his head and looks more like a New York 'Blood-tub' or a 'plug-ugly' than a major general of the U.S. Volunteers."

Butler was, if it's conceivable, even more scathing in his appraisal of Grant than his cavalry officer was of him. Asked about the nation's first lieutenant general, Butler didn't hesitate. "He's dull and ignorant," said the man who knew he was widely called "Beast." After a thought pause, he continued, "Grant no more comprehends his duty or his power under the Constitution than does a mongrel dog."

~~~

Confederate Maj. Gen. Lafayette McLaws was candid in his analysis of his colleague destined to become famous—or infamous—at Gettysburg. Said he: "James Longstreet is a humbug—a man of small capacity who is very obstinate, not at all chivalrous, exceedingly conceited, and entirely selfish."

~~~

Confederate Lt. Gen. Daniel H. Hill was widely known to have a low opinion of cavalrymen in general and their leaders in particular. He made an exception in the case of one man who entered the war without military training or experience.

In an official report, he praised Nathan B. Forrest without restraint: "If again placed on a flank, I would ask no better fortune than to have such a vigilant, gallant, and accomplished officer guarding its approaches."

Union Maj. Gen. Abner Doubleday, one of half a dozen men who won rapid promotions after having helped defend Fort Sumter, honored Maj. Robert Anderson as a soldier but questioned his views on the burning issue of the war era. As commander of the installation, Doubleday admitted, "he was neither timid nor irresolute."

"Unfortunately," continued the major general, "he desired not only to save the Union but to save slavery with it. He could not read the signs of the time and see that the conscience of the nation and the progress of civilization had already doomed slavery to destruction."

Alfred T. Andreas of Illinois, who fought under Sherman, never forgave newspaper reporters for having once branded his commander as insane. That verdict was absurd, insisted Andreas, who said:

> Sherman was one of the few geniuses of the war. A great thinker, always planning, never idle, he gave his enemy no rest.
>
> Clear-headed, with great foresight, always grasping the situation, he dealt telling blows. He took many hazards. When he cast the die, he boldly took the consequences.
>
> His idea of war was *strategy*. He counted every life in his keeping as though it was of his own kindred.

Sherman, who was perhaps the closest friend Grant ever had, chose words carefully when asked to give his appraisal of the man who was his junior in years but his senior in rank.

"Grant's whole character was a mystery even to himself," said the man who captured Atlanta. "He exhibited a combination of strength and weakness not paralleled by any of whom I have read in ancient or modern history."

Edwin M. Stanton replaced Simon Cameron as U.S. secretary of war early in 1862. Soon he found himself one of the most despised of the civilians who played a leading role in the war. McClellan, confiding in his wife, wrote that "Stanton is without exception the vilest man I ever knew or heard of."

Lincoln's private secretary, John Hay, refused to deliver papers to Stanton unless ordered to do so by the president. "I would rather make a tour of a smallpox hospital" than ask him for a courtesy, he said.

No other war maker was so widely vilified as was Abraham Lincoln. Contemptuous of the president's announced policies, the abolitionist Benjamin F. Wade announced that Lincoln's views on slavery "could only come of one who was born of 'poor white trash' and educated in a slave State." Secretary of the Treasury Salmon P. Chase, who had his own eyes on the White House, characterized his leader as "greatly wanting in will and decision, in comprehensiveness, in self-reliance, and clear, well-defined purpose."

Henry Ward Beecher, the nation's most famous clergyman in 1861, denounced the president from the pulpit. According to Beecher, the chief executive lacked any spark of genius and possessed "not an element of leadership, not one particle of heroic enthusiasm." Fellow abolitionist Wendell Phillips described Lincoln as "a second-rate man" and charged his "slackness" with "doing more than the malice of Confederates to break up the Union."

Governor John A. Andrew of Massachusetts, who was among the first to commit himself fully to the war effort, castigated the man for whom he raised regiments of volunteers. "Besides doing my proper work," wrote Andrew, "I am sadly but firmly trying to help organize some movement, if possible to save the President from the infamy of ruining his country."

Soon the Massachusetts leader sent one of his top aides to confer with Lincoln. Reporting about his visit, Henry Lee said just what Andrew wanted to hear. As he sat waiting, Lee recalled, "I grew more and more cross to think that this Western mummy of a rail splitter should sit in Washington's chair."

Editors of the Richmond *Examiner* made clear their feelings about the Confederate head of state and his aides. "It will be for Congress," they said, "to repair, as it best can, the mischief done the public service by a weak and impracticable executive."

With Richmond declared to be in serious jeopardy, newspapermen asserted that this was due to Jefferson Davis's "long course of trifling conduct, childish pride of opinion, unworthy obstinacy, official obtuseness, conceit, defiance of public opinion, imperiousness and despotic affectation."

Confederate Congressman H. S. Foote of Tennessee made a December 1863 speech in which he offered colleagues his appraisal of their president. Said the lawmaker of Jefferson Davis:

> The President never visited the army without doing it injury; never yet that it was not followed by disaster.
>
> He was instrumental in the Gettysburg affair. He instructed Bragg at Murfreesboro. He has opened Georgia to one hundred thousand of the enemy's troops and laid South Carolina liable to destruction.
>
> I charge him with having almost ruined the country, and will meet his champion anywhere to discuss it.

As if to tell the world that Richmond had no monopoly on ineptness, Congressman Frank Blair of Missouri urged that the primary obligation of every Unionist was "to stop fighting Jeff Davis and turn in on our own Government and make something of it." According to the lawmaker, soon to become a Federal brigadier, all Confederate leaders taken together had not harmed the nation half as much as "the cowardice, ignorance, and stupidity of Lincoln's administration."

Until 1860–65, no American had ever been generally reviled by subordinates and appointees as well as political foes. "Whittled down to size" by evaluations of men whose views were respected, Abraham Lincoln was made the subject of scores of cartoons—many of which have not yet lost their sting.

Part Five

BEYOND
THE HEADLINES

Twenty-five

ATROCITY, WAR FEVER, OR JOURNALISTIC HYPE?

Leslie's Illustrated of August 3, 1861, gave Northern readers an alleged insight into Southern attitudes. A woodcut showed a Confederate shell bursting on a Federal artillery train; accompanying text implied that the choice of target was deliberate.

This was an early example of a widespread policy, probably spontaneous and unplanned, under which stories of imaginary or undocumented atrocities were circulated. Most gained currency in the North, but scarcity of newsprint didn't prevent a few from gaining credence in the South.

On June 7, 1862, *Harper's Weekly* was heavily illustrated with sketches that depicted the handiwork of Confederates. Six separate pieces of handicraft were displayed: a goblet made from a Yankee skull; a paperweight cleverly fashioned from the jawbone of a Yankee soldier; a reading desk "formed of a whole skeleton of one of Lincoln's hired minions"; a necklace and a head wreath of Yankee teeth; and a cake basket created from ribs of Union soldiers.

An Office of Brig. Gen. Jacob D. Cox's staff reportedly picked up a letter on a battleground four miles below Charles Town. According to the *Philadelphia Bulletin* of August 2, 1861, the Confederate document read in part:

> Mat:—If there is any engagement, break my little trunk open, and take out my Bible and prayer-book.
>
> The news is that the enemy is coming up on both sides of the river. The orders are to scalp all we can get near to.
>
> J. W. M. Sherry,
>
> Captain of Boone Rangers

At Baxter Springs, Kansas, William C. Quantrill's raiders surprised a group of one hundred Federals under Maj. H. S. Curtis. During the October 6, 1863, engagement, more than sixty soldiers died. According to contemporary reports, raiders wearing blue uniforms systematically mutilated the bodies of the dead.

A Federal force reached Gunnell's farm near Dranesville, Virginia, on December 6, 1861. Having described the owner of the place as a "bitter secessionist," Brig. Gen. George A. McCall continued his official report. According to the report, Gunnell and his nephews "shot two stragglers of General Bank's division, and left them for the hogs to devour."

Lt. Asa B. Isham of the Seventh Michigan Cavalry considered secessionists to have become "brutalized" by the time the conflict was a few months old. Union soldiers who were taken prisoner didn't have a chance, said Isham, who wrote: "Upon the battle-field, they [prisoners] were beaten, shot, or bayoneted, made the recipients of the most vile and blasphemous epithets, and robbed of personal property, jewelry, money, pocket articles, mess utensils, blankets, over-coats, hats, coats, pants, or boots; in not a few instances stripped nearly naked."

<hr />

Readers of the Irontown *Register* were among the first to learn details of the "Guyandotte massacre." According to the Pennsylvania paper, Virginia seces-sionists boasted that "they had thrown eight or nine men off the bridge, into the Guyandotte River." John S. Everett was described as having stood "gun in hand, active in shooting men as they came to the shore in swimming across."

<hr />

An exclusive story in the New York *Tribune* of August 7, 1861, told how citi-zens of Memphis treated a young lady from Maine. Waiting to take a train headed for Cairo, Illinois, she was overheard by the railroad fireman to say to some Northern men, "Thank God! We shall soon be in a land where there is freedom of thought and speech."

Her spontaneous outburst, said the New York newspaper, triggered a quick reaction: "The fellow summoned the Vigilance Committee, and the three Northern men were stripped, and whipped till their flesh hung in strips. Miss Giernstein was stripped to her waist, and thirteen lashes were given to her bare back."

<hr />

Native Americans, rather than Cotton Belt secessionists, figured in an account published by the Albany, New York *Journal*. Describing affairs in strife-torn Missouri, the newspaper said that even a woman is prone to "cast off her femi-nine nature and become quite savage."

A wealthy female owner of slaves, said the *Journal*, made contact with a band of Cherokees that had come to the region to fight for the Confederacy. She then "publicly offered the Indians a large reward if they would bring her

'Yankee free-soil' scalps enough to make a counterpane for her bed. There is no mistake about it."

An account of Missouri action in the Albany, New York, *Journal*, quoted "a gentleman of the highest respectability in Illinois." According to a letter said to have been written on October 26, 1861, a railroad bridge near the border of Illinois "was undermined by the rebels." As a result, "Scores of men, women, and children were suddenly sent into eternity, and great numbers, who were not killed outright, were maimed for life."

Still quoting from its unidentified correspondent, the Albany newspaper told readers: "Scenes equally brutal, though not so destructive, by wholesale, of human life, are every day perpetrated by the 'Secesh' of Missouri. A more cowardly set of savages does not exist."

Lt. Joseph E. Osborn of an unidentified Federal unit was the source of an account about everyday life of encamped Confederate soldiers.

A sutler, said Osborn, was caught in the act of selling some of his wares to a group of Union soldiers. Though he admitted his guilt and begged for mercy, "he was chopped to pieces until there remained no piece larger than his head."

Not all atrocities were attributed to secessionists. Col. James A. Mulligan of the Twenty-third Illinois Regiment watched his men smash resistance in Lexington, Missouri, on August 18, 1861. The enemy, he said, had taken possession of a house used as a hospital and had filled it with sharpshooters.

When this turn of events became known, Mulligan ordered two companies of his men to storm the improvised hospital with this result: "They rushed gallantly across the intervening space, burst open the doors, took possession of the house, and killed every Confederate soldier found inside."

～∞～

Confederate Maj. Gen. W. W. Loring submitted a formal report to his secretary of war on August 21, 1862. Writing from Salt Sulphur Springs, Virginia, he said that Federal forces at Meadow Bluff shot a captured private named Robinson after he had laid down his arms.

When the matter came to the attention of Jefferson Davis, he disposed of the issue in a single sentence: "The statements are so improbable as to prevent credence."

About the same time, Col. Albert Sigel of the Missouri Militia submitted a report that was never seriously questioned. According to it, two bushwhackers—Blakely and March—were captured near Springfield. Believing himself under orders "to annihilate the outlaws and to bring in no prisoners," Sigel reprimanded members of the squad responsible for the capture.

Sigel later wrote that Lt. William C. Kerr, who headed the band responsible for the episode, took him to mean that the captives should have been executed. Hence he "took the two prisoners out of the guard tent and shot them."

～∞～

According to the New York *World* of September 12, 1861, any man near St. Louis in a Federal uniform was in mortal danger. "Mrs. Willow and a free colored woman named Hanna Courtena were arrested yesterday for selling poisoned pies to the soldiers at Camp Benton."

～∞～

An encounter at Sacramento, Kentucky, was reported at length in the Raleigh, North Carolina, *Spirit of the Age*. Cavalry headed by Confederate Col. Nathan

Bedford Forrest clashed with three hundred Hessians at an obscure spot in the border state.

According to a report widely circulated in the North, Capt. Albert G. Bacon of the Federal force was shot through the window of a house in which he had taken refuge. Instead of receiving first aid, Bacon was seized and taken away by his captors. Soon Confederates "rifled the pockets" of Bacon, then "stripped him of his watch" and left him in the woods to die.

Purportedly quoting from a Southern paper on November 20, 1861, the Cincinnati *Times* relied on information said to have been furnished by J. L. Shumate of New Madrid, Missouri. When the village of Fredericktown was evacuated, "the Northern Goths and Vandals burned a portion of it." Then, according to the unidentified Southern newspaper: "They pillaged the Catholic Church, arrested some of the ladies of the place, forcibly tore their ear-bobs from their ears and rings from their fingers, and offered them other indignities too hateful to mention."

Looting, pillaging, and wholesale destruction of property took place throughout the war. Neither side considered these actions comparable to murder. In part because newspapers were scarce, atrocity stories by Confederates are fewer than those circulated by Federals.

Carroll County, Missouri, lore has it that Captain John T. Worthington of the militia made a foray from Fayetteville late in 1861. He reputedly boasted of having killed twenty-two males too old or too young to fight for the secessionist cause.

Several newspapers published graphic accounts of action at Bolivar heights, Virginia, on October 16, 1861. Only a correspondent of the Washington *Star* reported post-battle actions of Confederates.

According to the capital's newspaper, Rebels abandoned their position hurriedly. When Federal troops occupied it, they made a gruesome discovery: "The rebels disgraced themselves more than ever by taking off the clothing, rifling the pockets, and then running their bayonets through the federal killed!"

That genuine acts of atrocity were committed by soldiers and civilians on both sides is beyond question. Yet no incident is so fully documented that every detail is clear.

At Fort Pillow, Tennessee, on April 12, 1864, Union Maj. Lionel F. Booth commanded a garrison made up of just under 300 white soldiers and more than 250 blacks from two units.

Assaulted by 1,500 Confederates under Brig. Gen. James R. Chalmers, the earthworks didn't have a chance. Booth was killed early in the fighting, so command devolved to Major William F. Bradford.

When he received a demand for surrender, Bradford stalled for time. With smoke signaling the approach of a river steamer, Gen. Nathan B. Forrest— who had arrived in time to direct some of the fighting—demanded surrender. Bradford refused, so Confederates stormed the works.

Forrest reported that 14 of his men were killed, and 86 were wounded. Among defenders of the fort, 100 were wounded, about 225 were killed, and an equal number were captured. Of the 262 blacks who were engaged, less than 60 were taken prisoner.

"Massacre!" screamed the Northern press.

Led by Benjamin F. Wade, members of the Committee on the Conduct of the War conducted a formal investigation. Some of the testimony they gathered is suspect; as early as the aftermath of First Bull Run, the same committee published atrocity reports that have never been substantiated.

Regardless of where the truth lies, there is little doubt that the action of Confederates at Fort Pillow can be branded as "uncivilized." Whether there was concerted action leading to planned mass murder remains an open question.

Documentation concerning actions of Federal troops in the West is equally sparse. With troops withdrawn from the Indian Territory in order to fight hundreds of miles to the east, many of the Sioux went on a rampage. Led by Little Crow, they allegedly killed an estimated 850 whites in the valley of the Minnesota River.

In mid-September, a band of about 1,800 white settlers set out to punish the Sioux. At Wood Lane on September 23, Little Crow and his warriors were soundly defeated. About 1,500 warriors were captured, but no one knows how many were killed.

Captives were subjected to a drum-head military trial, which resulted in the conviction of 337 warriors. In Washington, Abraham Lincoln reviewed evidence and pondered the verdict. He pardoned 299 men who were under the sentence of death, but sent 38 to the gallows in the nation's largest mass hanging.

Whether the Native Americans who were executed late in December 1862 were guilty, while their comrades were innocent, is a question unlikely to be resolved. There is little evidence that Federal authorities took into account the manner in which the withdrawal of troops affected the Indian Territory.

Were the Union's actions concerning the Sioux an atrocity at least as heinous as that at Fort Pillow, or did the fevered climate of war justify actions taken in Minnesota and in Washington?

Twenty-six

"SILENT BATTLES" DEFY EXPLANATION

Capt. George A. Thomas Thayer of the Second Massachusetts Infantry was unhappy at being away from the military action in June 1863. Hence he found "the sound cannonading near Fredericksburg, ten miles away" to be "a not unwelcome break" in his tedium. Cpl. Lucius W. Barber of the Fifteenth Illinois Infantry recorded having heard "the heavy notes of artillery" when fifteen miles from Vicksburg.

Riding toward Cedar Creek on the morning of October 19, 1864, Union Maj. Gen. Philip H. Sheridan frequently stopped his big black horse, Rienzi. Leaning forward in the saddle, he listened to sounds of battle twenty miles away and tried to assess their meaning.

Scores of other persons said they heard the boom of cannon and the rattle of muskets from a distance of ten miles or more. Union Capt. Ephraim E. Otis insisted that the first artillery fired at Shiloh were heard twenty-eight miles away. From Stones River, according to the Federal officer, clear sounds of cannon were heard forty miles away at McMinnville, Tennessee.

During the First Battle of Bull Run, Mary Todd Lincoln heard strange noises. She went to the roof of the White House, where she thought she could listen more effectively. After changing positions several times, she decided that the sounds were coming from the west. Not until hours later, however, did the First Lady learn that she had dimly heard the noise of battle about forty miles away at the hamlet of Manassas, Virginia.

Other civilians testified that they also knew "something strange was happening" at a distance. Some residents of Pittsburgh heard from a distance of 140 miles the cannonade that preceded Pickett's charge at Gettysburg.

Other firsthand reports deal with a phenomenon still not understood. At least half a dozen times, witnesses said, it was impossible to hear the sounds of battle from a nearby point. Sometimes termed "acoustic shadow," this effect led to what puzzled commentators call "silent battles."

Recalling the Federal bombardment that reduced the Confederate fortifications at Port Royal, South Carolina, in November 1861, S. H. Prescott wrote:

> The transport my regiment was on lay near enough inshore to give us a fine view of the whole battle; but only in some temporary lull of the wind could we hear the faintest sound of firing.
>
> The whole atmosphere seemed to move in a body, giving sound no chance to travel against it.
>
> A portion of the siege batteries were no more than two miles from the camp [we later established], but at times the firing from them and the enemy's replies could only be heard faintly.

Confederate Brig. Gen. R. E. Colston observed the March 9, 1862, *Monitor/Merrimac* battle from a vantage point only a few hundred yards away. He and "a great number of people from the neighborhood" soon found themselves bewildered. According to Colston:

> The cannonade was visibly raging with redoubled intensity; but, to our amazement, not a sound was heard by us from the commencement of the battle.
>
> A strong March wind was blowing direct from us toward Newport News. We could see every flash of the guns and the clouds of white smoke, but not a single report was audible.

At Gaines' Mill (Cold Harbor), Virginia, the head of the Confederate Bureau of War, Robert G. H. Kean, distinctly saw musket fire from both of the forces engaged in the Chickahominy Valley—less than two miles wide. He watched intently as batteries of artillery on both sides "came into action and fired rapidly."

Reporting his June 27, 1862, astonishment, Kean wrote: "looking for nearly two hours at a battle in which at least 50,000 men were actually engaged, and doubtless at least 100 pieces of field artillery, *not a single sound of the battle* was audible."

The terrain, he said, was a swamp with hills on both sides. So he concluded that the silent battle was due to "conditions capable of providing several belts of air, varying in the amount of watery vapor and probably in temperature."

Confederate Brig. Gen. Evander M. Law heard of the strange things that took place at Gaines' Mill, so he interviewed a number of witnesses.

They told him that it was easy to distinguish the lines of battle by means of smoke, "but it was all like a pantomime. Not a sound could be heard, neither the tremendous roar of the musketry nor even the reports of the artillery."

Another Confederate general, Joseph E. Johnston, said of the same event that "unfavorable condition of the air" prevented him from hearing the musketry at his position on the Nine Mile Road. As a result, for a time he was under the mistaken impression that the opposing forces were involved in an artillery duel only.

A similar phenomenon was important at Iuka, Minnesota. Union Maj. Gen. William S. Rosecrans described himself as being "profoundly disappointed at hearing nothing from the forces on the Burnsville road," where a battle was raging at a distance of about two miles.

Only a few miles away, Maj. Gen. E. O. C. Ord and his staff waited impatiently. They had received from Ulysses S. Grant a set of orders that directed them to join Federal forces at Iuka. Grant was quite specific, however; no movement was to get under way until officers heard the firing that would signal an assault by forces under Rosecrans. Ord heard nothing, and did not move. In his Sept. 19, 1862, report Ord noted that "we didn't hear any sounds of the battle past p.m."

Some analysts have concluded that a brisk wind blowing from the north, combined with the lay of the land, created "a pocket of silence" that prevented sounds of furious fighting from reaching the site at which Ord's division was encamped.

Less than sixty days later, another "silent battle" kept Union Maj. Gen. Don Carlos Buell in ignorance. At Perryville, Kentucky, three Federal divisions began a battle with Confederates about 2:00 P.M. on October 8. At Buell's headquarters, situated less than three miles from the scene of action, the Union commander and his aides heard nothing unusual.

Once Buell cocked his head, listened intently, and remarked that "the skirmishers are wasting too much ammunition." Only when a courier arrived from the Ninth Ohio Regiment did the Federal commander learn that many of his men were engaged in full-scale battle with big guns roaring.

Capt. Ephraim A. Otis, a Buell aide, said that neither the general nor members of his staff had any idea that batteries of artillery were in action within what would be considered normal hearing range.

Joseph E. Johnston may have been the only officer of top rank on either side to comment on the phenomenon of acoustic shadow in an official report.

In October 1862, Federal forces moved to a battlefield made famous during the Peninisular campaign. Union sources identify the clash that followed as Fair Oaks, while Confederate reports list it as Seven Pines. There Confederate Maj. Gen. Gustavus W. Smith waited anxiously for sounds of battle on the Williamsburg Road. During about three hours he and his aides heard "occasional firing of cannon," but little musketry. Hence they concluded—mistakenly—that "no real attack was likely to be made that day."

About noon on May 31, Johnston moved his headquarters to a site near Old Tavern and waited to hear the sounds of battle. Gen. Robert E. Lee paid him a visit at 3:00 P.M. and commented that he believed he detected musketry in the distance. Johnston seems to have responded, rather casually, that Lee must have mistaken an exchange of cannon fire for volleys from small arms. Not until a courier arrived an hour later did the Confederate commander learn positively that a battle was raging. He and his aides, inside a small house, had heard nothing. This despite the fact that staff officers waiting nearby were sure they heard the sounds of full-scale battle, not simply an artillery duel.

In his June 24 official report (delayed because of an injury) Johnston gave what to him seemed to be a plausible explanation of his actions that day:

> I had placed myself on the left of the force employed in this attack [upon troops led by U.S. Brig. Gen. Erasmus Keyes], that I might be on a part of the field where I could observe and be ready to meet any counter-movements which the enemy might make against our center or left.
>
> Owing to some peculiar condition of the atmosphere the sound of musketry did not reach us. I consequently deferred giving the signal for General Smith's advance until about 4:00 o'clock, at which time Maj. Jasper S. Whiting returned, reporting that it [the conflict] was pressing on with vigor.

How much acoustic shadow contributed to the large number of casualties at Fair Oaks—more than 11,000—no one knows.

According to theories suggested by observers of "silent battles," wind and air created layers or pockets that did not transmit sound. Probing for a scientific explanation, John B. DeMotte concluded that "varying density of the air" was more important than wind in causing "this strange acoustic opacity."

To this day, no one has offered a satisfactory explanation of the fact that numerous veteran fighting men saw the flash of guns, but heard no sounds; and others close to action said they were strangely shielded from hearing it as usual.

The roar of guns at Port Royal, South Carolina, was heard in St. Augustine, Florida—but not by soldiers on transports no more than two miles away.

Under some conditions, were sounds really barred from passing through air? Or did brain activity sometimes create a temporary psychological deafness?

Until new evidence is found, those questions remain without definitive answers.

Twenty-seven

ABOLITION OF SLAVERY NOT THE UNION GOAL IN 1861

Within days after Confederates fired on Fort Sumter, Union military leaders had to decide what to do with slaves who came into their lines. Although some later changed their minds, the stance of many differed little when the war ended.

One week after having been made a major general of U.S. Volunteers, Benjamin F. Butler offered assurance to Governor Thomas H. Hicks of Maryland—a state in which slavery was legal: "I am anxious to convince all classes of persons that the forces under my command are not here in any way to interfere with, or countenance any interference with, the laws of the State," he wrote.

Far to the west, Maj. Gen. George B. McClellan addressed an open letter "To the Union Men of Western Virginia." In it, he solemnly promised:

> Notwithstanding all that has been said by the traitors among you that our advent among you will be signalized by interference with your slaves, understand one thing clearly—not only will we abstain from all such interference, but we will, on the contrary, with an iron hand, crush any attempt at insurrection on their part.

At Fort Monroe, Maj. Gen. John E. Wool reported to U.S. Secretary of War Simon Cameron a few weeks after the battle of Bull Run in September 1861. He had put many runaway slaves to work, he said, and they were busy building "a new redoubt, railroad and other roads, bridges, etc."

Cameron favored this method of dealing with "all negro men capable of performing labor." Ordering that such persons be forwarded to McClellan he said, "They can be usefully employed on the military work in this vicinity [Washington]."

In Kansas City, replying to an inquiry from Brig. Gen. S. D. Sturgis, the commander of the Kansas Brigade, James H. Lane, made his position clear on October 3, 1861: "My brigade is not here for the purpose of interfering in anywise with the institution of slavery. They shall not become negro thieves, nor shall they be prostituted into negro catchers. The institution of slavery must take care of itself."

In Kentucky, also considered to be part of the West, Brig. Gen. William T. Sherman heard the disturbing news that Russian-born Col. John B. Turchin had permitted "some negro slaves" to take refuge in his camp. This would never do, scolded Sherman. Citing "the laws of the United States and of Kentucky," on October 15 he instructed Turchin that "all negroes shall be delivered up on claim of the owner or agent."

Sherman's verdict was echoed in early November by Maj. Gen. John A. Dix. Writing to Col. H. E. Paine of the Fourth Wisconsin, he ordered him not to interfere "with persons held to servitude." To make sure that there could be no misunderstanding, Dix ended his letter with a blunt directive: "You will not receive or allow any negro to come within your lines."

Almost simultaneously, Brig. Gen. A. McD. McCook consulted his superior about treatment of "contraband negroes" in Kentucky. Writing from Louisville, Sherman replied that he had received "no instructions from Government."

Therefore he ruled that "the laws of the State of Kentucky are in full force, and negroes must be surrendered on application of their masters or agents." What's more, he added, "you should not let them take refuge in camp."

By late November 1861, Maj. Gen. Henry W. Halleck was in command of the Department of the Missouri. Writing to Col. B. G. Farrar, provost marshal general, he stipulated that no citizen of the state should be debarred "from enforcing his legal rights to the services" of a band of sixteen blacks. Fugitives to whom he referred had taken refuge with the army led by Maj. Gen. John Charles Frémont.

One week after Farrar got his instructions, James B. Fry acknowledged receipt in Louisville of Brig. Gen. George H. Thomas's order by which "it is forbidden to receive fugitive slaves into camp."

Thomas later became an advocate of the use of black soldiers, for which he received high commendations. Many of his fellow generals in blue scoffed at his change of stance.

Seeking to clarify fully the vexatious issue of what to do with runaway slaves, on December 26, 1861, Maj. Gen. Henry W. Halleck took the time to prepare a formal ruling, the purpose of which was:

> To prevent any person in the Army from acting in the capacity of negro-catcher or negro-stealer.
>
> The relation between the slave and his master or pretended master is not a matter to be determined by military officers. One object in keeping fugitive slaves out of our camp is to keep clear of all such questions.

Seeking to make his verdict unequivocal, Halleck issued a General Order calling for any officer who harbored runaway slaves to be subject to severe disciplinary action.

When the struggle moved into 1862, attitudes toward slavery remained, for the most part, unchanged. Writing from Cairo, Illinois, on January 19, Brig. Gen. Ulysses S. Grant made his position clear to a subordinate who was on the way to take command at Fort Jefferson, Kentucky.

"On your arrival," instructed Grant, "all negroes who have flocked into camp will be permitted to return to their masters."

By early February, Halleck was ready to modify his ruling concerning slaves. In separate communications to Grant and to Brig. Gen. George W. Cullum, he no longer ordered that camps be kept free of runaways. Instead, he now considered it proper to "find contrabands, and put them at work to pay for food and clothing."

John A. Rawlings, assistant adjutant general, quickly implemented this decision. On February 26, he instructed all officers within Grant's command to identify slaves who had worked upon Confederate fortifications. These, he instructed, should not be released to their masters but "employed in the quartermaster's department for the benefit of the Government."

Many civilians, ready to fight for the Union, saw slavery in the same light as did military officers. On May 15, 1862, Senator Joseph A. Wright of Indiana presented to his colleagues a petition from citizens of his home state.

Hordes of ordinary folk, said the Hoosier senator, were eager for Congress to "stop the agitation of the negro question and attend to the business of putting down the rebellion."

One week after Wright spoke in the U.S. Senate, members of the Seventy-ninth New York Regiment wrote home about action they considered surprising. While marching through the streets of Washington, they saw civil authorities who were "provided with judicial papers" seize two runaway slaves.

Unable to break ranks to save the fugitives, New Yorkers ruefully reported the incident to folks back home. Slaves captured on the streets of the capital, they said, were "soon placed beyond the possibility of rescue."

George B. McClellan, though generally aware of Abraham Lincoln's personal views, feared that he might yield to political pressure. Confident that he knew the views of his men well, the commander of the Army of the Potomac wanted nothing to do with abolition.

Hence on July 7, 1862, he sent the president a letter of warning. In it he urged that "a declaration of radical views, especially upon slavery, will rapidly disintegrate our present armies."

There is no certainty that McClellan or any other Federal general had carefully read the March 4, 1861, inaugural address of their commander in chief. Had they turned to words of the new president, any question that the conflict was launched in order to free the slaves would have been resolved.

There was only one dispute between regions, said Abraham Lincoln. That dispute grew out of the fact that the Republican party was on record as opposing the geographical extension of slavery.

Early in his lengthy address, the man from Illinois stipulated that he personally supported the Fugitive Slave Law. To remove any doubts about where he stood concerning property rights of slave holders in regions where "the peculiar institution" already existed, he added:

> I aver that, to my knowledge, no sub-division, or individual, of the Republican party has ever avowed, or entertained, a purpose to destroy or to interfere with the property of the Southern people.
>
> For myself, I can declare, with perfect certainty, that I have never avowed, or entertained any such purpose; and that I have never used any expression intended to convey such a meaning.

Military leaders who issued impromptu proclamations declaring some slaves of Missouri and the deep South to be free were promptly squelched by their commander in chief.

Letters and speeches of Abraham Lincoln make it clear that he considered retention of Kentucky and other border states in the Union to be far more important than emancipation.

"Radical Republicans" who advocated immediate and total emancipation were vocal and influential in Congress. Because the president did not endorse their views, friction between the administrative and legislative branches of the Federal government soon reached a high level and remained there for the duration of the war.

Despite the philosophical change experienced by Maj. Gen. George H. Thomas and some other Union generals, many of their comrades fought to the end—not for abolition and for civil rights of blacks—but for preservation of the Union.

Sherman's capture of Atlanta is acknowledged to have contributed significantly to Lincoln's re-election in 1864. Sherman's subsequent March to the Sea is widely hailed as a saga of military daring and skill. Yet comparatively little is said about racial views of "the man who made Georgia howl."

While advancing toward Atlanta, he repeatedly rejected suggestions that blacks be incorporated into his forces. Even recruitment of them for service in some unspecified Federal unit would be a source of annoyance to him, he repeatedly wrote.

As he rapidly approached Savannah and the end of the long March to the Sea, large bands of runaway slaves were following his men in blue. Providing them with food made the march more difficult, and some former slaves were making nuisances of themselves.

Brig. Gen. Jefferson C. Davis of Sherman's army arrived at a neat solution to the problem of dealing with these camp followers. With some men in blue vowing that the smell of the sea was in the air, they reached Ebenezer Creek on December 8, 1864.

Despite the fact that it was not called a river, the stream was broad and deep. Davis had pontoons laid down by his engineers so that his men could cross. Then he quickly ordered the makeshift bridge lifted, leaving blacks who had followed the army for days stranded on the other side of the Ebenezer.

The emancipation of slaves in *Confederate territory but not in Union territory* was proclaimed on January 1, 1863. Framed for military purposes, the measure was not prompted by a desire to achieve racial and social justice.

Despite the motives behind its promulgation, the Emancipation Proclamation moved the nation in the direction of racial equality. Coupled with reluctant plans to use blacks as soldiers, it also proved to be the single most potent military measure of the Civil War.

Part Six

THE UNUSUAL
AND BIZARRE

In recent decades the phrase "friendly fire" has been elevated into nearly universal use. To err is human, and the fighting men of the Civil War on both sides were as human as they come. So logically a struggle lasting more than fourteen hundred days would include many instances of friendly fire.

The chapter that follows which deals tersely with friendly fire has come from a wide reading over a period of years. To find out more about this aspect of the conflict, the only way is to stumble across it through general reading. There are no sources other than the compilation included here. Much the same thing can be said about banishment, deportation, and fragging. Be prepared, therefore, for a few surprises in the pages to come.

Twenty-eight

BANISHMENT AND DEPORTATION

During colonial days, a persistent troublemaker was likely to be banished from the colony. Widely practiced, the punishment was borrowed from the Old World, where lawmakers didn't hesitate to engage in the wholesale deportation of convicts. Maybe because this punishment was linked with British tyranny, the Founding Fathers steered shy of it. The Constitution refers to the numerous types of punishments, but banishment and deportation are not among them. Constitutional silence, however, did not inhibit Federal and Confederate leaders, both political and military, as the record shows.

Pioneer detective Allan Pinkerton was sometimes called "a man who was born chock full of suspicions about his own parents." Whether or not that assessment is correct, he had been in and around Washington only a short time before he was sure that someone in the capital was providing a steady flow of vital information to the enemy. Surveillance plus checks of letters and telegrams soon implicated Mrs. Rose Greenhow O'Neal, an attractive widow whose conversation and other charms were fabled.

On August 23, 1861, Pinkerton placed her under house arrest. When he felt that he had confirmation of his suspicions, he managed to have her taken to the Old Capitol Prison. This Sixteenth Street Building was once the seat of the Federal government but had been converted recently into a house of detention. Rose Greenhow O'Neal was escorted there by a military guard.

It was not difficult to discover how O'Neal had managed to gain access to reports and recommendations that came from the highest levels of government. Her parties were the talk of Washington, attended by everyone who was anyone. No one knew how many highly placed officials she had entertained, but the list was believed to be long and very, very heavy with brass.

A large packet of love letters was discovered during a search of her home. Uniformly signed only with the initial "H." they may have been penned by Sen. Henry Wilson of Massachusetts. The evidence was not conclusive, since the cunning widow may have forged the missives in an attempt to involve Wilson should she be challenged about her activities.

Established in the Old Capitol Prison with her eight-year-old daughter and a few other women, the widow O'Neal was a political prisoner in the custody of the Department of State. Even so, she boldly continued her correspondence with Confederates. Much evidence supports the view that the Federal debacle at Bull Run stemmed in part from the fact that O'Neal had informed Brig. Gen. P. G. T. Beauregard of the Federals' plans.

That she was guilty of aiding and abetting the enemy, there was not a shadow of doubt. Yet no one, from Lincoln to the midlevel clerks in the State Department, wanted to initiate action against her. If O'Neal were to be tried in court, all sorts of embarrassing secrets were likely to emerge. Whether or not they had shared her bed at times, men who had confided secrets to her were likely to have extremely red faces if she should take the witness stand.

After a shakeup in the Lincoln administration, the responsibility for political prisoners was shifted to the War Department. Brig. Gen. John A. Dix and Judge Edwards Pierrepont were chosen as commissioners to examine civilians held in custody. Soon they were aided by the Bureau of Military Justice, headed by Judge Advocate General Joseph Holt.

Dix, Pierrepont, and Holt—along with Secretary of War Edwin M. Stanton —held only one conference on Rose O'Neal. She was guilty of treason. If tried, she would be convicted and sentenced to hang. Before the noose could be placed around her lovely neck, however, she was sure to talk . . . and talk . . . and talk. Her revelations would prove even more embarrassing than the July 1861 defeat at Manassas Gap, Virginia. In this dilemma, a secret top-level decision was made. Instead of giving O'Neal her day in court, she would be banished from the Union for the duration of the conflict.

By the time the judge advocate general had trumped up a vague legal precedent for the unconstitutional punishment, six friends and allies of the prisoner joined O'Neal in the Sixteenth Street prison, Mrs. C. V. Baxley and Mrs. Rosanna Augusta Heath Morris were neither as beautiful nor as clever as O'Neal, but they too were dangerous to the safety of the republic. Hence they shared the fate of their friend and colleague.

In June 1862, an officer of the First U.S. Volunteer Cavalry, heading a guard of six men, reached the Old Capitol. Accompanied by the warden, they led the three women to Fort Monroe, Virginia. After a period of detention in the only Virginia installation to remain in Federal hands throughout the war, the trio solemnly swore not to return to Union soil. They were then led to the Confederate lines and ceremonially released.

As the central figure in the first U.S. case in which a citizen was banished, O'Neal occupies a special niche in the annals of the period. She subsequently went to England and returned on the blockade-runner *Condor*. Nearing the coast, the ship was forced aground by vessels of the Federal blockade. Jumping from her ship to avoid capture, O'Neal drowned near Wilmington, North Carolina, on October 1, 1864.

Deportation consisted of involuntary physical departure from home, but it did not require deportees to leave the country. Where martial law was declared, it may have been legal. Few commanders, however, bothered to make formal declarations of martial law; they simply exercised absolute command over areas they controlled.

No other woman attracted as much notice as did Rose Greenhow O'Neal, but numbers of them were banished or deported by leaders on both sides. One of the first to be forced from her home was Phoebe Drew of Fairview, Arkansas. Her husband, a Unionist, fled into the swamps. Hence Phoebe and her three small children were made to leave the state in June 1861.

***

In 1862, as military commander of New Orleans, Union Maj. Gen. Benjamin F. Butler became incensed when Mrs. Eugenia Philips was seen to laugh at the moment a Union officer's funeral train was passing her home. Butler immediately sent her into exile on Ship Island off the Mississippi Gulf Coast as punishment for "unpatriotic levity."

***

Near Memphis, Belle Edmonton was banished in 1863 from the region by Union officials. Her crime consisted of having waved a Confederate flag at a boatload of prisoners.

In divided Missouri, Puss Whitty of Jackson County was reputed to have shot a Federal lieutenant in the arm before fleeing into the woods. When authorities captured her, she was banished from the state.

***

At Vicksburg on December 27, 1863, Brig. Gen. James B. McPherson banished five women. Having "acted disrespectfully toward the President," Kate Barnett, Ella Barrett, Laura Latham, Ellen Martin, and Mrs. Moore were ordered to leave Union lines within forty-eight hours.

McPherson followed with a warning that "all person, male or female, who by word or deed or by implication do insult or show disrespect to the President, the Government, or the flag of the United States, or to any officer or soldier of the United States shall be fined, banished, or imprisoned, according to the grossness of the offense."

~~~

Drastic punishment of men by Federal officers started at least as early as August 1861. Brig. Gen. John Pope, who then controlled part of Missouri, decided that he'd seen too much of irregulars and bushwhackers. A proclamation reprinted in the *Washington Republican* banned illegal assemblages and warned that all persons "taken in arms against the United States" would be sent to Mexico.

At Saint Louis, Maj. Gen. Henry W. Halleck, who had declared martial Law, banished merchant Samuel Engler from the Department of Missouri in January 1862. One month later editor Edmund J. Ellis of the *Boone County Standard* was banished from the state.

~~~

Commanding the Army of Virginia in July 1862, Pope seems to have consulted Abraham Lincoln. Apparently with the president's approval he issued General Order No. 11. Terms of the proclamation required Virginia citizens to take an oath of loyalty to the United States. Failure to take such an oath, said the military commander, would bring immediate punishment: "those who refuse shall be conducted south beyond the extreme pickets of this army and be notified if found again anywhere within our lines or at any point in the rear they will be considered spies and subject to extreme rigor of military law."

~~~

On April 13, 1863, Maj. Gen. Ambrose Burnside was commander of the department of the Ohio. From his headquarters he ordered Southern sympathizers deported to Confederate lines. Anyone found guilty of aiding the enemy, added the Union general, would receive an automatic death penalty.

During the first week of 1864 persons identified only as making up "a band of Southern sympathizers" were banished from Knoxville, Tennessee.

In 1861 Virginia lawmakers passed an ordinance directed at "persons holding office under the Government of the United States." All such were labeled as aliens and enemies and ordered to be "forever banished from the state" as traitors. Within days, editors of the *New Orleans Delta* were rejoicing at the "contemplated expulsion of all citizens of the United States from the Confederate States."

There was no systematic way to enforce this plan, so no one knows how many people were ordered to leave Confederate soil. At San Antonio in August 1861, records show that J. R. Ritchliff and W. P. M. Means appeared before a military commission and were required to leave the country.

Undeterred by the difficulty of enforcement, in November 1862 the Confederate Senate began debate on a special bill that would authorize Jefferson Davis to order all persons "who were loyal, and adhered to the United States Government" to depart from Confederate soil within forty days. This treatment of "alien enemies," conceded Confederate Secretary of War G. W. Randolph "was equivalent to banishment."

Military commanders had enforcement power that civilian lawmakers lacked. Hence most enforced removals occurred in occupied territory. This process began shortly after the fall of Fort Sumter and continued for the duration. Strangely, it had had little attention and cannot be documented by use of standard indexes except when names of commanders and locations are known.

At Key West, where firm Union control never relaxed, on September 16, 1861, Bvt. Maj. William H. French issued a proclamation giving civilians sixty days in which to take an oath of allegiance to the United States. All citizens of the island, their families, and the families of residents who had relatives in Confederate service were told they'd be removed if they did not take the required oath.

In Missouri, site of more battles than any other state except Virginia and Tennessee, Confederates and Confederate sympathizers around Saint Louis were herded into Camp Jackson. In December 1861, they were given the choice of taking an oath of allegiance to the Union or being banished into Southern territory.

Brig. Gen. Thomas Ewing Jr. of Ohio was responsible for the first mass deportation of civilians. Commander of the District of the Border, which included part of Missouri, he issued his General Order No. 11 during the spring of 1863. Under its terms, residents of four Missouri counties believed to include Southern sympathizers were ordered to leave their homes. Hundreds of people, including numerous Unionists, obeyed within the fifteen-day grace period Ewing had stipulated. Supported by Lincoln, the general from Ohio promised to execute all violators of this order.

No one knows exactly how many were involved in this mass deportation. It excited indignation and anger in the North as well as in the South, however. Artist George Caleb Bingham protested Ewing's action with a large painting depicting the flight of the innocents.

In July 1862, the Federal provost marshal of Memphis, Tennessee, ordered "all persons connected with the rebel army or government to leave the city with their families within five days." At least 130 residents of the river city "were provided with passes to go to the South." Though his name was directly attached to the directive, Maj. Gen. William Tecumseh Sherman—a foster brother of Thomas Ewing—was responsible for the deportation.

Simultaneously, the Federal commander sent his Forty-sixth Ohio Infantry Regiment to destroy houses, farms, and crops for fifteen miles below the city on the west bank of the Mississippi River. River boats soon came under fire from marksmen concealed on riverbanks. In reprisal, Sherman announced that each such incident would cause families of ten Confederates to be evicted from the city even if they had taken the oath of allegiance.

At Louisville, forces under Confederate Brig. Gen. Simon G. Buckner threatened the safety of the city. Alarmed Unionists called a mass meeting and demanded that all men between the ages of eighteen and forty-five enroll for service in militia companies. "All who refuse shall be sent to the North," warned the directive issued by civilians.

In Camden County, North Carolina, Unionists informed Lincoln that they could raise two regiments of volunteers. They'd move to do so, they promised the president, once he gave them permission to drive all Rebel families out of the county.

Civilian threats were sometimes meaningless because there were no enforcement mechanisms. In the case of military officers, among whom Maj. Gen.

William Tecumseh Sherman exceeded his peers, enforcement of an order was easy.

Approaching Atlanta, he became incensed upon learning that a textile factory at Roswell flew a French flag. In reprisal for what he considered a subterfuge, he ordered more than four hundred women employees sent north with their children. The terminus of their enforced journey by rail was Louisville, where they disappeared from the record.

Another textile factory on Sweetwater Creek near Atlanta employed about half as many women as did the Roswell facilities. These women too were dispatched to the North and dumped in a strange city or cities without money or resources. Like the Roswell women, few of them were able to return home after the war; for practical purposes, they simply vanished.

Once Sherman succeeded in cutting the rail lines into Atlanta, the heavily fortified city fell. He soon announced plans to turn it into a Federal military base that he called "a western Gibraltar." To implement these plans, he said, it was necessary for all civilians to depart immediately. Those who wished to go north could do so; others would be escorted south to the rail station of Rough and Ready and turned loose upon the countryside.

Lt. Col. William G. Le Duc was assigned the job of making—for once— an accurate tally of persons driven from their home by Sherman's order of September 4, 1864. According to Le Duc's records, 1,651 civilians—men, women, and children—were forced to leave Atlanta and go south. Unlike the textile workers from Roswell and Sweetwater Creek, the majority of these people eventually were able to return home.

These mass deportations were dramatic and emotional but relatively unheralded by the press. The banishment of a former Congressman from Ohio, however, attracted far more public interest.

Less than a month after Maj. Gen. Ambrose Burnside had used his Order No. 38 to forbid persons within his Department of the Ohio to express sympathy for the Southern cause, on May 4, 1863, a crowd of twenty thousand gathered to hear a speech by Clement L. Vallandigham. The former officeholder said that he "spit upon the Burnside order and trampled it under his feet." Denouncing Lincoln as a dictator, he called for an armistice that would end the fighting.

Late that night soldiers under Burnside's command broke down the door of Vallandighman's residence and carted him off to a military prison. Tried by a commission of eight officers, he was convicted of "publicly expressing sentiments designed to hinder suppression of rebellion."

Lincoln was placed in the difficult position of deciding whether to support the harsh military verdict or to set it aside. Concluding that the planned punishment of Vallandigham would do more harm than good, he directed that the culprit be banished into Confederate territory.

Placed aboard the gunboat *Exchange* at Cincinnati, the former lawmaker eventually reached the headquarters of the Union army in Murfreesboro, Tennessee. Since he still strongly voiced his loyalty to the Union whose policies he challenged, he found himself unwanted by Secessionists. Ordered off Confederate soil, he made a long and circuitous journey to Canada as the only man banished from both the United States and the Confederate States.

Whether individuals or masses were involved, most forcible evictions were illegal; at best, some could be considered extralegal. Yet emotions ran so high in both the North and the South that few persons protested measures that would not have been tolerated earlier. The brief abolition of habeas corpus in Confederate territory and the repeated abolitions of this right by Federal authorities caused both segments of the divided nation to come perilously close to military dictatorships.

Twenty-nine

SELF-INFLICTED CASUALTIES

Friendly fire, called by any name, is seldom mentioned in the official records. Letters and diaries of soldiers and occasional newspaper accounts reveal that men began shooting their comrades less than a month after Fort Sumter. They didn't stop until after Appomattox.

During the entire conflict, men in blue and gray turned their muskets or artillery upon their own troops more than sixty times. About half of the documented cases are reported here, in roughly chronological order.

Believing no enemy force to be near, the Third New York Infantry approached a dense forest in the region known as Big Bethel, near Hampton, Virginia, early on the morning of June 10, 1861. Following orders of Maj. Gen. Benjamin F. Butler, everyman wore a white band on his left arm to identify him as a member of the Federal force.

Marching along a narrow road in route step, troops led by Col. Frederick Townsend believed themselves to be two hours behind another Federal unit. Brig. Gen. Ebenezer W. Peirce and staff of the Massachusetts militia had joined them at midnight to lead a reconnaissance toward Yorktown.

Suddenly "a well sustained fire of small arms and canister" caught these ninety-day volunteers by surprise. Not until the turmoil subsided did Townsend learn the dreadful truth about the unexpected ambush. Men of an advance party, led by a Lieutenant Colonel Washburne of the First Vermont Infantry, had fired on their comrades. Col. John E. Bendix of the Seventh New York Infantry stopped the shooting as soon as he could.

Townsend submitted two reports about the tragedy. According to the first, two men were killed, three were dangerously wounded, and four officers and twelve privates sustained minor injuries. Townsend's second report indicated that the unplanned engagement between the two groups of Union soldiers led to twenty-nine casualties. They were the first to know casualties from friendly fire in the Civil War.

At Big Bethel, the use of green troops in early morning fog, dense woods, and lack of distinctiveness in uniforms proved fatal. This combination, or a variant of it, often linked with heavy smoke or dust, occurred repeatedly. In rare instances, a unit carried a false flag or had no flag.

Many times artillerists unwillingly fired at the enemy over the heads of their own infantry and could only hope that they had aimed high enough to miss them. In the emotional intensity of battle, men often fired without having had a good look at their targets.

Frequently the survivors did not learn until later that the deadly lead and iron rained upon them had come from their comrades. Few summaries of such incidents were published at the time they occurred because the men present were often so horrified at what had taken place that they gave only terse reports concerning casualties—or said nothing at all.

About the time the New Yorkers were being felled by their Vermont colleagues, two additional Federal groups were in motion ten miles southeast of Big Bethel. Both groups had been dispatched to seize the strategic area bordering on Hampton Roads.

One body of troops left their Newport News camp well before daybreak; the other departed from Fort Monroe half an hour later. They encountered each other before the sun came up and each unit fired on the other. Officers attributed the costly blunder to "nervousness of green troops in a dangerous situation" and did not report their casualties.

Fairfax Court House, Virginia, was the scene of several early clashes that were usually classified as skirmishes. According to the *New York Evening Post*, a deadly encounter took place on July 5, 1861. Said the newspaper report published far to the north: "This morning the rebel troops stationed at Fairfax Court-House, VA., were advancing upon the Federal lines, when a regiment of their infantry fired by mistake upon a company of their cavalry, killing seven or eight men and wounding several others."

By mid-July some military analysts were sure that a battle of magnitude would occur shortly, and Manassas Junction, Virginia, seemed the likely spot.

On July 18, the Eleventh Virginia Infantry moved toward the rivulet known as Bull Run. Desultory cannon fire from Federal forces frightened men never before involved in battle. Then soldiers, wearing motley uniforms set out to cross the stream.

James Franklin Jr. watched as Brig. Gen. James Longstreet's brigade moved forward to meet the enemy, with many men dressed in civilian garb. Almost simultaneously, Confederate Brig. Gen. Jubal A. Early led the Twenty-fourth Virginia Infantry toward the point of conflict.

Franklin wrote that as Early's men came closer to the conflict, confusion took over: "Just as their line approached the edge of the bushes they mistook our men [of the Eleventh Virginia] for the yanks and some of them fired. Gen. Longstreet, being between his brigade and Gen. Early's line, jumped off his horse to keep from being shot. His horse ran off and we thought the general had been killed." Two years later, Longstreet was wounded by Confederate troops during combat in the Wilderness.

~~~

Soon after the first battle of Manassas had begun in earnest, members of the Fourth South Carolina Volunteers mistakenly fired upon the unit known as the Louisiana Tigers. Angry Tigers then wheeled and returned the fire until Maj. Chatham R. Wheat restored order to his troops. Leading the Tigers, officially known as the First Louisiana Special Battalion, Wheat ordered his men to turn their attention to a large body of Federals and to charge at the double. Although the assault proved to be costly, for the moment it stopped the exchange of fire between two Confederate units.

~~~

Confederate Allen C. Redwood of the Fifty-fifth Virginia Infantry blamed much of the chaos at Bull Run on the lack of standardized uniforms. "So variegated were the costumes on both sides," he wrote, "that both Confederates and Federals frequently fired upon their own men. There are instances recorded where the colonel of the regiment notified his supporters to which side he belonged before daring to advance in front of them."

Analyzing the carnage, historian Francis Trevelyan Miller added, "Since the South had regiments in gray uniforms and many of the men of the North were clad in gray, fatal mistakes occurred and soldiers fired upon their own friends." No one knows how many men were killed or wounded by friendly fire on July 21, 1861.

~~~

Soon afterward a reporter for the *Jefferson City (Mo.) Evening News* described a set of blunders he termed "a second Bethel affair." On September 18, the steamers *War Eagle, White Cloud,* and *Desmoines* set out on an expedition designed to show the flag to Southern sympathizers. Fighting men aboard the river craft were from the Eighteenth, Twenty-second, and Twenty-sixth Indiana Regiments. One contingent of Federals set out for Glasgow, the other for Lexington, Missouri.

The commanders of the separate units were not in communication. Late on the evening of their second day, both leaders sent scouting parties toward Glasgow. Said the newspaper report: "The parties met in the woods, a short distance from where the boats were lying, and the scene at Great Bethel was re-enacted. Mistaking each other for enemies they commenced firing, and for some ten or fifteen minutes the firing was incessant. Before they found out their mistake, three troops of the Eighteenth and one of the Twenty-second were killed, and seven or eight were wounded. Among the wounded was Major [Thomas B.] Tanner of the Twenty-second; the wound is a severe one, and he is not expected to live."

Tanner survived, becoming a lieutenant colonel and taking another serious wound at Stones River. Left on the field this time, he was captured by Confederates under the command of Brig. Gen. St. John Liddell.

※

Three months after Bull Run, another incident was more precisely reported than was the first major battle. Said the *Washington National Intelligencer* on September 30: "This morning, about one o'clock, as some of the Federal regiments were advancing in the neighborhood of Munson's Hill, VA., Colonel Owen's Irish regiment mistook a portion of Colonel [Edward D.] Baker's for secessionists, and commenced firing upon them. The fire was returned, and before the mistake was discovered nine men were killed and about twenty-five wounded. Among the killed were three officers."

Lt. Col. Dennis O'Kane of the Sixty-ninth Pennsylvania Infantry noted the affair in a rare official report. According to him, men of the regiment were aroused at 11:15 P.M. and ordered by Brig. Gen. William F. "Baldy" Smith to be moving by midnight. Few officers were then aware of the great danger attached to a night movement of any sort.

To make matters worse, both officers and men "were in entire ignorance of the purpose or direction of the movement," O'Kane noted. The sudden appearance of unidentified skirmishers about 1:30 A.M. led to the deadly exchange of fire between the Federal units.

≈≈≈

On the night of October 9, 1861, Confederate Brig. Gen. Richard H. "Fighting Dick" Anderson led about one thousand men and a lone newspaper correspondent to Santa Rosa Island, Florida. By staging his assault before daylight, he hoped to break up the Federal batteries protecting Fort Pickens.

As reported in the *Atlanta Intelligencer*, excited soldiers quickly became disordered. "One cause of the confusion," said the newspaper account "was the strange land we had to climb over and the deep bogs we had to wade."

Union reinforcements from the fort threw attackers into wild confusion. During their chaotic withdrawal, the newspaper correspondent didn't know whether the Confederates had won a victory or suffered a defeat. As published, however, his account was clear concerning a central aspect of the disorganized fray: "*We shot down our own friends in numbers.* Indeed, I think as many of our men were shot by friends as by foes. Night skirmishing is a dangerous business, especially in an unknown country, as was the island of Santa Rosa." Col. Harvey Brown of the Fifth U.S. Artillery estimated Confederate losses during the melee at no fewer than 240 killed or wounded.

≈≈≈

According to the *Boston Transcript*, a few hours after the Florida debacle another body of Confederates set out to attack Federal forces in and around Paducah, Kentucky. "The rebels had divided their forces," newspaper readers were informed, "and in the excitement fired into each other. They then fled, each party taking the other for the National cavalry."

At Belmont, Missouri, a new and highly dangerous variable became central to fatal friendly fire. On November 7, 1861, the town became the target of a joint operation by infantry units supported by Federal gunboats.

When the attacking forces withdrew to the safety of the Mississippi River, Col. N. B. Buford and the Twenty-seventh Illinois Infantry were left on shore. Buford and his men set out for Charleston and reached Bird's Point without incident.

Suddenly Buford had to modify his plans, for gunners on the river boats were not aware of his movements. "To avoid the effect of the shells from the gunboats that were beginning to fall among his men," a Federal report said, "he took a blind path to the river" where he was able to board a steamer.

As the fall of 1861 yielded to winter, officers on both sides expressed confidence that there would be no exchanges of fire between comrades. Their optimism was premature. Close to the spot at which two Federal units fired upon one another near the tip of Virginia's southernmost peninsula, Confederate troops made the same blunder five month later. In its issue of November 16, 1861, the *Memphis Appeal* reported: "Two parties of rebel troops met on the peninsula, above Newport News, Va., and mistook each other for enemies. Brisk firing at once commenced and a number on each side were killed and wounded before the mistake was found out. Among the killed was Major Bailey, of Mobile."

A new year was barely under way before men learned to their dismay that fatal mistakes had not been eliminated. Opposing forces met on January 19, at Mill Springs, Kentucky, also known as Logan's Cross Road. An observer later said that "a moment or two of wild confusion seemed to be an eternity."

Confederate Brig. Gen. Felix K. Zollicoffer took a quick look at the Federal Fourth Kentucky Regiment and thought it to be one of his own units whose men were firing on their friends. His spurs dug into the sides of his horse so he could quickly rectify the error.

When the general came close to the body whose fire he believed should be redirected, he shouted to its leader and pointed to the left with a warning to change directions. "Of course," Col. Speed S. Fry of the Fourth Kentucky is said to have replied. He then lifted his musket to fire a single shot that dropped Zollicoffer from his saddle.

On February 8, 1862, a joint land-sea force of Federals hit Roanoke Island, North Carolina. They scored a decisive victory at the cost of only 260 casualties. Records and diaries fail to indicate how many of these were caused by Confederates and how many were due to friendly fire.

Spanish-born Col. Edward Ferrero of the Fifty-first New York Volunteers, later a brevet major general, said that he "commanded the men to lie down in order to avoid the shower of bullets from our own troops." These bullets, he wrote, came from men of the Ninth New Jersey and Ninth New York Regiments. With a presence of mind rare under such circumstances, Ferrero directed his bugler to "Cease Fire!" Once the clear notes of the instrument were heard above the sounds of battle, all the troops in the vicinity stopped firing on their comrades.

One week later another joint force set out to capture Confederate-held Fort Donelson on Cumberland River. This time, Union gunners were responsible for a gross error that came close to sinking one of their own vessels.

Cmdr. Henry Walke of the USS *Carondelet*—destined to figure in many engagements—penned two short reports. According to them, men aboard the USS *Tyler* fired a shell that exploded a short distance astern of the *Carondelet*. Iron penetrated the case mating of the warship, but it escaped disaster.

At Pea Ridge, Arkansas, confusion of the wildest sort reigned on March 7, 1862. Early in the day's fighting, Federal gunners shelled their own troops. Hours later as dusk approached, both Confederate and Union artillery batteries were for a time trained upon men in blue. A battalion of the Twenty-fifth Illinois Regiment, let by Maj. Frederic Nodine, was hardest hit by the barrage from Federal gunners.

Rival bands of Cherokees had been brought into Confederate service. Those led by Stand Watie came willingly, but others had been coerced into the ranks. During heavy fighting, these groups separated and began firing at one another. Unlike most instances in which soldiers shot their comrades by accident, this action was deliberate. When nightfall brought an end to the day's struggle, *New York Herald* reporter Thomas W. Knox filed a grim report. "In camp on that night," he said, "everything was in confusion."

Accounts of the *Monitor-Virginia* battle focus on the revolutionary nature of the clash between the two ironclads. Survivors were, however, bitter in their denunciation of both the carelessness and the inaccuracy of the Union gunners.

On Saturday afternoon, March 8, 1862, the CSS *Virginia* steamed in Hampton Roads, heavily defended by Federal batteries on shore. Two tiny gunboats, the *Beaufort* and the *Raleigh*, served as escorts for the mighty vessel.

Almost as soon as she was within the waterway, the *Virginia* headed toward the wooden Federal fleet. When the thirty-gun USS *Cumberland* was rammed, she began taking on water rapidly and sank about 3:30. An hour later, having been forced aground, the USS *Congress* surrendered.

Capt. Franklin Buchanan, commander of the Confederate marauder, saw that the *Congress* would soon sink. Her decks were crowded with seamen, he noted. Hence he signaled for men aboard the *Beaufort* and the *Raleigh* to rescue those about to drown. In addition to the Federals, many aboard the Union vessel were prisoners of war who had survived the heavy shelling of the ironclad.

An estimated twenty to thirty prisoners of war soon crowded into the Confederate gunboats with some of their captors. Union shore batteries then opened up on those who were fleeing from the doomed *Congress*. Almost simultaneously, the guns of the sinking warship were turned on the lifeboats holding both Union and Confederate fighting men.

Lt. Robert D. Minor of the *Virginia* was wounded by what the Confederates denounced as "that foul act of treachery." Displaying little concern for himself, Minor angrily testified that shells from the Federal guns on shore "killed some of their own men, among them a lieutenant."

More friendly fire occurred when the USS *Monitor* arrived the next day. W. F. Keeler, paymaster of the Federal "cheese box on a raft," insisted that two of the twenty-three shots that hit the vessel came from the USS *Minnesota*. Naval gunners seeking to sink the Confederate vessel aimed too low and blasted the ironclad that had come to rescue them, Keeler said.

Big Bethel, Bull Run, and Pea Ridge provided spectacular demonstrations of friendly fire in engagements on land; hence many commanders learned to take precautions. During three days of fierce fighting at Shiloh, they learned that the problem had not been solved completely.

On April 6, 1862, Federals of the Orleans Guard went into battle wearing splendid dress blue uniforms. When the action became heavy, these men were easy targets for a hail of Confederate bullets. One by one, they turned their uniforms inside out. Yet after this change had been effected, men no longer easily identified as belonging to Union units became targets of comrades still boldly displaying their blue.

Viewed from the perspective of Richmond, casualties among the Orleans Guard were minor in importance compared with the loss of one man in gray. Widely known as the South's most able commander, Gen. Albert Sidney Johnston was struck by a nearly spent Minié ball while directing front-line operations.

Aides failed to realize that the six-foot Kentuckian's leg was bleeding profusely. A large artery just below their leader's knee joint had been severed, but little blood was immediately visible. As a result, Johnston bled to death without getting medical attention. Those who examined the body came to a reluctant conclusion. From the location and angle of the wound, it appeared likely that one of the Confederate leader's own men might have fired the accidental, fatal shot.

～～

On May 8, 1862, the president of the United States was exposed to hostile gunfire for the first time. Aboard a steam tug, Abraham Lincoln was near Sewell's Point, eager for a firsthand look at the way in which riverboats could deal with Confederate shore batteries near Norfolk.

By using the USS *Monitor*, *Susquehanna*, and *E.A. Stevens*, the Federals hoped to make short work of land-based foes. As they steamed toward their objective, men aboard the *Stevens* were keenly aware that they were less than one mile behind the president. Careful to avoid hitting his tug, they elevated their Parrott gun to lob shells into the shore batteries.

Lincoln escaped without a scratch, but vessels that made up the little flotilla did not fare equally well. Men aboard the *Monitor* listened with horrified amazement as shrapnel from the *Stevens* screamed toward the ironclad. Some shells fired from the gunboat exploded prematurely and fell far short of their objectives on shore.

Aboard the *Susquehanna*, crew members saw a spanker take a direct hit from the rifled gun of their sister vessel. "Only an act of Providence saved Abraham Lincoln from a random shell fired by one of his own gunboats," a participant in the action concluded.

～～

On June 1, opposing forces prepared for a brisk skirmish at Strasburg, Virginia. In predawn darkness, firing from the rear created a wild stampede by Confederates who fled from rain-soaked tents. Men of the Sixth Virginia Cavalry rushed through the camp of the Second Virginia Cavalry before the latter knew what was happening.

Continuing their hasty flight, some members of the Sixth Cavalry burst into a clearing occupied by men of the Seventh Louisiana Infantry. Busy cooking their breakfast, the startled members of the Louisiana force, sure that the enemy had caught them off guard, delivered a volley against the Virginia cavalrymen.

At Corinth, Mississippi, the general officer of the day of Brig. Gen. John Pope's army learned how suddenly friendly fire can erupt. Maj. Frank J. Jones of the Sixth Ohio Infantry noted in his journal that at daybreak "all was quiet."

Suddenly men throughout the Union force were horrified to receive word of another tragedy caused by some of their comrades. Describing the last hour of the victim, Jones wrote: "He was inspecting the picket line and testing the qualities of a soldier stationed at one of the most dangerous points. Notwithstanding the challenge given him, he continued to advance—and paid the penalty of his rashness by receiving a mortal wound at the hands of this faithful soldier. The officer was popular, and his death was deeply lamented."

A trio of memorable incidents near Malvern Hill, Virginia, occurred on July 1, 1862. When Federal gunboats on the James River opened fire, "all their shot landed in or close by a Union battery."

Describing the debacle later, Maj. Gen. Fitz-John Porter said that the accidental killing proceeded for some time. It stopped only when a member of the Signal Service flashed an urgent message to commanders of gunboats: "For God's sake stop firing."

Porter admitted that he never learned what took place as a result of one of his orders of the same day. At his direction, three batteries headed toward Crew's Hill with instructions to "join in the fight if necessary, but not to permit the advance of the foe, even if it must be arrested at the risk of firing upon friends."

By dusk, Confederate units were, if possible, in greater confusion than the Federals. Without authorization, one of Brig. Gen. John B. Magruder's officers went to the front to try to separate two brigades. Eventually he managed to station them almost a mile apart. Yet as light dimmed rapidly, forces commanded by Brig. Gen. Joseph B. Kershaw and Brig. Gen. Paul J. Semmes were fired upon, not from the enemy in front, but from the rear. How many of the five thousand dead and wounded were casualties of friendly fire, no commander dared estimate.

The largest single-day casualty list of the war occurred on September 17, 1862, part of which stemmed from an epidemic of friendly fire. Of the estimated twelve thousand men in blue who fell that day, about twenty-two hundred went down in a corn field near Antietam during a period of twenty minutes.

Federal officers never liked to admit that some men became so panic-stricken that they ran from their enemies. Survivors never wavered in their insistence that when this happened, Union gunners opened fire on chaotic masses in which many of their own colleagues were intermingled with temporarily victorious Confederates. On the Joseph Poffenberger farm, about four hundred men were killed or wounded in a matter of minutes. Many of them were casualties of two volleys fired from Federal regiments. While trying to flank a stone wall, men of two units in blue thought they were facing the enemy, so they leveled their fire at one another.

Maj. Gen. Joseph K. Mansfield, who later received a mortal wound that day, was horrified at witnessing an action he was powerless to stop. Men of the Tenth Maine Infantry halted briefly in a field bordered by Smoketown Road. They spotted a band of soldiers scurrying for cover in the East Woods, so they quickly opened fire. Mansfield tried to order them to cease fire, but confusion was so great that the message never reached them. By the time the men from Maine had emptied their guns, those stragglers in blue who were not lying on the field had made it to safety in the woods.

At another center of chaotic action, men of the Fifty-ninth New York Infantry were told to stop a frontal assault by Confederates. Hastily reloading their guns and without having had a signal, they fired almost in concert—directly into the backs of the men of the Fifteenth Maine Infantry. Col. John W. Kimball of the target regiment raced to the side of Maj. Gen. Edwin V. Sumner. "For God's sake," he reputedly shouted to commander, "tell the New Yorkers to cease fire; they're killing your men as fast as the enemy!"

On the Mumma farm during the same day's action, men of the Fourteenth Connecticut Infantry halted briefly near the edge of another corn field. A picket spotted men running toward them, so a spontaneous but ragged volley was fired. Only when men in advance of the rest reached the line of soldiers in blue did the Connecticut troops learn that they had cut down comrades under the command of Brig. Gen. Max Weber.

Even veteran soldiers manning some Union batteries added to casualties caused by friendly fire that day at Antietam. With darkness rapidly approaching, gunners of a Maryland battery decided to get off a few more shots. Seeking to fire over the heads of troops making up a regiment from Maine, they underestimated the range. As a result, their first round took out four Federals, and their second knocked a lieutenant from his horse.

Barely halfway through the war, the toll from friendly fire was mounting rapidly. Instead of abating, it plagued combat units on both sides for another eighteen months. Irwinville, Georgia, was the site of the last documented instance.

On May 10, 1865, scattered forces led by Brig. Gen. James H. Wilson converged on a party of fleeing Southerners who included Jefferson Davis. With the capture of the Confederate president only minutes away, cavalrymen in blue were in a fever of excitement.

Men of two regiments found what they believed to be clues and raced toward them independently. As they approached their target they opened fire, not upon Confederates, but upon one another. In this final instance of fatal friendly fire, two Federal riders died and a number of their comrades were wounded.

Probably the most famous instance of friendly fire occurred in May 1863 near the hamlet of Chancellorsville, Virginia. A single shot by a soldier in gray may have been one of the most decisive of the millions of shots fired during the war.

Lt. Gen. Thomas J. "Stonewall" Jackson was executing Robert E. Lee's audacious plan that led to a stunning Confederate victory on May 4, 1863. With the attack having started late in the afternoon of May 2, Jackson and several of his staff had ridden out between the lines to reconnoiter that night. The lines between the two armies, however, were not clearly delineated, and with reports that Union cavalry were patrolling the woods, a North Carolina unit opened fire on a cluster of riders moving toward them. A single ball shattered Jackson's left arm. The arm was amputated, but the general developed pneumonia while he was being removed from the area as a consequence of his wound. The man whom Lee called his "strong right arm" died a short week later, the most celebrated and important victim of Civil War friendly fire.

Thirty

ACCIDENTALLY ON PURPOSE

Men under the command of Brig. Gen. Nathaniel Lyon swore never to forget that he ordered them to fire on civilians during a Saint Louis riot. Although friends and relatives of those who were killed donned blue because they loved the Union, they admitted they'd like to see Lyon dead.

Haters of the commander had plenty of opportunities to act during chaotic fighting at Wilson's Creek, Missouri, in August 1861. When the career military officer dropped from his saddle, dead before he hit the ground, it was impossible to know who had fired the fatal bullet. A rumor, undocumented but widespread, suggested that the battle had provided an opportunity for one of his men to settle an old score.

Despite the fact that a man put his life on the line when he wrote about execution-style killings, some clear-cut reports were penned. Although an older term than friendly fire, fragging had not yet entered general use at war's end. Regardless of what it was called, there is no question that it flourished.

Hatred of callous and brutal commanders was behind many a sudden death. Others stemmed from resentment at unit reorganizations. This often occurred when a regiment or a brigade was overmanned while others had not met their quotas. Men shifted into strange units under officers for whom they had not voted were prone to respond with challenges or violence.

Some fractious words that were never translated into fatal action were too serious to be ignored. Strangely, many more threats and murders from within the victim's command show up in Federal letters and diaries than in Confederate sources.

Tempers were on edge among men of the Seventy-ninth New York Infantry after the battle of Bull Run. Out of three hundred officers and men in its ranks, at least sixty did not survive the first battle of the war. Comprised largely of soldiers who were proud of their Scottish blood, the regiment suffered what even U.S. Secretary of War Simon Cameron labeled as an abuse of power.

Hoping to soothe frayed feelings, Washington instructed the unit's acting commander, Lt. Col. Samuel M. Elliott, to prepare for an election of a new commanding officer. It was imperative, he was told, to replace Col. James Cameron, a casualty of the Manassas fray. As in many Federal units, the top staff officer of the Seventy-ninth would be chosen, not by a vote among the ranks, but by a conclave of commissioned officers.

With the elections set for the afternoon of August 13, 1861, enlisted men grumbled louder than ever. Many of them declared that they'd serve under no colonel unless he was properly elected.

Seventy-two hours before the all-important election, Col. Isaac Stevens arrived at the camp and took command. Papers showed that he had been appointed from Washington on July 30. A West Point graduate and veteran of the Mexican War, he immediately made it clear that he was a spit-and-polish professional soldier who would tolerate no nonsense.

Six officers, including Maj. David McClellan and Capt. Thomas Barclay, resigned when Stevens took charge. At a dress parade following their departure, the men of the regiment were told by Stevens that they must move their camp to Maryland immediately. Their anger was exacerbated by their having earlier received an unauthorized promise that they would be sent to New York City for reorganization.

Before dawn on August 14, three-fourths of the regiment had vowed that they would obey no order from Stevens. When he instructed the men to strike their tents, they stood motionless and jeered at him. Furious, the new colonel directed officers to do the job, preparatory to moving.

As junior officers stalked through the camp knocking supports from tents, a private lifted a loaded musket and pointed it at Lt. William Lusk, muttering, "It was appointed for at least one officer to die." Just as he pulled the trigger, a comrade knocked the weapon upward and away from the officer. Lusk, who wrote home about the incident, would have been the first documented victim of fragging had his foe's shot gone as intended.

~~~

A camp incident such as that which took place in the ranks of the Seventy-ninth New York was rare. One week prior to this dramatic near miss, Federals under Bvt. Col. E. R. S. Canby of the Tenth Infantry had clashed with retreating Confederates.

According to the *Rebellion Record*, the opposing forces met near Santa Fe, New Mexico. "A battle ensued, in which the rebels were routed. Col. Sibley [possibly misnamed by newspaper correspondents familiar with Federal Col. C. C. Sibley] was assassinated by his own men, who charged him with drunkenness and inefficiency."

~~~

On January 14, 1862, the *Cincinnati Gazette* reprinted a letter that had appeared earlier in the *Louisville Courier*. According to it, men making up the Irish Tigers from New Orleans nearly rebelled when two of their number were shot "for some trifling military offense."

The letter writer, who didn't dare attach his name to his report, continued: "As a sequel to the execution of the two 'Tigers,' by order of court-martial, I have to record that, yesterday morning, *the bodies of two officers of the Seventh Louisiana regiment were found with their throats cut.* They were the officers of the day and of the guard, at the time of the commission of disrespect by the 'Tigers,' and were instrumental in bringing them to punishment."

On March 1, the *Pittsburgh Chronicle* published a detailed account from a local soldier. Having frequently been in close contact with captured Confederates, said the writer, he was confident of a Federal victory very soon. This stemmed in part, he wrote, from the fact that "Gen. [Leonidas] Polk has not the confidence of a single man in the army. He swears like a trooper, and in case of a fight he will be the first to be shot, and by his own soldiers."

With Federal forces on the attack, former U.S. Secretary of War John B. Floyd was in command at Fort Donelson in Tennessee. Without notice, the man who was now a prominent Confederate turned his command over to Brig. Gen. Simon Buckner and made his escape, leaving Buckner to be forced into unconditional surrender by Brig. Gen. U.S. Grant.

Reporting the fashion in which the former cabinet member had saved his own skin, the *New York Times* reported, "The feeling was so strong against Floyd, that several of the confederate soldiers fired at him as he was leaving, and it is asserted by many that he was killed."

News of Floyd's death at the hands of his own men was premature. On March 11, Jefferson Davis relieved from command the reported target and transferred him into the Virginia militia.

Fighting in the Shenandoah Valley under the leadership of Stonewall Jackson, Brig. Gen. C. S. Winder was said to be targeted for death by his own men. He punished soldiers right and left, once ordering thirty of them to be bucked and gagged simultaneously.

This punishment, commonly inflicted by both sides, was seldom life-threatening. A culprit was gagged, usually by having a stick pushed into his mouth. With hands and feet tied while he was sitting on the ground with knees drawn between his arms, he had a tree limb inserted over his arms and under his knees.

"This fellow won't ride away from our next battle," Winder's men whispered to one another. In spite of this rumor, the general survived both the Valley campaign and the Seven Days. At the start of the Cedar Mountain action, he was so sick that he went into battle in an ambulance. Official reports say he was killed by Federal artillery on August 7, 1862. Veterans who had served under him were never positive that this account of his death was accurate.

Col. Thomas T. Heath of the Fifth Ohio Cavalry received a new recruit late in July 1862. Calling himself Bully Butcher Boy, the new member of the regiment soon found himself punished by buck and gag.

Unable to form words, Bully Butcher Boy fumed and snorted while forced to remain motionless for hours in front of his new comrades. As soon as he was released from his punishment, he rushed behind his colonel's back and mouthed a silent promise: "First time we get into the smoke, Little Colonel, I'll empty your saddle!"

Though Heath survived the war, he did not forget the incident from which he learned never to turn his back upon his men during battle.

⚶

Educated men in the ranks of the Fifth Iowa Infantry described Col. W. H. Worthington as "a military martinet." In September 1862, the officer, who knew most of his men hated him, scouted an enemy position and then started back to his own lines. A picket stationed behind a tree saw him coming, stepped into the clear, and fired a bullet that struck the colonel in the middle of his forehead.

Arrested and tried, the killer was acquitted but the verdict convinced only a minority of men in the regiment. Many of them wrote home about the incident, stressing their conviction that Worthington—who had received many threats—had been murdered in cold blood.

About the time Worthington died, Federal Brig. Gen. William "Bull" Nelson was the subject of a plot. His nickname grew out of the way he roared orders and obscenities to his men. Described as having "an imperious temper, demoniac energy, and brutal manners," he boasted that he once "personally cut down some Union men who fought badly."

Many of the men in his command were Hoosiers who had known each other since boyhood. According to the *Cincinnati Enquirer*, they banded together and swore to kill Nelson the next time they went into battle.

Nelson, however, did not take a bullet in the back. Brig. Gen. Jefferson C. Davis, a subordinate with a fiery temper who had grown up in Indiana, quarreled with the intemperate Nelson in public. On the day before Union troops were scheduled to march south, Davis murdered Nelson in a Louisville hotel.

Brig. Gen. Thomas Williams, a native of New York who grew up in Michigan, entered the U.S. Army after graduating from West Point in 1837. Professional soldiers learned to lie under his dictatorial leadership, but the volunteers whom he commanded from 1861 to 1862 did not.

While posted in North Carolina, he twice fell into carefully prepared traps that his men labeled "pitfalls." After having quarreled with many of his officers, he was transferred to the West. During the August 5, 1862, battle of Baton Rouge, Williams died in action.

A widely circulated story, never documented, asserts that he was killed by artillery rather than by small-arms fire. According to this account, the tyrannical brigadier was seized by a group of his own men, who held him in front of a cannon, before signaling for it to be fired at the enemy.

Confederate Brig. Gen. Thomas R. R. Cobb acquired a reputation as an abuser of his soldiers during the Seven Days and at Second Bull Run in July and August 1862. He led his brigade to Fredericksburg, where he died under strange circumstances on December 13. Oral tradition asserts that there was no doubt that he was shot from behind by one or more of his own men.

Union Maj. Gen. Frank P. Blair Jr., brother of a member of Lincoln's cabinet, was widely blamed for murders in the streets of Saint Louis. Although he was not present when Nathaniel Lyon's men cut down civilians on those streets, the evidence supports the view that his policies helped to create the crisis that led to the riot.

Some soldiers in blue, though devoted to the Union, never forgave Blair for his role in the mass tragedy. As a division commander in the Seventeenth Corps during the Atlanta campaign, he realized that he was the subject of pent-up anger.

Recalling that period, Capt. Chester G. Higbee of the Twelfth Wisconsin Infantry later wrote: "Finally, a man (I think from the Sixteenth Wisconsin) fired at the general in open daylight and was arrested and it was said by the guards that the soldier frankly told General Blair that he intended to kill him. This ill-feeling was so general that I have often wondered why General Blair continued in command of that corps."

Six feet tall and inordinately proud of the number of horses killed under him, George A. Custer became a brigadier general at the age of twenty-three. His promotion meant that numerous older men, who considered him a stranger, were forced to serve under him.

Custer stripped some officers of their rank, ordered one to a court-martial, and sent culprits to the gallows on the slightest provocation. As a result, men he dubbed "western ruffians" came close to staging a mutiny.

Custer pretended to be oblivious of the dissidence; not so his wife, Libby. According to her, a stream of threats came to their home. Staff members, whose tents were pitched on the lawn before the Custer home, "tried to persuade the general to lock the doors and bolt the windows." Custer survived the war but went down at the Little Big Horn in 1876 at the hands of Native Americans.

※

At least one Union officer reversed the usual pattern of fragging by killing a subordinate. A sergeant of a Pennsylvania regiment reputedly defied Col. Samuel P. Spear of the Eleventh Pennsylvania Cavalry. "Damn you," he's believed to have told the colonel, "you have drafted us, but you can't make us fight."

Hours after the verbal clash, Spear shot and killed the rebellious sergeant without the presence of witnesses. When charged by the *Wilkes-Barre Union* with having murdered a subordinate, Spear refused to comment.

※

Even an enlisted man was not immune from the danger that a comrade would treat him as though he were a member of an enemy force. Pvts. John Rowley and Jerome Dupoy of the Seventh Connecticut Infantry quarreled, then fought with knives. Dupoy got the better of his comrade and left him with a series of deep flesh wounds.

Rowley put his knife aside but swore that he'd find a chance to get revenge. It came during the February 1864 battle of Olustee, Florida. When Dupoy was killed instantly by a single shot in the head, a court-martial was convened. Through its verdict, Rowley became the only man known to have been executed for having killed a member of his own company.

※

Brig. Gen. Jefferson C. Davis, the unpunished killer of Brig. Gen. William Nelson, commanded the Seventeenth Corps during Sherman's march from Atlanta to Savannah. Near the coast, Davis was forced to build a pontoon bridge to get his men across Ebenezer Creek. Once over, he destroyed the bridge to prevent escaped slaves, or contrabands, from continuing to follow his force.

Dr. James C. Patten, a corps surgeon, labeled these actions of his commander as "dastardly." To his journal he confided that he'd have Davis hanged if he had the power to do so. He ended his account of the matter by saying: "There is great indignation among the troops. I should not wonder if the valiant murderer of women and children should meet with an accident before long." The expectations—or hopes—of Patten were never realized; Davis survived until 1879.

According to Sgt. Maj. H. W. Manson of Dale's Confederate Sharpshooters, an unidentified Federal was unfortunate. At what Manson called "point blank range of less than forty steps," he saw "a tall, angular Federal" fall when he turned a Sharpe's rifle upon him.

Two days later, a wounded prisoner walked into a hospital tent where the Confederate was working temporarily. He instantly recognized the man he had dropped and found that his ball had hit his opponent's collarbone. To his surprise though, the most visible wound was near the back of the jaw of the soldier in blue.

Questioned, he tried to seem casual as he explained to Manson that after having been knocked down by the Confederate rifle ball, "Some of our own cowardly fellows shot me in the jaw when I got up."

Logic asserts that for every instance of fragging reported, there must have been many more similar incidents. From private to brigadier general, few on either side of the conflict were 100 percent sure they wouldn't be dropped by calculated fire from a comrade in arms.

Thirty-one

THINGS THAT COULDN'T BE COUNTED

After every battle, commanders wanted a reasonably accurate casualty count, an all-important matter in an official report. Since there was no way to ascertain the number of opposing soldiers who had been wounded, many generals employed a formula. They multiplied the known dead by six or seven to estimate the total casualties in an opposing force.

Naturally, most or all leaders of armies, corps, and brigades tried to minimize their own losses and magnify the losses of the enemy. Accuracy could be attained only by a tally of rosters in a given command, and this activity was seldom pursued in the aftermath of a major battle.

Arms, legs, heads, and other body parts were all-important to men who lost them, but they are rarely mentioned in military records. Letters, diaries, and memoirs are the only significant sources of information about these things that were of monumental significance to those who left them behind.

Enemy fire consistently severed arms, legs, and heads, not only from bodies of soldiers, but also from their mounts. William W. Loring spent much of the war as a Confederate brigadier, functioning with only one arm—he had left the other about three miles from Mexico City. A spent bullet knocked him unconscious in the September 12, 1847, battle of Chapultepec, so he always joked that he got off lightly, as he might have lost his head instead of his arm.

337

Irish-born Thomas Sweeny marched off to Mexico with the First New York Volunteers. In the 1848 battle of Churubusco he lost his right arm. Habitually keeping his empty right sleeve folded, the professional soldier reached the rank of captain on January 19, 1861, and just four months later became a Federal brigadier.

After every major battle, surgeons went to work with saws. More often than not, huge piles of severed limbs accumulated wherever they worked.

At Gettysburg, Federal medical officers were more meticulous than usual. They dumped amputated limbs into big barrels that were buried soon after they were filled. Months later, when decomposition of flesh was complete, the barrels were dug up and sent to the medical college in Washington. Used in teaching, these bones meant that many a veteran contributed to a doctor's education without knowing about it.

Inevitably, the conflict produced tens of thousands of severed body parts that disappeared without a trace. In a few instances, something is known about these byproducts of battle—with hair dominating the record.

Members of the Twelfth Mississippi Infantry were too late to be able to brag about helping to win a smashing victory at Bull Run. Members of the regiment spent the night of Sunday, July 21, traveling between Lynchburg and Manassas, Virginia. They didn't reach Manassas Junction until the first big encounter of the war was over.

One member of the unit, Pvt. T. G. Dabney, never tired of telling how astonished he was when he reached the field of battle. "We jumped off our train near a cluster of little shacks that were being used as field hospitals," he recalled. "It was impossible for a fellow who had never been in conflict to take his eyes off bloody dismembered limbs that had accumulated in huge piles."

On the second day at Gettysburg, Union Maj. Gen. Daniel E. Sickles took a direct hit from a Confederate shell. Within thirty minutes a surgeon had finished amputating his mangled leg.

Sickles loudly demanded that it be preserved in alcohol, but he soon became tired of it and donated it to the U.S. Army Medical Museum. Tradition says he visited his leg several times during the postwar years but never remained with it more than a few minutes.

At Stones River Pvt. John Long achieved distinction, of a sort. Confederate iron and lead mangled one of his legs so that there was no hope it could be saved. Unwilling to wait for a surgeon to act, the wounded man in blue pulled out his pocketknife and went to work. Long is the only soldier positively known to have amputated what remained of his own leg.

During the battle of Port Hudson, a round from a Union battery blew off the leg of Capt. R. M. Boone. Aware that he had only a few minutes to live, the Confederate artillery officer made a dying request. Records do not indicate whether or not men of his battery complied with it. His last wish, he said, was to have his severed leg stuffed into one of his guns and shot toward the enemy.

Union Col. Ulric Dahlgren, who was killed in the Kilpatrick-Dahlgren raid on Richmond, had earlier acquired a splendid wooden leg. After his death the artificial limb went on display in the window of a department store in the Confederate capital.

It stayed there only briefly, however. Confederate Lt. James Pollard, head of the unit that ambushed Dahlgren, soon lost his own leg. He claimed Dahlgren's as prize of war and tried to have it fitted for him. Finding that he couldn't use that piece of Federal wood himself, Pollard gave the leg to amputee John N. Ballard, who wore it for the duration of the war.

Struck by a Union shell at Brandy Station, Confederate Capt. William Farley was soon found by a rescue squad whose members made ready to take him to a field hospital. As he was lifted upon the litter, Farley gestured vigorously and with all the breath he could muster made a poignant plea: "Don't leave my leg lying in this pasture," he implored. "Hand it to me, so I can take it with me."

During the Confederate retreat from Nashville in 1863, a gun was accidentally discharged. The shot hit a Private Allen of the Thirty-sixth Alabama Infantry with such force that the only hope of saving his life lay in immediate amputation.

Chaplain L. M. Hutton agreed to remain with the soldier after the hasty surgery. Soon the pair of stragglers was captured by a Federal unit.

Recalling the memorable day, Hutton said that as soon as he saw the blue-coats coming, his first act was to bury Allen's leg. He didn't have time, however, to erect for it even a crude wooden marker of the sort often used on battlefields.

Near Adairsville, Georgia, Federal surgeons established a field hospital in the loft of what had once been a fine brick store. They treated a few wounded

Confederates as well as their own men, with surgery being the most common procedure. Upon evacuating the impromptu surgical theater, they were charged with having buried severed limbs of Union soldiers while deliberately leaving behind "the amputated leg of an unfortunate rebel."

Alfred R. Waud, a native of England, is believed to have executed more Civil War sketches than any other artist during the war. In 1862 he moved from the *New York Illustrated* news to *Harper's Weekly*, whose readers quickly came to look for his signature. Waud followed the Army of the Potomac in all of its major campaigns and often sent to New York sketches of everyday events in the lives of soldiers.

At an unidentified field hospital the artist saw surgeons at work, using the stump of a big tree as an operating table. A man whose right leg had just been amputated was being taken away on a stretcher.

Editors frequently lauded Waud for the accuracy of his work. This time, however, they considered him to have been too meticulous. Readers would be appalled at the horrors of war if his surgical sketch should be published as he submitted it, the management decided.

Unwilling to discard a vivid illustration, staff artists were told to turn the wounded man around to that the stump of his leg wouldn't be seen. It was this revised version that was published for wartime viewing. Yet the original piece of art, with the bandaged stump of a leg clearly visible, eventually found a home. It is preserved in the Library of Congress.

Arms were probably severed from bodies even more frequently than legs. Sometimes action took place with no surgery involved. After the battle of Antietam, a survivor proudly discussed the deadly work done by guns of Federal Battery B.

Every time a cannon roared, he said, the gunner's aim was so precise that debris briefly filled the air. Ripped haversacks and broken handguns became almost commonplace as they rose, and then dropped back to the ground. In one instance, recalled the Union gunner, "A severed arm still covered with a gray sleeve shot 30 feet into the air before it gently spiraled back toward the point at which the fellow who once relied upon it was lying upon his back."

Also at Antietam, Lt. Ezra E. Stickley of the Fifth Virginia Infantry suffered irreparable losses. When recuperating from injuries, he bemoaned having left behind a splendid horse and all of his personal belongings. Even worse, he said, when brigade surgeons took off his mangled right arm they casually tossed it under a kitchen table instead of saving it for him.

By far the most notable of severed limbs once went into battle by the side of Stonewall Jackson. At Chancellorsville, when he was hit in the left arm by fire from his own men, the wound required the arm's amputation. Had complications not developed, however, he might have survived the battlefield injury.

After Jackson's death, relatives and admirers saw to it that his severed left arm was given a respectful burial in the graveyard of the Lacy family near Chancellorsville. Soon a gravestone—believed to be the only one of its kind— was erected to mark the last resting place of Jackson's arm.

Hair, whether from the head of a combat victim or not, was valued as a souvenir. That's why the Louisiana Historical Association was glad to receive the gift of an envelope containing hair from the head of Jefferson Davis.

Headed for the gallows, convicted spy Marcellus Clarke (who frequently disguised himself as "Sue Mundy") borrowed a knife from a guard. When he had carefully severed a big hank of his hair, he made the "last request customarily afforded to a man about to die." The hair, he instructed, should be transmitted to men who made up the raiding company he once commanded "and carefully divided among them."

In a gesture of quite different nature, partisan raider John S. Mosby once cut off a lock of hair. Packaged for transmission along with a letter, he dispatched it to the White House in Washington.

There's no certainty that Abraham Lincoln ever saw the Confederate hair sent to him to emphasize threats that the president was likely soon to have his head shaved as a preliminary to his execution.

Richard Slade, a private who fought in gray, rejoiced at his good fortune. During a furious battle he received a direct hit but was uninjured except for a shattered left hand.

Writing to his loved ones, Slade told them of his injury and added: "It looks hard to see them take off legs & arms & cut men into pieces—but thank God, they got only a little part of me."

Jesse James, who fought briefly as a Confederate partisan, managed to dodge Federal bullets. Probably while engaged in target practice, he clipped off the end of one of his fingers. Though the body part involved was tiny, it eventually proved to be important. That missing fingertip was vital to identification of James's body when he was murdered in 1880.

Union forces involved in an early expedition aimed at coastal installations in North Carolina had never "seen the elephant," a phrase meaning that one had been in combat. An amphibious force that landed in near darkness spent the night without shelter and the next morning marched toward a Confederate fort.

When the Southerners' big guns began to boom, men in blue fell right and left. One of them, an unnamed captain, was apparently uninjured except that he lost his head when he fell.

Awed comrades, surveying the headless body of their friend, wondered what had happened. They eventually agreed that a cannon ball had created so strong a wind that it decapitated the man whose head it barely missed.

In Kansas, one of William C. Quantrill's raiders was so ruthless that he became known as Bloody Bill Anderson. After having formed his own band of partisans, he frequently led them into Missouri.

Near the hamlet of Orrick, he failed to realize that Union forces were waiting to ambush him. As soon as he came within range of their guns, his body was riddled with lead.

Victorious Federal soldiers dumped the body of the guerrilla fighter into a cart and hauled it to the village of Richmond, Missouri. They triumphantly mounted Bloody Bill's severed head on the highest telegraph pole in the area.

Anderson's one-time commander was treated with even less respect. After Confederate reverses in 1864, Quantrill set out for Washington with the avowed purpose of assassinating Lincoln.

He never came close to fulfilling his objective. While hiding out in Kentucky he was discovered by Federal troops and wounded. Quantrill died of his wounds three weeks later on June 6, 1865, in a prison hospital. He was buried in an unmarked grave. Logically, that should have ended his movements, but it did not.

Years later, biographer Albert Castel learned that twelve years after Quantrill's death the guerrilla leader's mother received permission to move the remains to a family cemetery. For this undertaking she enlisted the aid of William C. Scott, a long-time friend.

Believing himself to have been handed a bonanza, Scott stole Quantrill's skull and several bones from his arms and legs. They didn't attract the interest he expected and no one offered a fancy price for the relics. As a result, the bones of the Kansas border ruffian eventually went to the state historical society in Topeka. Quantrill's skull didn't accompany them, however. For reasons unknown, it wound up in the collection of the Dover Historical Society in Delaware.

More than thirty years after the hostilities ended, the Louisiana Historical Society published a list of relics presented to it by twenty-three donors during a period of just three months.

Among the 130 items with which private owners parted was a gift from Mrs. Charles L. Ball of Saint Louis. Because of "its historical significance," she some-what reluctantly sent to the society "a lock of hair of Gen. [Felix K.] Zollicoffer, clipped by her father while the General's body was in the hands of the Federals, who killed him.

Another item in the same inventory came from Mrs. W. H. Adams. She described it as "one iron fork, with handle made from the bone of a dead Federal soldier." According to the donor, this trophy was given to Pat Barrow, her father, during his 1863 imprisonment in New Orleans.

At least one famous animal contributed to the small store of body parts about which we know at least a little. After the battle of Bull Run, a captain in the Federal Topographical Engineers bought a wounded horse that he named Baldy.

Baldy took his owner to Fredericksburg and Chancellorsville, then to Pennsylvania and Gettysburg. He survived his master by a few years, and at his death executors of the estate of Maj. Gen. George G. Meade had the horse's head mounted—complete with mane.

Eventually presented to Philadelphia's War Library and Museum, the head of Meade's horse became a fixture at meetings of the Civil War Round Table in the City of Brotherly Love.

Quantrill's skull, Sickles's leg, and Jackson's arm, collectively, fall short of the importance of one small collection of body parts. Dried drops of blood, tiny fragments of bone, and bits of tissue make up this treasure trove. It represents samples salvaged from the body of Abraham Lincoln before he was prepared for burial.

Small as they are, these specimens have potential for unlocking a major riddle. By subjecting them to DNA tests, it is believed possible to learn whether or not the president was afflicted with Marfan syndrome. This condition causes elongation of arms and legs, often affects the heart, and can lead to early death. Because of the president's physical appearance, Lincoln may have been afflicted with the syndrome and might have had a very short life expectancy at the time he was assassinated.

Custodians of these bits and pieces that represent all that remain of Abraham Lincoln's body have so far refused to permit them to be tested. They may hold the solution to a puzzle that may never be solved.

Part Seven

THINGS CHANGE

L ife was relatively stable, almost static, when Alfred Lord Tennyson penned his "Locksley Hall." Yet even in that placid era he foretold: "Let the great world spin forever down the ringing grooves of change." Until the dawn of the electronic age, no period saw America and Americans change as rapidly as during the approximately fourteen hundred days of civil war. It would almost seem that earlier generations had been hoarding energy that would bring about innovations, and launch inventions. War released this pent-up store in such fashion that a torrent of change became a distinguishing mark of the period.

Thirty-two

DOWN THE RINGING GROOVES
OF CHANGE

Seven months after Confederates fired upon Fort Sumter, a headline in Horace Greeley's *New York Herald* proclaimed: *THE GREAT REBELLION A GREAT REVOLUTION.* Taking the long view, an editorial suggested, "Everything the finger of war touches is revolutionized." Even a hasty glance at a few areas of life—civilian as well as military—indicates that the statement was accurate.

Wandering from his native New York to the West, Gail Borden invented what he called a "meat biscuit" in 1851. Two years later he devised a way to reduce the bulk and increase the shelf life of milk. His 1856 patent for condensed milk evoked little or no interest; however, it is worth noting that in April 1861 Capt. Gustavus V. Fox included air-dried or "desiccated" food in his attempt to resupply Fort Sumter.

More than seventy-five thousand volunteers answered Lincoln's call for troops. Yet once they began to assemble, it became obvious that standard kitchen practices would be inadequate. Within months Borden's 1856 patent took on an importance beyond anything the inventor had envisioned. Anticipating an enormous demand, he opened a large "condensary" at Wassaic, New York.

Although initial interest was not as great as Borden had anticipated, following the September 1862 battle at Antietam, the U.S. Sanitary commission initiated an order for twenty-six hundred pounds. At the May 1863 battle of Chancellorsville, Robert E. Lee sent a supply of condensed milk and whiskey for the relief of wounded men in blue who were lying on the field and starving. By the time the conflict was three years old, inmates of Richmond's Libby Prison regarded Borden's product as a necessity.

Hundreds of thousands of soldiers were introduced to condensed milk during the conflict. Once veterans shed their uniforms, the innovation adopted as a military necessity became a staple in civilian life.

Footwear was as vital to both armies as condensed milk and other long-life foods. Members of infantry regiments who were continually on the march wore out shoes faster than new ones could be manufactured. Men fighting under Irvin McDowell, George G. McClellan, Ambrose Burnside, and other Union commanders had to have shoes to take the field against Confederates.

In 1860, an estimated 12,500 establishments made shoes; collectively they employed at least 120,000 workmen. At the time, a skilled cobbler could handcraft three pairs of shoes per day. Forced by necessity to change, the shoe industry abandoned traditional hand manufacture in small shops. Large buildings with lofts and abandoned cotton mills were equipped with stitching machines— power equipment that had been perfected by Lyman R. Blake in 1858 but had seen little use. Once war broke out, Blake's invention became of crucial importance in the North.

Mass produced under the leadership of Gordon McKay, the Blake invention was offered on generous terms. Any shoe manufacturer could modernize his shop for a down payment of five hundred dollars and a royalty of five cents for every pair of shoes stitched. Soon the average worker was turning out six or more pairs of shoes a day. As a result of this radical change in the industrial sector, most soldiers in blue remained well shod after thousands of their foes were forced to go barefoot because they had no shoes.

Clothing manufacturing was transformed within months after the conflict began. With seventy-five thousand men involved in the first Federal call for volunteers, the U. S. War Department had on hand a stock of clothing for only thirteen thousand soldiers.

Especially in Massachusetts, production of woolen uniforms literally exploded. At Lawrence, stockholders put about $2.5 million into building and machinery with which to enter this new field. Wartime dividends from this investment exceeded $3 million and the capital value of the original plant exceeded several times the 1861 figure.

Publisher Erastus Beadle envisioned a vast new market among common soldiers who often spent weeks in camp. Aided by editor Orville, J. Victor, he printed and distributed enormous quantities of dime novels about such characters as Dick Turpin and Red Rover. Today's paperbacks are lineal descendants of Civil War "yellow backs," as they were widely called.

Aboard the USS *Connecticut*, Cmdr. Maxwell Woodhull was faced with the problem of providing well-balanced meals for his men. Fresh beef was needed in huge quantities, so he reluctantly consented to let junior officers resort to a novel technique.

On October 4, 1861, Woodhull reported to U.S. Secretary of the Navy Gideon Welles concerning the innovation developed aboard his ship: "Doubtless you are aware the plan for preserving beef was a new and entirely untried one, on the grand scale attempted in this vessel. It consisted of what is called an ice and chill room, something in the style of a refrigerator on shore. I did not approve of it from the very first moment I saw it. I saw nothing but a great consumer of ice, without the corresponding amount of cold element promised from it. There were 400 quarters of beef hung on hooks and stowed together as close as possible. I did not believe that the cold air, even if ever so abundant, could penetrate the mass sufficiently to preserve it."

Having found himself to be wrong, Woodhull noted that the ice room worked wonders in preserving the ship's beef. The discovery was doubly significant in that the *Connecticut* was on station in Florida waters. Once the experiment became common knowledge, rooms refrigerated with ice were set up in every Northern city.

∼∼∼

The spiraling cost of the war created a fiscal crisis. There was not enough gold and silver in circulation to permit the free flow of commerce while military contracts were soaring in number and size.

U.S. Secretary of the Treasury Salmon P. Chase championed a radical change. Non-interest-bearing government notes were issued to serve as a medium of exchange in lieu of "hard money," or specie. Because they were printed in green ink on one side of the paper, these special war-issue notes were called "greenbacks."

Public opposition to the use of greenbacks was tremendous when they entered circulation. As a result, they depreciated in value and sometimes were traded at a rate of forty cents in gold or silver for a one-dollar greenback. Paper money with a face value of $450 million went into circulation as a result of a series of issues.

Late in 1865, with the war over, legislation was enacted to retire the greenbacks from circulation. Once the plan was initiated, a tremendous howl of public protest echoed throughout the land. People had become accustomed to paper currency and had decided that they liked it. As a result, legal tender issued during a wartime emergency became standard in the United States.

∼∼∼

Although civilian life changed swiftly and radically, the pace of change in military matters was faster and more sweeping. Nevertheless, numerous high-ranking Union leaders looked askance at new-fangled rifles. These weapons were more accurate than muskets, they conceded, yet their wholesale use was not easily approved. Rifles used ammunition too rapidly to suit purchasing agents.

Oliver F. Winchester of Massachusetts didn't intend to go into the manufacture of military rifles, despite the fact that the longtime manufacturer of men's clothing became president of the New Haven Arms Company in 1857. His firm produced fine sporting rifles for the wealthy clientele.

Tyler Henry, superintendent of the Winchester's arms manufacturing company, experimented successfully with rim-fire copper cartridges. At the U.S. War Department the new Henry rifle was not widely recommended, but thousands of individual Federal soldiers armed themselves with it at their own expense.

By war's end, the long-cherished musket was completely obsolete. Spurred by the success of Henry's weapon, Winchester began producing rifles in large quantities. As an indirect result of the Civil War, it was the new Winchester that came to be known as the rifle that tamed the West.

Coffee was high on the list of supplies most in demand by soldiers. Many Confederates were quickly forced to adopt crude substitutes, but Union soldiers insisted on the real thing.

Northern stockpiles of coffee beans were usually adequate to meet the demand, but many commanders balked at letting their men carry the bulky commodity. Wholesale merchants in a major port city, probably Philadelphia, devised what they considered to be a solution to the coffee problem.

Beans were ground to a fine powder, then mixed with sugar and milk to form a thick paste. Easily portable and not prone to spoil, a spoonful of paste and a cup of hot water generated a cup of coffee that a thirsty soldier would drink eagerly. Few civilians would today willingly down the brew, but it was this paste that presaged all modern forms of instant—or dehydrated—coffee.

It is acknowledged that naval warfare was suddenly and permanently altered as a result of an artillery duel between two vessels. Both the Federal *Monitor* and the Confederate *Virginia* (or *Merrimac*) were equipped with thick coats of iron. Their clash at Hampton Roads, Virginia, made wooden warships instantly obsolete; the Civil War innovation represented a giant and lasting step from naval designs and strategies that were centuries old.

Explosive devices not shot from small arms or artillery were a source of prewar interest. Crude kinds of hand grenades had been developed and had seen limited, restricted use. At Fort Sumter, Federal engineers filled huge barrels with gunpowder and planned to detonate them by using trails of powder.

It was not until the war became national in scope that someone devoted full time to experiments with special kinds of explosives. Confederate Brig. Gen. Gabriel Rains perfected a percussion cap so sensitive that it exploded on touch, igniting the powder with which it was connected.

At Yorktown, Virginia, many of the Rains devices were buried in front of Confederate positions. When men in gray withdrew, enemy forces advanced over ground strewn with primitive land mines. Forward movement came to an abrupt halt when a buried charge blew up, often wounding or killing those persons nearest it.

Union authorities were loud in their denunciation of the "infernal devices" that the Confederates had begun to call torpedoes. Their use was branded as a "savage mode of warfare." Yet Federal soldiers and scientists were busy developing new and more sophisticated torpedoes.

Arranged to float beneath the surface of water and to explode on contact, these were the torpedoes that Rear Adm. David G. Farragut damned at Mobile Bay. By war's end, both sides were producing and using torpedoes that could be exploded electrically. Both sides also succeeded in producing "clockwork bombs" whose explosion was predetermined prior to their placement.

Twentieth-century missiles and rockets of every variety, including those drawn to their targets by heat, are descendants of Rains's earliest torpedoes.

Pondering ways to accelerate communication between commanders on the battlefield, George W. Beardslee perfected a mobile telegraph unit. Albert J. Meyer, the chief signal officer of Union forces, was quick to adopt the new Beardslee system.

A typical unit, packed in a wooden box, was the heart of the Federal "flying telegraph train." Containing about five miles of insulated wire, this portable military telegraph was transported in two wagons. Beardslee's invention was so successful that by 1864 few Federal commanders used the time-honored courier rider. Instead, their communications consisted largely of telegrams.

The Southerners never came close to producing or using mobile telegraph systems that were competitive with those of the Federals. No one knows how much this factor contributed to the eventual collapse of the Confederacy, but the predecessor of portable two-way radios soon was in use by civilian field crews of many kinds.

New weapons galore came from the industrial North. Col. Hiram Berdan of the First U.S. Sharpshooters was responsible for at least a half-dozen innovations. One of them, a long-distance rangefinder, had a permanent effect upon the use of artillery throughout the world.

A Confederate officer devised a hand-cranked rapid-fire gun that could fire as many as sixty-five 1.57-inch shells per minute. Production facilities were so limited that this primitive machine gun is believed to have seen service only at the battle of Seven Pines.

Meanwhile, North Carolina native Richard J. Gatling perfected a gun designed to fire 250 rounds per minute. A few of them were used aboard Union warships and during the siege of Petersburg, but they had no significant impact upon the war. After the war, the physician who developed the first modern machine gun touted it as having been created to kill so rapidly that wars would cease to be waged.

Other less visibly dramatic changes than weapons development were taking place, and they had more profound long-range effects. For generations, it had been taken for granted that military nurses would be male members of fighting forces. This was about to change—forever.

Dorothea Dix arrived at the White House with a plan and a mission. Presidential secretaries John G. Nicolay and John Hay recorded their satisfaction at "the arrival of Miss Dix, who comes to offer herself and an army of nurses to the government gratuitously for hospital service." On June 10, 1861, she received a parchment unlike any ever before issued: for the first time the nation had a superintendent of U.S. Army nurses who was female.

Most veterans of military medicine reacted indignantly to Mother Dix's appointment. There were no general hospitals, but some of the larger installations had post hospitals. At Leavenworth, Kansas, there were accommodations for only twenty men.

Even after twenty-four members of the medical corps resigned to join the Confederacy, the U.S. Army still boasted a complement of twenty-seven surgeons and sixty-two assistant surgeons. With militia units due to serve only ninety days, many could not understand what had influenced U.S. Secretary of War Simon Cameron to establish a corps of female nurses.

That question became moot as the first Federal casualties reached Washington from the Manassas battlefield. Before the terrible carnage of the war ended, changing attitudes guaranteed that women would be welcomed to the nursing vocation.

Shortages of manpower opened other doors for women. A few bold spirits with good penmanship won early appointments as clerks in the U.S. Treasury Department. Soon women began to appear in the Patent Office and even in the U.S. War Department.

By early 1865, tens of thousands of women were government employees. Large corporations were beginning, grudgingly, to open their doors to a few women considered to be exceptionally capable. More than all other factors combined, the Civil War served as the foundation upon which the modern women's movement was erected.

A concurrent shift was also occurring at the highest levels of government. Founded from thirteen British colonies, the United States was for decades simply what the name implied: a union, or federation, of semiautonomous states.

Very early, it was clear to Lincoln and his colleagues that a loose conglomeration of political entities could not wage a successful war. Exerting what came to be called "war powers," the president took drastic actions that had the sanction of neither Congress nor the Constitution.

As the war progressed, the power concentrated in the Federal government expanded steadily. At the same time, rights and powers formerly relegated to the states were defined and limited. By the time Lincoln launched his campaign for a second term in the White House, the nature of the Union had been altered radically. With the central government now dominant, governors and legislators found themselves increasingly controlled from Washington.

This radical revision of the U.S. political structure soon began to advance with an impetus of its own. Federal programs, agencies, and regulations proliferated. Federal power loomed larger and larger in the everyday lives of ordinary citizens. In a real sense, the United States of the late twentieth century is the product of a radical shift in the bases of power that were initiated because they were essential to winning the war. If the debate on downsizing the federal government succeeds, subsequent changes could revert the federal-state relationship to its pre-Civil War state.

Thirty-three

THE NAMES WERE CHANGED

Were the Civil War record to include only the birth names of fighting men, the account might be hard to recognize. At least three dozen familiar names differ from those of the originals. Many alterations were deliberately made, often for understandable reasons. Most came about informally and were never made legal. Others were by-products of events over which the owners of the names had no control.

Regardless of why they were fashioned, the altered names rather than the originals appear in the record. An estimated three hundred women joined the fighting forces in disguise; only a fraction of their real and assumed names are known with certainty. In other cases, an informally modified name was treated as though it were legal.

When their first child was born at Point Pleasant, Ohio, in 1822, Jesse R. Grant and his wife, the former Hannah Simpson, had a ready-made name for him. Hiram Ulysses grew up not realizing that part of his name came from classical mythology. He was keenly aware, though, that his schoolmates jeered at it. After all, very few youngsters are saddled with names whose initials form a word so potent among juveniles as "HUG." To reduce the teasing, the young Grant transposed his names and became Ulysses Hiram.

At age seventeen he set his sights on the U.S. Military Academy and persuaded everyone he knew to write to Rep. Thomas L. Hamer on his behalf. Hamer, who was not personally acquainted with Grant, duly appointed him to West Point. Hastily preparing the necessary papers, the lawmaker inadvertently used the maiden name of Grant's mother on the submission to the academy's admissions office.

When Grant presented himself for enrollment at the Point, he was surprised to find that he had been enrolled as Ulysses Simpson Grant. Since the change was acceptable to him, he made no protest. Once the modified name was entered in the official military record, it was never again changed.

From that clerical mistake came U. S. Grant—an almost providentially bestowed coincidence, both with the initials of his country and with an early high moment for Union forces in the West when Grant offered no terms for surrender to the Confederates at Fort Donelson, Tennessee. "Unconditional Surrender" Grant drew headlines from that moment, through two terms in the White House, and into history.

❧

Hugh Judson Kilpatrick of New Jersey attended West Point fourteen years after Grant. Never having liked his first, baptismal name, which he considered effeminate, he casually introduced himself as Judson when his enrollment was being processed.

Busy with stacks of paperwork, the admissions clerks didn't bother to check the document attesting to the appointment of a farmer's son from Deckertown. With that annoying first name out of the way, Judson Kilpatrick graduated on May 6, 1861, and pinned on the insignia of a second lieutenant of artillery. Three days later he accepted a promotion to the rank of captain and was transferred from the U.S. Army to the Fifth New York Infantry.

In September, Kilpatrick was transferred again, this time to the Second New York Cavalry, and received another promotion. As a brigadier general, he led mounted men in every important action within the eastern theater of the war. Once having feared that he'd be called a sissy, Kilpatrick drove his men and horses so furiously that he came to be known as "Kill Cavalry."

Cadet Arnold Jones became uncomfortable with his surname some time before his 1837 graduation from West Point. Substituting the name of his paternal grandmother for that of his father, he became Arnold Elzey. Immediately after Fort Sumter he changed uniforms, becoming a Confederate lieutenant colonel. Just one year later he was Brigadier General Elzey.

Still another West Point cadet underwent a change of name at the academy. Born in Gates County, North Carolina, Laurence Simmons Daker received a congressional appointment in 1847. Reporting for his first day of classes, when the roll was called, he discovered that a War Department clerk had altered his name to the more familiar spelling of Lawrence.

Service on the frontier in the U.S. Mounted Rifles ended when he switched uniforms. As colonel of the First North Carolina Cavalry, the Confederate officer led his men so effectively that he became a brigadier in just over a year.

Some future officers who never attended military academies became new persons figuratively when they enlisted for war service. Julian Scott of Vermont, a musician only fifteen years old, watched helplessly as he was given a middle initial by a clerk.

Carried on muster rolls as Julian A. Scott, the drummer boy became a stretcher bearer when men of his regiment were wounded. At age sixteen he received the Congressional Medal of Honor for gallantry under enemy fire.

John A. Drummond of Galveston, Texas, volunteered for Confederate service when he was about the same age as Scott. Fearing that his father would learn what he had done and would have him discharged as being underage, he enlisted as John Anderson. His father didn't discover the subterfuge until too late, so Anderson fought through much of the war as a member of the Davis Guards.

*

Frederick Henry Dyer was also under the legal age to enlist. Calling himself Frederick H. Metzger, in September 1863 he gained a berth as a musician in Company H of the Seventh Connecticut Infantry.

Dyer's unit fought at Olustee, Drewry's Bluff, the Bermuda Hundred, Chaffin's Farm, New Market Heights, Fort Fisher, and numerous other places. Mustered out on July 20, 1865, he settled in Philadelphia and built up a printing business.

Success in business wasn't enough for the veteran who changed his name in order to enlist as a boy. Aware that there was no reliable source of information about all Federal units, he decided to compile one. During five years in which he lived as a hermit, Dyer put together by hand a colossal *Compendium of the War of the Rebellion* that remains the standard work of its kind after more than eight decades.

*

Half a dozen or more fighting men modified their names into forms that made them seem to be descended from ancestors who lived in the British Isles.

*

Julius Szamvald became a lieutenant in the Austrian army, then joined a revolutionary movement that was crushed. As a refugee he spent time in both England and Germany before coming to the United States as journalist Julius Stahel. An organizer of the First German Rifles, he became a brigadier general of U.S. Volunteers on November 12, 1861.

Henry Beeger emigrated from Germany before the war. Calling himself Henry Bertran, he joined the U.S. Army because of the high pay scale it offered. After five years as a member of the Second Artillery, he tired of monotonous life in tiny camps and deserted. At the outbreak of conflict, the man from Germany became a first lieutenant in the First Wisconsin Infantry. Promoted grade-by-grade until he became a colonel, he was the only deserter to become a brevet brigadier as a reward for his services during the Civil War.

Unlike Beeger, George Pforr didn't settle for half-measures when he decided to anglicize his name. Calling himself Charles W. Anderson, he joined Company K of the First New York Cavalry.

Anderson didn't volunteer until February 1864, but he won a Congressional Medal of Honor a year later. At war's end he signed up for a hitch in Company M of the Third U.S. Cavalry and remained in uniform for a dozen more years. Discharged in April 1878, he settled in Staunton, Virginia, where his wife, his children, and his neighbors knew him only as George Pforr.

Determined to serve in the Eighth Texas Cavalry, Charles Pelham Ten Eyck was sure that his name would lead to hazing. Presenting himself as Charles T. Pelham, he fought with distinction until he was fatally wounded by a Federal ball.

His grieving parents successfully petitioned the Texas legislature to change the name of their only grandson. As a result, Charles Pelham Ten Eyck Jr. became known as Charles T. Pelham.

Born in the Ohio River town of Wheeling, then still a part of Virginia, Jesse Lee Renault desperately wanted to attend West Point. Fearful that foreign-sounding surname associated with a sly fox would be an impediment, he began calling himself Jesse Reno.

Jesse graduated eighth in his class from the Point, a class that included Thomas J. Jackson, George Pickett, and George B. McClellan. These three fellow cadets compiled military records more impressive than that of the boy from Wheeling. After fifteen years in the U. S. Army, he became a brigadier general of U.S. Volunteers.

Yet the man who was killed at Fox's Gap, Virginia, on September 14, 1862, has a special monument of sorts. Alone among members of the West Point class of 1846, his name appears on the map of the United States. Had he not deliberately changed his name, today's Reno, Nevada, might have been Renault.

Ivan Vasilovich Truchinoff became a professional soldier in his native Russia and rose to the rank of colonel in the Imperial Guard. Upon settling in Chicago in 1856, he decided to do something about his name. As John Basil Turchin he soon found work in the engineering department of a railroad successfully sued by attorney Abraham Lincoln of Springfield.

Following the outbreak of war, Turchin left the Nineteenth Illinois Infantry. Perhaps because his wife made a personal appeal to Lincoln, the man whose subordinate called him "the Russian Thunderbolt" received a commission as a brigadier general.

Ferdinand Heinrich Gustav Hilgard left his native Bavaria in 1853. Hoping to become a journalist, he changed his name to Henry Villard and became a Washington correspondent for a number of major newspapers. By 1863 he was a valued member of the staff of Horace Greeley, whose *New York Herald* was perhaps the most widely circulated paper in the nation.

Edward W. Hincks of Boston won a seat in the state legislature while quite young. Just ten days after Fort Sumter he decided to volunteer for military service but wanted to be regarded as a "genuine American."

With a single letter dropped from his name, Edward Hinks launched his military career as a second lieutenant in the famous Second Cavalry, U.S. Army. Less than eighteen months later, the man who considered his legal name to sound "distinctly foreign" was a brigadier general of U.S. Volunteers.

At least one professional soldier altered his name so that he would seem to have a pronounced foreign ancestry. Washington Carroll Tevis of Pennsylvania graduated from the U.S. Military Academy in 1849. Within a year he sensed opportunity abroad, so he changed his name to Nessim Bey and became a *bimbachi* (major) in the Turkish army.

The outbreak of the Civil War induced him to return home and volunteer for service as C. Carroll Tevis. As a lieutenant colonel of Delaware and Maryland units, he compiled a long combat record. Congress accordingly made him a brevet brigadier general.

Other relatives made decisions that affected the lives of at least four youngsters. At the request of an uncle, Alexander Slidell, an officer of the U.S. Navy, added the name Mackenzie to his surname. His son was named Ranald Slidell Mackenzie. Immediately upon graduating from West Point in 1862, Ranald became an assistant engineer in the Ninth Corps. By 1864 he had been promoted to the rank of brigadier general of U.S. Volunteers, later becoming both a U.S. Army brevet brigadier and a brevet major general.

A youthful Cherokee, Galagina, studied in Connecticut at a school that received financial aid from Revolutionary War officer Elias Boudinot. With the permission of the veteran of Washington's army, Galagina changed his name to that of his patron.

When a son was born to him in 1835, the boy did not take a tribal name but was known as Elias Cornelius Boudinot. He was secretary of the Arkansas convention that voted for secession. After having served as a representative of the Cherokee Nation, the man whose name sounded like that of a colonial of European background became a lieutenant colonel in a Confederate regiment of Cherokees.

Spanish-born George Ferrugut changed his name to Farragut when he fought in the American Revolution. While stationed at New Orleans, he became closely associated with Cmdr. David Porter.

Porter later took youthful James G. Farragut into his home and reared him as a foster son. In gratitude, the man whose surname had been changed by his father voluntarily altered his baptismal name to honor Porter. As a result, David G. Farragut took to the sea and became the first U.S. naval officer to be awarded the rank of full Admiral.

Attorney Charles R. Sherman of Ohio considered the Native American warrior Tecumseh to be one of the greatest men of the region. He named his son in honor of the Shawnee chieftain. Relatives found the boy's name cumbersome, so they abbreviated it to Cump.

When Cump was nine years old, his father died suddenly, leaving his widow and eleven children all but destitute. Relatives and friends took the children into their homes and reared them as though they were their own.

Cump was adopted informally by wealthy Thomas Ewing, a neighbor. Soon Ewing insisted that the boy be baptized formally, decreeing that Cump must have "a proper Christian name." Since the day chosen was the feast day of Saint William, at Ewing's orders the priest christened the boy William Tecumseh.

The boy went on to be one of the most effective Union generals of the Civil War. Although he customarily signed all military documents as W. T. Sherman, among relatives and intimates he continued to be known as Cump or Cumpy.

Not all who changed their names or had them changed were male. At least four women gained fame or notoriety under names of their own choosing. Clarissa Harlow Barton of Oxford, Massachusetts, tolerated her name while she was a schoolgirl. When she went to Washington to apply for a position in the U.S. Patent Office, however, she listed herself simply as Clara. Once selected, the shortened version of her name remained with her for the rest of her life. As a result, many a person who reveres the founder of the American Red Cross is not aware that, properly speaking, she should be remembered as Clarissa Barton.

A daughter born to slaves of Dorchester County, Maryland, worked as a maid, a field hand, a cook, and a woodcutter. Most other slaves on the plantation knew her simply as Aramenta, daughter of Harriet Greene.

Long before she became the wife of John Tubman, a free black, she had taken her mother's name and was known as Harriet. A leader in the Underground Railroad, Harriet Tubman helped an estimated three hundred slaves to freedom and is renowned as "the Moses of her people."

Largely forgotten today, Cincinnati native Delia Swift changed her name when she moved to New Orleans at about age thirteen. As a prostitute, pickpocket, and skilled mugger, Bridget Fury was well known locally.

Imprisoned in 1858 for murder, she was still behind bars when the city fell into Union hands. One of the first decrees from the new military governor, George F. Shepley, was a blanket pardon of all persons convicted prior to the Federal occupation. Elevated to the level of a folk heroine because of a self-chosen name that was strangely fitting, Bridget Fury was briefly notorious throughout much of the nation.

—

Ethelinda Eliot of Goshen, New York, was a descendant of John Eliot, known as "the apostle to the Indians." As an adolescent she began contributing poetry to newspapers and magazines.

Since she regarded her surname as "tame and commonplace," she customarily signed her lines as Ethel Lynn. At age nineteen, after becoming the bride of William H. Beers, her pen name became Ethel Lynn Beers.

One of her many Civil War poems first appeared as "The Picket Guard" in the November 30, 1861, issue of *Harper's Magazine*. Remembered for its vivid first line, "All quiet along the Potomac tonight," the poem is seldom recognized as the product of a woman who chose for herself an elegant-sounding name. Instead, "All Quiet Along the Potomac" is usually thought to be the work of a veteran in blue who spent many nights on picket duty.

—

When a recruitment officer came to an Ohio town, a boy of ten decided he wanted to join the fight. His chances of being accepted as a drummer would be enhanced, he believed, if he had an important-sounding name. So John Clem hastily fabricated a middle name—Lincoln.

In April 1862 the nation came to know him as Johnny Shiloh. He seems to have been a drummer for several units before being added to the muster roll of Company C of the Twenty-second Michigan Infantry. At the battle of Chickamauga he won national fame, but that was not enough to gain admission to West Point at war's end. Brushed aside as having an inadequate education, the man who named himself for the president of the United States remained in uniform until his 1916 resignation as a major general.

〰️

Elihu Washburn of Maine began thinking about a career in politics before he was twenty years old. To make his name "properly elegant," he added an *e* to the end. Three of his brothers refused to follow his example. Although each of the trio of Washburns achieved national prominence during the war years, it was Elihu Washburne who was U.S. secretary of state before becoming the U.S. minister to France.

〰️

Born at Saint Augustine, Florida, young Edmund Kirby Smith fought through the Mexican War after graduating from West Point. He changed uniforms in 1861 and became a Confederate colonel of cavalry. Successively in command of a number of Confederate departments, he decided that Smith was too common a name to demand the respect he deserved.

Long predating the modern trend toward hyphenating names, he began calling himself Edmund Kirby-Smith. Although never made legal formally, it is his self-chosen modified name that appears in many reference works today.

〰️

Morgan Lewis Smith of New York was at least as contemptuous of his surname as was Kirby-Smith. Enlisting in the U.S. Army as Martin L. Sanford, he became a drill instructor. Five years' experience in that capacity made it easy for him to raise the Eighth Maine Infantry In 1861.

Correctly anticipating that his men would elect him to serve as their colonel, he resumed his legal name. The name of Martin L. Sanford appears nowhere in the lists of Civil War officers, but Morgan L. Smith became a brigadier general of U.S. Volunteers about one year after Fort Sumter.

Harriet Bailey, a slave on a Maryland plantation, became pregnant by a white man whose identity was not known. When her son was born, she decided to give him a truly sonorous name: Frederick Augustus Washington Bailey.

Years later, after having purchased his freedom, Harriet's son decided to sever his ties with the past. At the suggestion of a friend, he borrowed a sur-name from Sir Walter Scott's *Lady of the Lake*. A skilled orator and publicist, the man now known as Frederick Douglass was the only African American of his era to become an advisor to U.S. presidents.

Without having reasons so compelling as those that persuaded Frederick Bailey to change his name, Robert B. Smith of Virginia took similar action. Moving to Florida, he joined the staff of the *Tallahassee Floridian* as Robert Benjamin Hilton.

Hilton—or Smith—advanced professionally in journalism while also study-ing law. As owner and editor of the *Savannah Georgian*, he returned to Florida to become captain of the First Florida Infantry. Earlier having been elected to Congress, but never having been seated, he now won a seat in the Confederate Congress. After hostilities ceased, the lawmaker with an assumed name launched a new career as a judge.

Few U.S. lawmakers of the period were as influential as Sen. Henry Wilson. Having succeeded to the seat of nationally famous Edward Everett, Wilson was involved in many Washington intrigues. He was among the prominent men believed to have been lovers of Confederate spy Rose Greenhow O'Neal; earlier he had helped Clara Barton to gain her position in the patent office as a pioneer female employee of the U.S. government.

An ardent admirer and a staunch friend of Lincoln, Wilson engineered passage of an all-important congressional measure that granted Lincoln after-the-fact sanction of numerous irregular actions. Many lawmakers were wary of approving the measure, so the vote on the bill was stalled repeatedly.

With the special session about to end, a bill was introduced to boost the salaries of U.S. soldiers. In the aftermath of Bull Run, no senator or member of the House of Representatives would have dared vote against this measure. Wilson craftily attached a last-minute rider to the bill that conferred extraordinary war powers upon the first Republican president.

Long after he had shown himself to be a master of political maneuvering, Massachusetts voters discovered that their senator had been born in New Hampshire as Jeremiah Jones Colbaith. He had changed his name when he moved to the Bay State in 1833 and began work as a shoemaker.

An aristocratic Creole from Louisiana may have changed his name more often than any other notable of the Civil War. Born as Pierre Gustave Toutant-Beauregard, he deleted the hyphen while he was still quite young. Later he stopped using Pierre to become plain G. T. Beauregard.

By the time he had begun to win fame as a Confederate general, the man from Louisiana had restored the first segment of his baptismal name. Widely known as P. G. T. Beauregard, he insisted that his friends simply call him Peter.

Beauregard was famous in the South as the hero of both Fort Sumter and Manassas, but his name was never so widely familiar as was that of a native of England. When Henry Carter came to New York in 1848, he changed his name legally to Frank Leslie for reasons he never revealed.

Frank Leslie's Illustrated Newspaper competed with the famous *Harper's Weekly* to portray the war on paper. Because of its tremendous impact—still significant after many decades—his newspaper and its woodcuts and engravings made the name of Frank Leslie widely familiar.

Also a native of the British Isles, John Rowlands was a cabin boy on a merchant vessel. When it reached New Orleans shortly before the outbreak of the Civil War, Rowlands jumped ship. A wealthy merchant, Henry Morton Stanley, adopted the eighteen-year-old in 1859. As a gesture of gratitude to his benefactor, the runaway changed his name and also became known as Henry Morton Stanley.

Stanley's Civil War career—one of the most varied and colorful on record—turned him toward the field of journalism. Eight years after shedding his uniform, he received a prized commission. James Gordon Bennett of the *New York Herald* put him in charge of an expedition to find an English doctor believed to be lost in central Africa. It was there that the journalist offered a greeting that was soon familiar throughout the Western world: "Dr. Livingstone, I presume?"

Thirty-four

THEIR MOTHERS WOULDN'T
HAVE KNOWN THEM

Joseph Howard of the *New York Times* was in or near Willard's Hotel in
Washington, D.C., very early in the morning of February 23, 1861, when
Abraham Lincoln arrived from Springfield. A telegram informed his editors
that the president-elect had reached the capital wearing "a Scotch plaid cap and
a very long military cloak, so that he was entirely unrecognizable."

Howard's headline-producing account was based on the fact that warnings
of assassination had reached Lincoln in Philadelphia. As a result, a last-minute
change of schedule sent him through Baltimore at an hour when no one was
expecting him.

There had been no attempt at disguise, however. A soft wool hat given to
Lincoln in New York was worn instead of his customary tall, stiff hat. Still,
the peculiar hour and the story in the *Times* triggered hundreds of newspaper
accounts. Numerous cartoons published before the first shot of the war was
fired alleged that Lincoln had reached Washington so carefully disguised that
no one who saw him would recognize him.

⌇

Strangely, another story of a chief executive in disguise surfaced around the
time the last shots of the war were being fired. Northern newspapers reported
that Jefferson Davis had been dressed as a woman at the time of his capture in

372

Georgia. On May 27, *Harper's Weekly* depicted Davis in a long dress and sur-rounded by Federal soldiers. Like the Lincoln story and the ensuing cartoons, this scene was a fabrication, too. When Davis was apprehended on May 10, he had been dressed for riding and had thrown a raincoat over his shoulders.

Clement L. Vallandigham of Ohio was probably the most notable political figure who tried to disguise himself. Having been banished to Confederate ter-ritory, the one-time pacifist editor found himself unwelcome and unwanted. So the articulate advocate for peace went to Canada.

Ohio Democrats were outraged at the treatment of their former congress-man. At a state convention, they nominated him for governor by a vote of 411 to 11. Partly because Lincoln actively worked for his opponent, Vallandigham lost the election by one hundred thousand votes in the October 1863 election.

Weary of exile, Vallandigham decided to return to Ohio in June 1864. For this momentous journey, the man whose face was familiar throughout the North stuffed a pillow under his clothing and tied on a set of false whiskers. When an account of his disguise became public, Lincoln mocked Vallandigham's attempt to conceal his identity.

Although he succeeded in ignoring arrest orders and reached Ohio, Vallandigham never again played a notable role in national politics. Edward Everett Hale used him as the model for the central character of his short story "The Man Without a Country."

Throughout the war, men and women of the North and of the South played ludicrous or thrilling roles in disguise. In Saint Louis, Capt. Nathaniel Lyon wanted a firsthand look at a nearby Southern military camp. On May 9, 1861, the veteran U.S. Army officer turned into "old Mrs. Alexander, a soci-ety matron who liked to wear bombazine and a heavy black veil." Sometimes described as having disguised himself as a farm woman, Lyon did pose as a woman of wealth. He probably borrowed the clothes from the mother-in-law of Rep. Francis P. Blair Jr.

Regardless of where he secured his elaborate dress and bonnet, the disguised Lyon climbed into a carriage with a black driver. Since the real Mrs. Alexander was well known for her eccentricities, the officer made a leisurely tour of Camp Jackson without incident.

According to the *Memphis Appeal*, a Confederate scouting party led by a Colonel Looney left Chattanooga in late November 1861. "They captured fourteen horses, and took one hundred Lincoln men prisoners," the newspaper reported. A Unionist ruffian known only as Holloway "managed to make his escape by clothing himself in female attire."

In divided Kentucky, guerrilla bands flourished. One of them was led by prosperous but tiny Marcellus J. Clarke. According to the *Louisville Courier*, he was frequently disguised as Sue Mundy and continued a double life until March 15, 1865. As he swung from a gallows after a hasty "citizens' trial," there was no doubt that the guerrilla leader was male.

Recent studies indicate that tales about Sue Mundy's exploits were greatly exaggerated by reporters for the *Louisville Daily Journal*. Even if that is the case, few men were as successful as Clarke had been in maintaining a long-time pretense at being an attractive woman.

Capt. Frank H. Mason of the Twelfth Ohio Volunteer Cavalry was a member of the force that captured men who had fought under Confederate Maj. Gen. Joseph Wheeler. Near Atlanta, following Johnston's surrender in North Carolina, Wheeler and his raiders were surrounded and trapped.

Because a captured slave in the group wore the uniform of a Confederate Major general, a Federal officer became suspicious. Soon he discovered that Wheeler had exchanged clothing with his valet in a futile attempt to be identified as a contraband, or a rootless slave. After his disguise had been exposed, Wheeler was sent to Fort Warren as a prisoner of war.

Only a handful of men are known to have disguised themselves as former slaves. One band, whose names were not preserved, successfully made it out of a temporary prison in Saint Louis by using burnt cork on their hands and faces.

Brig. Gen. Schuyler Hamilton, commander of the Federal military district in which the escape occurred, took quick steps to prevent more Confederates from using the same ruse. He directed that the prison's doctor examine all inmates and "to exclude from the prison all negroes," for whom a temporary shelter was arranged elsewhere.

Col. Richard Thomas of the Virginia Volunteers fared better than did the Confederate cavalry leader who tried to pose as a runaway slave. His caper in disguise began in June 1862, when a plan was made to seize the USS *Pawnee*. The warship's armament made conventional capture impossible. Thomas therefore decided to seize a small steamer, the *St. Nicholas*, with the hope that he might approach his target without raising an alarm.

Capt. George N. Hollins of the Confederate navy, dressed as a woman companion, went along as chief aide to Thomas. Other volunteers were dressed as workmen. Concealing their weapons in tool boxes, these "laboring men" went aboard the *St. Nicholas* at three or four different points.

When the little steamer reached Point Lookout, Maryland, a woman in a hoop skirt came aboard and registered herself as "a French lady named Zarvona." Officers of the little steamer were honored to have aboard so exotic a passenger and expressed disappointment when she said she must go to her cabin and rest.

Soon after "Zarvona" went below, a Confederate Zouave wearing a brace of pistols climbed on deck. His men pulled out their weapons and took over the ship with little or no resistance. Learning that the *Pawnee* was not at her customary berth, the seized vessel was taken up the Rappahannock River toward Fredericksburg and transformed into the CSS *Rappahannock*.

Leading only four men from the *Rappahannock*, "Zarvona" soon boarded a larger passenger steamer where "she" was quickly recognized. By the time a company of Federal infantry had swarmed aboard, the French "lady" had seemed to vanish. After a ninety minute search, however, "she" was found curled up in a bureau drawer. Once flushed from hiding, the "lady" was revealed to be Thomas. So much publicity followed this incident that the man who had posed as a woman was for a time the most celebrated prisoner in Federal captivity.

At least one man who served a brief term as an irregular soldier did not gain any fame until after the fighting had ceased. Small of stature and having little or no beard, smooth-skinned young Jesse James sometimes disguised himself as a woman to scout Federal positions.

Pvt. Benjamin F. Stringfellow of the Fourth Virginia Cavalry had light-colored hair and weighed less than a hundred pounds. To Capt. John F. Lay that seemed to make him an ideal candidate for the risky job of spying.

Properly dressed he was described by admiring comrades as "making a really attractive girl." Wincing slightly as he walked, Stringfellow went into Federal-occupied Arlington, Virginia, several times. The information he gathered is said to have proved especially useful to Confederate Gen. P. G. T. Beauregard.

Confederates who made the northernmost raid of the war knew that they were risking their lives. Preparing to rob the banks of Saint Albans, Vermont, Pvt. William Teavis decided to don women's clothing. Some of his comrades jeered at his lack of courage, but Teavis was the only raider to get through the North without being detected.

⸙

For Secret Service agents and spies, disguise seemed to come naturally. Allan Pinkerton, who worked for Maj. Gen. George B. McClellan, claimed frequently to have spent days behind Confederate lines with his face and clothing so altered that even his mother would not have recognized him. His firsthand account is not supported by independent sources. He gave no hint of the way that a man from Chicago could disguise his voice and visit Memphis without detection.

⸙

Confederate spy Thomas N. Conrad had a voice so booming that it was useless to attempt to alter it when he penetrated Federal lines. His most conspicuous facial features were a huge mustache and a beard, carefully described to Federal commanders with whom he was likely to come in contact.

Conrad somehow turned what seemed a liability into an asset. He managed to alter his facial hair so that when in disguise he was not recognized by friends who had known him for years.

⸙

According to the *Louisville Journal* of November 30, 1861, an unidentified Confederate colonel was arrested at Paducah, Kentucky, "Dressed like an ordinary farmer, in conversation he appeared not very bright." When he became excited, his use of language changed so drastically that a fellow traveler asked the provost marshal to take him into custody.

⸙

During heavy fighting in Missouri, Federal leaders had urgent reasons to send dispatches from Sedalia to Independence. Since the region was heavily pocketed with Confederates, it was decided to seek volunteers for the ninety-mile mission.

Two Hoosiers, Pvts. Marshall Storey and William Waters, offered to undertake the long and dangerous journey. With dispatches hidden in their hats and boots, they assumed the role of refugees.

Once they were ordered to halt by the leader of a band of jayhawkers, guerrilla fighters with Unionist leanings who used the war for their own purposes. Waters whispered to Storey, "Go along with me!" Pretending to be half-witted, the Federal soldier stammered that he was taking his brother home after a stay in Saint Louis.

His self-chosen role as a half-wit proved so successful that Waters tried to climb aboard a beautiful black pony belonging to a Jayhawker. When pulled from the animal's back he picked up a stick and pretended to challenge the owner to a fight.

With the laughter of their would-be captors ringing in their ears, the two Hoosiers left the band of jayhawkers and reached Independence with their messages intact.

Confederate Capt. Julius de Lagnel tried a similar ploy. Separated from his unit during heavy fighting in West Virginia, he stumbled upon a cabin in the mountains.

During three days in his refuge, de Lagnel carefully studied the mannerisms and speech patterns of the mountain family. He then set out to rejoin his comrades. Frequently stopped by Union pickets and guards, his "mountain accent and crackerish ways" convinced them that he was a farmer hunting livestock who had wandered from his pasture.

One of Pinkerton's agents, Pryce Lewis, posed as an English gentleman travel-ing for pleasure. Wearing tweeds and flourishing a cigar case ornamented with an ivory British lion, he had no difficulty in deceiving Secessionists of western Virginia during June 1861.

Lafayette C. Baker of the National Detective Police made several forays into Confederate territory. He drove a photographer's wagon and carried along the increasingly familiar tools of the trade. According to his reports, the Confederates from whom he gathered information were too interested in what the photographer was doing to ask questions about his identity.

Little is known about John Burke, a man who tried to spy for both sides, except that he had a glass eye and that he gave himself the honorary title of captain. It was the missing eye that enabled him to alter his appearance radically. When he left his glass eye behind to go on a mission, even close acquaintances failed to recognize him.

Confederate scout Henry B. Shaw (sometimes known as Capt. C. E. Coleman) took on the name and attire of an itinerant doctor so he could go back and forth between lines in Middle Tennessee.

Near Chambersburg, Pennsylvania, Confederate Col. Ashby Turner passed as a "horse doctor," or veterinarian, to spy for Stonewall Jackson.

Disguised as civilians, Capt. W. F. Brown and ten members of the Confederate Marine Corps took passage on the steamer *Ike Davis*. Once away from Federal installations, they seized the vessel and took it to Matagorda Bay, Texas, as a prize of war.

Federal soldiers proved equally adept at playing the same game. Capt. Peter Haggerty disguised himself as an organ grinder to go into Baltimore daily to gather information for Maj. Gen. Benjamin F. Butler. During one of his forays he learned that several tons of gunpowder had been stored on Calhoun Street. This information helped convince Butler that he should establish martial law in the city that seemed to be filled with secessionists.

After the battle of Wilson's Creek, Brig. Gen. Franz Sigel dressed like a Texas Ranger. Wearing a blanket over his uniform and topped by a yellow slouch hat, he passed through Confederate outposts without being challenged.

Members of Ohio regiments who volunteered for special service under James J. Andrews were not so fortunate. Dressed as civilians, they seized the locomotive *General* and set out to disrupt the railroad linking Atlanta with Chattanooga. After a ninety-mile chase, Andrews's raiders were captured.

Because they were not in uniform, seven Union soldiers who posed as Confederate civilians were sentenced to die. Their mass execution in Atlanta was the railroad center's largest such event ever.

Richard Yates, wartime governor of Illinois, launched his military career at Bull Run. Late in the conflict he attracted the attention of Maj. Gen. Philip Sheridan, who requested him to organize a body of "special scouts." Actually spies, the fifty-eight men who made up Yates's band frequently risked the gallows by donning Confederate uniforms in pursuit of information or other behind-the-lines actions.

Confederate Maj. Gen. James Ewell Brown "Jeb" Stuart took the same risk near Falling Waters, Virginia (now West Virginia). Unwilling to trust the skill and judgment of his subordinates, he wore a Federal uniform to scout the countryside ahead of his force.

Confederate Brig. Gen. Robert S. Hoke was in desperate need of a way to stall Federal forces entrenched near Drewry's Bluff, just north of Richmond. Explaining that the risk of death was great, he asked for a volunteer to undertake a special mission.

Pvt. Halifax R. Wood, age eighteen, immediately stepped forward. Hoke handed him a Federal uniform and issued verbal instructions. Hoke gathered no information, but the disguised Confederate made his way to the headquarters of Maj. Gen. Benjamin F. Butler and excitedly reported having seen a large force of Confederates landing on the James River. Having delivered the false message, the Confederate beat a hasty retreat to the safety of his own line.

Also near Richmond, French soldier of fortune Victor Vifquain devised an outlandish scheme to end the war. With three companions, he donned a heavy disguise and headed toward the Confederate capital. Although his identity was not discovered, he was turned back by pickets before he could carry out his mission: to capture Jefferson Davis, president of the Confederacy.

In Richmond, Davis personally approved a plan submitted to him by Congressman Duncan F. Kenner of Louisiana. Kenner would travel to Europe in disguise and discuss with various government officials the possibility of abolishing slavery in the Confederacy in return for diplomatic recognition.

Knowing that he would have to pass through New York to reach his objective, Kenner resorted to an elaborate disguise. He made his long journey safely and without being recognized—but accomplished nothing. Realizing that the fate of the Confederacy had been sealed on battlefields, the European leaders were no longer interested in the possibility of extending diplomatic recognition to the new nation.

A few months after the start of hostilities, a special agreement between the two opposing forces exempted military surgeons from capture. Capt. Harry White of a Pennsylvania regiment decided to take advantage of this special opportunity.

As a prisoner of war, at City Point, Virginia, White went aboard a Confederate steamer carrying a small black valise that held a few surgical instruments. He successfully passed himself off as exempt from imprisonment until the captain of the vessel found his name on the list of officers not eligible for exchange. "Harry White, come forth!" bellowed an officer in gray. Momentarily forgetting his disguise, the officer from the Keystone State stepped from the ranks and ruefully relinquished his little black bag.

Henry B. Shaw, a steamboat clerk intimately acquainted with Middle Tennessee, headed a band of spies who worked for Confederate Brig. Gen. Benjamin F. Cheatham. Disguised as a rural physician recently having accepted a gray uniform, he called himself Dr. C. E. Coleman.

Union forces didn't know that Coleman was an aide to Gen. Braxton Bragg, so they permitted the doctor to wander through their lines at will. Coleman and others who made up a special body of scouts always wore Confederate uniforms when on a mission. If captured, the uniform would allow them to be treated as prisoners of war rather than as spies.

⌁

Chaplin J. D. Rodgers of the Twenty-third Indiana Infantry may have heard of the caper pulled off in Missouri by fellow Hoosiers. Whether that was the case or not, he was immediately suspicious when an elderly gentleman boarded a vessel at Henderson, Kentucky.

Dressed like a farmer, the man started a conversation with Rodgers and acted dull-witted. In a moment of excitement, however, the rhythm and pitch of his voice made a decided change. At Paducah, therefore, Rodgers called the attention of the provost marshal to the man who was playing the role of a dullard.

Questioned, the old farmer turned out to be a Confederate colonel who had participated in the battle of Bull Run. He was immediately taken into custody, but his name and unit were not recorded.

⌁

Federal scout Henry H. Young and a band of more than fifty men made numerous successful forays into Confederate territory disguised as Southern soldiers.

⌁

Capt. Alexander M. Shannon and handpicked men of the Eighth Texas Cavalry pursued a similar course. Wearing blue uniforms, they gathered information on movements of Federal troops in Tennessee and Georgia.

⌁

All correspondents had been barred from the funeral service for Maj. Gen. Philip Kearny, killed by a Confederate bullet on September 1, 1862. Joseph Howard of the *New York Times* had earlier written a bogus account of Lincoln's pre-inaugural journey in disguise. This time, he donned a surplice and carried a prayer book to cover the ceremony and give readers a firsthand report of the funeral.

A few women proved to be at least as resourceful and skillful as the men who had disguised themselves. Several authorities agree that the Civil War saw enough women fighting in uniform to make up several companies. Some of them seem never to have been discovered; others were identified under strange circumstances.

A Brooklyn girl known only as Emily dressed as a young boy and enlisted in a Michigan regiment as a drummer. After she was fatally wounded during the second day's fighting at Chickamauga, a male nurse attempting to bandage her wound discovered her secret.

Loreta Velaques of New Orleans dressed as Lt. Harry Buford so she could accompany her husband to war. Said to have served briefly as a company commander under Confederate Brig. Gen. Bernard Bee at Manassas, her comrades in arms learned her secret a year later. According to her colorful memoirs, she then became a secret agent.

Like Velaques, Florena Budwin posed as a man so she could go into battle with her husband. Both were captured and sent to the military prison at Andersonville, where he died. Florena somehow survived and was sent to another Confederate prison at Florence, South Carolina. When she was caught up in an epidemic of illness, the doctor who discovered her sex offered her a special room plus food not served to ordinary prisoners.

~~~~

Albert J. Cashier of the Ninety-fifth Illinois Regiment fought at Vicksburg, Nashville, and Mobile. Fifty years after enlisting, Cashier was injured in an automobile accident. At a hospital, Cashier was discovered to be a female. Questioned, she admitted nothing except that she was of Irish birth and was really named Hodgers.

~~~~

An even later discovery took place in 1934 near Shiloh National Military Park. Digging in his garden, Mancil Milligan found a quantity of human bones. He eventually learned that he had stumbled upon the unmarked grave of nine Federal soldiers killed in the battle.

While Milligan's find evoked wide interest in the region, it was not until pathologists examined them that a more interesting discovery was made. One set of bones belonged to a female, probably killed or fatally wounded by the Minié ball that lay close to her ribs.

Investigation failed to identify the woman who died at Shiloh. According to some authorities, however, she was the only female positively known to have been killed in combat.

~~~~

No other woman who posed as a man quite equaled the exploits of Sarah Edmonds. Calling herself Franklin Thompson, she enlisted in the Second Michigan Infantry on May 14, 1861. Having escaped injury at Antietam, she contracted malaria a few months later. Knowing that a medical examination would prove her undoing, she deserted and for a time worked as a spy.

According to her account, in this role she often wore "a wig of real Negro wool" to play the role of a male slave. So disguised, she claimed to have visited Richmond several times.

In 1884 Sarah attended a regimental reunion minus her disguise as Franklin Thompson. Former comrades persuaded her to petition Congress for revocation of her conviction as a deserter and to file for a veteran's pension. She seems to have won both contests, for some records of the Grand Army of the Republic suggest that Sarah Emma Edmonds was its sole female member.

At about the time Jefferson Davis was falsely accused of trying to hide his identity by dressing as a woman, several notable Confederate leaders were traveling in disguise. Judah P. Benjamin, whose last post in the Richmond government was that of secretary of state, headed for Mexico after the capital fell. Since he spoke excellent French, he passed himself off as a Frenchman named Bonfal. Successively posing at different times as a sea cook and an ordinary farmer, the disguised former cabinet official reached Florida and found passage to England.

Maj. Gen. Jubal A. "Jubilee" Early also believed that he could find a haven south of the border. Famous—or infamous—for his Washington raid of 1864, he knew that his face was widely known. Permitting his beard to become scruffy, he reached Mexico wearing overalls and a straw hat appropriate for the dirt farmer he pretended to be.

Thirty-five

NAVAL CHAOS

M any battles were known to Confederates by one name, to Federals by
another. The nomenclature of armies was an additional source of confusion; for example, the Army of the Tennessee was made up of men wearing
blue, while the Army of Tennessee was a Confederate force.

Difficult as it was and still is to keep straight the many names used on land
for the same event or similar reference, these are easy when compared to naval
affairs. There were no standard procedures with respect to a change of possession.
Following purchase or capture, a vessel's name might be retained or it might be
altered. Frequently modified in naval records, but not always changed in civilian
mercantile annals, the names of ships were a source of frustration to the officers
whose duty it was to get them right.

Purchased by Rear Adm. Hiram Paulding in 1862 for $25,000, the *Nuestra
Senora de Regla* displaced 376 tons. Men who stumbled over the name of the
side-wheel steamer were delighted when she was recommissioned as the USS
Commodore Hull.

Numerous men were honored by Federal authorities when their names were given to newly completed vessels or those purchased after having been in operation for months or years.

At the New York prize court, $331 was paid in 1863 for the captured ship *Hettiwan*. When it was launched under the Stars and Stripes, it bore the name *Percy Drayton*. Drayton had commanded the *Pocahontas* at the 1861 battle of Port Royal, facing Confederate guns under the command of his brother, Confederate Brig. Gen. Thomas F. Drayton.

The War Department obligingly transferred to the U.S. Navy the steamer *Lancaster*. When it became a member of the famous Ellett Marine Brigade, officials turned to a Revolutionary hero from abroad and called it the *Kosiuszko*.

The citizens of the great river city seemed not to have protested when the *Saint Louis* was renamed to honor another European Revolutionary War hero, *Baron De Kalb*. As a tribute to the Marquis de Lafayette, the name of the *Fort Henry* was scrapped in favor of his. Earlier, the vessel had been registered as the *Alick Scott*.

Rated at 512 tons, the *Ethan Allen* commemorated still another hero of the American Revolution. When put to use fighting Confederates, it became the USS *Commodore Barney*.

Nearly twice as large, the *Atlantic* was purchased at New York in August 1863. Once it became the property of the U.S. Navy, its name was changed to honor *Commodore Read*.

When captured by the USS *Pursuit*, the 460-ton *Florida* became a prize of war. Purchased for $28,500 at an auction, the one-time Confederate ship became the USS *Hendrick Hudson*.

Annals of the period say little about Ben Williams. Still, he must have been pleased when his name was bestowed upon a sailing vessel familiar on many waterfronts as the *Mediator*.

One of the most unusual changes involving a noteworthy person was made at Key West. There the Navy Department secured from the prize court the schooner *Priscilla C. Ferguson*. Despite the fact that a general by the same name had watched over the bombardment of Fort Sumter and had commanded Confederate forces at the first battle of Manassas, the 101-ton sailing vessel became the USS *Beauregard*.

Launched in 1819, a vessel called the *Alabama* was viewed askance once the state for which it was named withdrew from the Union. Yet it was not until 1864 that it belatedly became the USS *New Hampshire* in honor of one of the few states that was nearly 100 percent loyal.

Early in the struggle, the schooner *Savannah*, a privateer out of Charleston, was captured. Condemned by a New York prize court, it was sold to the U.S. Navy for just $1,250. Armed with two 9-inch Dahlgren smoothbores and an 11-inch rifled cannon, the one-time Confederate vessel was added to the Potomac River Flotilla as the USS *Chotank*.

Another privateer proudly bore the name of the Confederate governor of North Carolina. Captured, the *A.D. Vance* soon became the *Winslow* and then the USS *Frolic*.

Indian names abounded among warships built for the U.S. Navy on contract. Only a few vessels captured or purchased were given new names from this source during the war years, however.

Purchased at Boston in 1855 for $55,000, the sailing sloop-of-war *City of Boston* was renamed *Despatch*. Five years later, with the attack on Fort Sumter a probability, the *Despatch* became the *Pocahontas* in honor of the Indian princess of Virginia's early colonial days.

Ulysses S. Grant used the *New Uncle Sam* in his expedition against Fort Donelson, Tennessee. Despite its role in that significant Federal victory, the 902-ton side-wheel steamer became the USS *Black Hawk* in December 1862.

Less than half the size of the vessel familiar to many as the *New Uncle Sam*, the screw steamer *Westernport* was big enough to hold four 32-pounder guns and one 24-pounder. Before the former mercantile vessel went to war, though, she became the USS *Wyandotte*.

Ironically, the retention of old names was often a source of as much confusion as would have resulted from changes. In an alphabetized sampling of major Union vessels, the first letter reveals these potential problems:

- Three vessels were called *Aries*.
- Half a dozen bore the name *Arizona*.
- *Arkansas* was honored by three ships and *Arletta* by two.

- Sailors served aboard five vessels called *Arrow* and two that were named *Artist*.
- The name *Ascension* was at the bows of three ships.
- Ten Federal vessels of widely varying size and strength were called the *Atlantic*.
- A figure of classical mythology gave his name to two ships called *Atlas* and three were called by the Latin-derived name of *Augusta*.
- *Aurora* was painted on four vessels, while there were two each of *Avenger*, the *Avon*, and the *Azalea*.

Animals fared better than Native Americans when new names were bestowed upon Federal ships. The purchase of the wooden stern-wheel steamer *Rachel Miller* added significantly to the strength of the Mississippi River Flotilla. Soon after changing hands at Cincinnati, its feminine name was dropped in favor of the USS *Reindeer*.

A distant relative of the reindeer was commemorated when the 162-ton *Countess* was named the USS *Elk*.

Measuring 158 feet 8 inches in length, with a beam of more than 30 feet, the *Fanny Barker* became the USS *Fawn* as soon as she was equipped with six 24-pounder howitzers and entered Federal service.

Built at Cincinnati, the *Florence Miller* No. 2 caught the eye of Adm. D. D. Porter, who paid $32,000 for her. When she became the property of the U.S. Navy, the riverboat entered her new career as the USS *Moose*.

The *Emma Brown* became the USS *Gazelle*, and the *Ohio Valley* was transformed into the USS *Ibex*.

Possibly the existence of the Confederate raider known as the *Alabama* led the new Federal owners of an 80-ton schooner named *Alabama* to rechristen it as the USS *Fox*.

Compared with the Federal records, those concerning Confederate ships are skimpy. Yet Richmond leaders were responsible for perhaps the most memorable of all changes of ships' names. When an attempt was made by the Federals to burn the USS *Merrimac* to prevent its capture, its name had already been shortened form the original *Merrimack*. Converted by its captors into the first American ironclad read for battle, it became the famous CSS *Virginia*. Because a majority of early writers about the switch from wooden to iron vessels were from the North, the salvaged ship that bore the name of a Confederate state is still widely identified as having been the *Merrimac*.

Compared with many Federal vessels, the armament of the CSS *Savannah* was puny; she was mounted with only one 32-pounder smoothbore. Formerly the *Everglade*, this 53-ton warship created new confusion when she became the *Oconee* in August 1863.

Once called the *Leopard*, a privateer trying to outrun half a dozen blockaders failed to make it into Charleston Harbor. In desperation, its captain burned the splendid *Stonewall Jackson*, thereby failing to deliver 40,000 army shoes, 200 barrels of saltpeter, and several artillery pieces.

A sister vessel, the CSS *Stonewall*, went through the war relatively unscathed. She then ended her service in Japan as the *Hijms Allzuma*.

Launched as the *Dragon* and renamed the *Torpedo*, a sleek river vessel received a special honor in 1864. She was selected to convey Confederate Vice President Alexander H. Stephens to Hampton Roads to engage in conversations aimed at achieving what Confederates considered an honorable peace.

When captured by the raider *Alabama*, the bark *Conrad* was promptly put under the Stars and Bars as the privateer *Tuscaloosa*. Earlier, Confederate acquisition of the *Giraffe* led her to become the *Robert E. Lee*.

Built in Boston, the 387-ton *Enoch Train* was a fixture around the New Orleans water front. Purchased for $100,000, she was given a protective coat of iron but only one 32-pounder carronade when converted into the CSS *Manassas*. No match for a powerful Federal warship, she was sunk in a battle below New Orleans after just three months' service in the Confederate navy.

When Southerners became the owner, the *Oreto* was renamed the CSS *Florida*. After an epoch-making voyage as a blockade-runner loaded to the gunwales with weapons and military supplies, the renamed *Fingal* reached Savannah. Soon afterward she became the CSS *Atlanta*.

Confederate purchasing agent James Bulloch, who accompanied the *Fingal* on her first voyage, wangled the purchase of numerous fine British-built vessels. One of them, built simply as *#290*, became first the *Enrica* and then the *Alabama*, the most famous cruiser to prey on Union shipping.

Despite the impact of the *Alabama*, Bulloch's most famous purchase in England was the swift raider initially known as the *Sea King*. Equipped with both sails and a 250-horsepower engine, this teak-plated clipper was rated at only 1,018 tons.

Commanded by Lt. James I. Waddell and renamed in honor of a Virginia valley, the *Shenandoah* captured thirty-eight prize before being surrendered at Liverpool in 1865. Later purchased by the sultan of Zanzibar, the one-time raider went down in the Indian Ocean in 1879 under a third name that was not preserved in Western records.

Seeking to resupply Maj. Robert Anderson and his men at Fort Sumter, President James Buchanan dispatched the *Star of the West* to Charleston in January 1861. She was turned back by fire from cadets at the Citadel military college but was present at several other engagements before being captured.

Joyful Confederates went through formal ceremonies renaming the vessel the CSS *Saint Philip*, and then ruefully decided to sink her. She went down in Mississippi's Tallahatchie River as part of an effort to block its channel to Federal vessels.

⹊⹊⹊

Like the *Alabama*, the CSS *Theodora* sailed under two earlier names. When launched, the 500-ton sidewheel ironclad privateer was called the *Carolina*. Before becoming a member of the Confederate fleet, she was for a time listed as the *Gordon*.

⹊⹊⹊

U.S. Secretary of the Navy Gideon Welles or one his top aides must have had a penchant for blossoms. One after another, several names of vessels were changed in favor of flowers.

Purchased in 1862 from a veteran tar who had given his surname to his ship, the little 117-foot *Schultz* became the USS *Columbine* as soon as she was acquired by the U.S. Navy.

⹊⹊⹊

Secured at New York in 1863, the screw steamer *Governor* would seem to have had a satisfactory name. Not so, said Washington. Hence the far from dainty 198-ton vessel was renamed the USS *Camelia*.

⹊⹊⹊

On August 24, 1863, the very day she was purchased from A. H. Cunningham, the 82-ton *Ajax* became the USS *Carnation*. Acquired a few weeks later from J. Howe and C. W. Copeland, their 123-foot *Meteor* was immediately dubbed the USS *Cowslip*.

Apparently the use of feminine names was not welcomed in some circles. Brand new and sheathed with yellow metal, the tugboat *Alice* of Philadelphia became the property of the U.S. Navy in July 1864. The ink on the ownership papers was hardly dry before the 122-foot screw streamer was renamed the USS *Aster*.

Mary Grandy seemed an appropriate name for a 321-ton screw steamer while she was operated by Copeland and Howe. Days before workmen mounted a 30-pounder Parrott gun and two 12-pounder rifles upon the one-time merchant ship, she became the USS *Bignonia*.

In almost monotonous fashion, long-familiar names of purchased and captured vessels, many of them feminine, were scrapped—often in favor of flowers. Some of such changes were:

- *Heliotrope* instead of *Maggie Baker*
- *Acacia* in lieu of *Vicksburg*
- *Geranium* for *John A. Dix*
- *Violet* rather than *Martha*
- *Peony* for *Republic*
- *Jonquil* in lieu of *J. K Kirman*
- *Fuchsia* instead of *Kiang Soo*
- First *Hornet* and then *Cuba* for *Lady Stirling*
- *Clarence* in lieu of *Coquette*
- *Albion* for *Lucy R. Waring*

Some names of flowers bestowed upon vessels formerly bearing other titles include: *Gladiolus, Anemone, Hydrangea, Daisy, Jasmine, Pansy, Rose, Daffodil, Tulip, Periwinkle, Hollyhock, Dahlia, Primrose, Honeysuckle*, and even *Phlox*.

Imagine a tar-blackened seaman explaining to his wife or sweetheart that he was serving aboard the *Periwinkle* or the *Heliotrope*!

Numerous as they were, flowers accounted for only a fraction of new names for ships. Officials of the U.S. Navy selected many forts, generals, and battle sites when they renamed vessels. They also honored six states, eleven cities, and four birds—the petrel, curlew, oriole, and grosbeak.

Decades later this welter of double and triple names belonging to ships of every size and type remains a source of considerable confusion. It is apparent that the upper echelons of the U.S. Navy substituted many flower and animal names for those of women. In the process of having scores of vessels reregistered, they agreed to use only three feminine names: Pocahontas, Anna, and Emma.

A particularly puzzling change took place when the U.S. Navy acquired the bark *Abd-el-Kadir*. It's small wonder that the name was immediately changed, but records fail to indicate why the new Federal owners sent it to war as the USS *Ammonoosuo*.

Part Eight

NOTORIOUS
AND NONESUCH

In sheer magnitude, the Civil War is in a class by itself. No other U.S. military involvement comes close to challenging its stupendous statistics. An estimated 623,000 Americans died during about 1,400 days of conflict. Only about one-third of them were combat fatalities, yet some or many who died took part in so many clashes that they lost count. Frederick H. Dyer, who devoted a great part of his life to compiling Union data, identified about 13,000 of these. Listed in order of diminishing size, they range from battles and engagements to actions and combats, sieges, skirmishes, affairs, reconnaissances, scouts, and "other military events." So many men and women took part in so many military and civilian affairs that ultimate achievements or events were inevitable.

Thirty-six

FIRST TIMES

A majority of Confederate leaders and most of their foes in blue held that the first shot of the war was fired in Charleston Harbor on April 12, 1861. Lincoln, commander in chief of U.S. forces, had a different view. It was his contention that no state had actually seceded; although eleven claimed to have done so, according to the president, they were still in the Union. Traditionally, war was regarded as a conflict between two sovereign states. Since the independence of the Confederacy was not recognized, Lincoln termed the sectional struggle an insurrection. It came about, he said, by "a combination of forces too powerful to subdue by ordinary means."

So viewed, the April artillery duel between Federal and Confederate forces didn't start a war. Thus it was impossible to label the initial shell fired at Fort Sumter as having been first in the war.

Pennsylvania-born James Buchanan, Lincoln's predecessor in office, was adamant in his insistence that only Congress could declare war. He wasn't interested in a verbal subterfuge to justify sending troops to the South. More than anything else, Buchanan wanted peace. In a bid to secure that peace, Buchanan reluctantly endorsed the plans of his top military advisers. As a result, the merchant ship *Star of the West* was sent to Charleston Harbor with supplies and reinforcements for Maj. Roberts Anderson and his tiny garrison at Fort Sumter.

Having received advance warning that the ship was en route, the Secessionists were prepared. When the vessel entered Charleston waters early on the morning of January 9, 1861, cadets from the Citadel military academy manning a battery on Morris Island, close to the Federal installation, placed a shot across the ship's bow. By many standards, that shot was the first of the war. The records are clear and precise; it was fired by Cadet George W. Haynesworth.

Full-scale military action would have followed this first shot in January had Lincoln, who was committed to the preservation of the Union at all costs, occupied the White House. Had that happened, Haynesworth would be much better known today.

Debate over the identity of the man who launched the first shell toward Fort Sumter began very early and has never completely subsided. Many of his admirers credited this honor to Edmund Ruffin of Virginia, an ardent Secessionist who went to Charleston hoping to participate in the fireworks. Much evidence suggests that Ruffin was offered the opportunity to begin the shelling, but he shook his head in refusal. Three or four other prominent Confederates have been identified as firing that first shot in April, but the evidence is inconclusive. An unidentified member of a Secessionist battery probably fired the shot that led Lincoln to try to put down an insurrection.

At least two members of the Fort Sumter garrison, both of whom later became prominent, claimed to have fired the first shot at a Confederate battery. Subsequently a brigadier, Jefferson C. Davis claimed that the honor belonged to him, but those comrades in arms who detested him discounted his report.

Career artillerist Abner Doubleday, then a captain, insisted that he was the first to fire upon Southerners who were trying to drive the Federal forces from Fort Sumter. After the conflict was over, Doubleday wrote a volume of *Reminiscences* in which he said the honor was indisputably his. Doubleday was made a major general in 1862, and his postwar book was widely circulated. Maybe because of these factors, the man who had nothing to do with the invention of baseball is usually identified as the first to return the Confederate fire.

If it was Doubleday and not Davis who fired the first shot from the Federal fort, it was a dud. Doubleday admitted, "My first shot bounded from the sloping roof of the battery opposite without producing any apparent effect." Regardless of how effective his fire may have been that day, he was promoted one month later, again on February 3, 1862, and once more just nine months later. After the 1863 battle of Gettysburg, Major General Doubleday was relieved of field duty and assigned to a desk job for the duration.

No one has been identified as the person who fired the first shot at the first battle of Manassas (or Bull Run), but Confederate Brig. Gen. Richard S. Ewell is believed to have been the first to lead his men into battle there. According to his report, Ewell's brigade was made up of Robert E. Rodes's Fifth Alabama Infantry, John J. Seibels's Sixth Alabama, and Horatio Seymour's Seventh Louisiana. Four companies of cavalry and a battery of artillery accompanied the infantry.

On the morning of July 21, 1861, Ewell followed his orders to hold himself "in readiness to advance at a moment's notice;" As a result, he and his men may have been first to arrive at what became the first major battleground of the war.

Confederate historians say that the first artillery shot at Manassas roared from the mouth of a 30-pounder Parrott gun at about 5:00 A.M. It is credited to a battery commanded by Capt. J. Howard Carlisle, who failed to record the name of the gunner.

Many persons interested in the largest of American wars think of Bull Run as being the first battle. Yet more than two weeks earlier, opposing infantry clashed at Philippi, Virginia (now West Virginia).

As battles go, the first encounter didn't amount to much. Federal forces attacked Confederates under Col. G. A. Porterfield just after daybreak on June 3. Outnumbered at least two to one and taken completely by surprise, Porterfield's men threw down their muskets and fled. The Confederates' departure from the first encounter between opposing troops was so rapid that the jubilant victors bragged that the skirmish constituted "the Philippi Races." Porterfield was censured and then relieved of his command.

Philippi put another first into the record books: after the battle, Pvt. Jim Hanger became the first man to have a leg amputated during the Civil War.

⁓⁓⁓

The clash at Philippi wasn't significant enough to be labeled a battle, and the bluecoats took a terrific beating at Manassas. Hence many analysts hold that the first Federal battlefield victory came at Mill Springs, Kentucky, little more than a year after cannon turned back the *Star of the West*. Part of the irony of the Union win lies in the fact that the Bluegrass State had officially declared itself to be neutral.

Some residents of the region in which the Confederates suffered their first significant defeat were not positive about its site. Many of them knew the place called Mill Springs, but most Federal records list it as Logan's Cross Roads. Others believed that the battle in the neutral state occurred at Beech Grove, otherwise known as Sunset.

In his *Compendium of the War of the Rebellion*, Frederick H. Dyer—almost as well known for his conservative use of language as for his accuracy—listed the January 19, 1862, conflict as having occurred at Fishing Creek.

⁓⁓⁓

There's little or no debate about the fact that the first decisive Union victory in a pitched battle west of the Mississippi River was won at Pea Ridge, Arkansas. Confederates who admitted having been defeated there in March 1862 preferred to call the place Elkhorn Tavern.

Facts about the origin of baseball and the first shot fired from Fort Sumter are debatable, but there is no such discrepancy about Alexandria, Virginia. On May 24, 1861, Col. Daniel Butterfield of the Twelfth New York Militia led his men across Washington's Long Bridge before dawn. That made him the first Federal commander to set foot on Confederate soil during the hostilities. Throughout the North, the man remembered as the composer of "Taps" was hailed as a hero.

Many who joined in his praise conveniently forgot much that Lincoln had said in his First Inaugural Address. Speaking to the divided nation on March 4, 1861, the first Republican president said that the power of his office would be used "to hold, occupy, and possess the property, and places belonging to the government, and to collect the duties and imposts." Then he made a brief but solemn promise. Beyond doing what was necessary to accomplish these stated objectives, he said, "There will be no invasion—no using of force against, or among the people anywhere."

Less than two months later, that comment by the chief executive of the nation was exploded by artillery fire in faraway Charleston Harbor. As a result, Butterfield had the distinction of leading the first Federal troops to enter Virginia.

In the case of the soldiers in gray, the first invasion of enemy soil did not occur until September 5, 1862. It was neither planned nor led by Robert E. Lee. Troops under the command of Thomas J. "Stonewall" Jackson crossed the Potomac River at White's Ford, near Leesburg. Unlike the Federals who advanced upon Alexandria in silence, the confident Confederates sang at the top of their voices. The tune chosen by the first Southerners to enter Northern territory was "Maryland, My Maryland!"

Brig. Gen. Adam R. "Stovepipe" Johnson led the first successful Confederate invasion in the western theater. With only a handful of men, he penetrated Kentucky's Green River region south of Owensboro. So much alarm resulted from the 1862 raid that Indiana Gov. Oliver P. Morton sent an urgent telegram to Washington requesting more Federal cavalry be sent to the state immediately to prevent Johnson's crossing the Ohio River. Morton's plea for help arrived too late; Stovepipe and his ragged band had already struck at Newburgh, Indiana, and retired into Kentucky.

A few months earlier, Capt. Ezra Taylor of Battery B, First Illinois Light Artillery, filed the first official report of its kind. In it he reported a November 7, 1861, skirmish at Belmont, Missouri. Five men had been wounded: in each case, the rank and full name were given. Three horses were shot on the field, and two others sustained serious leg injuries.

Taylor's meticulous report, which reveals a great deal about the needs of a fighting force, then enumerated two sets of data always significant to a commander but seldom listed in detail:

> Left on the field: 2 caissons, 1 baggage wagon, 2 sets artillery lead harness, 1,000 ball cartridges for Colt's revolver, 200 rounds ammunition for 6-pounder guns, 25 double blankets, 20 canteens, 5 coats, 3 caps, 15 Colt's revolvers, 5 horse blankets, 6 sabers, 5 lanterns, 3 shovels, 1 overcoat, 2 currycombs and brushes, 2 fuse-gouges, 60 friction primers, 2 camp kettles, 20 cups, 1 leg guard, 1 sponge and rammer, 6 whips, 20 haversacks, 2 pick-axes, 4 felling axes, 1 trail handspike.
>
> Captured from the enemy: 120 horses, 1 mule, 1 6-pounder brass gun, 1 12-pounder brass howitzer, and some fragments of artillery harness, and sundry small articles captured by individual, not of any particular value to the service.

Taylor and his men went into action armed with four 6-pounder field guns, two 12-pounder howitzers with gun limbers and caissons complete. Guns and officers required 81 horses and 14 mules. Ammunition carried into the fight consisted of 1,000 rounds for guns and howitzers and 1,000 pistol cartridges. During the encounter, 114 Federal gunners fired 400 rounds on the field, lost 200, and returned from the action with 400.

In his *Compendium of the War of the Rebellion*, Frederick H. Dyer, who termed the meeting an "engagement," reported that six Federal units from Illinois and one from Iowa were also involved in addition to Taylor and Battery B: Dollins's Independent Cavalry Company; Delan's Adams County Cavalry; the Twenty-second, Twenty-seventh, Thirtieth, and Thirty-first Illinois Infantries; and the Seventh Iowa Infantry.

Dyer didn't attempt to compile Confederate statistics, and those who have made an effort to do so have found the records to be woefully lacking. Federal casualties included 80 killed, 322 wounded, and 99 missing.

Three days later, in another action, a man was leading troops despite the fact that his offer to serve the Union had been initially ignored. Having worn a blue uniform through the influence of the congressman whose district included Galena, Illinois, Ulysses S. Grant had earlier "seen the elephant" in Mexico as a captain. Elihu B. Washburne's protégé experienced his first Civil War combat on Missouri soil, not far from Benton.

Confederates didn't win their first major victory in the West until September 1863. Their hour of glory came at Chickamauga, in southeastern Tennessee. Confederate Gen. Braxton Bragg failed to follow up his win and soon was so badly beaten at Chattanooga that he was removed from command.

Three weeks after Virginia had been invaded, men of seven Union regiments marched most of the night to reach the neighborhood of Great Bethel. Also called Big Bethel, Virginia, the region was known to have about twelve hundred Confederates under the command of Col. John G. Magruder.

An estimated twenty-five hundred Federals launched their attack under the command of Brig. Gen. Ebenezer W. Peirce. Although tiny by comparison with later clashes, the ensuing combat is often listed as the first battle of the war. When the dust settled, Magruder announced that the ratio of Federal to Confederate casualties was more than nine to one.

According to the Confederate Military History, Maj. Henry C. Carter of Richmond entered the record book at Great Bethel. He was credited with having fired the first cannon discharged during a "regular engagement" on Virginia soil.

<hr />

At Gettysburg, the first battle in which more than forty thousand casualties occurred, the first shot is said to have been fired by Lt. Marcellus E. Jones of the Eighth Illinois Cavalry. For the record, the weapon he used was neither a musket nor a rifle, but a carbine, one of the standard weapons of Federal cavalry.

Henry Raison of the Seventh Tennessee Infantry is regarded as the first Confederate to die in the greatest of all American battles.

West Point graduate William T. Sherman, class of 1840, was in command of a brigade at Manassas in 1861. For the man destined to gain fame and infamy as the leader of the March to the Sea, the July battle constituted his first experience of combat.

<hr />

During early action in Virginia's western region, now West Virginia, one of Sherman's opponents saw his first action of the Civil War. A professional soldier who had graduated from West Point in 1829 and had won slow advancement in the thirty-two years prior to the war, he did not achieve the rank of colonel until 1861.

Changing uniforms and accepting a new commission, Robert E. Lee led Virginia state forces at Conrad's Mill on September 11, 1861. It was at this remote point that he first commanded men under fire.

No longer a professional soldier without combat experience, Lee planned and executed the remainder of the Cheat Mountain campaign in western Virginia. His admirers sometimes fail to remember that this campaign ended in defeat for Lee's forces.

No pure cavalry engagement occurred until horsemen met at Kelly's Ford, Virginia, on March 17, 1863. This first battle of its sort resulted in only 211 casualties. One of them was Maj. John Pelham, called "as grand a flirt as ever lived" and nicknamed "the Gallant Pelham." In gratitude for his services, he received a posthumous promotion to the rank of lieutenant colonel.

Ten weeks after the action at Kelly's Ford, the largest cavalry battle in North America occurred at Brandy Station, Virginia. About ten thousand men on each side took part in the conflict that led to nearly one thousand Federal casualties and more than five hundred Confederate.

The impact of the battle was greater than these data suggest, however. Despite the losses by the soldiers in blue, Brandy Station demonstrated for the first time that Federal cavalry could fight as well as Confederates on horseback.

Reams Station, also in Virginia, was the point at which two battles took place. During the second one, Confederate Capt. Shade Wooten of North Carolina racked up a record that was never challenged.

Although the August 24–25, 1864, conflict produced more than three thousand casualties, Wooten was not among them. Three times he saved his life by throwing dirt at the eyes of a foe who was about to shoot him.

Alfred Ely of New York was the first sitting congressman to be captured in battle. Along with scores of other Washington celebrities, he couldn't resist riding out to see the action at Manassas Gap in July 1861.

While an inmate of Richmond's famous Libby Prison, Ely was picked for an especially demanding task. When the names of captured Federal officers were put into a hat, Ely drew them out one by one to determine which of them would become hostages for the safety of Confederate seaman threatened with death for the crime of piracy.

Brig Gen. Robert S. Garnett achieved immortality of a sort by becoming the first general officer on either side to die of battle wounds. During a July 13, 1861, action at Corrick's Ford, Virginia (often identified as Carrick's Ford), the brigadier in blue was mortally wounded while attempting to withdraw his skirmishers from the field.

Garnett was by no means the first soldier to die. That honor went to Pvt. Daniel Hough of the First U.S. Artillery. According to Abner Doubleday, Hough was killed at Fort Sumter on April 14, 1861, when a cannon went off prematurely during a salute to the flag.

Purely accidental and not due to Confederate fire, the death was attributed to spongers who failed to extinguish fire inside the piece before it was reloaded. Hough's right arm was blown off, and he quickly bled to death.

Hough wore the uniform of a regular in the U.S. Army. Just five days after his death, four ninety-day volunteers from Massachusetts were the first soldiers to die in combat—of a sort.

Marching through the streets of Baltimore, men of the Sixth Massachusetts were pelted with stones by pro-Secessionist civilians. A musket was fired, and men on both sides emptied their guns indiscriminately.

Pvts. Luther C. Ladd, Sumner Needham, Charles A. Taylor, and Addison O. Whitney were killed immediately or received mortal wounds. At least three times as many civilian residents of the Maryland city died as a result of the fray.

May 7, 1861, brought a first event of quite different nature. On that day an unidentified private in Company G of the Eighth New York Infantry carefully prepared his musket for action. He then sat down against a wall, rested his chin on the muzzle of his weapon, and tripped its flintlock. As a result he became the first Civil War soldier to die by his own hand.

Col. Elmer Ellsworth of the New York Fire Zouaves, or Eleventh New York Volunteers, was the first Federal commissioned officer to die. Ellsworth had just removed a Confederate flag from the roof of a hotel in Alexandria, Virginia, when the proprietor, James T. Jackson, shot him at close range on the stairway. Pvt. Francis E. Brownell promptly shot and killed Jackson.

So closely linked with Lincoln that he could be termed a favorite of the family of the commander in chief, Ellsworth's death caused the White House to be draped in mourning. Throughout the North he was lauded as a martyr for the righteous cause and labeled as "a war hero" despite the fact that he had never been in combat.

Capt. James H. Ward was the first Union naval officer to die in combat. As commander of the Potomac Flotilla, the twenty-eight-year veteran led an attack on Confederate batteries at the mouth of Aquia Creek. During the artillery duel that followed, Ward took a direct hit and died immediately. His failed mission was designed to keep the river open and end the Confederate blockade of Washington. Records of the period are so chaotic that Ward's death is variously reported to have taken place on June 1, June 17, and June 27, 1861.

Shortly before or after Ward became a war hero, the name of Lt. John Greble of Company B, Second U.S. Artillery, went into the record books. One of the twenty-five hundred men who went to Big Bethel, Virginia, on June 9, 1861, under the leadership of Brig. Gen. Ebenezer W. Peirce, Greble became the first officer of the U.S. Army to die during the Civil War.

His battery had delivered only about a dozen rounds against the enemy before he was killed in action. Admirers saw to it that he received a succession of posthumous promotions that eventually catapulted him to the rank of lieutenant colonel.

Cyrus W. James of the Ninth New York Cavalry is listed as the first man to be killed at Gettysburg. He probably died not knowing that a cavalryman of the Eighth Illinois would be credited with firing the first shot and starting the largest battle of the war.

At Gettysburg, Federal Maj. Gen. John Reynolds was the first but not the last general to be killed or mortally wounded during the mammoth three-day struggle.

Albert Sydney Johnston, whose gray collar carried the three stars of a full general, was the first commander of an army to die in combat. While directing frontline operations at Shiloh, he was hit in the leg and bled to death before the wound was recognized as serious.

Only Maj. Gen. James B. McPherson was Johnston's counterpart of sorts in blue. Dropped by Confederates while on reconnaissance near Atlanta, the commander of the Army of the Tennessee died on the spot.

A little-known encounter took place two days before "the Philippi Races." John Q. (or R.) Marr, a Virginia Military Institute graduate, became captain of the Warrenton Rifles when he formed the unit.

Early one morning in June 1861, a few members of Company B, Second U.S. Cavalry, galloped through the village of Fairfax Court House, Virginia. As they raced along the road, they fired a few shots at random. Struck in the chest, Marr became the first Confederate officer to die in combat.

Since both Fairfax Court House and Philippi were minor skirmishes, another name soon appeared on the roster of heroes in gray. Pvt. Henry L. Wyatt of Company A, First North Carolina Infantry, was felled by a Federal volley as the first battle of Manassas got under way. Consequently, he became the first Confederate soldier to die in battle.

While reconnoitering near Elkwater Bridge, Virginia, on September 13, 1861, Lt. Col. John A. Washington was killed. News of this tragedy in the mountains of Randolph County brought mourning to Virginia troops.

Washington, a long-time friend of Robert E. Lee, was the first member of his commander's family to die in combat. He fell early in Lee's fatally flawed first field campaign for the Confederacy.

Today several Civil War battlefields are heavily dotted with markers commemorating the men who fought there. Whether fashioned from granite or copper, these tributes are latecomers. A monument erected in September 1861 in memory of an Eighth Georgia Infantry officer was the first battlefield tablet erected for a fallen Civil War soldier.

Thirty-seven

CLAIMS TO FAME

At least one out of every ten Confederate soldiers alive after Appomattox seems to have claimed to have been involved in the last gasp of the Lost Cause. Some of these doings show up in official documents, but many do not. Practically all of them have produced historical markers that were erected by state or local organizations. This subject is a challenge. To deduce the truth, the language used to describe a last military encounter has to be analyzed and the evidence sifted.

On December 6, 1911, Bvt. Maj. Gen. J. Warren Keifer of Ohio addressed a band of veterans. In his closing remarks he modestly indicated that his command was responsible for the capture of Robert E. Lee's oldest son. Powerfully built and standing six feet, two inches tall, Confederate Maj. Gen. George Washington Custis Lee was made a prisoner three days prior to his father's surrender to Ulysses S. Grant.

Describing the capture of the high-ranking prisoner, Keifer said that it took place on April 6 "at Sailor's Creek, Virginia, the last field battle of the war."

No matter what terminology is used to label it, the fracas that occurred at Sayler's Creek was a lot more than a skirmish. Federal forces suffered about twelve hundred casualties before forcing nearly eight thousand men in gray to surrender.

Keifer was a colonel on April 18, 1865, when he compiled his official report at Burkeville, Virginia. In it he does not mention capturing Lee, saying only that the division of Custis Lee was "known to have participated in the battle."

Four days earlier at the same village, Pvt. Harris S. Hawthorn, Company F, 121st New York Volunteers, appeared before Judge Advocate H. E. Hindmarsh of the First Division, Sixth Corps, to sign a sworn statement. According to it, Hawthorn was "the first person [officer or enlisted man] who seized or captured General Custis Lee, of the Confederate Army, in the engagement of the 6th of April."

His regiment, known as the Orange and Herkimer, was attached to the Second Brigade, First Division, Sixth Corps. When Lee was captured during the "last field battle," Keifer was a brevet brigadier at the head of the Second Division, Sixth Corps.

Three days after Sayler's Creek, with the surrender ceremonies at Appomattox having been completed, fierce fighting was under way near Mobile, Alabama. Forces under Edward R. S. Canby, a major general of U.S. Volunteers, attacked Fort Blakely at 5:30 P.M. on April 9.

Ranks of defenders included a brigade of boy reserves charged with holding the Confederate right flank. When attacked by sixteen thousand men in blue, they withered under fire and surrendered after twenty minutes of fighting. Federal casualties were about six hundred, but Canby considered that a small price to pay for thirty-four hundred prisoners and more than forty captured guns.

Confederate Maj. Gen. Richard Taylor commanded the Department of East Louisiana, Mississippi, and Alabama at the time of the capitulation at Blakely. Five days earlier he had decided to accept the surrender terms offered by Canby. Hence he met the Federal commander at Citronelle, Alabama, on May 4, to make the agreement official.

It wasn't until May 8 that paroles offered to his men were accepted. So Taylor insisted that the surrender occurred on that day. He consistently described it as "the surrender of the last major Confederate force east of the Mississippi River."

More than a month later, at Palmito (or Palmetto) Ranch on the Rio Grande, five hundred Confederates under Brig. Gen. James E. Slaughter fought against a band of sixteen hundred soldiers in blue.

Texas Rangers, whose commander was known as Rip Ford, made a futile charge at what survivors described as "a headlong gallop." On the Federal side, most of the fighting was done by men under the command of Col. T. H. Barret. To his dying day, Barret insisted that his Sixty-second U.S. Negro Regiment took the honors in the last battle of the war.

Based partly upon Barret's claim, the death of Pvt. John J. Williams is regarded as the last Union combat fatality. A member of the Thirty-fourth Indiana Infantry, he fell before Confederates claimed victory on May 13, 1865.

Survivors of the struggle at Bentonville, North Carolina, scoffed at claims originating far to the west. On March 19, 1865, they were waiting for Federal troops to make a move and were delighted to see Maj. Gen. Henry W. Slocum's Army of Georgia in the distance.

The Confederates made three separate assaults in a struggle that ended after sunset, but they were repelled each time. Union officers failed to compile a careful tabulation of the casualties. Two days later, another clash at Bentonville was recorded as a Federal victory.

As a result, many authorities describe the North Carolina conflict as being "the last significant Confederate effort to halt Sherman." Confederate Lt. Gen. Wade Hampton, the Southern authority most often quoted, called Bentonville the "last general battle."

Although an estimated 2,650 Confederates were captured at Bentonville, there was no formal surrender of a major body of troops. That made it possible to erect a historical marker near the western edge of the state. The plaque reads:

> *NEAR THIS SPOT*
> *THE LAST SHOT OF THE WAR*
> *BETWEEN THE STATES*
> *WAS FIRED UNDER THE COMMAND OF*
> *LT. ROBERT T. CONLEY*
>   *OF THE CONFEDERATE ARMY*
> *MAY 6, 1865*
> *ERECTED BY*
> *UNITED DAUGHTERS OF THE CONFEDERACY*
>   *OF THE DISTRICT OF NORTH CAROLINA*
> *1892*

A freestanding bronze tablet on South Main Street in Waynesville bears the message:

> *GEN. JAMES G. MARTIN'S ARMY*
> *OF WESTERN NORTH CAROLINA,*
> *LAST CONFEDERATE FORCE IN THE STATE, SURRENDERED*
> *HERE*
> *ON MAY 6, 1865.*

Regionally famous, Martin's "surrender" took place on the day Jefferson Davis moved south from Sandersville, Georgia, knowing that Federal cavalry were closing in on him.

In the contest for the honor of being the last to surrender, Confederate Gen. Edmund Kirby-Smith disputed any claims made by others who fought in gray. His Trans-Mississippi Department had been cut off from Richmond by the 1863 fall of Vicksburg, hence the area had become known as "Kirby Smithdom."

Kirby-Smith led his forces to Galveston late in May and reached a tentative surrender agreement with Federal leaders. On June 2, 1865, formal surrender ceremonies took place, after which he claimed to be the last Confederate general officer to surrender and then left the country for Mexico.

Stand Watie, however, seems to have the stronger claim to be the last Confederate general to surrender. Watie fought at Pea Ridge, Arkansas, as a Confederate colonel of the Cherokee Mounted Rifles and took part in numerous engagements late in the war. On May 8, 1864, he became the only Native American to receive a commission as a Confederate brigadier.

Soon after learning that Lee had surrendered, Watie took to the hills. More than thirteen months after his elevation in rank, on June 23, 1865, Watie surrendered to Federal authorities.

Months earlier, Federal Maj. Gen. John M. Palmer faced what he considered to be a unique situation in Kentucky. Trying to get the better of irregulars, or bushwhackers, he put Edwin Terrill at the head of a band he described as "Federal guerrillas."

Terrill and his ragged followers were responsible for the May 1864 capture of William C. Quantrill. Some of the men who had followed Quantrill from Kansas escaped and successfully eluded their pursuers for months. Fourteen weeks after Appomattox, they rode into the outskirts of Louisville and handed over their weapons. Many residents of both Kansas and Kentucky insist that these men, whose names were not preserved, were the last Confederates to surrender.

Archibald H. Thomson of the Twelfth Ohio Infantry would have scoffed at others who claimed to have affected the last capture of Confederates. At Sweetwater, Tennessee, he thought he had only one more job: completion of the final muster rolls. Suddenly he was ordered to lead twenty-five men to Chattanooga to collect some cattle belonging to the government.

On or about August 17, 1865, Thomson was told that the cattle had been stolen by a band of irregular Confederates whose leader was known only as Gatewood. Moving toward the region, the Federals were ambushed.

Thomson later said that he confronted the Confederates with nothing but a revolver. When he raised his weapon, twenty-five carbines were leveled on the gang. The guerrillas surrendered without a fight.

According to Thomson, the Federal exploit in Tennessee ended the war, since he was convinced that he had gained the last surrender of a Confederate force.

Maj. Aaron P. Brown of the Georgia State Militia saw things differently, of course. He was the surgeon in charge of a field hospital at Upson, and the stream of sick and wounded men diminished only slightly after Appomattox.

Brown continued to perform surgery and to administer laudanum and other drugs until a band of Federal cavalry entered the village where the doctor was still in uniform. They surrounded his tiny hospital and leveled their weapons. According to Brown, he regarded it as futile to resist, so he gave up his patients to the men in blue. The physician said, "My August 23, 1865, capitulation against overwhelming odds constituted the last surrender of Confederate troops."

Thirty-eight

DISTINCTIVELY OBSCURE

Observers on the bank of the Tennessee River could hardly believe their eyes. An immense fleet, known to be under the command of Ulysses S. Grant, was moving in the direction of a site soon to become memorable—Shiloh.

An awed Confederate managed later to make a list of the names of the vessels. He found it to include 14 armed river boats and 153 steamboats of every imaginable size and build. T. M. Hurst insisted that nothing in history equaled this fleet. Even the Spanish Armada, he said, did not exceed it in number. According to Hurst, the vessels of Grant's expedition "were not exceeded in tonnage by any flotilla that ever broke the foam."

Both the USS *Lexington* and the USS *Tiger*—believed to be the first gunboats ever to appear on the Tennessee River—were included in the Federal fleet. In addition, according to Hurst, one vessel had a unique asset. Only the little steamer *Glendale* was equipped with a calliope.

Unique maritime events abounded, and many of them took place upon the rivers of the South. Lt. F. S. Conover, commander of the USS *Isaac P. Smith*, chafed at being assigned to patrol the Stono River near Charleston. Bored with running up and down the tiny waterway, his men drew a crude figure of a Confederate soldier and placed it on Johns Island to use for pistol practice.

Barely half a mile from the improvised pistol range, Confederates were enraged at seeing the improvised target. Late in January 1863, under cover of darkness, they managed to haul at least four guns close to the bank of the river.

Maj. Charles Alston concealed his battery under a huge live oak tree. From this concealment, on January 30, the Confederates opened fire upon the heavily armed Federal vessel. Return fire raked the hidden position as the vessel increased speed to remove itself from the range of the Confederate guns.

Carefully directed fire from shore, combined with luck, caused three hits to the boilers of the Federal vessel. Hopelessly disabled the *Isaac P. Smith* became the only warship to surrender to a field battery. Within weeks, the 453-ton warship joined Confederate vessels in the defense of Charleston.

Every man aboard the CSS *Arctic* knew that she was a huge floating battery rather than a warship. When completed on November 30, 1863, the iron-plated monster mounted only three guns. Yet she entered the record books as the only Confederate vessel to have more than six hundred names on her muster roll. Despite her formidable manpower, the *Arctic* became useless when Wilmington, North Carolina, fell to Federal forces in 1865.

One month after the fall of Fort Sumter, a lookout aboard the screw steamer USS *Mohawk* (earlier the *Caledonia*) spotted an unusual vessel. Obviously so heavily loaded that it could not move rapidly, the large bark seemed to be headed for Key West.

Hailed, the ship proved to be the slaver *Wildfire*. Conveyed to New Orleans after it quickly surrendered, the vessel with a cargo of almost five hundred Africans was the only ship of its kind to be captured during the war.

Also in a class by itself, the *Hattie* was a vessel of quite different character. During her brief life, this blockade-runner made at least sixty successful runs. No other blockade-runner even came close to evading pursuers as many times.

Despite Confederate awe at the size of Grant's Tennessee River fleet, a long-standing Federal record was set in the eastern theater. At the age of thirty-six, Maj. Gen. George B. McClellan showed far more daring upon water than upon land. Having determined to move the Army of the Potomac from Washington to the peninsula of Virginia, he commandeered every available ship. In March 1862, his troops successfully landed and began a campaign that came within miles of Richmond. Castigated by Lincoln for having "the slows," McClellan's swift movement constituted the largest movement of troops by water until immense Allied fleets were assembled for action during World War I.

Confederates never came close to assembling an amphibious force the size of McClellan's army. Yet the self-styled independent nation that launched a war before acquiring a navy achieved rare distinction. Thousands of vessels took part in the four-year struggle. Of them, only the 790-ton cruiser *Shenandoah* succeeded in circumnavigating the globe while millions were fighting on land.

A sister vessel's impact was even more significant than the achievements of the Confederate raider. She is famous for having fought the *Monitor* to a draw in the world's first engagement between ironclads. Many an admirer of the CSS *Virginia* didn't know that she was the only famous warship to be built from a wreck that had been earlier burned almost to the water line.

Income from revenue collected at ports of entry was vital to the United States until 1861. That's why the Revenue Service had its own fleet of twenty-four vessels. Of these, the *Harriet Lane* was in a class by itself. She was the only side-wheel steamer used prior to the war to collect duties on imported goods.

Hundreds of armed vessels operated on the high seas, in rivers, and in harbors. Only one warship was stationed in the Great Lakes, however. Rated at 582 tons, the side-wheel steamer USS *Michigan* plowed through the waters of Lake Erie on a regular schedule.

Her armament consisted of a single gun that was considered adequate. Late in February 1865, however, U.S. naval authorities decided that the fire-power of the lone patrol boat was inadequate. With the conflict nearly over, the *Michigan's* battery was enlarged by a 30-pound Parrott rifle, five 20-pound rifles, six 24-pound guns, and two 12-pounders.

Launched at Erie, Pennsylvania, in 1844, the Civil War vessel, renamed *Wolverine*, was still operating in 1915.

Coxswain John Cooper of the USS *Brooklyn* was the target of a hail of Confederate fire during the battle of Mobile Bay. He fought with such conspicuous bravery that he was awarded the Medal of Honor.

When he was subsequently assigned to shore duty, the building in which Cooper worked caught fire. Wind blew the flames into other structures, some of which held stockpiles of ammunition. Aware that a wounded soldier was likely to burn to death, Cooper raced through exploding shells to rescue him.

Again he received the Medal of Honor, becoming the only member of the U.S. Navy to receive two such decorations.

David D. Porter launched his maritime career at the age of eleven and, following the capture of Vicksburg, rose to the rank of rear admiral in 1863. As commander of the North Atlantic Blockading Squadron, Porter was a key figure in successive Federal assaults against Fort Fisher, North Carolina. When the last big installation of its sort surrendered, Admiral Porter received the Thanks of Congress for his victory. Earlier exploits had earned him two citations of this sort, making him the only officer of the U.S. Navy to be thanked formally by Congress on three separate occasions.

Numerous one-and-only records were scored on land. Although many towns and cities were besieged, only one large Union army was bottled up by the Southerners. Having withdrawn into Chattanooga in 1863, Federal forces were cut off for many days from their sources of reinforcement and supply.

Woodlawn National Cemetery at Elmira, New York, is believed to be the only site in the nation where fighting men in both blue and gray lie in a mass grave. Seventeen members of the Federal Eleventh Veteran Reserve Corps are buried there, along with about fifty Confederates. Men who were wearing gray at the time of their death came from at least eight North Carolina regiments, six Virginia units, and six Georgia regiments.

How did so many dead soldiers from such diverse units wind up in New York? On July 15, 1864, the worst railroad accident in U.S. history up to that time occurred near Shohola, Pennsylvania. An Erie Railroad head-on collision took the lives of all but one of the thirty-seven men on a prison train.

All Seventeen Union soldiers who died served as guards. Each of them was buried in his own coffin, probably fashioned from the wood of the wrecked railroad cars. The prisoners didn't fare so well; but crude boxes were built to hold four bodies each.

An elaborate monument stands near the burial trench, at least seventy-five feet long, in which blue and gray uniforms were intermingled. Scanty records make it impossible to know whether or not the names chiseled in stone—Union on one side of the marker, Confederate on the other side—are accurate.

—※—

Records concerning Richmond's Chimborazo Hospital are both accurate and detailed. Once it was completed, it was years before any other medical facility challenged it for first place in size.

Spread over an estimated 120 acres, at its peak Chimborazo included nearly 200 buildings. Since 150 of these were medical wards, the Confederate institution could house 4,800 sick and wounded men.

—※—

At its peak the U.S. Military Telegraph Service used hundreds of men. Only one of them, J. C. Van Duzer, is mentioned in the record as having been a combat officer.

Col. Anson Stager, head of the telegraph service, once received a confidential message from Van Duzer. According to it, Maj. Gen. Ulysses S. Grant had ignored traditional lines of authority when he appointed an aide for Stager without consulting the colonel.

Soon learning that someone had challenged the appropriateness of his appointment, Grant quickly identified Van Duzer as the culprit and ordered him to a guardhouse. Civilian telegraph operators threatened to walk off the job unless Van Duzer was released. Grant broke up the strike by ordering close confinement for any man guilty of "contumacious conduct."

Since the conflict revolving around Van Duzer involved civilian employees, the matter could not be classified as mutiny. Yet the only combat officer of the U.S. Military Telegraph Service was applauded by his comrades as the only man to defy Grant and escape severe punishment.

—※—

After reaching its maturity, the U.S. Army Signal Corps was often regarded as a rival to the telegraph service. Not so at its beginning, however.

Maj. Albert J. Myer, who entered the U.S. Army as an assistant surgeon, became a signal officer on June 27, 1860. His new post was created especially for him by Congress, and after the appointment he found himself to be the only member of the corps.

U.S. Brig. Gen. Justus McKinstry's distinction—if that is the right label to confer upon him—was quite different in nature. He was the only general to be dismissed from the service for mishandling funds.

An 1838 graduate of West Point, he had an unblemished record of twenty-two years of military service. Because he could move beyond his peacetime rank by transferring into the U.S. Volunteers, he took that step on September 2, 1861.

As chief quartermaster in the Department of the West, McKinstry was responsible for purchasing huge quantities of food, uniforms, and supplies. Many with whom he dealt had little interest in the conflict except as an opportunity for easy money. Some of these manufacturers and dealers specialized in "shoddy," the term used for blankets, tents, and garments made from cloth that quickly deteriorated in use. One such dealer with whom McKinstry did much business, the firm of Child, Pratt, and Fox, reaped a windfall of just under $1 million in a matter of months.

Accused of having lined his own pockets by purchasing huge quantities of shoddy, McKinstry was arrested, tried, convicted, and cashiered in 1863.

Camp Chase, near Columbus, Ohio, was the site at which a regiment was organized very early. Mustered into service on June 11, 1861, men of the Twenty-third Infantry left for Benwood, Virginia (now West Virginia), on July 25.

By war's end, the regiment had participated in scores of actions, ranging from a minor skirmish at Cross Lane, Virginia, on August 26, 1861, to South Mountain and Antietam.

When veterans were mustered out on July 26, 1865, every man of the regiment knew that relatives and descendants would be proud of him. What they could not foresee was that of the multitude of regiments in the Union army, only the Twenty-third Ohio Infantry included two future presidents: Rutherford B. Hayes and William McKinley.

Numerous military departments under Federal control were merged with others or dissolved. Only one, the Department of Texas, was given to the Confederacy by its commander.

Brig. Gen. David E. Twiggs, a distinguished veteran of the Mexican War, was strongly sympathetic to the Southern cause. Known to many of his officers as "the Bengal Tiger," he repeatedly requested instructions from Washington during the early weeks of 1861.

No orders came, so on February 18 the Tiger engaged in a brief ceremony with Col. Ben McCulloch, commander of Confederate troops in Texas. Twiggs formally turned over every fort and outpost in the department, along with two thousand soldiers, all of his equipment, and all U.S. Army funds on hand.

By May 22, the long-time veteran of Federal fighting forces was wearing the uniform of a Confederate major general, having been dismissed from Union service twenty-one days earlier. Twiggs was the oldest and most senior U.S. Army officer to switch uniforms. He also was the only Federal brigadier to surrender to Confederates substantially more than 10 percent of all men in the U.S. Army.

James J. Andrews is believed to have been born in Finland and to have been named Andreas Johan Kars. He probably fought in the Russian army before coming to Kentucky about 1850. Experienced in undercover work—or capable of convincing others that he was experienced—Andrews became a spy for the Union.

In 1862 he devised a plan to disrupt the flow of goods from Georgia into the other Confederate states. At the head of twenty-two Ohio soldiers who volunteered for the mission, he tried to cut the Western and Atlantic Railroad. Rainy weather and an exceptionally persistent railroad conductor foiled his plans. He and many of his men were captured; several were executed, but the survivors were among the first recipients of the Medal of Honor.

Andrews became the only civilian raider to be remembered because of failure.

North Carolina's Fort Fisher was a tempting target as 1865 began. A December expedition led by U.S. Maj. Gen. Benjamin F. Butler fizzled before it could gain the fort, leaving the port of Wilmington as the Confederacy's last gateway to England and Europe.

Frustrated, Lt. Gen. Ulysses S. Grant established a special eight-thousand-man "provisional corps" headed by Brig. Gen. Alfred H. Terry. Terry's only assignment was to take Fort Fisher.

Given a free hand to assault or besiege the Southern fortification, Terry persuaded naval authorities to put more than fifty warships at his disposal. Since they were armed with at least six hundred guns, their bombardment was expected to weaken the Confederate defenses and facilitate an amphibious landing.

For the first few hours on January 12, things went according to plan. With the warships firing as rapidly as possible, thousands of men landed on the beach just south of Wilmington. In an all-out assault on January 15, hand-to-hand combat lasted for hours.

At the height of the frenzied fighting, the Ninety-seventh Pennsylvania Regiment was the first to plant its flag on the Confederate parapet. Col. Galusha Pennypacker, commander of the forces that included the Ninety-seventh, received a nearly fatal wound while personally accompanying the flag.

Pennypacker was immediately given a brevet as a brigadier and was formally promoted to that rank a month later. This action, which required congressional sanction, made the man from the Keystone State the youngest general officer in blue. When the new brigadier general celebrated his birthday in June, he "achieved his majority," that is, he was twenty-one years old and then eligible to vote.

~~~

Isaac Murphy was never quite sure how he came to be chosen as a delegate to a special convention held in Arkansas. He'd been a surveyor, teacher, lawyer, and was one of the multitude who had gone to California during the gold rush. Regarded by friends and neighbors as "uncommonly outspoken," he had made no secret of his allegiance to the Union.

At the call of the governor, a secret session of the convention convened on May 6, 1861. With seventy members present, sixty-nine voted in favor of the ordinance of secession. Undaunted, Murphy refused to budge from his position and cast his lone vote against the measure. His action made him the only documented member of a Southern convention who openly defied every other delegate.

~~~

Early in April 1864 the Federal Army of the Potomac appeared stymied. Plans called for movement across the James River near Wyanoke Landing. At this point the river was about twenty-one hundred feet wide. Tidal currents had cut some channels to a depth of fifteen fathoms. To amateurs and veterans alike, it seemed impossible to devise a way by which tens of thousands of men could cross the water.

Maj. J. C. Duane, an experienced pontonier, was put in charge of a hand-picked crew of 450 army engineers. Assisted by Capt. G. H. Mendell, Duane sketched a temporary bridge that would be supported by three schooners. The materials were assembled and the plans completed, but work did not start until orders were received just before noon on June 15.

With the first schooner anchored and two others moving toward strategic spots, Duane started putting pontoons together. By using 101 of them, he managed to reach the opposite shore of the river in eight hours. No other pontoon bridge built during the conflict came close to this one in length.

The crossing of the army was completed early on the morning of June 18. When every man was over, the only improvised bridge of the war to exceed two thousand feet in length was broken into three sections. Treated as rafts, the sections were floated to Grant's headquarters at City Point, Virginia.

From his pulpit in Brooklyn, New York, Henry Ward Beecher vigorously denounced slavery. Translating words into action, he raised funds that enabled opponents of slavery to move to Kansas, where settlers would decide whether to form a free or a slaveholding state.

Violence erupted in the territory early in the 1850s and mounted in intensity as the years passed. Generally known as Bleeding Kansas, it was in this territory that John Brown perpetrated a massacre and developed his plans to create a new nation of former slaves.

In distant Brooklyn, Beecher found more and more persons willing to underwrite the antislavery movement in Kansas. Positive documentation is lacking, but the evidence confirms that wagonloads of crates were shipped west marked "Beecher's Bibles." Since many or all of these shipments contained rifles, the action made Beecher the lone prominent clergyman to fight slavery with the most advanced weapons money could buy.

Maj. Innis N. Palmer of the renowned U.S. Second Cavalry had no idea that his name would go into record books on July 21, 1861. He only knew that his provisional battalion of seven cavalry companies drawn from three regiments was expected to drive the Confederates from the Manassas battlefield.

When the day ended and the Federal forces were in full flight back to Washington, Brig. Gen. Irvin McDowell who had been a major three months prior, discovered that Palmer's men had been his entire cavalry force at Manassas. As a reward for being the only leader of Federal mounted units in the first real battle of the war, Palmer was given a brevet promotion. Two months later the honorary rank was made permanent and Brigadier General Palmer led brigades to Yorktown, Williamsburg, and Seven Pines.

Godfrey Weitzel of Ohio, an 1855 graduate of West point, chafed at the slow promotion rate that characterized the army in time of peace. Although the outbreak of war brought a host of rapid promotions, he failed to gain advancement. As a result, he transferred to the U.S. Volunteers in August 1862 and was made a brigadier. Within two years he was Major General Weitzel, USV.

One month after achieving that rank, Weitzel was given command of the newly organized Twenty-fifth Corps. His men were the first Federals to enter Richmond in 1865 after the Confederate capital was abandoned. That was enough to make his name honored in the North and despised in the South. The intensity of sectional reaction was heightened by the fact that Weitzel headed the only corps of African Americans in the U.S. armed forces.

Pvt. Henry Brown of Darlington, South Carolina, is renowned as having been the only regularly enrolled man of African descent who fought in the Confederate forces of his state. Brown was not issued a musket or rifle; he carried a drum.

Since his combat service was in a class by itself, South Carolina citizens later decided to extend to him another unique honor. A monument fifteen feet tall was erected to his memory, the only memorial of its sort in the Old Confederacy.

Confederate Maj. Gen. Earl Van Dorn fought throughout two years of war without achieving special distinction on the battlefield. Fame of a sort came to the Mississippi native after he moved his division into Middle Tennessee, where he discovered a particularly charming young woman living in Spring Hill.

Soon the 1842 graduate of West Point was seen in the village and at his camp with the Maury County woman he found fascinating. She proved to be the moving force behind events that gave the Confederate officer a unique distinction. On May 7, 1863, he died, not in battle, but from a single shot delivered by Dr. George B. Peters. The action by the Tennessee physician made Van Dorn the only general officer of the Civil War to be killed in uniform by a jealous husband.

While proudly wearing his gray uniform, Pvt. Edward D. White was one of thousands captured by the Federals during the Vicksburg campaign. When he surrendered at Port Hudson, there was nothing unusual about the fact that he was required to give his parole not to resume fighting until regularly exchanged.

White would today be forgotten were it not for the fact that he exchanged regular garb for a black robe thirty years after the end of the war. When he took his oath of office, the man from Louisiana's La Fourche Parish became the only former prisoner of war to serve as an associate justice of the U.S. Supreme Court.

Debate concerning the origin of the familiar nickname bestowed upon Confederate Brig. Gen. Thomas J. Jackson is not likely to subside. No one knows for certain what Brig. Gen. Barnard Bee meant when he said that Jackson stood "like a stone wall" at Manassas. Earlier, as an instructor at the Virginia Military Institute, the man who became immortalized as Stonewall had been called Old Blue Light and Tom Fool.

Bee's comment may have been a compliment, but some suggest it was an insult. Whatever the case, after July 21, 1861, "Old Blue Light" was forgotten as "Stonewall" scored victory after victory. From that day on, the Manassas battlefield to the end of the war, his brigade was known officially as the Stonewall Brigade. That made it the only brigade in gray to be designated by an officer's nickname.

George W. Johnson of Kentucky, a plantation owner and attorney, scoffed when the state's elected leaders announced that the state would be neutral in the sectional struggle. He sought and won election as the first head of the provisional Confederate government established by the Bluegrass State.

Chafing at civilian life while the fighting was escalating, Johnson volunteered his services to Confederate Gen. Albert Sidney Johnston. Enrolled as an adviser without a uniform, he was later transferred to the staff of Maj. Gen. John C. Breckinridge.

Johnson accompanied the former vice president of the United States to the battlefield at Shiloh, where a horse was shot from under him early in the struggle. Demanding an opportunity to fight rather than to advise, within hours he enlisted as a private in the First Kentucky Infantry.

Private Johnson was struck during his first day of fighting and died on April 9. Had he known of his unique niche in the story of the Civil War, he would have smiled at the honor of being the only governor to die of Civil War battlefield wounds.

French-born Victor Jean Baptiste Girardey, reared in Georgia and Louisiana as an orphan, hurried to enlist when Jefferson Davis called for volunteers. By October 1861, he was a lieutenant and became a captain just three months later.

Captain Girardey fought during the Seven Days battles and at Chancellorsville and Gettysburg without special distinction. His moment came at Petersburg, where he acted without orders and led two brigades in resisting Union forces in the battle of the Crater.

Girardey's Petersburg exploit was brought to Lee's attention, and the general saw to it that the native of France received a third promotion. This time, he became the only Confederate to jump four ranks—from captain to brigadier general.

Hundreds of clergymen left their flocks to go to the battlefield with the units mustered from their villages and towns. Most of them served faithfully in obscurity.

Not so the Reverend T. L. Duke of the Nineteenth Mississippi Regiment. Near Fredericksburg, Virginia, men of Brig. Gen. Carnot Posey's brigade wavered during hand-to-hand fighting. Duke seized a musket, raced to the front of his regiment, and there "mainly directed the movements of the skirmishers."

As a result, the Mississippi clergyman became the only Confederate chaplain to be cited officially for gallantry in battle.

Thirty-nine

ONE OF A KIND

When President Lincoln called for seventy-five thousand volunteers to serve for ninety days, the response was immediate and overwhelming. As the conflict dragged on, however, Washington was forced to adopt a system of conscription. Quotas were assigned to states, and individuals were chosen for service by means of a lottery, or "draft."

Tens of thousands of men who didn't want to go to war after having been drafted hired substitutes to take their places. Among those to do so was a Buffalo, New York, resident who later occupied the White House: Grover Cleveland. Bur Cleveland was not the first chief executive to hire a wartime substitute.

Although the action was a symbolic one, Lincoln hired a substitute to serve in his place. Unlike John D. Rockefeller and J. Pierpont Morgan, who also hired substitutes, the president was not subject to the draft. Lincoln never explained his action. Pennsylvania native John S. Staples accepted at least five hundred dollars—well above the normal rate—to put on a Federal uniform and fight as Lincoln's substitute.

~~~

Matthew Brady of New York is the best known Civil War photographer. After having tried to become a painter, he opened a daguerreotype studio. Specializing in portraits, he achieved enough success to establish a branch studio in Washington.

By the time Fort Sumter had been fired upon, Brady had developed a skill in the new wet-plate photographic process. Although extremely slow by today's standards, the use of wet plates was suitable for battlefield use. Hence the New Yorker hired a corps of assistants to follow Federal troops wherever they went.

It is doubtful that Brady was responsible for any familiar images taken in the field; his sight was failing rapidly by 1861. Yet he put his name upon thousands of photographs taken by Timothy O'Sullivan, Alexander Gardner, and other photographers. As a result, more wartime images are credited to Brady than to any other photographer. Properly speaking, most of them should be credited to the Brady Studio.

New Hampshire native Benjamin F. Butler moved to Massachusetts and became a powerful figure in the Democratic Party. A successful criminal lawyer, he took command of Massachusetts Volunteers three days after Lincoln's call for volunteers following the debacle at Manassas Junction.

Within a month Butler was wearing two stars and is now remembered as having been the first of Lincoln's so-called political generals. Some analysts attribute his appointment to the president's political acumen; after all, a leading Democrat couldn't simultaneously fight Confederates and oppose Republicans at the polls.

Regardless of the factors that led the president to honor him, Butler soon became the only Union general to be condemned across Europe. International reactions stemmed from the most violent of several controversial actions. As military head of occupied New Orleans, he was the only Union general to order the execution of a civilian.

Shortly after New Orleans had surrendered, William B. Mumford, a professional gambler, tore down a U.S. flag that had been raised at the former U.S. Mint building and dragged it through the streets. When Butler's troops arrived to occupy the town, the general was informed of Mumford's actions and ordered the gambler's arrest. Tried and convicted of treason, Mumford was hanged on June 7, 1862.

Robert Anderson was praised as a national hero in the North, but Com. James Armstrong was branded as a traitor. Armstrong had served twenty-eight years in the navy when on May 29, 1861, the *New York Courier and Enquirer* called for his dismissal in disgrace.

Prior to Anderson's surrender of Fort Sumter, Armstrong had given up the U.S. Navy Yard at Pensacola, Florida, on January 12, 1861, without a struggle. At Charleston, victorious Secessionists told Anderson he was free to go where he pleased; at Pensacola, Armstrong became a captive.

Alone among naval officers of high rank, the New Jersey native had surrendered an important installation long before the outbreak of civil war. When released by his captors, Armstrong was court-martialed and suspended from duty. At war's end, the sole officer of his rank to be humiliated by Secessionists and Unionists alike was promoted to the rank of captain.

Relatives and acquaintances of Hinton R. Helper did not laud him during the time of tension that preceded the siege of Fort Sumter. In 1857 he financed the publication of a little book that he called *The Impending Crisis of the South: How to Meet It*.

Born and reared in North Carolina, he knew just enough about the North to realize that the sectional gap was immense and growing. To Helper, it seemed self-evident that the decisive difference between the two regions stemmed from the fact that the working population in the North was free, while a majority of workers in the South were enslaved.

Part of the paradox of the tarheel's achievement stems from the fact that this southerner who condemned slavery was an avowed racist. His zeal for the abolition of slavery stemmed from an eagerness to help poor white laborers.

Despite this factor, his book was received with enthusiasm in the North, where an estimated 14,500 copies were sold. With the election of 1860 approaching, the Republican National Committee printed and distributed about 100,000 copies of an abbreviated and expurgated version. Because Congressman John Sherman of Ohio endorsed much that Hinton had written, he was defeated in a contest for the vital post of Speaker of the House.

Another Republican political leader, William H. Seward of New York, gave a commendation of sorts to the Hinton volume, which is believed to have been a significant factor in his razor-thin defeat when members of his party gathered in Chicago to choose a presidential nominee. Motivated solely by economic considerations, the antislavery racist who vented his frustration by writing a book is the only author known to have helped put Lincoln into the White House.

An adopted son of Cmdr. David D. Porter, David G. Farragut received a commission as midshipman at age nine. Born in Tennessee, the career naval officer was living in Virginia when the war began. Many residents of Norfolk soon made it clear that a man known to harbor strong Unionist sentiments was not welcome in the port city.

Disgusted and angry, Farragut moved to the North, where he soon found that high-ranking officials were also suspicious of him because of his southern background. Porter, who insisted that his foster son was loyal, had the ear of the assistant secretary of the navy, Gustavus V. Fox. Together they persuaded the secretary of the navy, Gideon Welles, to give Farragut a chance. When the suspect captain was put in charge of the West Gulf Blocking Squadron, he soon captured New Orleans, the largest city in the Confederacy.

Two years later Farragut led Federal warships into Mobile Bay. Despite the presence of numerous floating mines, or torpedoes, he won a stunning victory. As a reward, the rank of vice admiral was created and awarded to him. In 1866 another new rank was established especially for Farragut, and he became the first full admiral in the nation's history. Not bad for a man whose loyalty had been questioned just five years earlier.

South Carolina plantation owner Wade Hampton had no military training or experience, but he was eager to fight. He raised volunteers who formed units of infantry, cavalry, and artillery that made up a hybrid organization known as Hampton's Legion.

Colonel Hampton was awarded the stars of a brigadier after ten months of service and became a major general in September 1863. His last promotion came sixty days before the surrender at Appomattox, after which he led Gen. Joseph E. Johnston's cavalry to resist Sherman's armies advancing through the Carolinas.

When the last major army in gray surrendered at Durham's Station, North Carolina, Hampton returned to South Carolina as the only Secessionist who was stripped of more than three thousand slaves as a result of the war.

Before Hampton began recruiting men for military service, numerous Southerners suffered other big losses. One after another, members of the House of Representatives and the U.S. Senate gave up their seats. With the size of Congress greatly reduced, a man from Tennessee stubbornly clung to his place after his state seceded.

Because he became a conspicuous figure in Washington when his Southern colleagues went home, Andrew Johnson became well known to Lincoln. Picked as the running mate for the president who was seeking a second term, Johnson became chief executive following Lincoln's assassination. That forced him to preside over the early years of Reconstruction.

Had he not been notoriously stubborn, Johnson would not have remained in the Senate as its lone member from the South. This trait also caused him to become the only president to be impeached.

Long before that momentous event took place, he was the only future chief executive unable to write at the age of seventeen. A one-time apprentice to a tailor, Johnson acquired that skill from sixteen-year-old Eliza McCardle. They married on May 5, 1827, without dreaming that the eighteen-year-old bridegroom was going to the altar at an earlier age than any other future president.

London-born Edward D. Baker saw a political opportunity when statehood for Oregon was looming. Earlier he had been a member of the Illinois house of representatives and an organizer of the Republican Party in California. During his Illinois years he formed a close friendship with attorney Abraham Lincoln, so that the man from Springfield chose Edward as his second son's name.

Seated as a U.S. senator from Oregon late in 1860, Baker yearned for military service when war erupted. His friend in the White House offered to make him a brigadier, but he declined the commission because acceptance would have forced him to give up his seat in the Senate.

Late in the summer of 1861, the man from England, Illinois, California, and Oregon turned to Pennsylvania. When offered to become their colonel, the soldiers of the Seventy-first Pennsylvania Infantry, popularly known as the California Regiment, made it clear that they were itching to fight.

By this time Baker had received a major general's commission from Lincoln, which he neither accepted nor declined. Hoping for a brilliant military victory that would enhance his career, Colonel Baker blundered into a disastrous fight at Ball's Bluff, Virginia. On October 21, 1861, this ambitious wanderer and intimate of the president became the only sitting U.S. senator to die on the battlefield.

Another Federal colonel carved a niche for himself larger than that of Baker, but he never held political office. An inveterate inventor, mechanical engineer Hiram Berdan of New York City was considered by some northerners to be "thoroughly unscrupulous and unreliable."

Nevertheless, for a dozen years before the war he was touted as the top rifle shot in the United States. His fame was such that when the conflict began, it was easy for him to recruit enough volunteers to fill two regiments, dubbed Berdan's Sharpshooters.

Colonel Berdan of the First U.S. Sharpshooters probably entered the recruitment business to develop new markets for his military inventions. His men could be identified at a glance; they wore green coats and green caps adorned with black plumes. Instead of carrying muskets, they were armed with .52-caliber Sharps rifles.

Officers and men who made up the body claimed, probably correctly, that they eliminated more Southern soldiers than any other force of comparable size. Especially proud of often silencing Confederate batteries with their powerful rifles, more than one thousand of the twenty-six hundred sharpshooters were killed or wounded during four years of constant action.

At Chancellorsville and at Gettysburg their leader went into battle at the head of a brigade. In the mellow mood of postwar generosity, Congress awarded two brevets to Berdan, brigadier general and major general.

Apparently initially motivated by the desire to make money from the sale of his inventions, Berdan did not succeed in that effort. Instead, the force he raised and led became one of the most memorable of those who wore, well, at least a bit of blue.

Although Henry M. Stanley found fame when he discovered David Livingstone in Africa, years earlier he had engaged in a series of actions that may have been without parallel. At the age of twenty and infected with "war fever," Stanley abruptly quit his job to enlist in the Sixth Arkansas Infantry. Along with numerous comrades captured at Shiloh, he was sent to a prison near Chicago.

Life at Camp Douglas was harsh, and there seemed to be no prospect of release. Hence the Confederate combat veteran became a "galvanized Yankee" by taking an oath of allegiance and exchanging his gray uniform for a blue one. Soon discharged because of illness, he went to New York and enlisted in the U.S. Navy. Stanley, also known as John Rowlands, is the only serviceman known to have served in the Confederate Army, the Union army, and the U.S. Navy. His unique military career came to an end when he jumped ship at a New Hampshire port early in 1865 and became a deserter.

With 1860 seen as a crucial political year, Vice President John C. Breckinridge of Kentucky was a candidate for the presidency. Although he didn't come close to winning in November, he garnered more than 1.4 million popular votes. Eleven states gave him seventy-two electoral votes—almost one-fourth as many as Lincoln, because one American in sixteen voted for him.

In March 1861, he succeeded John J. Crittenden as a senator from Kentucky, but he resigned from the Senate to accept a brigadier's commission in the Confederate army. Promoted to major general in April 1862, he remained in uniform until February 4, 1865, when he became Confederate secretary of war. After the war, Breckinridge left the United States for three years, traveling to England and Canada. In 1868, he returned to Kentucky and practiced law for seven years, until his death in 1875.

Breckinridge's fame was of a sort that no other former vice president has matched, although Aaron Burr came close. He was the only former vice president to take up arms against the United States.

Jesse Bright's name seldom appears on any list of notable Civil War figures. In view of his record, that omission is remarkable.

Bright hailed from Indiana, where Lincoln spent many of his boyhood years. He was a state legislator and a lieutenant governor before going to Washington in 1845. During fifteen years in which he gained seniority, Bright three times served as president pro tem of the Senate, despite the fact that he had made numerous political enemies, some of whom were prominent in his own Democratic Party.

On December 16, 1861, lawmakers who sensed that something unusual was about to happen, crowded into the chamber. A letter dated March 1, 1861, and written by Bright was read into the record. According to it, Bright's friend Thomas B. Lincoln had made a significant improvement in firearms.

The letter would have stirred no interest had it not been sent to Montgomery, Alabama, and addressed to "His Excellency Jefferson Davis, President of the Confederation of States."

The fact that a U.S. senator had recognized the separate legal identity of the seceded states caused a turmoil in the Senate. Bright's colleagues devoted most of twenty working days to debate concerning the terse memorandum. Bright made a long and vigorous speech in his defense and found more supporters than his record would have caused him to expect.

In the end, the term "President Jefferson Davis" was too much for Bright's colleagues to accept. Repeatedly, the president of the United States had underscored his verdict that no secession had taken place. Bright was expelled formally in February 1862, the first senator to be removed by his colleagues.

Because he served for a decade as a Methodist circuit rider, William G. Brownlow was known as a "Parson." Turning to another vocation, he founded a little newspaper known as the *Elizabethton (Tenn.) Whig*. Soon he took his publication to a larger city, where it became *Brownlow's Knoxville Whig*.

Though his journalistic pursuits, the former clergyman found an audience and a following. He made the most of his leadership opportunities when war broke out, planning and perhaps participating in the burning of several railroad bridges.

Driven from East Tennessee as a well-known bridge-burner, parson Brownlow forayed into the North. Highly successful as a speaker at recruitment rallies, he sold an estimated one hundred thousand copies of a little book with a big title, *Sketches of the Rise, Progress, and Decline of Secession; with a Narrative of Personal Adventures Among the Rebels.*

When Union troops gained the advantage in East Tennessee, Parson Brownlow returned with the first wave of men in blue. He soon reestablished his newspaper as the *Knoxville Whig and Rebel* and at war's end became governor of the state.

Brownlow's most unusual claim to fame stems from his frequently announced views. No other chief executive of a former Confederate state was both an ardent supporter of the Union and a fiercely vocal opponent of the abolition of slavery.

Indiana-born Ambrose E. Burnside graduated from West Point in 1847 and was assigned to the artillery branch of the service. His Mexican War duties consisted only of garrison assignments, but he was later wounded while fighting Apaches in New Mexico.

During his recuperation he devised a way to improve breechloading carbines. His invention had such potential that he resigned from the army and became a weapons manufacturer in Rhode Island.

With the outbreak of the war, he became a major of the First Rhode Island Infantry on May 2, 1861—a command he held only one month. After having led a brigade at the battle of Manassas, Burnside accepted a brigadier's rank in the U.S. Volunteers.

His successful leadership of the North Carolina Expeditionary Corps (from December 1861 to April 1862) repeatedly put his name into headlines. Probably as a result of the publicity gained from his penetration into Secessionist territory, Lincoln offered to put the Hoosier at the head of the Army of the Potomac. Burnside declined, believing that he lacked adequate experience. When Lincoln's patience with George B. McClellan was exhausted following the battle of Antietam, the president again approached Burnside and made it clear that he expected immediate acceptance.

Perhaps reluctantly, Burnside took command over the most powerful Federal army in the country. Now remembered more for his facial hair than for his successes on the battlefield, Burnside's ineptness demonstrated that he— not Lincoln—was right about his ability to lead an army.

Veteran newspaper correspondent Sylvanus Cadwallader of the *New York Herald* wore a coonskin cap when he was attached to Grant's forces in August 1862. Fellow journalists initially saw nothing special in Cadwallader, but within a year they discovered that he was one of the best of their vocation.

On Mississippi's Yazoo River, aboard the USS *Diligence* in June 1863, Cadwallader encountered a drunken Grant. He ushered the general to his stateroom and disposed of the commander's whiskey. Later aided by Col. John A. Rawlins, Cadwallader is credited with preventing Grant's dismissal.

His action earned Grant's appreciation and respect because Cadwallader refused to make anything of the story. In return, Grant treated the journalist as though he were a member of the commander's official staff and rescinded the requirement for Cadwallader to submit his dispatches to a military censor prior to forwarding them on to his editors.

The *Herald* correspondent was very visible at Appomattox. Alone among the newspapermen who hovered around the surrender ceremonies, Cadwallader's dispatches were transmitted immediately to his New York office.

Kentucky-born Robert Anderson may have been assigned to command in Charleston Harbor because he once owned slaves and was the husband of a Georgia girl. Foes of U.S. Secretary of War John B. Floyd publicly charged that this was the case when Anderson's 1860 appointment was made public.

Regardless of what motives lay behind Floyd's decision, the southern-born professional soldier elevated duty above sectional loyalty. Moving his force into powerful but never-used Fort Sumter, he was a primary character in the drama that led to the outbreak of war.

After spending nearly three days on the receiving end of an artillery duel, Major Anderson was promoted to the rank of a Federal brigadier general. He was the only officer to jump two grades in rank immediately after surrendering his post.

English political leaders made only perfunctory attempts to hide their disdain when Charles Francis Adams Sr. reached London. He presented his credentials, was duly recognized as the U.S. minister to Great Britain, and tried to ignore the snubs.

Boston-born Adams, courtly in appearance and manners, soon made a friend. He was just the sort of person Prince Albert of Saxe-Coburg-Gotha enjoyed, so he spent considerable time with him. Largely through the influence of Queen Victoria's consort, the American succeeded in his primary mission. Despite widespread sympathy for the Confederacy, he managed to prevent Parliament from recognizing the South as an independent nation. This, in turn, thwarted Secessionists who had planned to form military alliances with European nations at odds with the United States.

Adams also managed to put an end to British sales of warships to Confederates. Often overlooked today, his influence upon the outcome of the American conflict was second only to that of Lincoln. It was his patrician heritage, however, that made the minister unique. Among the sons of U.S. presidents, only Charles Francis Adams—son of John Quincy Adams and grandson of John Adams—played a prominent role in the civil war.

Nathan Bedford Forrest grew up without a trace of formal schooling. In much the same fashion as Lincoln, but to a far less degree, he managed to educate himself. To keep the records needed by a livestock dealer, sixteen-year-old Forrest had to learn mathematics as well as how to read and write.

Forrest made enough money from cattle to support his family and soon had enough capital to enter the slave trade. Purchases of land in increasingly larger tracts enabled him to become a cotton planter of significance. As a result, Nathan B. Forrest accumulated assets of at least $1 million, a very large amount for that time. When he enlisted in the Seventh Tennessee Cavalry, he may have been the Confederacy's only millionaire private.

Soon he raised a cavalry battalion of his own and was rewarded by promotion to lieutenant colonel. Sometimes engaged in pitched battles but more often leading raids, the self-taught cavalry leader did not surrender until he learned that Lee had capitulated at Appomattox. In postwar years, he was a railroad president and a founder of the original Ku Klux Klan, which he left when he found the Klan's methods too brutal for his tastes.

Wealthy beyond the dreams of most southerners, Forrest occupies a Civil War niche that belongs to him alone. No other man who fought in either gray or blue enlisted as a private and surrendered as a lieutenant general.

Part Nine

THE MONEY TRAIL

M aj. Gen. William Tecumseh Sherman's terse "War is all hell" summation of the Civil War was neither overstatement nor hyperbole. A divided nation had exhausted almost every resource in the struggle that concerned manpower, industry, and inspiration.

Love of the union was an ingredient that may have been as potent as sectional pride. Fierce resentment of directives from Washington was another essential contributor to the mix that exploded at Fort Sumter. These factors and many more combined to make the Civil War not only possible but inevitable. In looking at it from the perspective of several generations, we tend to emphasize such virtues as courage, self-sacrifice, obedience to orders, inventive ingenuity, and readiness to die in defense of home and region.

An essential ingredient, often overlooked, was money. Money played so many roles, some of them unobtrusive, that without it there would have been no war. It was the grease that made the wheels of the Federal and Confederate war machines move more or less smoothly.

The amount of money expended from 1861 to 1865 is startling. This is magnified when the relative value of a dollar then and now is taken into account. By the most conservative estimate, in the last decade of the twentieth century the purchasing power of $1 very roughly corresponds to $2^{1}/_{2}$¢ or 3¢ during the Civil War. Thus without taking into account wartime inflation or the depreciation of Confederate currency, a single wartime dollar bought the equivalent of $33 to $40 today.

Forty

BIG TICKETS TO SMALL CHANGE

U.S. animals, wagons, tools, clothing, ordnance, and commissary stores surrendered to Confederates in Texas before the surrender of Fort Sumter were valued at $1,209,500. U.S. Brig. Gen. David E. Twiggs, sometimes known as "Old Davy," surrendered all federal property without firing a shot. An itemized evaluation shows that the lost material included 1,800 mules and 950 horses whose combined value was $232,500.

During the fiscal year that ended on July 1, 1862, money expended for the Union military effort averaged $1,300,000 per day. During the same period, annual Federal expenditures for pensions and for Indians totaled only $3,102,985.50.

Philip Kearney was by no means the wealthiest of military leaders. Yet he may have been the man who pocketed the largest amount of cash without working for it. When his grandfather died in 1836, the future U.S. brigadier inherited substantially more than $1,000,000—almost enough to pay for one day of the war during its first year.

Samuel Colt patented the first of many revolvers in 1836, but his manufacturing company floundered, then failed. Revived by the Mexican War, in 1861 and 1862 his Patent Arms Manufacturing Company sold 107,000 .44-caliber weapons to the U.S. War Department. These sales alone netted $1,375,000 for the inventor-manufacturer.

According to the *Philadelphia Press*, Southern pride reached an apex of sorts late in 1861. During three months, the Northern journal reported, the seceded states contributed $1,515,898 to the Confederate armies.

During the fiscal year that ended on June 20, 1862, the U.S. government received $1,795,331.78 from "direct taxes" imposed upon the states. Since levies were made upon seceded states that refused to pay, their arrears created an enormous problem for them during the early months of Reconstruction.

Convinced that numerous Secessionists were still on the Federal payroll, Lincoln didn't trust conventional procedures. Although military supplies were desperately needed, he feared that the money would not be used properly.

As a result, the president took unprecedented action. He drew a voucher upon the U.S. Treasury in the sum of $2 million. Then he turned the cash over to John A. Dix, George Opdyke, and Richard M. Blatchford. No security, or bond, was required of these three civilians who were told to buy as many essentials for the war effort as they could.

Responding to the ensuing criticism, the president sent a special message to Congress on May 27, 1862. In it he insisted: "I believe that by this and similar measures taken in that crisis, some of which were without any authority of law, the Government was saved from overthrow. I am not aware that a dollar of the public funds thus confided without authority of law, to unofficial persons, was either lost or wasted."

～～～

Before New Orleans fell into Federal hands in April 1862, local leaders saw that surrender was near. Officers of major banks, a contemporary report claimed, packed $2 million in gold and currency into nine barrels labeled as beef. This consignment was then shipped up the Red River by commercial steamer.

～～～

In August 1863 the steamer *Ruth* had a special cargo aboard in the form of U.S. funds amounting to $2.5 million. When the vessel caught fire on the Mississippi River, flames raced through it so rapidly that not a single dollar was saved.

～～～

A congressional committee reported in 1863 that the cost of the war to the Federal government had reached $2.5 million a day.

～～～

After draft riots rocked New York City in July 1863, Mayor George Opdyke received from the city council a new ordinance authorizing payment of "commutation," or reparation, to persons whose property had been damaged. Eventually vetoed by the chief executive of the nation's largest city, the $2.5 million involved was estimated to be enough "to cover a substantial part of the losses occasioned by public resistance to military conscription."

～～～

During the conflict, expenditures for the U.S. Military Telegraph Service amounted to $2,655,500. Until 1863 the cost of providing and using the system was only $22,000 per month. It increased to $38,500 per month during that year, and in 1864 soared to $93,500 per month.

Published twenty-five years after the war's end, *War of the Rebellion—Official Records of the Union and Confederate Armies* ran to 128 volumes. The cost of the enterprise, completed in 1890 after having been inaugurated by U.S. Secretary of War Edwin M. Stanton, ran to $2,858,514.67.

In May 1862 Com. Andrew H. Foote received a gratifying report. According to it, until that date the cost of building and maintaining the flotilla of Federal gunboats on the Mississippi River was a bit under $3 million.

On August 13, 1863, Federal forces launched a raid into central Mississippi. Starting from LaGrange, Tennessee, cavalry and mounted infantry struck Oxford and Grenada. This foray produced one of many paths of destruction; although minor by comparison with others, it was estimated by the *Rebellion Record* to have destroyed Confederate property valued at not less than $3 million.

The cost of the war mounted more rapidly than did casualty figures. By 1865, military expenditures of the U.S. Government reached a total just under $4 million a day.

Initially violently opposed by many military leaders, the U.S. Sanitary

Commission received $4,813,750.64 from July 17, 1861, to July 1, 1865. Expenditures came to $4,530,774.92. Since it was impossible to keep records concerning the exact value of supplies sent to battlefields, hospitals, and camps, they were estimated at an even $15 million.

From 1861 to 1865 mills owned and operated by the DuPont family produced gunpowder for the Federal government valued at $6,861,922.

Two of the most active and successful Confederate vessels, the *Florida* and the *Alabama*, captured or destroyed ships and cargoes valued at $12,498,033.

Federal recruitment was comparatively haphazard until a Bureau for Enrollment and Conscription was organized on March 17, 1863. Brig. Gen. James B. Fry, serving as provost marshal general of the agency, reported that prior to the bureau's establishment, 1,356,593 men entered the Federal military establishment at an average cost of $34.01 per man, or a prebureau cost of $11,026,910. This amount greatly exceeded the $4,613,772 Fry and his subordinates spent in recruiting 1,120,621 men at an average cost of $9.84 per man.

At war's end, the United States demanded that Great Britain make reparation for ships and cargoes taken by Confederate raiders built in the United Kingdom. Eleven vessels were said to have inflicted damage amounting to $19,021,000.

If the report of the commissioners concerning British-rooted damage to U.S. shipping was accurate, the total was surprisingly close to that of the 1860 tax apportionment of all thirty-four states. From Alabama through Wisconsin, taxes claimed by the states amounted to $19,637,126.

Union paymasters reached the vicinity of Knoxville just as an artillery duel commenced. Fearful that any money they disbursed might fall into enemy hands, these officers "sat by the side of their twenty or thirty millions of dollars" until they were confident of a Federal victory.

Prior to the war, angry Southerners were correct in charging that the chief source of revenue for the U.S. government was the Customs Service. Since industry was concentrated in the North, goods imported into the agricultural South accounted for the bulk of receipts for a twelve-month period reported as having been $49,056,897.62. During the same time the sale of public lands brought to federal coffers only $152,293.77.

Except in unusual circumstances, soldiers in blue were expected to be paid at ninety-day intervals. During periods of continuous fighting, it often proved impossible to maintain this schedule. As a result, newspapers reported late in January 1863 that "paymasters left Washington this week to deliver part of the $60 million in overdue pay to Union soldiers."

Data concerning the value of industrial production in the South during the war were not preserved. Within the Union, shoes were used in such immense quantities that their manufactured value was calculated to have been $91.9 million.

Surprisingly, textiles manufactured in the North during the war years surpassed shoes by only a small margin. With uniforms included, their value was just $115.6 million.

⁓⁓⁓

Although there was comparatively little fighting on the seas during 1865, expenditures for the U.S. Navy that year amounted to $123 million.

⁓⁓⁓

Food required an even bigger outlay than did shoes. During the fiscal year 1863–64, the Federal government appropriated $140 million to feed the army.

⁓⁓⁓

During the peak year of 1862, an estimated six thousand blockade runners defied the U.S. Navy to enter and leave Confederate ports. The value of the goods brought to the seceded states from England and Europe during the entire conflict has been estimated at around $200 million.

⁓⁓⁓

Top officials of the U.S. Navy were pleased when final tabulations of wartime expenditures were made. According to them, warships and their batteries and crews accounted for only 9.3 percent of the total cost of the war to the Federal government. If that figure is correct, the Union expended only $314 million for enterprises that included the blockade, which is considered to have been one of its most successful efforts.

⁓⁓⁓

To boost enlistment in Federal armed forces, a system of bounties was developed very early. Men who volunteered to serve for ninety days in 1862 received $25 from Uncle Sam, while those who signed up for a year got twice as much. Rising throughout the conflict, the bounty paid to a five-year volunteer after March 1863 was $400.

Most states, many cities, and numerous villages paid additional bounties. Total cash handed out as bounty payments probably exceeded $70 million.

Jay Cook, only forty years old at the outbreak of the conflict, became the chief financial adviser to U.S. Secretary of the Treasury Salmon P. Chase. Soon he was made the sole agent for the sale of U.S. government bonds to both public and private investors.

During a single six-month period, Jay Cook and Company sold government paper whose face value exceeded $850 million.

Federal paymasters were required to keep meticulous records, usually in duplicate or triplicate. On October 31, 1865, their disbursements that had begun on July 12, 1861, were tabulated. During this period, officers and men of the U.S. Army received $1,029,239,000. New York City topped this figure. According to the *Journal of the Board of Alderman*, the municipal government paid for equipping regiments with arms and ammunition and for relief of soldiers' families in the amount of $1,038,378,000.

Late in 1865, the directors of a principal railroad of the Confederacy issued a report on its wartime losses. The cost of the conflict to the Georgia Railroad and Banking Company was listed at $2,232,528.71

All estimates of the value of slaves freed during and after the conflict are suspect. One yardstick is found in congressional records. At the insistence of the president, lawmakers offered to reimburse owners in the amount of $67,644,900 on condition that all slaves would be freed.

In 1860, according to *The Statistical History of the United States*, there were 3,953,760 slaves in the country. If a "reasonable" figure of $400 per slave is used to factor the total cost of the population, then that figure would be around $1.6 billion.

In 1865 the national public debt was about $75.01 per person, or a total of $2,677,929,000. In 1861, when Maj. Robert Anderson moved his command to Fort Sumter from Fort Moultrie, a levy of $2.06 per person would have wiped out the federal debt of $64,844,000.

The total cost of the war in which an estimated 4,178,000 men fought cannot be calculated with accuracy. Federal records, considered to be reasonably accurate and complete, indicate that the outlay of the Union reached at least $3.02 billion. Since property losses were much greater in the South than in the North, the conflict may have cost the Confederates $4 billion.

That $7 billion total is almost equal to the appraised value of all real and personal property in every state in 1850. In terms of the purchasing power of the 2010 dollar, the Civil War cost 39 trillion.

During one of the times when U.S. Maj. Gen. William Tecumseh Sherman had Memphis under his control, an enterprising merchant brought in two boxcars filled with merchandise but marked as "Relief Association." When Sherman discovered the ruse, he confiscated the shipment.

A Federal officer who witnessed the proceedings reported that the confiscated goods were sold within twenty-four hours, yielding $8,000 to the U.S. government.

~~~

When the patriotic citizens of New York's Oneida County wanted to aid the war effort, wealthy Charles Wheelock organized the Ninety-seventh New York Volunteers. Once he was elected colonel of the outfit, he assumed all responsibility for the dependents left by the soldiers. According to the *New York Tribune*, Wheelock parted with "upward of nine thousand dollars out of his own pocket towards the support of the families."

~~~

On May 21, 1863, a band of guerrillas rode into Pittsburg, Missouri. Soon they discovered that a local bank was a depository for state funds. Before sundown, they departed "carrying with them eleven thousand dollars belonging to the State."

~~~

In April 1864, a band of about a thousand men in blue marched down a bank of the Tennessee River toward Decatur, Alabama. Serving under the command of Brig. Gen. John W. Geary, they halted for the night at a hamlet near Bridgeport. When the soldiers entered the tiny town, they discovered and seized "mail and seventeen thousand dollars in Confederate money."

~~~

Many of the folk who lived in the mountains of western Virginia were more than ready to create a new state. Backed by Lincoln, they established West Virginia.

This movement, seldom recognized as a form of secession from the Old Dominion, couldn't operate without cash. Hence the dissidents seized $30,000 in Virginia funds to begin to implement their independence.

The money had been deposited in the Exchange Bank of Weston, where it was placed to the credit of the Western Lunatic Asylum. Civilian-soldiers who seized the cache "aroused the drowsy population by playing 'The Star-Spangled Banner' before demanding the cash."

Since a detail of men from the Seventh Ohio Infantry had assisted the rebellious West Virginians, they were rewarded by the man who called himself governor of the new state. Francis H. Pierpont, soon to be recognized in Washington as governor, gave the soldiers 10 percent of the money they helped to seize. "Thus was the Restored Government organized," Boyd B. Stutler wrote many years later, "the most unusual state that ever belonged to the Union."

Late in September 1860, a Federal provost marshal issued a proclamation in Saint Louis to announce that $33,000 belonging to Cherokees had been "confiscated to the use and benefit of the United States."

The money involved represented a portion of the annual annuity promised to the Cherokees at the time of their removal from Georgia to Oklahoma.

According to the *New York Herald* of August 18, 1860, an unidentified band of U.S. troops staged a successful raid at Sainte Genevieve, Missouri. Some readers of the eastern newspaper were surprised to learn that $58,000 was seized.

R. C. Gridley of Nevada unsuccessfully solicited gifts for the U.S. Sanitary Commission, having specified to his friends and neighbors that he wanted them to be generous.

Refusing to be foiled in his effort to raise money for the organization of volunteers, Gridley tried a novel scheme. He put a twenty-pound sack of flour into a benefit auction. The gift changed hands several times, each seller following his example of contributing the purchase money. Gridley's flour eventually boosted the resources of the Sanitary Commission by $3,500 a pound for a total gift to the agency of $70,000.

∼∽∼

When North Carolina attorney Jacob Thompson was the chief Confederate agent in Canada, he was not required to give a detailed accounting of money sent to him. After the war, however, Judah P. Benjamin, one-time Confederate secretary of the treasury, became suspicious and hinted that he would request an audit of Thompson's books. This prompted the Tarheel to turn over to former Confederates about $60,000.

After Benjamin ceased to ask questions, Thompson took the remaining $113,000 from his accounts and spent the next few years living luxuriously in Europe.

∼∽∼

Confederate Maj. James Nocquet had been selected to safeguard funds that were designated for a number of military construction projects. Shortly after the November 25, 1863, battle of Missionary Ridge, he was seen making his way toward Federal lines. His progress was somewhat slow, as he carried with him an estimated $150,000 that aides of Gen. Braxton Bragg had planned to spend on roads and defensive works.

∼∽∼

Near Kearneysville in what had become West Virginia, Confederate raider John S. Mosby directed his men to tear up a section of railroad track. Soon a passenger train of the Baltimore and Ohio Railroad hit the trap at full speed.

The waiting Confederates headed straight toward a baggage car believed to be transporting two U.S. Army paymasters. When they pried open the door of the car, it took the bandits in uniform only a few minutes to scoop up $173,000 before they burned the train.

Famous—or infamous—as the Greenback Raid, this exploit took place in a gorge on October 13, 1864. The jubilant Southerners returned to their base to the strains of music produced by two fiddlers who knew only one tune, "Malbrook Has Gone to the Wars."

Saint Albans, Vermont, was the site of the northernmost Confederate raid of the war. On October 19, 1864, Lt. Bennett H. Young led a band of about twenty-five volunteers into the town that lay only fifteen miles south of the Canadian border.

Three banks were robbed, yielding a total of $201,522. Within days more than one-third of the stolen money was recovered.

U.S. Maj. Gen. Benjamin F. Butler learned that some of the banks of New Orleans held considerable sums. Citing a congressional act of July 17, 1862, as his authority, he seized Confederate funds believed to be in excess of $250,000.

On March 14, 1861, members of the provisional Confederate Congress adopted a resolution of thanks directed to "the convention of the State of Louisiana." It lauded "the patriotic liberality" of lawmakers whose metropolis was New Orleans.

Earlier, Confederates of the port city had seized from U.S. authorities a "bullion fund" in the amount of $389,267.46. It was soon turned over to the Confederate government by A. J. Guirot of the Louisiana State Depository. At Montgomery, delighted Secessionists soon learned that $147,519.66 more would come their way. This sum represented U.S. customs collections at New Orleans after January 31 of the year in which war broke out.

~~~

Confederates were not the only ones to seize cash in New Orleans. As military governor of the city, Union General Butler concluded that funds held by the Dutch consul had been sent for safekeeping by Southerners who planned to purchase war supplies.

Disregarding diplomatic immunity, he ordered Federal troops to raid the consulate, taking from it $800,000.

~~~

South Carolina led the way in seizing Federal installations within the borders of seceded states. F. C. Humphreys, storekeeper of military supplies, made no attempt to resist when armed men surrounded his building on December 30, 1860.

The value of the arsenal, which occupied the whole of a city block, is unknown. In addition, Secessionists seized weapons that ranged in size from pistols to cannon. The value of more than twenty-two thousand pieces of ordnance acquired that day by the Palmetto State was conservatively estimated to be "well in excess of $350,000."

~~~

Once it was certain that an armed conflict would take place, Southern leaders made it known that they were in desperate need of cash. As a result, the state of Alabama made a loan of $500,000 to the central government then established in Montgomery. Had this money not been available, Confederate troops would have been unable to meet the Federal invaders of Virginia soil at Manassas.

~~~

Confederate units led by Maj. Gen. J. E. B. Stuart descended upon Federal headquarters on August 22, 1863. As Union Maj. Gen. John Pope had been comfortably established at Catlett's Station for some time, several money chests were stored there.

Members of Stuart's Ninth Virginia Cavalry made off with Pope's personal belongings, some of his horses, and his dispatch book. In addition, they took the contents of the Federal money chests, approximately $520,000.

※

Commanders of warships that made up Federal blockading squadrons had orders to seize cotton whenever possible. So much of it accumulated that U.S. Secretary of the Treasury Salmon P. Chase decided it was time to do something with it.

Thus Hiran Barney, a Federal cotton agent in New York, was authorized to sell everything in the Federal warehouses. In February 1863, he reported that he had sold 3,325 bales of cotton. Additional cotton that had not been ginned was estimated at 1,779 bales. Net proceeds to the Federal government amounted to $696,562.

※

An ardently pro-Confederate, former governor Sterling Price of Missouri took command of state troops in 1860. He captured Lexington, Missouri, in September 1861 and triumphantly reported having found $900,000 that Federals had earlier taken from banks in the state.

In addition to the cash, Price seized commissary stores whose estimated value was $100,000. Reporting to Gov. Claiborne F. Jackson, he said this raid netted well over $1 million since he seized "over 3,000 stand of infantry arms and about 750 horses."

※

En route to Falmouth, England, the commercial vessel *B. F. Hoxie* carried papers showing that her cargo included a quantity of expensive logwood. She was seized by a privateer in June 1863 at a point described as "latitude twelve degrees north, longitude thirty degrees."

When men from the crew of the raider *Florida* broke open the hold of the captured vessel, they found that in addition to wood she carried silver bars and thirty tons of silver ore. The bars were appraised at $500,000, and the ore was estimated to be worth about the same.

Gov. Oliver P. Morton of Indiana personally led recruitment campaigns that sent regiment after regiment into Federal service. Since the state included thousands of Democrats who opposed the war, legislators balked at providing the funds needed for Morton's troops.

An impasse was reached when it became evident that the Hoosier chief executive had to choose between only two alternatives. He could disband many of his regiments or he could find way to circumvent the state legislature. Morton therefore borrowed more than $1 million to spend on pay, uniforms, muskets, and artillery.

Michigan responded eagerly when Lincoln issued his first call for volunteers. Historically, its lawmakers had provided an annual appropriation of only $3,000 for the twenty-eight militia companies of the state.

On May 7, 1862, with civil war a certainty, the legislature hurriedly passed a magnanimous fiscal act. Under its terms, the state that earlier begrudged $3,000 a year for military purposes authorized the governor to raise ten regiments and float a loan of $1 million to arm and equip them.

On September 3, 1861, Unionist readers of the *National Intelligencer* were gratified by a detailed report concerning the activities of a federal official described as the "surveyor of the port of New York." During the five months immediately following the surrender of Fort Sumter, this official had seized eight ships, seven barks, and ten other vessels "owned wholly or in part by rebels." The value of the twenty-five privately owned ships confiscated in the port of New York was reported to be more than $2 million.

⁓

On September 15, 1863, Union Rear Adm. David D. Porter sent a special report to Washington describing some minor military actions. One of these occurred near Bolivar, Tennessee, where three Confederate paymasters had been captured. Escorted by thirty-five men, the money carriers had been headed toward Little Rock with $2.5 million. Although the entire sum was captured, it did not affect U.S. balance sheets since men in gray were to be paid in Confederate currency.

⁓

After 1861, British investors owned most blockade-runners. A postwar summary indicated that "total loss to owners who ventured in the business was in the neighborhood of $30 million."

⁓

Under a series of congressional acts, the U.S. Treasury was authorized to issue interest-bearing notes during the 1850s. On January 1, 1861, Federal obligations incurred through distribution of these notes amounted to $17,387,011.64.

When Lincoln issued the call for volunteers, fiscal authorities switched from notes to bonds. More than two weeks before the first battle of Manassas, a "loan bill" passed the U.S. House of Representatives. When five issues of bonds authorized before the first major battle had been sold, the U.S. national debt increased by $250 million.

Soon after Appomattox, the ladies of Montgomery, Alabama, formed a Memorial Association. Twenty-five years later, the body passed a resolution authorizing erection on Capitol Hill of a monument to the state's Confederate dead. The cost, when completed, was not to exceed $45,000.

To help raise the money, the ladies "gave an entertainment for the great monument, in which all alike are interested." This fundraising event brought to the memorial Association a net profit of $143.85. Presumably their other efforts met with greater success since the monument is there today.

Soldiers in gray who were stationed in San Antonio at war's end knew that the city was a depository for Confederate silver. They raided the government vault, divided the silver among themselves, and each man became richer by $160.

When the USS *San Jacinto* was wrecked in 1865, what was left of the vessel was sold. An auction resulted in a gain for the U.S. Treasury of $224.61.

After the U.S. Government resorted to enforced conscription for military service, a man in any Northern state could hire a substitute. During 1863, in nearly every part of the Union, a fellow who agreed to go to the battlefield in place of a draftee pocketed at least $300.

Throughout the Cotton Belt, desperate need for gunboats induced women to hold fairs to raise money. At Tuskegee, Alabama, a different approach was tried in early 1862. Five ladies used columns of the *Advertiser and Register* to reach the general public. The newspaper reported that: "The patriotic ladies of Tuskegee desire to be represented in the enterprise that has for its object the protection of their dearest rights. For this purpose they have canvassed the community, and have secured cash subscriptions to the amount of $303.95, together with a donation of three bales of cotton."

At Pensacola, Confederates met in hand-to-hand combat with Federal soldiers during the fall of 1861. A letter written from the scene of the action reported, "We killed about one hundred of them, and lost heavily in killed and wounded on our side, but I do not know the exact number."

Pockets of Federal dead were quickly emptied, the letter writer added. Loot included "coats, hats, caps, swords, and a fine pair of navy pistols." Even better, in the opinion of the writer, "One of our men got three hundred and forty dollars in cash."

While bank employees in Saint Albans, Vermont, were being held at gunpoint by Confederate raiders, a local merchant came to pay off a note. Sam Breck was quickly spotted as carrying cash in his right hand. Hence the soldiers pushed him into a backroom of the bank, relieved him of the cash, and added $393 to their take.

The adjutant general of the U.S. Army, Samuel Cooper, became a tormented man before the outbreak of war. Born and reared in New Jersey, he graduated from West Point in 1815 and soon married a Virginia belle. With war looming, he decided in early March 1861 to join the Secessionists.

Cooper became a brigadier on March 16 and was the moving force behind the organization of the Confederate army. Soon he received a commission making him a full general, ranking from May 16. As the senior general officer of forces in gray, Cooper did more than anyone except Davis and Lee to keep the Confederacy alive.

By 1870 he was a "dirt poor farmer" in Alexandria, Virginia, who was barely able to subsist. Vividly conscious of Cooper's monumental labor for the Lost Cause, Lee solicited contributions from veterans.

Former Confederates who responded to the appeal from the one-time commander of the Army of Northern Virginia sent him $300. With a personal gift from Lee added, "the Samuel Cooper Relief Fund" reached a total of $400.

Pennsylvania-born mechanic Samuel Ruth took a course opposite to that of Cooper. When the war began, he had lived in Virginia for many years and was regarded by neighbors and fellow workers as a true-blue supporter of the Confederacy. By this time he had become superintendent of transportation for an all-important railroad that ran from Richmond to the Potomac River by way of Fredericksburg.

Ruth successfully hid his strong Unionist sentiments for months, then secretly made contact with Federal military leaders. For at least two years, he served as a spy who fed to Washington vital information about railroad movements.

After the surrender at Appomattox, he dropped the pretense, admitted what he had done, and applied for compensation. Early requests from Ruth seem to have been ignored, but his claim for having rendered services worth $40,000 was eventually processed. From the capital, the spy whose life was daily laid on the line for two years received a check for $500.

Forty-one

PAYDAY SOME DAY

A widely circulated report has it that South Carolina was the only state that did not raise a single regiment for Federal service. Despite its prevalence, the account is not correct. From January to July 1863, four regiments of South Carolina infantry were raised to fight Confederates. Both the First and the Second South Carolina Infantry (African Descent) saw limited combat service.

Organized at Hilton Head in June, the Third South Carolina Infantry (African Descent) spent more than seven months there on post duty. Moving to Jacksonville, Florida, in February 1864, during March it became the Twenty-first U.S. Colored Troops.

Sgt. William Walker of Company A was disgruntled when he learned that regulations called for men in blue to be paid only at ninety-day intervals. To make matters worse, no paymaster appeared after members of the Third South Carolina had drilled and drilled and drilled for that long period. Members of the regiment devised a song whose melodious refrain was simply, "P-a-a-y-day, some d-a-a-y!"

Col. Thomas W. Higginson, destined to gain fame and die with the Fifty-fourth Massachusetts Infantry, sympathized but could do nothing. In his diary he noted that the pay issue "impaired discipline, relaxed loyalty, and has begun to implant a feeling of sullen distrust" among black soldiers.

Walker, who was exempt from conscription, had volunteered and enrolled on April 24. By August he was so angry that he was charged with using threatening language when addressing an officer. Soon a court-martial was convened and the man who wanted only to be paid was put on trial. Convicted, he was reduced to the rank of private and sentenced "to be shot to death with musketry."

On February 29, 1864, Walker paid with his life for having waged a one-man fight to get the U.S. government to pay a just debt.

One man whose pay came from the U.S. government never complained that his money would arrive some day. It invariably came to Abraham Lincoln on schedule, at the rate of about $70 a day or $2,083 per month.

Lincoln's $25,000 per year was princely in comparison with all military and most civilian salaries. His wife, however, seems to have been a compulsive buyer, whose spending sprees packed the White House closets with shoes and garments that were never worn. Despite the idiosyncrasies of Mary Todd Lincoln, the frugal president had accumulated about $90,000 by the time he was felled by a bullet from John Wilkes Booth's derringer. After the president's death, unredeemed salary warrants worth $4,044.67 were found in his desk.

In 1862 Edwin M. Stanton of Ohio was approached about becoming U.S. secretary of war. When he learned that the position paid $8,000 annually his initial reaction was negative. "I can't afford to give up a thriving law practice for such a sum," he said.

After deciding to join Lincoln's cabinet, Stanton chose Peter H. Watson to be assistant secretary of war. For $3,000 a year and some prestige, Watson often worked more than one hundred hours a week.

Confederate Secretary of State Judah P. Benjamin was paid $6,000 a year in 1862. His chief clerk, L. Q. Washington tried to make ends meet on $1,750 a year—in Confederate currency already depreciating rapidly.

When the provisional Confederate Congress was organized at Montgomery, Alabama, the elected representatives were given a per diem allowance of $8 a day. In 1861, many of them collected a total of about $450.

This situation changed rapidly, despite the fact that no member of the body had significant seniority. In April 1862 the *Richmond Whig* berated Southern lawmakers for accepting "about five thousand four hundred dollars per annum from the public treasury." As a result, raged the newspaper, a man whose only risk came from harsh words received about $2,700 more for a year's service than did a colonel on the battlefield.

Neither editorials nor public opinion had any effect. Knowing that the collapse of the Confederacy was near and with their government deeply in debt, Confederate lawmakers boosted their own salaries to $16,500 per year.

Members of the Maryland legislature did not fare nearly so well as did Confederate congressman. In 1861 they were paid $4 a day to try to keep the divided state out of war.

About the time of Lincoln's first inauguration, the Confederate provisional Congress tackled the difficult question of military structure and pay. It was comparatively easy to decide to authorize formation of one corps of engineers and another of artillery, plus six regiments of infantry and one of cavalry.

Starting at the top, lawmakers provided for the selection of four brigadiers, each to be paid $3,612 per year. A chief aide-de-camp, with the minimum rank of lieutenant, would start at $125 per month.

Some officers in other branches of Confederate service were initially paid more than infantry officers of the same rank. In 1861 an infantry colonel drew $195, while a colonel of artillery received $210 monthly. Pay of a major ranged from $150 in the infantry to $162 in the cavalry.

For their surgeon general, the Confederate lawmakers provided $3,000 per year "plus fuel and quarter." In the U.S. Army a surgeon with ten years of military experience was eligible to draw $200 per month, but one who had practiced for only nine years received $162 per month.

Commanders of an army in the field were allowed an extra $100 per month. Anticipating the possibility of a struggle much longer than was then foreseen in Washington, lawmakers assembled at Montgomery voted to give an extra $9 per month to every commissioned officer who reached the five-year service mark.

A sergeant or master workman of a Confederate engineer corps was eligible for pay at the rate of $34 per month, while corporals and overseers received $20. An infantry private was paid $11 per month plus clothing and one food ration per day.

Two years later, with merchants often refusing to accept Confederate currency at face value, the pay for men in gray was substantially the same. A general, regardless of grade, still received $301 monthly. Some disgusted privates grumbled that their commanders received $1 per month for the services they rendered, with the balance thrown in "to please them." By war's end, a full general in gray was due to receive Confederate currency in the amount of $328 per month.

Many officers' pay was supplemented by a formal scale regarding the number of horses allowed for their use. Assistant surgeons received two animals at government expense, and generals of all ranks were allowed four. Cavalrymen under the rank of first lieutenant were required to provide their own mounts.

Battlefield experience soon demonstrated the necessity or desirability of using persons not initially listed as military personnel. Hence by 1863 Confederate armies were paying hospital stewards $20 or $21 per month and a hospital matron received all of $6 per month. Chaplains, added as an afterthought, received $80 per month, according to *Regulations for the Army of the Confederate States*.

Although the Confederate Marine Corps was never large, it was elite. Lawmakers initially envisioned it as comprising not more than 621 men and commanded by a major. With authorized strength boosted to 1,000, this body finally included about 525 men.

By the time the corps attained that size, the pay of privates had been increased from $11 per month to $15. A marine corporal received an extra $2 per month, and a first sergeant's pay swelled to $24 monthly. Since a colonel's pay was considered to be generous, in the marine corps it remained at $195 per month.

Many a Confederate would have been amazed at the actions that led to William Walker's execution. Scores of units fought, marched, and fought again for more than a year before receiving a single dollar.

Men in blue sometimes fared no better. Pvt. Alfred S. Roe of the Ninth New York Heavy Artillery never forgot nor forgave. Long after the war ended, he lamented, "I never saw any of Uncle Sam's wages between January '64 and March '65."

Volunteers rushed to form Anderson's Cavalry (later the Fifteenth Pennsylvania) at Carlisle, Pennsylvania, in November 1861. This high-profile unit was formed to provide an escort and a headquarters guard for Brig. Gen. Robert Anderson of Fort Sumter fame. Now a brigadier in Kentucky, Anderson was delighted to receive volunteers from the Keystone State. These Federals were paid nothing until December 1862, more than thirteen months after having first mounted their horses and flourished their sabers.

Theory—and regulations—called for Federal units to be mustered for pay at sixty-day intervals. Paymasters were supposed to be on hand the last day of February, April, June, August, and October. Perhaps as a sort of year end or Christmas bonus, the final payday of a calendar year was often scheduled for December 5. Many factors operated to prevent timely payments, however.

Union Maj. Gen. John C. Frémont didn't like the idea of asking men to fight without pay. After having made repeated futile requests to the War Department, he dispatched an urgent letter to Lincoln on July 30, 1861. In it, the man who had won civilian fame as "the Pathfinder" said that a U.S. depository in Saint Louis held "$300,000 entirely unappropriated."

Frémont had asked the official in charge to release $100,000 to the paymaster of the Western Department but was curtly refused. Reporting to the president, the man who in 1856 had been the first Republican candidate for the White House announced: "This morning I will order the Treasurer [in Saint Louis] to deliver the money in his possession, and will send a force to take the money, and will direct such payments as the exigency requires. I will hazard everything for the defense of the department you have confided to me, and I trust to you for support." If Lincoln acknowledged this imperious demand that soldiers be paid, his reply has vanished; it does not appear in his *Collected Works*.

Frémont's plan to seize and dispense these funds may have failed. In December, editors of the *Missouri Democrat* berated the War Department because members of the Twenty-seventh Missouri Infantry still had received no pay.

Bureaucrats of the War Department devised an ingenious scheme to juggle payments in favor of the U.S. Treasury. Having failed to smash the Army of Tennessee, U.S. Maj. Gen. William T. Sherman decided to capture Atlanta.

Sherman fired off a series of telegrams to the paymaster general in Washington, first requesting and then demanding that his troops be "mostly paid in checks on New York." On September 30, 1864, the general received a telegram from Maj. Gen. Henry W. Halleck that outlined a system devised for deferring payday.

Halleck, the U.S. chief of staff, informed Sherman that half of what was owed to Union soldiers was to be paid in the form of interest-bearing treasury notes or bonds. Such a remittance, he pointed out, "not being a legal tender by law, cannot be deposited and checked against." This meant that although soldiers who had followed Sherman from Chattanooga to Atlanta were paid in full legally, they could not use the money for weeks or months.

Women of the U.S. Sanitary Commission, no longer willing to see soldiers go penniless for months, established a "back-pay agency." Civilian volunteers took the soldiers' papers, ensured that they were in proper order, and learned how to knock on the right doors in Washington. A single branch of this agency sometimes received $20,000 from the capital in a single day.

Gov. John A. Andrew of Massachusetts was frustrated with the notorious delays in the army's paying its soldiers. In early 1863, he proposed that the state legislature empower the state treasurer to borrow funds to make pay advances to the men of Massachusetts serving in the Union army whose pay from Washington was late. The measure was approved. At the time, the pay for the First Massachusetts Cavalry was more than $200,000 in arrears.

At first, Lincoln was successful in opposing prisoner exchanges. Since he argued that no state had seceded, an exchange of prisoners would seem to elevate the Confederacy to the level of nationhood.

Practical considerations eventually forced him to abandon this point of view. Once the distinction was made, Federal authorities took action that granted prisoners of war the same pay they would have received if they had been on normal duty.

When misconceptions about the conflict began to clear and the country realized that the war would be a much longer affair than many had at first expected, lawmakers on both sides began to adjust the pay of soldiers. The pay of Union privates jumped from $11 to $13 per month in 1861 and eventually reached a peak of $16. Meanwhile, a private in gray saw his pay raised from $11 to $18 per month. At the time this increase took effect, in much of the Confederacy a pair of shoes cost $125 and coffee was hard to find at $12 a pound.

Some Native Americans who volunteered to fight in gray fared even worse than their Anglo counterparts. When Confederate Brig. Gen. Albert Pike authorized the raising of regiments during the fall of 1860, Creeks, Choctaws, and Cherokees responded with considerable enthusiasm. Their zeal for the Confederate cause, however, began to evaporate when they found that neither arms nor pay had been arranged for them. A disgusted officer later acknowledged that "with the exception of a partial supply for the Choctaw regiment, no tents, clothing, or camp and garrison equipage was furnished to any of them."

Federal officers were initially paid much less than their Southern counter-parts. A brigadier received $124 per month and a major general was paid $220 monthly. Cash designated for colonels ranged from $95 to $110, depending upon the branch of service in which a man fought.

Pay differential for majors was $10 monthly, from $70 (infantry and artil-lery) to $80 (cavalry, ordnance, and engineers). Many a captain yearned to move from the infantry into the cavalry in order to boost his monthly pay from $60 to $70.

Unlike enlisted men, Federal officers were not issued rations in addition to cash. This often forced a man wearing stars on his shoulders to send out a ser-vant or two to forage for him. This situation fostered widespread looting from civilians, regardless of their loyalty or lack of it.

After a Union officer pocketed $600 during a calendar year, the balance of his salary was subject to what Washington called "special duty" of 3 percent. This highly effective device constituted the prototype of today's income tax withholding from wages and salaries.

Originally designated at ninety days, terms of enlistment in Federal forces were frequently and rapidly extended. By the time Grant closed the jaws of his mili-tary trap upon Lee, five-year volunteers were being enrolled.

A recruit who signed up for a sixty-month hitch was promised—but did not always get—clothing in addition to cash. Regulations called for such a person to achieve during his five-year hitch the following equipment: two blankets, thirteen pairs of trousers, eight coats, fifteen flannel shirts, eleven pairs of drawers, twenty pairs of stocking, five hats, twelve caps, and, at three-month intervals, one pair of booties). In 1863, the *Revised Regulations for the Army of the United States* stipulated that "mounted men may receive one pair of boots and two pairs of bootees instead of four pairs of bootees."

In addition to having preferential treatment for their feet, Union cavalrymen who provided their own mounts and gear were paid for them during much of the conflict. An initial allowance of 50¢ per day for this purpose was quickly reduced to 40¢. Eventually, having accumulated enough of its own horses to meet the need, the War Department dropped this special allowance.

Privates on both sides were promised one ration per day in addition to cash. Within Federal forces, any soldier of that rank could use as much as $42 worth of clothing in twelve months as a supplement to his pay. If he exceeded the annual limit, the cost of extra clothing was deducted by a paymaster.

Anyone who managed to spend a year on active duty without using his full clothing allowance was supposed to receive the difference in cash. Thus one of the typical activities following a battle was the systematic stripping of clothing from the dead.

After the Federal disaster at Manassas, a military nurse—almost always male—was paid at the rate of 40¢ per day plus one food ration.

Under the terms of a congressional act of July 17, 1862, Lincoln was authorized to employ African Americans "for the suppression of this rebellion." He was given a free hand to establish a system of organization with which to use them, but the act made no provision for their compensation.

William Whiting, solicitor of the War Department, handed down a ruling on April 25, 1863, stating that "persons of African descent who should be employed under the law should receive $10 per month and one ration each per day, of which $3 might be paid in clothing." For practical purposes, this established the pay of a black volunteer at a trifle over half that drawn by a white comrade.

Racial tensions in the North mounted when a few free African Americans discovered that if they volunteered they would not receive the same bounties promised to whites. So serious was this matter that a congressional committee made a study, resulting in a special report about "Colored men and their relation to the military service."

The ambiguous language of the report complicated matters even more. With Federal draft laws in effect, the U.S. solicitor general was requested to look into the question of racially mixed substitutes. The opinion stated: "In compliance with special instructions from the President, an order was issued on the 20th of July, 1863, directing that men of African descent should only be accepted as substitutes for each other."

Thus Northerners could not avoid service in the Union army by hiring free blacks to fight for them. In many cities, African Americans would have accepted $200 gladly (two-thirds of the going rate) to serve as a substitute for a draftee.

Although still on the books, this provision was not being enforced in 1865. By that time, African-American soldiers were paid at the same rate as whites.

Pay for a maritime service was generally higher than for service on land. A Confederate admiral drew $6,000 per year, and when commanding a squadron a captain was listed at $5,000. For other sea duty, a captain's pay dropped $800 per year. Yet while on leave or awaiting orders, such an officer drew $250 per month.

With five years' experience (usually most of it in the U.S. Navy), a Confederate commander on sea duty drew $2,825 per year. While awaiting assignment or on leave, such an officer received only $187.50 per month.

By January 1, 1863, *The Register of the Navy of the United States* reported that Federal naval officers had received significant raises in pay. At sea a commander drew $2,800 yearly, while a captain was paid $3,500. When a man moved from the rank of captain to commodore, his sea duty pay jumped $500 yearly.

For the newly created rank of rear admiral, the U.S. Navy Department provided $5,000 during sea duty. A rear admiral took a 20 percent cut in pay when he was assigned to shore duty, and other wearers of naval brass faced approximately the same differential.

For reasons never fully explained, the commanding officer of a warship whose pay was only $1,500 annually was also allowed one food ration per year without charge. Should such an officer take on the chores of paymaster, he drew an extra $200 a year.

A Federal surgeon on duty at sea drew $2,200 a year for five years, but this rose to $3,000 annually after twenty years of service. A chief engineer was paid at the rate of $150 per month for five years, but after fifteen years was boosted to $216.66. A naval gunner started at $1,000 per year and after twelve years reached a peak of $1,450.

Two sets of persons were at the bottom of the inverted pyramid that made up the pay scale of the U.S. Navy. A powder monkey, or "water boy," received $10 a month plus rations. Since this position called for sailors of a small, short stature, some of these youngsters had been recruited at nine years of age.

Once a shooting war got under way, these juveniles had competition for the position from older and larger African Americans. In September 1861, U.S. Secretary of the Navy Gideon Welles released a directive, stipulating that "persons of color, commonly known as contrabands, may be enlisted as 'boys' at $10 per month and one ration per diem."

Civilian pay varied wildly, with geographical location and skills being major variables. Andrew Carnegie started as a bobbin boy in a Pennsylvania cotton mill and was paid $1.20 for a workweek of seventy-two or more hours.

Working in the sprawling Washington arsenal, a boy of twelve to sixteen years of age was paid, not by the hour, but by the piece. It took most of them a full day to put together 650 cartridges. As the need for ammunition grew more critical, the pay rose from about 60¢ a day to 75¢. Much piecework was also done at the U.S. Patent Office. In 1861 a typical employee received 80¢ for the skilled and laborious job of sewing a book by hand.

With plans underway for establishing the Gettysburg National Cemetery, another big job had to be done piece-by-piece. Thousands of bodies were exhumed at an average rate of $1.69 each.

A man working as a civilian medical corpsman for Federal forces was likely to be paid $20.50 monthly. Both the remuneration and the risk compared favorably with those of Pennsylvania coal miners, some of whom were lucky to get $275 per year and others who received as little as 50¢ per day.

In many sections of North Carolina and Tennessee, poor whites were glad to work for $110 a year plus food and clothes. Along the northwestern frontier of the United States, pay was substantially higher. A dependable workman could command as much as $14 a month in cash.

In cities along the eastern seaboard, a laborer with few skills was often paid $20 per month. At Elmira, New York, a veteran gravedigger received twice that amount.

Pay scales were almost always lower in the South than they were in the North. In New Orleans early in 1861 boys were lucky to earn 50¢ a day, while adult women often were paid 75¢ and unskilled men drew $1 a day. Some skilled workers received as much as $9 for a six-day workweek.

Carpenters working on the CSS *Mississippi* in 1861 were ordered off the job because they had banded together and demanded the impossibly high wage of $4 a day.

With a large proportion of young men in uniform, contractors who furnished fuel for wood-burning locomotives boosted their workers' wages to $3 a day, occasionally paying even more than that.

Newspaper members of the Southern Associated Press found themselves in the same bind by 1863. Fees for weekly reports of three thousand to four thousand words jumped to $12.

Veteran reporters and artists for widely circulated eastern newspapers fared even better. From the large dailies, they customarily drew $25 a week plus expenses. Winslow Homer was a conspicuous exception to the general rule. His work was in such demand that he was paid $60 a page.

A future major general, James A. Garfield, served for four prewar years as president of Ohio's Hiram College. In addition to his administrative duties, he lectured and taught penmanship. Garfield's salary was set by the college board of trustees at $80 per month.

When the famous Pony Express was launched in 1860, it was destined to survive only eighteen months, falling victim to rapidly expanding telegraph networks. A rider who went through Indian country from Saint Joseph, Missouri, to San Francisco in ten days was promised pay at the rate of $25 per month.

In New York, the 1862 annual report of the American Express Company reported that "two thousand men are in the regular employ of this company." The average salary was $600 per annum.

The Federal victory at Port Royal, South Carolina, made it easy for Northern entrepreneurs to come in and take possession of many large plantations. They soon discovered that they didn't know what to do with them. According to the *New York Tribune*, the new plantation owners promised to pay experienced overseers as much as $1,000 a year.

Salaries of the eight-man office working under the U.S. attorney general in 1861 ran to $20,500. Meanwhile, as confidential clerk to the commissioner of patents, Clara Barton was drawing $1,400 a year.

While the founder of the American Red Cross was working at the patent office, William Tecumseh Sherman took on the job of superintending the operation of the Saint Louis Car Company. This system of street transportation paid the future general $2,000 annually for his services.

Four years earlier another future general became chief engineer of the Illinois Central Railroad. In that capacity, George B. McClellan was paid $3,000 a year for three years.

At war's end, P. G. T. Beauregard returned to his native New Orleans, financially ruined. After serving as president of a railroad, the renowned former Confederate general became superintendent of the state lottery. In this position, he was paid $30,000 annually—20 percent more than Lincoln's wartime salary.

Forty-two

FOR THE RIGHT PRICE

One of the least expensive things any military unit took to the battlefield was an eagle. At Eau Claire, Wisconsin, the regiment initially known as the Eau Claire Badgers wanted a mascot. For $2.50 they purchased a young eagle and called it Old Abe in honor of the president.

✦✦✦

Union Adm. David D. Porter designed and built what was probably the least expensive craft of the war. He fastened two old lifeboats and a rotten flat-boat together. Scrap canvas covered the three-hundred-foot contraption, upon which he mounted a set of "Quaker guns" made from logs. For fake smoke-stacks the Federal officer used a pair of pork barrels.

When placed where currents would carry it toward Confederate posi-tions, the dummy ironclad created consternation when first spotted, but the Southerners soon saw that it posed no threat to them. It was not until much later that anyone outside of Porter's command knew that the cost of construc-tion was calculated at $8.63.

✦✦✦

In the North, pocket watches were prized by clerks, workmen, and sometimes by soldiers. The cost of such a timepiece climbed from $12 in 1861 to about $20 in 1863.

Before the start of hostilities, a target telescope could be purchased for about $20. The cost of less-expensive, mass-produced pieces ranged from $14 to $30.

———

When given his commission as a signal officer of the U.S. Army, Albert J. Myer compiled a list of essentials and their cost. A "complete set of day and night signal apparatus," he reported in July 1860, could be purchased for $30. Before the end of the year, the cost of these instruments ranged between $44 and $60.

———

Early telegraph lines erected for Federal forces were built on contract. In the mountains of western Virginia, the bids averaged about $45 per mile. In Missouri, the same work cost about $100 per mile.

———

Fearful that persons on the U.S. government payroll couldn't be trusted, Lincoln assigned early purchases of military goods to civilians. No one knows what they paid for a soldier's uniform and equipment, exclusive of weapons. When the Quartermaster's Department began to buy in quantity, a soldier could be put into the field for $50 plus the cost of his musket or rifle.

———

When Confederate Lt. James H. Young of the Forty-second Georgia Infantry was killed at Chickasaw Bayou late in December 1862, most of his possessions were sold at auction in Atlanta. Some of the prices fetched were: $25 for his saddle and shotgun, $80 for fifteen hogs, $35 for his watch, $100 for a cow and calf, $27 for two jars of lard, and $150 for a buggy and harness.

Whether working at home or in improvised mills, each person processing cotton had to have a pair of cards, a tool consisting of pieces of fine wire set in thick leather and mounted on a piece of wood. Used to untangle fibers before spinning, the pair cost 40¢ at Savannah in 1861. By 1865 the same tool was worth $30 in northern Mississippi.

By March 1862 "moveable electric trains" were in wide use by Union commanders. Each set of gear included two wagons, each carrying a Beardslee telegraph instrument. Reels, grounding rods, and splicing tools were included, along with enough insulated wire for the wagons to be stationed five miles apart. Mass production brought so quick a drop in cost that a complete field telegraph system could be purchased for $2,500 in 1862 in the North.

Small arms were considered essential for dress and parade if not for use in battle. A Federal cavalry saber, complete with sheath, usually cost about $7.

Dress swords, much in demand for ceremonial purposes, ran from a low of about $125 to a high of more than $2,500. Most elegant weapons of this sort were presented to high-ranking officers by citizens of their states or by men in their command.

Far more effective as weapons than mass-produced sabers or hand-worked swords, pistols turned out by Starr and by Colt brought about $25 in 1861. So many of them were produced that the price of Colt's army .44-caliber dropped to $13.75. By war's end, plenty of five- and six-chamber weapons were on the market at $12 or a trifle less.

Produced in quantity but never used in battle, pikes were probably the war's most useless weapons. In 1862 Gov. Joseph E. Brown of Georgia made it known that he wanted tens of thousands of pikes. At least one hundred manufacturing firms rushed to turn out the six- or seven-foot poles with twelve-inch pointed blades at about $5 apiece.

In 1862 a New Orleans firm contracted to furnish the Confederate secretary of war with seventy-five tons of gunpowder at 84¢ per pound in gold and silver. Although the conflict was little more than six months old, the company balked at furnishing powder for less than $1.14 per pound in Confederate currency. By the end of 1862 a one-hundred-pound keg of gunpowder smuggled into a seceded state from Europe brought about $300.

Before the war, a shipment of ten thousand muskets cost $2 each. If purchased in smaller quantities, the price was $2.50. Two years later, however, U.S. government officials proudly reported that the Springfield Armory could turn out muskets for about $9. Similar weapons produced by private firms in the North retailed in the $20 range.

Overseas, musket makers charged whatever the traffic would bear. Demand for smoothbores dropped sharply when rifled barrels came into general use, so a Prussian manufacturer dumped eighteen thousand weapons on the world market at $4 each.

At war's end, the Ordnance Department of the U.S. Army announced that any soldier who wanted to keep his weapon could do so for a price. By that time a musket of any kind, with or without accouterments, was valued at $6.

I. P. Lindsay, an employee of the Springfield Armory, developed and patented a vastly improved musket late in 1860. Limited numbers of the .58-caliber muzzleloaders that fired two shots were made and sold. One lot consisting of one thousand pieces went to the U.S. War Department in August 1864 at $25 apiece.

Prices declined steadily after 1860. For 1861–65 the average cost of a musket was only $14.93. With ramrod, bayonet, and other equipment added, many purchasers paid as much as $20 for "a rifled musket of Springfield pattern" that weighed almost ten pounds. Samuel Colt's first large order for this weapon came late in July 1861, calling for the delivery of twenty-five thousand Springfield rifles to the U.S. War Department.

Desperate for the necessary war matériel to sign contracts without haggling, War Department officials paid importer C. K. Garrison $27 each for ten thousand rifled muskets of the Liege variety.

Breechloading weapons with rifled barrels, or rifle-muskets, were abundant by 1862. Early in September, Herman Boker and Company of New York City offered a lot of one hundred thousand guns for $18 each.

During the war the Springfield Armory turned out immense numbers of .577-caliber rifle-muskets. With the output of private industries added, at least 1.5 million were produced.

Eli Whitney is credited with developing the use of interchangeable parts, causing the price of firearms to drop sharply. He believed that $20 was a reasonable price for a musket, and he agreed to produce twenty-five thousand for the military. Before the last rifled musket was ready for use, corporate records show that this contract resulted in a substantial loss for Whitney.

Breechloading rifles were viewed suspiciously by the U.S. War Department when they became available in quantity because it was thought that they'd use too much ammunition. Despite this factor, many individual soldiers and numerous companies or regiments on both sides purchased such rifles with their own money. Thousands were sold at $28 to $30 each.

When the Spencer repeating rifle was introduced, it initially brought $35. Prices dropped to $29 and then to $20. Battlefield use of this weapon and its competitors demonstrated that the muzzle-loading musket was obsolete. As a result, the U.S. War Department paid $28 each for sixteen thousand breech-loading carbines of the Gibbs variety.

Samuel Colt's revolving rifle brought $50 in 1857. Although the Colt rifle usu-ally cost $45, many who used this splendid weapon considered it worth twice as much as the best Gibbs ever made.

A Colt was cheap by comparison with the Telescope-equipped rifle hand-made in Boston by W. G. Langdon. A veteran maker of watches and clocks, Langdon's heavy rifle was designed especially for snipers. He finished only a few pieces, but sold twenty of them to the U.S. War Department for $150 each.

Immediately after the loss at Bull Run, U.S. Secretary of War Simon Cameron contacted an arms buyer in New York. It was imperative, he wrote, to take a fast ship to Europe and purchase one hundred thousand rifled muskets. In addition, Cameron wanted ten thousand carbines and the same number of revolvers. For the massive purchasing program he established a $2 million line of credit.

Confederate agents had already bought the best that England and Europe had to offer. As a result, the hurried trip yielded only fifteen thousand English-made Enfield rifles whose average cost was $18.45. An additional four thousand decidedly inferior French-made rifles were picked up at nearly $17 apiece.

For New York troops, the same purchasing agent secured twenty-five thousand Enfield rifled muskets, for which he paid only $16.70. Although large quantities of Austrian-made pieces were on the market at $10, comparatively few of these inferior weapons reached Federal forces.

~~~

U.S. manufacturers never forgot that superior rifles were in great demand. By 1864 a .44 Henry rifle with a fifteen-cartridge magazine was selling for $35.

Only a handful of wealthy soldiers could afford to buy the Whitworth target rifle. Imported by Tiffany's of New York, this handmade weapon, equipped with a telescopic sight, was considered a bargain at $1,250.

~~~

After the last bullet was fired, any Union combat veteran could buy a fine Spencer carbine from the War Department for $10. Other carbines were tagged at $8.

"Galvanized Yankees," or Confederates who took the oath of loyalty and changed sides, were mostly used for guard duty on the frontier. As a special reward for their services, in 1866 this small group of veterans was offered an opportunity to buy Springfield rifles for $6 each.

~~~

A few analysts have published estimates of the number of cartridges expended during the conflict. In the case of major Northern manufacturers, some accurate records are available. A report issued by the Winchester Company indicated that it produced 58,238,924 cartridges of the Spencer variety alone.

Bullets were produced in scores of types and varieties. When fighting forces withdrew from Gettysburg, early relic hunter J. M. Bush picked up 125 different kinds of bullets on the battlefield.

Ebenezer Starr, a carbine maker in Yonkers, New York, in 1861 put cartridges on the market at $24.95 per thousand. Six months later "musket shells" were bringing $150 per thousand in New Orleans.

When cartridges with flanged copper cases for use in carbines became available in quantity, three firms controlled the market. With demand from the War Department estimated to be 43,350,000 in 1864, manufacturers offered them in lots of ten thousand at a price of $280.

Horses constituted a source of major expense for the U.S. government and for some individual owners. During the summer of 1861 the War Department customarily paid an average of $120 per animal. Within two years, a healthy animal could not be purchased for less than $150. During 1864, the price in the North was stabilized at $170.

Robert E. Lee saw an attractive colt during the spring of 1862. Having purchased the animal for $200, he named him Traveller.

Since prices were not stabilized in the South, they soared to astronomical heights. In 1863, owners of stables in Richmond had no difficulty filling their stalls with animals whose owners paid $300 a month for their keep. Early in 1865 a Confederate cavalryman seldom found anyone willing to curry his mount for less than $400 in currency.

The cost of food for horses soared as the war dragged on. In the spring of 1861, plenty of corn was available in El Paso at $3.50 per bushel. By 1865 those few farmers who had managed to hoard a supply of grain doled it out for 25¢ to 50¢ an ear.

Civilians everywhere were caught in the price squeeze, which became far more acute in the South than in the North. Quinine was sold for $5 an ounce in New York in 1862, while the same quantity was eagerly grabbed up in South Carolina for $60. During the two years of conflict that followed, a Confederate lucky enough to find quinine for sale had to pay $400 to $600 an ounce. Meanwhile the typical country doctor in the South raised his fee for a house call from $1 to $30.

When flannel jumped to $20 a yard in Petersburg, many potential purchasers protested. Before the conflict ended, it was not unusual for a handkerchief to bring $20. Bonnets and hats became virtually unobtainable in the Confederacy; when a nice piece of headgear was brought in by a blockade-runner in 1864 it was likely to be priced at $500 or more.

Flour, a necessity for soldiers as well as civilians, provides an inflation index of sorts. Much of it was sold in barrels that held about 125 pounds. As late as the spring of 1862, a barrel of flour could be purchased in New York for $6; the same quantity cost about $25 on the New Orleans market. Six months earlier the price in New Orleans had been $18, but flour produced in Spain was available there at $10. By fall, the residents of Vicksburg found little flour on the market at $20 a barrel.

In Richmond, where price controls were attempted, a barrel of flour was worth $16 in October 1862. That was $4 less than the going rate at Fort Walla Walla in the Washington Territory.

By January 1863, newspapers in the Confederate capital were advertising flour at $25 per barrel. The inmates of Libby Prison, unable to purchase flour at market prices, were forced to pay $100 to $110. Far to the south, in occupied New Orleans, the price was $60 and rising.

During the winter of 1864, anywhere in the Confederacy, a person was lucky to find flour at only $275 per barrel. In Vicksburg, the price had passed $400, a price also common at many inland hamlets. Libby Prison inmates were told that the precious commodity was available in limited quantities at $900 per barrel in hard currency.

By 1865, Confederate officials were paying $1,000 per barrel. One of the worst riots to hit a Confederate city occurred in Richmond when housewives staged a bread riot to protest the high prices. They were dispersed only after Jefferson Davis threatened to call out the troops.

When turpentine glutted the New Orleans market early in 1862, it brought only $3 a barrel, while New York residents were glad to get it at $38.

Bacon was plentiful in Richmond during the spring of 1860, and sellers considered themselves fortunate to get 22¢ per pound. At Fort Walla Walla, the same bacon would have brought 30¢.

Inmates of Libby Prison in Richmond paid 75¢ for bacon during the fall of 1862 and $3.50 just one year later. Shortly before war's end, it jumped to the range of $6.50 to $7 per pound in the Confederate capital.

Salt purchased at Nassau for 60¢ a pound in January 1863 was worth $80 to $100 when it reached a Confederate port aboard a blockade-runner.

Fuel was almost as expensive as salt and quinine. Except in mining regions, where it was plentiful, coal cost about $4 a ton in 1860, rising to $12 and then to $20—when it could be found.

Wood that was worth 50¢ a cord before the war was almost unobtainable in 1865, when it brought $100 in Charleston. Persons living far from a source of wood were forced to buy it by the stick at $5, since sellers were unwilling to part with an entire cord at one time. Kerosene, relatively new on the market, was much more stable in price than were other sources of heat. It increased in price only 13¢ a gallon during four years of war—from 28¢ to 41¢.

During 1861, 99,863 bales of cotton were sold on the Savannah market. For this staple, the lowest price of the year was 4¢ a pound and the highest was 14 1/2¢. In June 1862, the price jumped to 50¢ in England.

Long staple or sea-island cotton was much less abundant than the upland or short staple variety. In 1863, only 7,114 bales of premium quality cotton were sold at Savannah, but the price varied from 8¢ a pound to 32¢ during the year.

Very little tobacco, prized by fighting men in both gray and blue, was produced in Union territory. Confederate fighting men who agreed to accept their pay in tobacco instead of currency usually got it at about $1 per pound.

So much of it was available in the South that an inmate of Libby Prison could get it at this price until 1862, when "navy plug" jumped to $2.50. Once

rampant inflation caught up with Southerners who had nothing but depreciated Confederate currency, tobacco was considered to be cheap at $15 a pound.

One of the least expensive Civil War items was also the most widely purchased.
Tens of millions of "rations," or allocations of food for a soldier or sailor for one
day, were bought, assembled, and distributed. In 1861 a Confederate ration
cost 35¢, but by 1865 the cost had soared to $2.50. Initially, a great many
Federal rations were secured at 14¢, but continuous increases in the volume of
purchases added to relatively little inflation in the North meant that increases
in the cost of this all-important commodity were reported only in fractions of
a cent.

Forty-three

RANSOMS, REWARDS, AND PRIZES

No one knows what commander conceived the idea of exacting a ransom for a captured town rather than burn it. Nevertheless, this concept proved to be profitable.

A Federal officer may have been the first to try this. From Hudson, Missouri, on August 19, 1861, a directive was sent "to Mayor and Authorities, City of Palmyra, State of Missouri." These officials were ordered "to deliver up to the military authorities of this brigade, within six days, the marauders who fired upon the train bound west on the Hannibal and Saint Joseph Railroad on the evening of the 16th instant, and broke into the telegraph office."

Since compliance was unlikely, the Union demands ended with an offer of ransom that read: "If the guilty persons are not delivered up as required, and within the time herein specified, the whole brigade will be moved into your county, and contributions levied to the amount of $10,000 on Marion County and $5,000 on the city of Palmyra." The order was signed by Brig. Gen. Stephen A. Hurlbut, "under direction of John Pope, brigadier-general, commanding North Missouri."

Confederate Brig. Gen. John McCausland added a refinement in July 1864. Having demanded a huge collective ransom from the citizens of Chambersburg, Pennsylvania, he then required individual residents and merchants to pay amounts ranging from about $150 to $750. McCausland failed to stress one clause of the agreement, if he mentioned it at all. Regardless of the ransom paid by an individual, if the town itself failed to come up with the entire sum demanded, the whole place would be torched.

Eager to retaliate for the Federals' burning of three Virginia homes, McCausland ordered the evacuation of the village and burned it to the ground. Years later, the state of Pennsylvania paid $1,628,431 to Chambersburg residents as compensation for their losses.

Confederate Brig. Gen. John Hunt Morgan had earlier employed a similar but simpler technique. During his July 1863 raid into Ohio, in Summansville and in Pomeroy he demanded that business owners pay ransoms to save their establishments. Unlike McCausland, Morgan spared the places whose owners paid; he didn't have time to destroy them.

Just before Morgan started toward Cincinnati, Confederate Lt. Gen. Jubal Early and his men took possession of the village of York, Pennsylvania. He would let the place stand, he told the residents, in exchange for payment of ransom. An accommodating Virginian, Early said he'd accept commodities in lieu of some of the cash he badly needed.

Late in the evening of June 28, 1863, the citizens delivered $28,600 in cash and many wagonloads of food, clothing, and shoes. As a result, the town not far from the state capital was returned to its residents intact.

Shortly afterward, Early's men reached Gettysburg and again demanded ransom, this time in the amount of $10,000. They believed the villagers were telling the truth when they said they had little or no money on hand. Thus the Confederates agreed to spare it in return for a ransom consisting of seven thousand pounds of pork, twelve hundred pounds of sausage, one thousand pounds of coffee, six hundred pounds of salt, one thousand pairs of shoes, five hundred hats, sixty barrels of flour, and ten bushels of onions.

While the residents of Gettysburg were trying to assemble the ransom, scouts reported that Federal troops were approaching. This time, the Confederate commander left so hurriedly that he took little or nothing with him. He returned later in a futile attempt to acquire shoes, and this second foraging party precipitated the battle of July 1–3, 1863.

On July 6, 1864, Early's lieutenant McCausland took possession of Hagerstown, Maryland. For a mere $200,000, he said, he would not reduce it to ashes in retribution for Federal depredations in the Shenandoah Valley. There was no way that the folk of Hagerstown could assemble that much money. They did their best, though, and put together $20,000. The Confederate grudgingly accepted it and rode away.

The following day, July 7, Early's troops moved into the tiny hamlet of Middletown, Maryland, and he offered to spare the town in return for a ransom of $5,000. The residents simply didn't have that kind of money, they explained. A hasty door-to-door canvas yielded $1,500. When that ransom was delivered, Middletown escaped the flames.

Headed toward Washington, believed to be lightly defended for a brief period, Early made a short detour. Crossing the Potomac at Sheperdstown, he reached Frederick, Maryland on July 9, 1864.

For a ransom of $200,000, he would bypass the town. Again the town population decided it was better to borrow than to burn, but Early lost a full day waiting for them to assemble the ransom. As soon as the money was delivered, he charged off to Washington. Some claim that the day's delay allowed the Washington defenses to be warned and better prepared for Early's attack.

Descendants of the townspeople who managed to satisfy Early worked hard for decades to pay off the debt they incurred to meet the ransom. It was a triumphant day when the last of Frederick's indebtedness was paid off eighty-seven years after the town had boosted Confederate coffers by $200,000.

*

At least one Federal officer seems to have used the ransom ploy to line his own pockets. As post commander at Natchez, Mississippi, Brig. Gen. James M. Tuttle sent his troops to arrest as many prominent citizens as they could find.

Once a man was in captivity, Tuttle contacted his relatives. He claimed to be holding a person suspected of treasonable activities, and demanded a ransom in order to release the suspect. Short of that, the person would be tried and might possibly face the death penalty.

Numerous reports, telegrams, and letters from and to Tuttle survive. Not one of them, however, includes even a hint as to the total ransom collected at Natchez or what was done with it.

*

Following long-standing custom, the captain of a captured ship was often permitted to pay a ransom to save it. Otherwise, the vessel was likely to be burned or taken into port and sold at auction.

On October 9, 1862, the Philadelphia-based *Tonawanda* fell prey to the

CSS *Alabama*. Capt. Theodore Julius entered into a formal written contract that stated in part: "I am held and firmly bound, and I do hereby bind Thomas P. Cope and Francis R. Cope, owners of the ship [*Tonawanda*] and cargo, their and my heirs, executors, and assigns, well and truly to pay unto the President of the Confederate States of America for the time being, at the conclusion of the present war between the said Confederate States and the United States, the sum of $80,000, current money of the said Confederate States, and the said ship *Tonawanda*, her tackle and apparel, are hereby mortgaged for the payment of this bond."

Also in October 1862, Capt. John Saunders ransomed the brigantine *Baron de Castine*. Based in Castine, Maine, the vessel was released when papers were signed by her captain. On December 5 the schooner *Union*, out of Baltimore, was ransomed for $1,500. Earlier, the bark *Investigator* was turned loose in return for a ransom bond of $11,250.

When Confederates captured the mail steamer *Ariel*, it was correctly judged to be worth far more than the big *Tonawanda*. The value of the vessel stemmed in part from the identity of its owner, Cornelius Vanderbilt of New York City. It was ransomed on December 9, 1862, by Capt. A. G. Jones on a promise of payment to the Confederacy of $261,000. Of this sum, $123,000 was considered to be the value of her cargo.

Rewards never reached the level of ransoms pledged for the release of great ships and their cargoes. Owners of runaway slaves frequently advertised for them and promised payment for their capture and return, but such reward offers seldom exceeded $500.

Former slave Harriet Tubman was in a category all by herself. After she had conducted numerous fugitives to Canada via the Underground Railroad, many in the South were eager to see her captured. A person would have collected rewards amounting to $40,000 had he managed to snare her.

≈≈≈

Because of the scarcity of food and the resulting need for austerity, citizens of the Confederacy were forbidden to engage in some activities that had been legal earlier. To foster enforcement, small rewards were offered to informers.

Among the Confederate states, ten enacted legislation limiting or outlawing the use of corn, grain, or fruit for purposes of distillation. In South Carolina, a person who reported a neighbor's operation of an illicit still was paid $250.

To encourage production of food crops, several states put quotas upon land that could be used to grow cotton or tobacco. These restrictions were customarily tied to the number of field slaves, or "hands," held by an owner.

Arkansas, the first state to enact legislation of this sort, forbade anyone to plant more than two acres of cotton for every field hand age fourteen or older. Florida limited growth of the fiber-producing plant to one acre per hand between the ages of fifteen and sixty. South Carolina and Georgia each set the limit of cotton fields at three acres for each field hand between the ages of fifteen and fifty-five.

Fines imposed for violation of these edicts ranged from $500 to $5,000, and any person who provided information leading to collection of a fine was usually rewarded with half of it.

≈≈≈

Rewards offered for the apprehension of fugitives ranged from huge amounts to small sums. Having stepped into the office made vacant by Lincoln's assassination, President Andrew Johnson was eager to capture Jefferson Davis. As a result, he offered a reward of $100,000, a sum eventually divided among men under the command of Union Brig. Gen. James H. Wilson.

As governor of Tennessee, William "Parson" Brownlow charged that former governor Isham G. Harris, a Confederate, was "a fugitive from justice who departed with all the state's belongings." Brownlow offered a reward of $100,000 for his capture. There is no record that it was ever paid.

In comparison with David and Harris, the reward offered for presidential assassin John Wilkes Booth seemed of small consequence. For his capture, U.S. Secretary of War Edwin M. Stanton offered only $50,000.

Stanton also offered to reward the captor of conspirators John H. Surran and David E. Herold in the sum of $25,000. A separate offer by Col. L. C. Baker of the War Department guaranteed a reward of $30,000 for Booth's capture. Baker's promise, which seems to have been issued without authorization, was based upon belief that Lincoln's killer had unsuccessfully tried to kill U.S. Secretary of State William H. Seward.

Booth was discovered at a Virginia farm and shot during his apprehension. Three officers pulled him from a burning barn and placed him on the porch of the farmhouse where he died. Each of the three officers claimed credit for the capture. For their role in Booth's capture, Capt. Everton J. Conger received $15,000, Lt. Edward P. Doherty received $4,250, and Lt. Luther Baker received $3,750. Sgt. Boston Corbett fired the shot that eventually killed Booth and received a reward of $1,653.85.

Although it was by no means the largest reward posted as an incentive to find or to reveal the whereabouts of a wanted man, the Booth reward is in a special class. All of it was eventually paid, while most other rewards either brought no results or were canceled because of technicalities.

In an aside to the story, a Maj. A. D. Robinson seems to have taken a personal interest in the manhunt for John Wilkes Booth. After the assassin's death was officially reported, he sent Boston Corbett a remittance of $100 that he labeled "a bounty for success in the search for Abraham Lincoln's killer."

During the years in which few persons were neutral and open hostility flourished, anyone and everyone seems to have been permitted to offer a reward for the death or capture of an enemy. In Atlanta, resident George Martin fled after having been charged with uttering "treasonable sentiments against the Southern Confederacy."

In 1861 a group of irate fellow citizens, headed by S. M. Manning, inserted an offer in the town's *Southern Confederacy* newspaper. In it they promised a reward of $250 "for the arrest of Geo. Martin, dead or alive."

Earlier, abolitionist William Lloyd Garrison had evoked the anger of Georgia lawmakers. Years before the outbreak of hostilities, the state legislature enacted a measure perhaps not expected to be taken seriously. Under its terms, any person who brought Garrison to the state was eligible to claim a reward of $1,000.

During fighting near Fort Pickens, Florida, the colorfully garbed members of William Wilson's Zouaves did not always conduct themselves as chivalrous gentlemen. Enraged Confederates blamed what they termed "atrocities" upon Wilson, who headed the unit officially listed as the Sixth New York Infantry.

In October 1861 Wilson's foes posted notices saying that "$5,000 is the reward for him, dead or alive." In a letter he dispatched to New York, Wilson reported, "They are exhibiting my hair and my head in Pensacola—the reward is already claimed."

Operating in western Virginia during the spring of 1862, Union Brig. Gen. Robert H. Milroy encouraged or permitted his men to ruthlessly pillage the area. Furious Confederates in the Tidewater region heard of his exploits and offered a reward of $7,500 for his capture.

❧

Confederate Lt. Charles W. Read commanded the commerce raider *Florida* during the spring of 1863. Partly as a result of daring, partly because of exceptionally good luck, Read managed to capture several small merchant ships, fishing schooners, and passenger boats.

Since most of the ships that Read burned were taken in New England waters, Boston merchants banded together and offered a reward of $10,000 for the capture of the Confederate seaman.

❧

An identical sum is reputed to have been offered by Jefferson Davis for the apprehension of Samuel Upson. The man had committed what the Confederate head of state considered to be an especially heinous crime. In Philadelphia, Upson counterfeited Confederate currency that was circulating in Richmond as genuine.

❧

Thomas Garrett of Delaware pretended to be amused when he learned in the prewar years that a price had been put upon his head. Active in work of the Underground Railroad, he was credited with having gained freedom for more than two thousand slaves. Since most of those he aided came from Maryland, the state offered a reward of $10,000 for his capture.

❧

Confederate statesman Clement C. Clay spent more than a year in Canada devising a plan for a negotiated peace. When that effort failed, he returned home and was widely believed to have been implicated in the assassination of Lincoln.

Because he voluntarily gave himself up, no one received the $10,000 reward that had been offered for Clay's capture. After having been held in prison for more than a year without trial, he was released.

~~~

Wealthy Richard Yeadon of Charleston was enraged when he learned of Union Maj. Gen. Benjamin F. Butler's actions in occupied New Orleans. Hoping to put an end to those goings-on Yeadon advertised an offer of a $10,000 reward. It would be paid in Confederate currency, promised the Charlestonian, "for the capture and delivery of the said Benjamin F. Butler, dead or alive, to any proper Confederate authority."

~~~

Lt. O. R. McNary of the 103rd Pennsylvania Infantry was stationed at Plymouth, North Carolina, during the spring of 1864. As acting superintendent of Negro affairs, he was busily engaged in recruiting former slaves for Federal military forces. According to McNary's postwar account, this activity so offended the Secessionists that an unidentified Confederate provost marshal offered a reward of $10,000 for him dead or alive.

~~~

President Andrew Johnson seems to have discounted reports that the Booth conspiracy originated in or near Washington. Believing that plans for Lincoln's murder had originated in Canada, he offered rewards for a number of prominent Confederates who had operated there.

Johnson's most generous promise was $25,000 to the person or persons who captured Jacob Thompson "within the limits of the United States, so that he can be brought to trial."

At Charleston in 1863, Confederate Brig. Gen. Thomas Jordan tried to do something about the menacing Federal warships of the Union blockade. Reportedly funded by the international firm of John Fraser and Company, Jordan announced that any person who could show he had been responsible for the sinking of an armored warship would receive a reward of $50,000. Two famous vessels were regarded as especially important. Hence Jordan increased the reward to $100,000 for the destruction of the USS *New Ironsides* or the USS *Wabash*.

Jordan's offers, generous as they were, only echoed others posted in October 1862 by the U.S. Navy Department. With at least a dozen warships searching for the Confederate raider *Alabama*, anyone who could show that he had destroyed the vessel could claim a reward of $300,000. Should a naval officer demonstrate that he was responsible for the capture of the Confederate vessel, a reward of $500,000 was promised.

Two quite different Civil War payments had the same name: bounty. The U.S. government, most states, and many cities and towns offered cash incentives to anyone who volunteered for military service. These bounties became so generous that a new business of bounty brokering evolved. Some brokers became wealthy from a portion of the bounties paid to men they persuaded to enlist— sometimes repeatedly and under assumed names.

Cash payments, usually small, were also offered for the apprehension of persons belonging to specified groups or classes. For example, military officials struggled with the problem of desertion long before the war broke out and offered bounties for the return of anyone who was absent without leave.

On September 7, 1861, the reward for the return of a deserter was reduced from $30 to $5 on grounds that the amount was adequate "to cover all the expenses of apprehension and delivery." Unfortunately, the cut-rate bounty "proved prohibitory to action, and the economy practiced was found in the end to have been expensive." Nearly two years later, with the problem mounting instead of decreasing, the bounty was doubled without producing significant results. During the fall of 1863 a bounty hunter once again received $30 for each deserter.

Before large-scale battles became frequent the *Mobile Advertiser* published a notice of an offer by the Confederate government. Under its terms, "a premium or bounty of $25 was offered for every prisoner captured and delivered to the authorities by privateers."

A Federal prison on Johnson's Island, Ohio, gained notoriety long before the Confederate prison at Andersonville made headlines. Johnson's island was three miles from land, and the prison was guarded by a fifteen-foot stockade plus an eight-foot ditch. Nevertheless, so many Confederates escaped that authorities fixed a bounty of $50 on escaped prisoners. Any citizen who captured an escaped prisoner was promised immediate payment.

Cullen M. Baker achieved a record, of sorts, by deserting from both the Confederate and the Union armies. He then recruited a band of followers and set out to pillage villages in Arkansas and Texas. Cullen was so successful that Gov. Clayton Powell offered a bounty of $1,000 for the capture of "Confederate irregulars," or guerillas.

At least as early as the fifteenth century, a captured ship was called a prize, this usage stemming from Latin and meaning "to seize." Civil War seamen took the label for granted and used it without explanations for the benefit of landlubbers.

In many instances a victorious captain was too busy to evaluate his capture carefully or lacked the knowledge to do so. Hence many prizes were sent to New Orleans or to Charleston by Confederates and to New York or Philadelphia by Federals, without having price tags placed upon them.

Two vessels captured by the CSS *Sumter* fell into this category. Seized off Puerto Cabello, Venezuela, the *Abby Bradford* went to New Orleans with an appraisal. Sent to "some port on the south side of the island of Cuba" by Raphael Semmes of the same raider, the *Joseph Maxwell* took no estimate of value with her. Until sold at auction, the worth of ships such as these was seldom recorded.

When possible, both Union and Confederate commanders preferred to establish the value of a prize before sending her into port. A system for dividing the money fetched by a capture had been in use for generations. Under its terms, the proceeds from a maritime prize were divided equally between pension funds for seamen and those who effected the capture. Men even remotely involved in a successful assault upon a ship received for their prowess the following allocations:

> Commanding officer of the fleet, 5 percent
> Commander of the victorious vessel, 5 percent
> Officers above the rank of master, 10 percent
> All other officers, 17 1/2 percent
> Petty officers, 12 1/2 percent
> Seamen, 35 percent

U.S. Secretary of the Navy Gideon Welles was instrumental in abolishing this schedule in 1862. After July 17, officers and seamen who participated in the capture of a prize were rewarded according to the rates at which they were paid.

⁓⁓⁓

Frank B. Butts, a paymaster's clerk in the U.S. Navy, was delighted when the blockade steamer *Flag* made a capture. His share of the prize money amounted to $49.97.

⁓⁓⁓

Aboard the USS *Nahant*, a powder monkey pocketed $176.16 as his share of the prize money paid by the U.S. government for the CSS *Atlanta*.

⁓⁓⁓

Surgeon William F. Hutchinson fared somewhat better. Aboard the U.S. steam sloop-of-war *Lackawanna*, he and his shipmates spotted what they believed to be a Confederate cotton carrier. When the steamer *Isabel* was captured, en route from Galveston to Havana, her hold was packed with 750 bales of cotton. Although the vessel itself was of little value, when the value of its cargo was added to the prize money, Hutchinson's share came to $750.

⁓⁓⁓

Youthful William Tillman, cook of the schooner *S. F. Waring*, fared a great deal better. Within weeks of the surrender of Fort Sumter, the Confederate vessel was captured by the privateer *Jeff Davis*. Six men from the *Davis* were put aboard the *Waring* as a prize crew. While most of them were asleep, Tillman went into action. After having killed three men, he persuaded the survivors to surrender.

Once the schooner was in the hands of the cook, soon to be labeled a contraband because of his racial background, he took her into port as a prize of his own. Tillman's exploit, unique in maritime annals of the era, brought him $6,000 in prize money.

❧

Union Adm. Samuel P. Lee of Virginia was distantly related to Robert E. Lee. Joining the U.S. Navy in 1827, he became known as a troublemaker during his first decade on the water. At the outbreak of war he was in command of the USS *Vandalia*, then in South African waters.

Lee did not see any action against the Confederacy and the blockade-runners until his ship returned to U.S. waters and joined the blockading fleet. During the next four years his ship compiled a record that no other came close to matching. Collecting shares totaling $109,689, Lee gained the most prize money in the struggle to drive the blockade-runners out of business.

❧

Officers and seamen in both gray and blue received part of the value of each prize taken by their vessels. One such prize, the sloop *Alligator*, was valued at just $50 when she was captured by the Federal gunboat *Tahoma*.

❧

On December 1, 1861, the crew of the USS *Penguin* rejoiced when the vessel reached New York with the captured schooner *Albion* (formerly the *Lucy R. Waring*) in tow. Since the blockade-runner based at Nassau carried a valuable cargo, her captors divided $100,000 in prize money.

❧

Among the most powerful of Confederate ships, the CSS *Atlanta* was one of the new class of ironclads against which wooden warships had no chance for victory. Because the vessel was considered so formidable, the crew of the Federal warship that captured it divided an even $300,000 in prize money.

~~~

Union tars who helped to capture the blockade-runner *Lady Stirling* were distressed when they lost at least seventy-five bales of cotton to a fire caused by their guns. They were elated, however, when they learned that the ship and its remaining cargo were worth $489,891.29.

~~~

That sum was topped on November 10, 1863, when the steamer *Memphis* was captured with a heavy load of weapons purchased abroad. Because her cargo was so valuable, this blockade-runner yielded $510,914.07 in prize money to the men of the USS *Magnolia*.

~~~

From 1861 to 1865, more than eleven hundred prizes, mostly blockade-runners, were captured by the U.S. Navy. Approximately one-fourth of them were lost at sea, but prize money awarded for those that made it into harbor exceeded $24 million.

On the other hand, there is no formal accounting of those ships that had been ransomed, no way to confirm that the bonds signed by captains of the captured vessels were honored after the vessels had been released.

~~~

Four vessels taken in the blockade were central to a vital and long-drawn legal contest. Owners of the *Amy Warwick*, the *Crenshaw*, the *Hiawatha*, and the *Brilliante* sued the government over their seizure. War had not been declared, they pointed out, so the taking of the ships as prizes was illegal.

This issue reached the U.S. Supreme Court in February 1863, after having been delayed so that three newly appointed justices could be seated. The legality of the conflict that the president termed an insurrection was threatened by the charges of the attorneys representing the owners of the four prizes. The quartet of separate actions were labeled "the Prize Cases." Hearings concerning the issue resulted in the only significant Supreme Court ruling during the Civil War.

The justices concluded that although never declared by Congress, a de facto state of war began on Friday, April 19, 1861. Five days after Federal forces surrendered at Fort Sumter, the president made public a proclamation designed "to set on foot a blockade of the ports from South Carolina to Texas."

Soon extended northward along the Atlantic Coast, the blockade was initially unenforceable. Yet the date of its proclamation, taken as having launched a war that existed without having been declared, was named as the starting point of the conflict. This verdict was reached by a five-to-four decision. The dissenting justices argued that a state of war did not exist until July 13, 1861, when Congress recognized that war existed without having been declared.

Once April 19 was legally established as the date on which the conflict began, persons whose ships were seized as prizes could not get compensation. Neither could an agent or agency of the U.S. government be sued for losses incurred after that date.

---— *Forty-four* ———

THE GOLDEN TOUCH

The English poet Thomas Hood died sixteen years before the outbreak of war across the Atlantic. In sixteen lines of a lengthy poem, the Englishman praised and berated gold. Two of the lines give a capsule summary of Civil War attitudes toward the most precious metal then known to western civilization: "Bright and yellow, hard and cold, / Heavy to get, and light to hold."

California was not the site of the earliest U.S. gold rush. It took place in regions destined to be included in the Confederacy—North Carolina and Georgia. So much of the yellow metal came from the hills of North Georgia that a branch of the U.S. Mint was established at Dahlonega. Since gold and silver coins made up the only U.S. legal tender prior to the Civil War, the national supply of metal was a critical issue. Production in California peaked between 1851 and 1857, then fell to an average of about two million ounces annually during the war years.

When the first shell exploded over Fort Sumter, gold pieces were abundant. Eagles, named for the design stamped upon them and first issued in 1795, were worth $10. A double eagle, issued by the U.S. Mint beginning in 1850, was twice as valuable. Half-eagles and quarter-eagles abounded, as did gold $3- and $1-coins. Anyone who didn't have a few pieces of gold in his pocket was indeed poor.

The outbreak of war soon led to hoarding, causing more and more gold coins to disappear from circulation. This situation was exacerbated when the U.S. Treasury began to print greenbacks that were not redeemable in gold.

This device, designed to multiply the perception of national wealth, led to depreciation of currency everywhere. In the Confederacy, the crisis reached monumental levels just before the surrender at Appomattox. In the Union, matters were not as bad, but they could have been a lot better in 1865 when $236 million in greenbacks were in circulation.

Despite the eventual success in converting money usage from metal to paper, during the Civil War Americans nevertheless valued gold more highly than ever before. Such a state of affairs inevitably triggered many ploys and capers. Although the amount involved varied widely, the yellow metal sparked intrigue wherever it appeared.

Washington was briefly exultant when gold was found in the Montana Territory late in May 1863. This find did not compare with the California strike, but it was sufficient to grease the wheels of the Federal war machine for a few days.

A correspondent of the *Richmond Sentinel*, while bemoaning the Federal godsend, was inspired by it. He challenged all loyal Confederates to turn their gold and silver plate over to the government. This "vast and unproductive fund," he wrote, "might be made to act a valuable subsidiary part in any well-digested scheme to restore the credit of the Treasury."

Despite his fervent appeal, there is no record that a significant amount of household gold was sent to Richmond. All through the seceded states, folk responded more readily when requested to turn in church bells so they could be used in making guns and ammunition.

By March 1863, citizens residing in the Confederate capital were offering $400 in currency for $100 in gold. Thirty days later, a person was lucky to get five double eagles for $500. In Atlanta a full year before Sherman arrived, a single eagle jumped in value to $121.10 in July 1863.

Clark Wright of the Ninth New York Zouaves wrote: "In September, 1861, $1.10 of Confederate money was equal to $1 in United States gold." By January 1865, it took $60 Confederate money to buy $1 in gold.

~~~

That did not mean the Confederacy was entirely without gold. When Jefferson Davis and his close associates fled from Richmond, they took with them a few wagons heavy with gold. Capt. Micah H. Clark, acting treasurer of the Confederacy, never said how much gold went south. Like everyone else, he probably did not know.

At Abbeville, South Carolina, the bullion is supposed to have been transferred to the care of Brig. Gen. Basil Duke. Since it was not with Davis when he was captured in Georgia, it was stolen or hidden somewhere in the South. To this day, hopeful hunters continue to pore over clues considered likely to point them to where the Confederate treasure was stashed.

~~~

Racing toward what he hoped would be freedom, Jefferson Davis soon outdistanced what was left of the Confederate treasury. A short special train bearing some or all of it reached Danville, Virginia, on April 5, 1865.

Men assigned to guard the treasure wanted to leave it in Danville, but no officer of the James River Squadron was authorized to accept it. As a result, the treasure train pulled out for Charlotte, North Carolina, still carrying an estimated $200,000 in silver and $300,000 in gold.

Although Davis was rumored to be in Charlotte, he could not be found. Again, guardians of the treasure were frustrated because no one was willing to accept it. As a result, the treasure train slowly snaked its way into the Deep South and oblivion.

~~~

Although no one knows exactly how much gold left Richmond hurriedly in April 1865, Lt. Warren H. Mead of the Sixth Kentucky Cavalry never forgot the exact amount he received ninety days later.

Captured and shipped from one stockade to another, Mead wound up at "Camp Sorghum," adjacent to Columbia, South Carolina. After guards instructed him, he drew a draft upon his father. The terms of the instrument made Lockwood Mead of Genoa Cayuga County, New York, liable for $50 in gold. In return for the draft, the prisoner of war was handed a blue slip of paper worth $399.99 in Confederate currency.

Mead turned the bulk of his money into extra provisions. With "a piece of poor fresh beef the size of a man's hand ranging in price from $14 to $17.50," during the fifteen days before the prisoners were liberated by Sherman's forces, Mead spent more than two hundred Confederate dollars on meat and sweet potatoes.

Surgeon William F. Hutchinson was serving a hitch on the USS *Lackawanna* at the time Mead found that a draft on his father was as good as gold. His vessel, part of the West Gulf Blockading Squadron, saw many a blockade-runner make it safely into port. A woman once visited the Federal warship under a flag of truce. Complimented upon the appearance of the calico dress she wore, the Texas woman tossed her head before responding, "It sure ought to look great. Last week it cost me my last $200 in gold." When that dress was purchased, food for an officer aboard the *Lackawanna* cost about twenty-five US dollars weekly.

In a little-known caper, a quartet of French adventurers left Washington late in March 1862. Their destination was Richmond, where they planned to kidnap Jefferson Davis. Traveling under assumed names selected from Alexander Dumas's *The Three Musketeers*, they reached Manassas without difficulty.

At the spot made famous in July 1861, "Porthos" managed to shoot himself in the hand with his pistol. That forced him to give up the adventure, but his companions pressed on toward their target.

Deciding that they could not make it without horses, the three remaining Frenchmen bargained with a Virginia farmer. The man had three good horses he was willing to sell, but he declined to take the trio's greenbacks. He did, however, provide them with mounts when they produced $300 in gold. As the farmer pocketed the specie, he pointed out the road to Fredericksburg as a gesture of goodwill. Neither the horses nor the goodwill did the trio much good; they were discovered by a Confederate patrol and returned to Washington.

Early in 1864, notorious guerrilla leader William C. Quantrill conceived a plot similar to that of the Frenchmen. With a handful of followers, he set out for Washington to kidnap or kill Lincoln. On May 10, in Kentucky, his men clashed with Federal troops.

Mortally wounded, the Ohio native who had earlier plundered Lawrence, Kansas survived for twenty days. Moaning on his deathbed, Quantrill produced a pouch crammed with what remained of his fortune.

When Kate Clarke, Quantrill's lover, visited the prisoner, he handed her everything he had—$500 in gold. Kate did not wait for him to die; she took the first coach to Saint Louis and used the gold to set up a brothel.

Robert Toombs, one of Georgia's wealthiest planters, saw much that he had accumulated evaporate. During his years as a Confederate brigadier and as the Confederacy's secretary of state, his fortune dwindled to about 10 percent of its prewar level. That did not prevent the fiery attorney from continuing to treat gold casually.

After the last Confederate cabinet meeting was held in Washington, Georgia, members of the Fourth Illinois Cavalry seized the town. Busy paroling prisoners, Capt. Lot Abraham barely looked up when a visitor approached him.

"My name is Toombs," he said as though he expected everyone to be familiar with it. "In passing my house a few days ago, Breckinridge threw down from his horse a meal sack. When I picked it up, it was found to be very heavy. That sack held $1,780 in gold and $3,400 in silver. Looks as though it might belong to your government; here, take it."

Startled, the Federal officer asked no questions. Had he done so, he might have concluded that the precious metal stuffed in the meal sack was part of the lost treasure of the Confederacy.

———

Spy extraordinary Rose Greenhow O'Neal went to England after being banished from the United States. Probably serving as a Confederate courier, she remained there until entrusted with top-secret papers. En route to Wilmington aboard a blockade-runner, O'Neal feared capture when a Federal vessel approached. With two companions she took to a rowboat.

Heavy seas sent the rowboat to the bottom as it came close to shore. O'Neal might have escaped had she not been wearing a money belt stuffed with at least $2,000 in gold. The precious metal claimed the life of the skilled and colorful espionage agent.

Tradition has it that a Confederate soldier found the body of the dead woman and emptied the fatal money belt. When he discovered her identity, he reputedly turned the gold over to the Confederate authorities.

———

After the surrender at Appomattox, Confederate Brig. Gen. Edmund Kirby-Smith, head of the Trans-Mississippi Department, had hoped to assist Jefferson Davis in his escape from the collapsing Confederacy. The Confederate president, however, was captured on May 10 in Georgia, and Kirby-Smith surrendered the last Confederate bastion on May 26.

Kirby-Smith had been holding $5,000 in gold for the former president's personal expenses. As his men had not been paid in weeks, the general took out

340 gold eagles to be divided "on salary account." The remaining gold was sent to Brig. Gen. Edward R. S. Canby in New Orleans as "the balance of the secret service fund of the Trans-Mississippi Department." Flat broke, Kirby-Smith borrowed $100 in Confederate currency with which to make his way home.

≈≈≈

Attorney Philip Phillips of Washington seems to have been ignorant of the activities of his wife, Eugenia. Having come under the influence of Rose Greenhow O'Neal, she had joined a spy ring early in 1861. Seized late in the summer, Eugenia and her sister were placed under house arrest n the O'Neal home.

Phillips, whose practice was limited to cases bound for the U.S. Supreme Court, spent at least three weeks cajoling prominent officials. Eventually the women were given permission to enter the Confederacy by way of Fortress Monroe.

Lt. Gen. Winfield Scott personally made arrangements for the former prisoners to take a steamboat headed for the South. As a gesture of personal appreciation for a respected attorney whose loyalty to the Union was never questioned, he permitted Phillips to leave the Federal capital with $5,000 in gold.

≈≈≈

At Catlett's Station, Virginia, J. E. B. Stuart staged a spectacular raid in August 1862. Leading fifteen hundred cavalrymen in gray, he seized the headquarters of the Army of Virginia.

Much of the loot found near the residence of Union Maj. Gen. John Pope was routine, but chests intended for use by paymasters were not. When he returned to his own lines, Stuart carried with him $20,000 in gold. To subordinates he confessed that he considered this haul to be far more exciting than the $500,000 in greenbacks also captured.

≈≈≈

Confederate Brig. Gen. James E. Slaughter was among claimants for the honor of having fought in the last battle of the war. After failing to score a victory at Palmito Ranch, Texas, he withdrew across the Rio Grande. There he soon sold his artillery to Mexican Maj. Gen. Tomas Meija, who paid for his purchase with $20,000 in gold.

Alabama cotton broker Zachariah Deas was known to be well off financially. When the state's Twenty-second Regiment was formed in the fall of 1861, Deas yearned to be its colonel. He found it easy to gain the coveted spot but was surprised to learn that his men were not ready to fight. Some of them had no weapons, and the rest were armed with muskets and squirrel rifles.

The regiment's leader immediately ordered a shipment of splendid Enfields, which he paid for with $28,000 in gold. A grateful government later reimbursed Colonel Deas with $28,000 in Confederate bonds that became worthless not long after they were printed.

Analysts of the northernmost of Confederate raids have uncovered aspects of the story that were unknown in October 1864. Bank records recently uncovered indicate that the men who robbed Saint Albans, Vermont, were hasty and careless, to say the least. Making their getaway to Canada, they left behind at least $50,000 in gold.

The soldiers who robbed the Vermont banks were also guilty of sloppy planning. Hence most of them were soon captured on Canadian soil and were found to be carrying $88,000 in U.S. currency.

Since the money was part of the capture, it became Canadian property. Public outcry north of the border soon forced the passage of unique legislation. Under its terms, three Saint Albans banks were eventually paid $50,000 in gold by the Canadian government.

Confederate Brig. Gen. Albert Pike was concerned during the harsh winter of 1861–62 that his men had not been paid for months. Trying to remedy the situation, he dispatched his son, Walter, to Richmond. When military officials were presented with demands from a leader they badly needed in the West, they expedited Walter's return to Arkansas with $63,000 in gold.

Federal forces seemed ready to pounce upon Pike's troops when the payroll funds arrived. Desperate to safeguard his money, the Confederate entrusted it to a slave known only as Brutus with instructions to hide it.

Two days after the March 7–8 battle of Pea Ridge, or Elkhorn Tavern, a solitary bedraggled black man guided his horse into the Confederate camp. When the slave handed over the gold-filled bag, he was rewarded with his freedom on the spot.

On May 27, 1862, Confederate Secretary of the Treasury C. G. Memminger drafted a unique memo to Jefferson Davis. He reported that $100,000 in gold that had been designated for the ordnance department had been seized in Mobile, Alabama, by Gen. P. G. T. Beauregard. The officer who had executed the general's order, Lt. Col. Frank H. Hatch, explained that this had been done to prevent the money's falling into enemy hands. Normally, when a Confederate horde was seized by Southern forces the money was returned to the treasury in Richmond.

As Military governor, Union Maj. Gen. Benjamin F. Butler ruled New Orleans with a high hand. Documents of the period strongly support claims that he considered any money he uncovered to be the property of the U.S. government.

At the office of the consul of the Netherlands, some of Butler's aides became suspicious when they noticed a number of kegs. An attempt to move a single keg evoked a one-word signal: Money!

Once in Federal hands, the keg that seemed strangely out of place in the office of a consul yielded $5,000 in gold. So did each of 159 other kegs seized in a violation of international law that enriched the U.S. Treasury by $800,000.

Weapons, quinine, shoes, and other badly needed commodities were the backbone of the blockade-running business. One of them, the *Giraffe*, was renamed the *Robert E. Lee* soon after having been purchased for the unusually large sum in 1862 of $160,000 in gold.

Officers and men aboard the new member of the Confederate fleet bragged that the steamer built in England was the fastest vessel afloat. That boast, seldom challenged, was repeated during twenty-one successful voyages. Before being captured she took to English markets at least seven thousand bales of cotton worth more than $2 million in gold.

With Confederate currency depreciating rapidly, Secretary of the Treasury C. G. Memminger concocted a scheme designed to create financial panic in the North. By buying gold in quantity and exporting it, he believed that he could create a fiscal crisis.

A plea to Southern sympathizers in loyal states was linked with the plot. Urged to convert paper money into gold and horde it, many citizens acted promptly.

At the same time, Confederate agent J. Porterfield went from Montreal to New York and began buying gold for export. He managed to ship about $2 million out of the country before a partner was arrested. This ended the Confederacy's great gold caper.

In May 1864, Joseph Howard, city editor of the *Brooklyn Eagle*, conceived a scheme designed to make himself rich almost overnight. His first step was to buy gold with every dollar he could borrow. Then he fed bogus news stories concerning a Federal call for an additional four hundred thousand men to numerous publications. Two of them, the *New York World* and the *Journal of Commerce* took the bait detailing military failures necessitating the draft. When readers absorbed the dismal news, many began to buy gold as a hedge against inflation. The price of gold jumped 10 percent in a single day. Now famous as the Gold Hoax, the plot masterminded by a newspaper editor did not make him rich. Instead, it sent him to jail for ninety days.

In Washington, the gold scare caused Lincoln to suffer one of the most serious embarrassments of his presidency. He *had* planned to issue just such a call as Howard described, but furor created by the Gold Hoax forced him to delay the proclamation for two months.

Conclusion

Gettysburg has produced a literature of its own—dozens of books and scores of articles plus television documentaries. Though no other narrowly-focused Civil War subject has been so frequently treated in great detail, books have been devoted to all campaigns and major battles plus most military events beyond the level of a skirmish.

Abraham Lincoln is the subject of an estimated 6,000+ books. Some top military and civilian leaders on both sides wrote autobiographies; all of them and many of their aides have been treated in one or more biographies.

Strangely, however, many of the "little things" and "minor persons" involved in approximately 1,700 days of conflict have been neglected. Lots of them, including some entries in this volume, are of curiosity value, only. Others were of far greater moment than space devoted to them in the past would suggest.

No previous book or magazine article has dealt in even reasonably full fashion with the way hostages affected public opinion and official views. Yet had not Confederates resorted to the use of hostages very early, there is a strong possibility that numerous naval officers and seamen would have been hung as pirates.

For weeks, Abraham Lincoln was positive that he would lose the election of 1864. The president was so certain of this outcome that he required his cabinet members to sign documents pledging their allegiance to the next chief executive—whoever he might be.

Lincoln's resounding victory enabled him to remain in office to pursue the war to the conclusion he had always stipulated. Men who led armies from what

he insisted upon labeling as "so-called seceded states" were forced into unconditional surrender because the strong peace movement in the North lost its vigor.

Lincoln's political triumph and the unconditional surrender of Confederates
was in large part due to achievements of two Union officers. Every casual reader
of Civil War literature knows that they were Ulysses S. Grant and William
Tecumseh Sherman—Grant's hand-picked commander of Federal forces in
what was then called the West.

Analysts are virtually unanimous in the verdict that the fall of Atlanta was
the 1864 turning point in public opinion and hence was the catalyst that
led to Lincoln's re-election. Few if any serious students of the war challenge
the conclusion that among Federal commanders, only Grant was capable of
achieving radical re-direction of military goals. It was Grant who demanded
that the Army of Northern Virginia must replace Richmond as the primary
target of Union forces. Small wonder that the man from Galena, Illinois, was
hailed as the savior of the nation.

Curiously, however, Grant's success may have stemmed at least in part from
an often-overlooked aspect of his career. His wife succeeded in staying with
him or close to him during many crucial months. In her absence, he had been
licked by the bottle while in earlier service on the west coast. Julia Grant may
have been "only a wife," but she contributed mightily to the victories of her
sober husband.

Newspaper stories concerning atrocities seem of little importance and less
believability when viewed from the distance of nearly 140 years. Yet in the
heated climate of the war years, these curious "little things" had a powerful
impact upon public opinion. Every man who read that bones of dead heroes
were desecrated or heard that Indian fighting men had taken scalps of fallen
foes had his backbone stiffened.

When factors such as this are underscored, it is hard to escape the conclusion
that each event and every person was significant. So viewed, many of the "curiosities" briefly treated in this volume loom to sudden and perhaps crucial
importance.

SELECTED BIBLIOGRAPHY

Abdill, George B. *Civil War Railroads*. New York: Bonanza, 1961.

Abraham Lincoln Quarterly. 15 vols. Urbana: University of Illinois Press, 1979–94.

American Annual Cyclopedia and Register of Important Events (Appleton's). New York: Appleton, 1861–65.

American Heritage. New York, 1948–95.

America's Civil War. Leesburg, VA, 1988–95.

Andrews, J. Cutler. *The North Reports the Civil War*. Pittsburgh: University of Pittsburgh Press, 1959.

_____. *The South Reports the Civil War*. Princeton, NJ: Princeton University Press, 1970.

Annals of the Civil War, The. Philadelphia: Philadelphia Weekly Times, 1979.

Army of the Potomac. *Report of the Joint Committee on the Conduct of the War*. Washington, DC: Government Printing Office, 1863–66.

Baker, LaFayette C. *History of the U.S. Secret Service in the Late War*. Philadelphia: L. C. Baker, 1867.

Ball, Douglas B. *Financial Failure and Confederate Defeat*. Urbana: University of Illinois Press, 1991.

Barnard, John G. *A Report on the Defenses of Washington*. Washington, DC: Government Printing Office, 1871.

Barton, William E. *President Lincoln*. 2 vols. Indianapolis: Bobbs-Merrill, 1933.

Basler, Roy P., ed. *The Collected Works of Abraham Lincoln*. 8 vols. New Brunswick, NJ: Rutgers University Press, 1963.

Bates, Edward. *The Diary of Edward Bates*. Edited by Howard K. Beale. Washington, DC: Government Printing Office, 1933.

Beller, Susan P. *Medical Practices in the Civil War*. Cincinnati: Betterway, 1992.

Benjamin, Marcus. *Washington During War Time*. Washington, DC: National Tribune, 1902.

Blue & Gray. Columbus, OH. 1984–95.

Boatner, Mark M. *The Civil War Dictionary*. Revised edition. New York: David McKay, 1988.

Brooks, Noah. *Washington in Lincoln's Time*. New York: Century, 1895.

Browning, Orville Hickman. *The Diary of Orville Hickman Browning*. Edited by Theodore C. Pease and James G. Randall. 2 vols. Springfield: Illinois State historical Library, 1925–33.

Butler, Benjamin F. *Autobiography and Personal Reminiscences*. Boston: A. M. Thayer, 1892.

Carpenter, Frank B. *Six Months at the White House with Abraham Lincoln*. New York: Hurd and Houghton, 1866.

Caffey, Thomas E. *Battlefields of the South*. New York: J. Bradburn, 1864.

Canby, Courtland, ed. *Lincoln and the Civil War*. New York: Brazillier, 1960.

Catton, Bruce. *The Coming Fury*. Garden City, NY: Doubleday, 1961.

_____. *Grant Takes Command*. Boston: Houghton Mifflin, 1968.

_____. *Mr. Lincoln's Army*. Garden City, NY: Doubleday, 1962.

_____. *Never Call Retreat*. Garden City, NY: Doubleday, 1965.

_____. *A Stillness at Appomattox*. Garden City: NY: Doubleday, 1953.

_____. *The Terrible Swift Sword.* Garden City, 1963.

Century Magazine. New York: Century, 1878–80.

Chase, Salmon P. *Diary and Correspondence of Salmon P. Chase.* 2 vols. Washington, DC: Government Printing Office, 1903.

Chestnut, Mary Boykin. *A Diary from Dixie.* Edited by Ben Ames Williams. Boston: Houghton Mifflin, 1905.

Civil War. Berryville, VA: 1982–94.

Civil War Chronicles. New York: American Heritage, 1991–92.

Civil War Times and Civil War Times Illustrated. Harrisburg, PA, 1959–95.

Confederate Veteran. Nashville, 1893–1932. *Cumulative Index.* 3 vols. Wilmington, NC: Broadfoot, 1986.

Connelly, Thomas L. *Army of the Heartland.* Baton Rouge: Louisiana State University Press, 1967.

_____. *Autumn of Glory.* Baton Rouge: Louisiana State University Press, 1971.

Coulter, E. Merton. *The Confederate States of America, 1861–65.* Baton Rouge: Louisiana State University Press, 1950.

Current, Richard N., ed. *Encyclopedia of the Confederacy.* 4 vols. New York: Simon & Schuster, 1993.

Cushman, Pauline. *The Romance of the Great Rebellion.* New York: Wynkoop & Hallenbeck, 1864.

Dana, Charles A. *Recollections of the Civil War.* New York: Appleton, 1902.

*Davis, Jefferson. *The Rise and Fall of Confederate Government.* Richmond: Garrett and Massie, 1938, 1881.

Davis, William C. *The Imperiled Union.* Garden City, NY: Doubleday, 1982–83.

_____. ed. *The Image of War.* 6 vols. Garden City, NY: Doubleday, 1981–84.

Devens, Richard M. *The Pictorial Book of Anecdotes and Incidents of thee War of the Rebellion.* Hartford: Hartford, 1866.

Donald, David. *Divided We Fought.* New York, Macmillan, 1952.

Dumont, Dwight L., comp. *Southern Editorials on Secession.* New York: Century, 1931.

Dupuy, R. Ernest. *The Compact History of the Civil War.* New York: Hawthorne, 1960.

Duyckinch, Everet A. *National History of the War for the Union.* New York: n.p., 1867.

Dyer, Frederick H. *A Compendium of the War of the Rebellion.* Des Moines: Frederick H. Dyer, 1908.

Early. Jubal A. *The Campaigns of Gen. Robert E. Lee.* Baltimore: J. Murphy, 1872.

Eaton, Clement. *A History of the Southern Confederacy.* New York: Macmillan, 1954.

Eisenchemiel, Otto, and Ralph Newman. *The Civil War.* Indianapolis: Bobbs-Merrill, 1947.

_____. *Why the Civil War?* Indianapolis: Bobbs-Merrill, 1958.

*Evans, Clement A., ed. *Confederate Military History,* 17 vols. Atlanta: Confederate 1899. (Two-volume index: Wilmington, NC, Broadfoot, 1987).

Famous Adventures and Prison Escapes of the Civil War. New York: Century, 1893.

Farrar, Fernando. *Johnny Reb.* Richmond: Nye, 1869.

Faust, Patricia, ed. *Historical Times Illustrated Encyclopedia of the Civil War.* New York: Harper and Row, 1986.

Fessenden, Francis. *Life and Public Services of William Pitt Fessenden.* 2 vols. Boston: Houghton Mifflin, 1907.

Fiske, John. *The Mississippi Valley in the Civil War.* Boston: Houghton Mifflin, 1900.

Foote, Shelby. *The Civil War.* 3 vols. New York: Random House, 1958–86.

Fox, Gustavus V. *Confidential Correspondence.* 2 vols. New York: De Vinne, 1918.

Freeman, Douglas Southall. *Lee's Lieutenants.* 3 vols. New York: Scribner's, 1972.

_____. *R. E. Lee.* 4 vols. New York: Scribner's, 1934–35.

Frost, Griffin. *Camp and Prison Journal.* Quincy, IL: Quincy Journal, 1867.

Fuller, John F. *The Generalship of Ulysses S. Grant.* London: Murray, 1929.

*Grant, Ulysses Simpson. *Personal Memoirs of U. S. Grant.* 2 vols. New York: C. L. Webster, 1885.

Guest, James W. *Love, Honor, and Civil War.* Columbia, SC: Palmetto Press, 1993.

Haguina, Parthenia. *A Blockaded Family.* Boston: Houghton Mifflin, 1888.

Hall, Charles B. *Military Records of General Officers.* C.S.A. New York: Lockwood, 1898.

Hamersley, Lewis R. *Records of Living Officers of the U.S. Navy and Marine Corps.* Philadelphia: Lippincott, 1870.

Hattaway, Herman, and Archer Jones. *How the North Won*. Urbana: University of Illinois Press, 1873.

Hay, John. *Lincoln and the Civil War, In the Diaries and Letters of John Hay*. Selected by Tyler Dennett. New York: Dodd, Meade, 1939.

Hertz, Emanuel. *Abraham Lincoln: A New Portrait*. 2 vols. New York: Liveright, 1930.

Ingraham, Prentiss. *The Two Flags*. New York: n.p., 1897.

Jackson, Florence. *The Black Man in America*. New York: Watts, 1972.

Jackson, John S. *Diary of a Confederate Soldier*. Columbia: University of South Carolina, 1990.

*Johnson, Robert V., and Clarance C. Buell, eds. *Battles and Leaders of the Civil War*. 4 vols. New York: Century, 1887.

Johnson, Rossiter. *Campfire and Battlefields*. New York: Civil War Press, 1967.

*Johnston, Joseph E. *Narrative of Military Operations During the Late War Between the States*. New York: Appleton, 1874.

Joint Committee on the Conduct of the War. *Report of the Joint Committee on the Conduct of the War*. 3 vols. Washington, DC: Government Printing Office, 1863.

Jones, Virgil. *The Civil War at Sea*. 3 vols. Wilmington, NC: Broadfoot, 1990.

Journal of the Confederate Historical Society. Essex, England, 1962–72.

Journal of the Southern Historical Society. 49 vols. Wilmington, NC: Broadfoot, 1990–92. 2-volume index.

Katcher, Philip. *The Civil War Source Book*. New York: Facts on File, 1992.

Ketchum, Robert M. *American Heritage Picture History of the Civil War*. Garden City, NY: Doubleday, 1960.

Knox, Thomas W. *Camp Fire and Cotton Field*. New York: n.p., 1865.

Koerner, Gustave. *Memoirs*. Edited by T. J. McCormack. 2 vols. Cedar Rapids: Torch, 1909.

Lanier, Robert S., ed. *The Photographic History of the Civil*. 10 vols. New York: Review of Reviews, 1912.

Lamon, Ward H. *Recollections of Abraham Lincoln 1847–1865*. Edited by Dorothy Lamon Teillard. Washington: 1911.

Leech, Margaret. *Reveille in Washington*. New York: Harper, 1941.

Lincoln, Abraham. *Collected Words*. Edited by Roy P. Basler. 9 vols. Brunswick, NJ: Rutgers University Press, 1953–55. (Earlier editions vary considerably from this one at some points, and some Lincoln documents in the *Official Records* are not identical with those collected here. Volumes published as supplements to the *Collected Works* are of little interest except to specialists.)

Long, E. B. *The Civil War Day by Day*. Garden City, NY: Doubleday, 1971.

Longstreet, James. *From Manassas to Appomattox*. Philadelphia: Lippincott, 1903.

Lossing, Benjamin J. *Lossing's Pictorial Field Guide to the Great Civil War*. Boston: Nagle 1889.

*McClellan, George Brinton. *McClellan's Own Story*. New York: Charles L. Webster, 1886.

McHenry, Robert, ed. *Webster's Military Biographies*. New York: Dover, 1978.

McPherson, James M. *Battle Cry of Freedom*. New York: Oxford, 1988.

*Meade, G. Gordon. *Life and Letters of G. Gordon Meade*. New York: Scribner's 1913.

Memoir of John A. Dahlgren, Rear-Admiral United States Navy, by His Widow. Boston: J. R. Osgood, 1882.

Meredith, Roy, and Arthur Meredith. *Mr. Lincoln's Military Railroads*. New York: Noreton, 1975.

Miers, Earl S. *The American Civil War*. New York: Golden, 1961.

Military Order of the Loyal Legion of the United States. 65 vols. 1883–1906. (In preparation, three-volume index, Wilmington, NC: Broadfoot.

*Miller, Francis Trevelyan, ed. in chief. *The Photographic History of the Civil War*. 10 vols. New York: Review of Reviews, 1912.

*Moore, Frank, ed. *The Rebellion Record*. 12 vols. New York: Putnam, 1861–63; Nostrand, 1864–68.

National Almanac and Annual Record, 1860–65. 6 vols. Philadelphia: n.p., 1860–65.

Neely, Mark E. *The Abraham Lincoln Encyclopedia*. New York: McGraw Hill, 1982.

Nevins, Allan. *Ordeal of the Union*. 2 vols. New York: Scribner's, 1947.

_____. *The War for the Union*. 4 vols. New York: Scribner's, 1959.

Nicolay, John G., and John Hay. *Abraham Lincoln*. 10 vols. New York: Century, 1890.

Official Documents of the Post Office Department of the Confederate States of America. 2 vols. Holland, MI: n.p., 1979.

Official Records of the Union and Confederate Navies in the War of the Rebellion. 30 vols. Washington: Government Printing Office, 1894–1927.

Perry, Milton F. *Infernal Machines*. Baton Rouge: Louisiana State University Press, 1965.

Phisterer, Frederick. *Statistical Record of the Armies of the United States*. New York: Scribner's, 1883.

Quarles, Benjamin. *The Negro in the Civil War*. Boston: Little Brown, 1953.

Quint, Alonzo H. *The Potomac and the Rapidan*. Boston: n.p., 1984.

Roller, David C., and Robert W. Twyman. *Encyclopedia of Southern History*. Baton Rouge: Louisiana State University Press, 1968.

Royster, Charles, *The Destructive War*. New York: Knopf, 1991.

Schurz, Carl. *Intimate Letters*. Translated and compiled by Joseph Schafer. Madison, WI: State Historical Society of Wisconsin, 1928.

Seward, Frederick W. *Seward at Washington, As Senator and Secretary of State*. 2 vols. New York: Derby and Miller 1891.

Sheridan, Philip H. *Personal Memoirs*. 2 vols. New York: Appleton, 1888.

*Sherman, William Tecumseh. *Memoirs of W. T. Sherman*. 2 vols. New York: Appleton, 1875.

Sifakis, Stewart. *Who Was Who in the Civil War*. New York: Facts on File, 1988.

*Southern Historical Society. *Southern Historical Society Papers*. 52 vols. Richmond, VA: Virginia Historical Society, 1876–1959. (Three-volume index, Wilmington, NC: Broadfoot, 1992.)

Stepp, John W., and I. William Hill, eds. *Mirror of War*. Washington, DC: Evening Star, 1961.

The Union Army: A History of Military Affairs in the Loyal States, 1861–66. 8 vols. Madison, WI: Federal, 1908.

War of the Rebellion: Official Records of the Union and Confederate Armies. 130 vols. Wilmington, NC: Broadfoot, 1991–95. 6-volume supplement.

Warner, Ezra S. *Generals in Blue*. Baton Rouge: Louisiana State University Press, 1964.

_____. *Generals in Gray*. Baton Rouge: Louisiana State University Press, 1959.

Welles, Gideon. *Diary of Gideon Welles*. 3 vols. New York: Houghton Mifflin, 1911.

An asterisk (*) indicates the work was subsequently reprinted in one or more editions.

INDEX